DETENTE AND DEFENSE
A Reader

DETENTE AND DEFENSE
A Reader

Edited by Robert J. Pranger

American Enterprise Institute for Public Policy Research
Washington, D.C.

ACKNOWLEDGMENTS

The publisher wishes to thank those who have given permission to reprint the following articles:

"In Thrall to Fear." From *The Crippled Giant*, by J. William Fulbright. Copyright © 1972 by J. William Fulbright. Reprinted by permission of Random House, Inc. Originally appeared in *The New Yorker*.

"Détente: An Evaluation." Reprinted with permission from *Survey*, Spring/Summer 1974 (91/92), pp. 1-27. © 1974 by *Survey* and Leopold Labedz.

"Is Détente Worth Saving?" Reprinted with permission. © 1976 by George Kennan and *Saturday Review*.

"The Bureaucratic SALTscreen." Reprinted with permission of *The Wall Street Journal*. © 1976 by Dow Jones & Company, Inc. All rights reserved.

"Choices." Reprinted with permission. © 1973 by *Foreign Policy*. "How to Look at the Soviet-American Balance" and "Soviet Strength and U.S. Purpose." © 1976 by *Foreign Policy*.

The following are reprinted by permission from *Foreign Affairs*:

"Can Nuclear Deterrence Last Out the Century?" (January 1973). Copyright 1972 by Council on Foreign Relations, Inc. "U.S. Foreign Policy: The Search for Focus" (July 1973). Copyright 1973 by Council on Foreign Relations, Inc.

"Détente or Entente?" (April 1975). Copyright 1975 by Council on Foreign Relations, Inc. "Assuring Strategic Stability in an Era of Détente" (January 1976). Copyright 1975 by Council on Foreign Relations, Inc. "Assuring Strategic Stability: An Alternative View" and "Strategic Stability" (April 1976). Copyright 1976 by Council on Foreign Relations, Inc.

Punctuation, capitalization, and other points of style have been altered in some instances for consistency or clarity.

ISBN 0-8447-3227-3

Foreign Affairs Study No. 40, October 1976

Library of Congress Catalog Card No. 76-44607

Printed in the United States of America

CONTENTS

General Introduction   *Robert J. Pranger*   **1**

PART ONE: OVERVIEW   **7**

1 Problems of Future American Foreign Policy   **9**

U.S. Foreign Policy for the 1970s:
Shaping a Durable Peace   *Richard M. Nixon*   9

In Thrall to Fear   *J. William Fulbright*   18

U.S. Power in Transition   *Charles Burton Marshall*   41

U.S. Foreign Policy:
The Search for Focus   *Zbigniew Brzezinski*   56

Choices   *Stanley Hoffmann*   75

America's Principled Role in World Affairs: A Realistic
Policy of Peace and Freedom   *Melvin R. Laird*   99

PART TWO: DETENTE   **111**

2 Basic Agreements on Détente   **113**

Basic Principles of Relations between the United States of
America and the Union of Soviet Socialist Republics,
29 May 1972   114

Treaty between the United States of America and the Union
of Soviet Socialist Republics on the Limitation of Antiballistic Missile Systems, 26 May 1972   117

Interim Agreement between the United States of America
and the Union of Soviet Socialist Republics on Certain
Measures with Respect to the Limitation of Strategic
Offensive Arms, 26 May 1972   122

Protocol to the Interim Agreement between the United States
of America and the Union of Soviet Socialist Republics on
Certain Measures with Respect to the Limitation of
Strategic Offensive Arms, 26 May 1972   124

Report of Secretary of State William P. Rogers on the
Strategic Arms Limitations Agreements, 10 June 1972   125

Joint U.S.-Chinese Communiqué Issued at Shanghai,
27 February 1972   141

Agreement between the United States of America and the
Union of Soviet Socialist Republics on the Prevention
of Nuclear War, 22 June 1973   145

Joint U.S.-Soviet Statement and Agreement Issued at
Vladivostok, 24 November 1974   148

3 Détente: Two Statements   153

Détente with the Soviet Union: The Reality of
Competition and the Imperative
of Cooperation   Henry A. Kissinger   153

Report to the Twenty-Fifth Congress of the
Communist Party of the Soviet Union,
24 February 1976   Leonid I. Brezhnev   178

4 Is Détente in the American Interest?   190

Détente: An Evaluation by a Group of Students
of Soviet and International Affairs   190

Détente on Entente?   Richard Rosecrance   215

Is Détente Worth Saving?   George F. Kennan   234

America: You Must Think about the World
Alexander Solzhenitsyn   243

Kissinger's Grand Design   G. Warren Nutter   257

PART THREE: DEFENSE   **273**

5 Defense: Selected Documents   **275**

U.S.-Soviet Military Balance: A Frame of Reference
for Congress   *Congressional Research Service*   275

The Permanent Challenge of Peace: U.S. Policy
toward the Soviet Union   *Henry A. Kissinger*   313

Annual Defense Department Report FY 1977   328

6 Is America's Defense Adequate?   **341**

How to Look at the Soviet-American Balance
Les Aspin   341

Soviet Strength and U.S. Purpose   *Amos A. Jordan,*
R. W. Komer, Les Aspin   350

The Bureaucratic SALTscreen   *Robert L. Bartley*   359

SALT Accords Debate   *Henry M. Jackson,*
J. William Fulbright, Alan Cranston   363

Assuring Strategic Stability   *Paul H. Nitze*   376

Assuring Strategic Stability: An Alternative
View   *Jan M. Lodal*   400

Strategic Stability   *Paul H. Nitze*   420

Can Nuclear Deterrence Last Out the Century?
Fred Charles Iklé   424

Contributors   **443**

GENERAL INTRODUCTION

Robert J. Pranger

If the international order has any coherence at all, it is primarily due to political organization. Many commentators have focused on the rise of economic interdependence and the ascendance of globalist values that transcend national parochialism. Surely, interdependency and cosmopolitan sympathies are increasingly important forces in world affairs and perhaps in the long run will spell the difference between a durable international peace, which accommodates vastly complex nations and peoples, and global chaos, caused by fragmented national self-seeking. Yet the actions of national governments, prompted by political interests, will determine how fast and how far international orderliness based on mutual dependency develops. A vision of a world order with minimal violence and a strong sense of community is itself a form of politics highly prized domestically as well as internationally: its achievement in global terms, no less than in local situations, will depend on what kinds of political decisions are made by national states. History might bring about a realization that human survival depends upon an international system governed to a greater extent by reason and law, but that realization must be translated into political activity, based largely on national decisions.

International relations today are a long way from a world community that channels interstate violence into effective central institutions of deliberation and adjudication. Politics in world affairs remains much as it has been for centuries: the most typical political practices are diplomacy and war. It is through these practices that more comprehensive international institutions might emerge, preferably as a result of careful negotiations rather than a nuclear exchange.

It is in this context—of evolving international order and of enlightened demands on nations to insure more dependable international institutions—that relations between the United States and the Communist powers, especially the U.S.S.R. and the People's Republic of China, are changing. This broad perspective of the developing rela-

1

tions between capitalism and communism has not always been appreciated. *Détente*, that catchall expression for eased relations between capitalist and Communist blocs, is often debated as an aspect of a relationship between adversaries instead of as a phenomenon of international evolution. In turn, decision-making centers, such as Moscow and Washington, are regarded as the only important actors, without much thought being given to the evolving status of these two capitals in the wider realm of the international order.

The importance of viewing détente from a global perspective should not diminish the fact that many important decisions with worldwide impact are made in Moscow and Washington. No one can compel the Politburo to realize that relations with the United States should aim for the greater good of the international system. Nor is there any divine intervention in the proceedings of the National Security Council that gives the participants a glimpse of supranational or transnational imperatives. In any event, universal truths are apt to be self-evident in different ways in America and Russia. National politics lies at the base of détente in all its aspects, from the most solicitous for the human race to the most narrow in unilateral self-interest.

Nonetheless, if political action is still largely confined to nation states, the political imagination need not be. Politicians may be enthralled by the application of narrow bilateral relations between Moscow and Washington to foreign policy more generally (either in praise or in condemnation), but these relations are part—and only part—of the sum of international relations. The American experience in the United Nations, the law of the sea conferences, the confrontations between rich and poor nations, and the regional conflict in the Middle East, to name only a few major arenas for U.S. foreign policy, give some hint of the range of important problems partly or largely outside the ambiance of détente, yet representative of substantial portions of evolving world affairs.

It might be said that a reciprocal relationship exists between a developing international order and national decision making. Détente fits into this reciprocity, in part shaping international order and in part being shaped by it. Yet, the chief instruments of international politics today—diplomacy and war—are still firmly in the hands of nations. And astride all other nations in the realms of diplomacy and war stand the United States and Soviet Union. Whether the international order develops dependable, authoritative institutions for governing the planet's common business, with minimal violence, will be determined in large measure by how those masters of force in Moscow and Washington (and to a lesser extent Peking) perceive their relationships *with each other*. The stakes in détente go well beyond national self-interest to global self-preservation, but most of the world can do little except await the outcome of superpower transactions.

Through the haze of diplomacy have come glimpses of a more globalist perspective in détente undertakings between the United States on one hand and the Soviet Union or People's Republic of China on the other. Agreements since early 1972 seem to fit into a general evolution of international relations away from the idolatry of national power, if only because of the peril of nuclear war to any that overextend such power. Yet, at the same time, it is not very clear how détente affects certain matters of great international consequence, such as human rights and the distribution of wealth, except for some vague spillover in ideological rhetoric.

Diplomacy and war remain central to the practical operation of the international political order, and the United States and Soviet Union dominate diplomacy and war, even in this age of new international issues and a moderated bipolar condominium. By a simple syllogism, it should follow that détente, now critical to the relations between the United States, the Soviet Union, and the People's Republic of China, should be vital to international politics in some way, and so it is. No reasonable person can deny this logic, so often propounded by official apologists. But what significance has this logic for the steady improvement of international relations? Only by giving some substance to détente—by answering the question of what détente is, in contrast to emphasizing the logic of détente—is it possible to see how détente functions in the evolution of international relations toward a more desirable system of minimal violence and enhanced global community.

Does détente actually improve or diminish the chances of reaching world peace and institutionalized global authority? To answer this question, there must be clearly defined values toward which the international system should evolve *and* a good understanding of how détente serves or hinders this evolution. Both views of détente, from the outside-in as a matter of importance for the international order and from the inside-out as a vital issue for national foreign policies, require consideration. Unfortunately, the discussion of détente has not yet become systematic enough to allow such consideration, though the debate does touch on these two viewpoints. Simplistic defenders of détente argue, by definition, that peaceful intentions constitute a step toward international peace. Sophisticated proponents

3

would add that a global order with minimal violence must have institutions as well as intentions. It is precisely on the issue of what significant institutional improvement in the international order has occurred during détente that the most prescient criticism concentrates. In the final analysis, the crucial debate between friends and foes of détente may well center on its significance for improving life in the international order, rather than on its contribution to better relations between the United States and the U.S.S.R. There is no simple equation that links the first issue with the second.

The ties between improved bilateral relations among adversaries and improved life in the international order are highly complicated. For those who espouse détente in American foreign policy, the metaphors of a "linkage" and a "web" have been used to picture a steady accumulation of cooperative activity, resulting from joint agreements and undertakings, that contrasts the present era with the cold war. Critics are skeptical, refusing to equate the metaphorical with the real. It should be noted, however, that complicated fields of intellectual endeavor, such as modern physics, have used metaphor effectively in their early stages of development to express radically changed concepts. As Niels Bohr noted in 1922, "when it comes to atoms, language can be used only as in poetry."[1] A similar case could be made for metaphorical foreign policy that somehow must account for and express dramatic world changes. Again, the critics of détente are skeptical that the changes have been dramatic and, in any case, insist that metaphors should eventually yield to accomplishments.

No area of evolving relations between the United States and the Soviet Union has received as much attention by those skeptical of détente as national defense. Reservations about détente have been expressed both by those who approach defense relations with the Soviet Union in strictly national terms and by those who question how détente might lead to diminished violence in world politics. There is little doubt that negotiations between Moscow and Washington on military issues, most notably in the strategic arms limitation talks (SALT), rest on the assumption that military power is more constrained in the evolving international system for a variety of reasons. Chief among these reasons appears to be the nuclear balance of terror between the United States and the U.S.S.R., which threatens these two superpowers with vast destruction. A simple equation is

---

[1] Werner Heisenberg, *Physics and Beyond: Encounters and Conversations*, trans. Arnold J. Pomerans (New York: Harper & Row, 1971), pp. 40-41; quoted in Robert J. Pranger, *Defense Implications of International Indeterminacy* (Washington, D.C.: American Enterprise Institute, 1972), p. 12.

inferred between this bilateral fear and the advancement of the international order toward less interstate violence: out of dread springs authority, as Hobbes noted.

Thoughtful students of the evolving constraints on military power, however, realistically note that military force is still a lively part of an international order where politics is deficient in its other forms.[2] In the past decade, there have been examples of astonishing military success by certain nations in pursuit of political objectives. And now there appears a tendency for militarily powerful states to add nuclear arms to their arsenals for reasons that seem less a function of fear than of national ambition. The nuclear balance between Moscow and Washington may well be calibrated under constant anxiety of mutual destruction, but do the same restraints apply to the proliferation of atomic weapons in the Middle East, Asia, and Latin America? What linkage is there between the United States–U.S.S.R. nuclear balance and the reduction of violence in the international order? With or without SALT, does the equation of "super" power with atomic weapons encourage or discourage nuclear proliferation? And does such proliferation add to the dangers of war in the international order, or does it deter war?

As in the case of détente in the sense of the stated principles of peaceful cooperation between capitalist and Communist nations, so also on the more specific subject of national defense there exists no simple formula that links bilateral relations—even among superpowers —with an evolving international system. In defense matters as in other areas of détente, the final debate between proponents and critics may well focus on how détente works to improve political organization in the international order itself. Where it is found that peacemaking between Moscow and Washington does not translate into peacekeeping within the international order more generally, serious questions will be raised about détente, both in principle and in terms of its current operations.

The readings in this book are organized into topics ranging from broad considerations of where the international political order is headed to specific questions about the national defense efforts of the United States and U.S.S.R. In the center of concern stands the policy of détente. This volume is designed to give a global perspective on

---

[2] See Kenneth Waltz, *Man, the State and War* (New York: Columbia University Press, 1959); Klaus Knorr, *On the Uses of Military Power in the Nuclear Age* (Princeton: Princeton University Press, 1965); Stanley Hoffmann, "The Acceptability of Military Force," in *Force in Modern Societies: Its Place in International Politics*, Adelphi Paper No. 102 (London: The International Institute for Strategic Studies, 1973), pp. 2-13.

détente as well as to provide information and analysis about the changing relations between the United States and the Communist nations.

PART ONE
OVERVIEW

1

PROBLEMS OF FUTURE
AMERICAN FOREIGN POLICY

U.S. FOREIGN POLICY FOR THE 1970s:
SHAPING A DURABLE PEACE *

Richard M. Nixon

In this report, former President Richard Nixon summarizes the reasons underlying the foreign policy initiatives pursued during the first four years of his Administration. Fundamental to these initiatives was the policy of détente with the Soviet Union and the People's Republic of China. The President argues that the expansive policies pursued by the United States during the postwar period had become seriously misaligned from current realities by the late 1960s, and this caused unnecessary difficulties in our international relationships. To correct these problems, a new international philosophy articulating viable policies was needed. America was to move away from a paternalistic to a cooperative view of its global mission, while continuing to undertake a major commitment toward the world for the pursuit of peace.

In January 1969, America needed to change the philosophy and practice of its foreign policy.

Whoever took office four years ago would have faced this challenge. After a generation, the postwar world had been transformed and demanded a fresh approach. It was not a question of our previous policies having failed; indeed, in many areas they had been very successful. It was rather that new conditions, many of them achievements of our policies, summoned new perspectives.

---

* Source: *U.S. Foreign Policy for the 1970s: Shaping a Durable Peace*, A Report to the Congress by Richard Nixon, President of the United States, 3 May 1973, pp. 2-10.

RICHARD M. NIXON

The World We Found

The international environment was dominated by seemingly intractable confrontation between the two major nuclear powers. Throughout the nuclear age, both the fears of war and hopes for peace revolved around our relations with the Soviet Union. Our growing nuclear arsenals were largely directed at each other. We alone had the capacity to wreak catastrophic damage across the planet. Our ideologies clashed. We both had global interests, and this produced many friction points. We each led and dominated a coalition of opposing states.

As a result, our relationship was generally hostile. There were positive interludes, but these were often atmospheric and did not get at the roots of tension. Accords were reached on particular questions, but there was no broad momentum in our relationship. Improvements in the climate were quickly replaced by confrontation and, occasionally, crisis. The basic pattern was a tense jockeying for tactical advantage around the globe.

This was dangerous and unsatisfactory. The threat of a major conflict between us hung over the world. This in turn exacerbated local and regional tensions. And our two countries not only risked collision but were constrained from working positively on common problems.

The weight of China rested outside the international framework. This was due partly to its own attitude and its preoccupation with internal problems, and partly to the policies of the outside world, most importantly the United States. In any event, this Administration inherited two decades of mutual estrangement and hostility. Here the problem was not one of a fluctuating relationship but rather of having no relationship at all. The People's Republic of China was separated not only from us but essentially from the world as a whole.

China also exemplified the great changes that had occurred in the Communist world. For years our guiding principle was containment of what we considered a monolithic challenge. In the 1960s, the forces of nationalism dissolved Communist unity into divergent centers of power and doctrine, and our foreign policy began to differentiate among the Communist capitals. But this process could not be truly effective so long as we were cut off from one-quarter of the globe's people. China in turn was emerging from its isolation and might be more receptive to overtures from foreign countries.

The gulf between China and the world distorted the international landscape. We could not effectively reduce tensions in Asia without talking to Peking. China's isolation compounded its own sense of insecurity. There could not be a stable world order with a major power remaining outside and hostile to it.

Our principal alliances with Western Europe and Japan needed adjustment. After the devastation of the Second World War, we had helped allies and former adversaries alike. Fueled by our assistance and secure behind our military shield, they regained their economic vigor and political confidence.

Throughout the postwar period our bonds with Europe had rested on American prescriptions as well as resources. We provided much of the leadership and planning for common defense. We took the diplomatic lead. The dollar was unchallenged. But, by the time this Administration took office, the tide was flowing toward greater economic and political assertiveness by our allies. European unity, which we had always encouraged, was raising new issues in Atlantic relations. The economic revival of Europe was straining the Atlantic monetary and commercial framework. The relaxation of tensions with the Communist world was generating new doctrines of defense and diplomacy.

The imperatives of change were equally evident in our Pacific partnership with Japan. Its recovery of strength and self-assurance carried political and psychological implications for our relationship. Its spectacular economic growth had made it the world's third industrial power; our entire economic relationship was undergoing transformation. The earlier paternalism of U.S.–Japanese relations no longer suited either partner.

The Vietnam war dominated our attention and was sapping our self-confidence. Our role and our costs had steadily grown without decisive impact on the conflict. The outlook at the conference table was bleak. The war was inhibiting our policy abroad and fostering dissent and self-doubt at home. There was no prospect of either an end to the fighting or an end to our involvement.

Although the historical imperatives for a new international approach existed independently, the war made this challenge at once more urgent and more difficult. More than any other factor, it threatened to exhaust the American people's willingness to sustain a reliable foreign policy. As much as any other factor, the way we treated it would shape overseas attitudes and American psychology.

The context for our national security policy was fundamentally altered. From the mid 1940s to the late 1960s, we had moved from

11

America's nuclear monopoly to superiority to rough strategic balance with the Soviet Union. This created fresh challenges to our security and introduced new calculations in our diplomacy. The U.S. defense effort remained disproportionate to that of our allies, who had grown much stronger. The threats from potential enemies were more varied and less blatant than during the more rigid bipolar era. These changes, combined with spiraling military costs and the demands of domestic programs, were prompting reexamination of our defense doctrines and posture. They were underlining the importance of arms control as an element in national security. They were also leading some in this country to call for policies that would seriously jeopardize our safety and world stability.

Around the world, friends were ready for a greater role in shaping their own security and well-being. In the 1950s and 1960s other nations had looked to America for ideas and resources, and they found us a willing provider of both. Our motives were sound, the needs were clear, and we had many successes. By 1969, scores of new nations, having emerged from colonial status or dependency on major powers, were asserting themselves with greater assurance and autonomy.

Four years ago, this growing capacity of friends was not reflected in the balance of contributions to security and development. This meant that others could do more, and the United States need do proportionately less, in the provision of material resources. More fundamentally, it meant that increasingly the devising of plans belonged outside of Washington. The sweeping American presence was likely to strain our capabilities and to stifle the initiative of others.

There were new issues that called for global cooperation. These challenges were not susceptible to national solutions or relevant to national ideologies. The vast frontiers of space and the oceans beckoned international exploration for humanity's gain. Pollution of air, sea, and land could not be contained behind national frontiers. The brutal tools of assassination, kidnapping, and hijacking could be used to further any cause in any country. No nation's youth was immune from the scourge of international drug traffic. The immediate tragedies of national disasters and the longer-term threat of overpopulation were humanitarian, not political, concerns.

At home we faced pressures that threatened to swing America from overextension in the world to heedless withdrawal from it. The American people had supported the burdens of global leadership with enthusiasm and generosity into the 1960s. But, after almost three decades, our enthusiasm was waning, and the results of our generosity were being questioned. Our policies needed change, not only to match new realities in the world but also to meet a new mood in America. Many Americans were no longer willing to support the sweeping range of our postwar role. It had drained our financial, and especially our psychological, reserves. Our friends clearly were able to do more. The Vietnam experience was hastening our awareness of change. Voices in this country were claiming that we had to jettison global concerns and turn inward in order to meet our domestic problems.

Therefore the whole underpinning of our foreign policy was in jeopardy. The bipartisan consensus that once existed for a vigorous American internationalism was now being torn apart. Some of the most active proponents of America's commitment in the world in previous decades were now pressing for indiscriminate disengagement. What was once seen as America's overseas obligation was now seen as our overseas preoccupation. What was once viewed as America's unselfishness was now viewed as our naivete. By 1969, we faced the danger that public backing for a continuing world role might be swept away by fatigue, frustration, and overreaction.

This Administration's Approach

We were determined to shape new policies to deal with each of these problems. But our first requirement was philosophic. We needed a fresh vision to inspire and to integrate our efforts.

We began with the conviction that a major American commitment to the world continued to be indispensable. The many changes in the postwar landscape did not alter this central fact. America's strength was so vast, our involvement so broad, and our concerns so deep, that to remove our influence would set off tremors around the globe. Friends would despair, adversaries would be tempted, and our own national security would soon be threatened. There was no escaping the reality of our enormous influence for peace.

But the new times demanded a new definition of our involvement. For more than a score of years our foreign policy had been driven by a global mission that only America could fulfill—to furnish political leadership, provide for the common defense, and promote economic development. Allies were weak, and other nations were young, threats were palpable, and American power was dominant.

By 1969, a mission of this scale was no longer valid abroad or supportable at home. Allies had grown stronger, and young nations

13

were maturing, threats were diversified, and American power was offset. It was time to move from a paternal mission *for* others to a cooperative mission *with* others. Convinced as we were that a strong American role remained essential for world stability, we knew, too, that a peace that depends primarily on the exertions of one nation is inherently fragile.

So we saw the potential and the imperative of a pluralistic world. We believed we could move from an environment of emergencies to a more stable international system. We made our new purpose a global structure of peace—comprehensive because it would draw on the efforts of other countries; durable because if countries helped to build it, they would also help to maintain it.

To pursue this fundamental vision, we had to move across a wide and coordinated front, with mutually reinforcing policies for each challenge we faced.

Peace could not depend solely on the uneasy equilibrium between two nuclear giants. We had a responsibility to work for positive relations with the Soviet Union. But there was ample proof that assertions of good will or transitory changes in climate would not erase the hard realities of ideological opposition, geopolitical rivalry, competing alliances, or military competition. We were determined not to lurch along—with isolated agreements vulnerable to sudden shifts of course in political relations, with peaks and valleys based on atmosphere, with incessant tension and maneuvering. We saw as well that there were certain mutual interests that we could build upon. As the two powers capable of global destruction, we had a common stake in preserving peace.

Thus, we decided to follow certain principles in our policy toward the Soviet Union. We would engage in concrete negotiations designed to produce specific agreements, both where differences existed and where cooperation was possible. We would work with Moscow across a broad front, believing that progress in one area would induce progress in others. Through the gathering momentum of individual accords, we would seek to create vested interests on both sides in restraint and the strengthening of peace. But this process would require a reduction in tactical maneuvering at each other's expense in favor of our shared interest in avoiding a calamitous collision, in profiting from cooperation, and in building a more stable world.

Peace could not exclude a fourth of humanity. The longer-term prospects for peace required a new relationship with the People's Republic of China. Only if China's weight was reflected in the international system would it have the incentive, and sense of shared responsibility, to maintain the peace. Furthermore, the time was past when one nation could claim to speak for a bloc of states; we would deal with countries on the basis of their actions, not abstract ideological formulas. Our own policies could be more flexible if we did not assume the permanent enmity of China. The United States had a traditional interest in an independent and peaceful China. We seemed to have no fundamental interests that need collide in the longer sweep of history. There was, indeed, rich potential benefit for our two peoples in a more normal relationship.

So we launched a careful process of private diplomacy and public steps to engage the People's Republic of China with us and involve it more fully in the world. We did so, confident that a strong, independent China was in our national interest; resolved that such a process need not—and would not—be aimed at any other country; and looking for a reciprocal attitude on the part of the Chinese.

Peace must draw upon the vitality of our friends. Our alliances with Western Europe and Japan would continue as major pillars of our foreign policy, but they had not kept pace with the changed international environment. We thus sought to forge more equal partnerships based on a more balanced contribution of both resources and plans.

America had been the automatic source of political leadership and economic power. Now we needed new modes of action that would accommodate our partners' new dynamism. The challenge was to reconcile traditional unity with new diversity. While complete integration of policy was impossible, pure unilateralism would be destructive.

Before, we were allied in containment of a unified Communist danger. Now communism had taken various forms; our alliances had stabilized the European and Northeast Asian environments; and we had laid the foundations for negotiation. We had to decide together not only what we were against, but what we were for.

Peace required the ending of an ongoing war. Our approach to the Vietnam conflict and our shaping of a new foreign policy were inextricably linked. Naturally, our most urgent concern was to end the war. But we had to end it—or at least our involvement—in a way that would continue to make possible a responsible American role in the world.

We could not continue on the course we inherited, which promised neither an end to the conflict nor to our involvement. At the same time, we would not abandon our friends, for we wanted to shape

15

a structure of peace based in large measure on American steadiness. So we sought peace with honor—through negotiation if possible, through Vietnamization if the enemy gave us no choice. The phased shifting of defense responsibilities to the South Vietnamese would give them the time and means to adjust. It would assure the American people that our own involvement was not open-ended. It would preserve our credibility abroad and our cohesion at home.

Given the enemy's attitude, peace was likely to take time, and other problems in the world could not wait. So we moved promptly to shape a new approach to allies and adversaries. And by painting on this larger canvas, we sought both to put the Vietnam war in perspective and to speed its conclusion by demonstrating to Hanoi that continued conflict did not frustrate our global policies.

Peace needed America's strength. Modifications in our defense policy were required, but one central truth persisted—neither our nation nor peace in the world could be secure without our military power. If superiority was no longer practical, inferiority would be unthinkable.

We were determined to maintain a national defense second to none. This would be a force for stability in a world of evolving partnerships and changing doctrines. This was essential to maintain the confidence of our friends and the respect of our adversaries. At the same time, we would seek energetically to promote national and international security through arms control negotiations.

Peace involved a fresh dimension of international cooperation. A new form of multilateral diplomacy was prompted by a new set of issues. These challenges covered a wide range—the promise of exploration, the pollution of our planet, the perils of crime—but they were alike in going beyond the traditional considerations of doctrine and geography. They required cooperation that reached not only across boundaries but often around the globe. So we resolved to work both with friends and adversaries, in the United Nations and other forums, to practice partnership on a global scale.

Above all, peace demanded the responsible participation of all nations. With great efforts during the postwar period, we had promoted the revitalization of former powers and the growing assurance of new states. For this changed world, we needed a new philosophy that would reflect and reconcile two basic principles: *A structure of peace requires the greater participation of other nations, but it also requires the sustained participation of the United States.*

16

To these ends, we developed the Nixon Doctrine of shared responsibilities. This doctrine was central to our approach to major allies in the Atlantic and Pacific. But it also shaped our attitude toward those in Latin America, Asia, and Africa with whom we were working in formal alliances or friendship.

Our primary purpose was to invoke greater efforts by others— not so much to lighten our burdens as to increase their commitment to a new and peaceful structure. This would mean that increasingly they would man their own defenses and furnish more of the funds for their security and economic development. The corollary would be the reduction of the American share of defense or financial contributions.

More fundamental than this material redistribution, however, was a psychological reorientation. Nations had habitually relied on us for political leadership. Much time and energy went into influencing decisions in Washington. Our objective now was to encourage them to play a greater role in formulating plans and programs. For when others design their security and their development, they make their destiny truly their own. And when the plans are their plans, they are more motivated to make them realities.

The lowering of our profile was not an end in itself. Other countries needed to do more, but they could not do so without a concerned America. Their role had to be increased, but this would prove empty unless we did what we must. We could not go from overinvolvement to neglect. A changing world needed the continuity of America's strength.

Thus, we made clear that the Nixon Doctrine represented a new definition of American leadership, not abandonment of that leadership. In my 1971 report, I set forth the need for a responsible balance:

> The Nixon Doctrine recognizes that we cannot abandon friends, and must not transfer burdens too swiftly. We must strike a balance between doing too much, and thus preventing self-reliance, and doing too little, and thus undermining self-confidence.
>
> The balance we seek abroad is crucial. We only compound insecurity if we modify our protective or development responsibilities without giving our friends the time and the means to adjust, materially and psychologically, to a new form of American participation in the world.
>
> Precipitate shrinking of the American role would not bring peace. It would not reduce America's stake in a turbulent world. It would not solve our problems, either abroad or at home.

Peace had a domestic dimension. Steadiness abroad required steadiness at home. America could continue to make its vital contribution in the world only if Americans understood the need and supported the effort to do so. But understanding and support for a responsible foreign policy were in serious jeopardy in 1969. Years of burdens, cold war tensions, and a difficult war threatened to undermine our constancy.

While new policies were required to meet transformed conditions abroad they were equally imperative because of the changing climate at home. Americans needed a new positive vision of the world and our place in it.

IN THRALL TO FEAR *

J. William Fulbright

J. William Fulbright, former U.S. senator from Arkansas and chairman of the Senate Foreign Relations Committee, discusses the Truman Doctrine as a force that shaped many crucial U.S. foreign policy actions from the time it was formulated in 1947, as a response to Communist activity in Greece and Turkey. He contends that the universal application of this doctrine during the following decades was inappropriate because it postulated only one principal motive for the actions of our antagonists, and he reviews several situations to demonstrate that this simplistic point of view was inaccurate. Seeing America at a turning point following the Vietnam War, Fulbright argues that the United States should embrace true internationalism through support of the United Nations as it was initially conceived.

For reasons still not wholly known and understood, the grand alliance of the Second World War broke up almost as soon as victory was won, and the powers that had called themselves "the United Nations" fell into the pattern of hostility, periodic crisis, and "limited" war that has characterized world politics for the last twenty-five years. At Yalta in February 1945, the United States, Great Britain, and the Soviet Union pledged to maintain and strengthen in peace the "unity of purpose and of action" that was bringing victory in war. Just over two years later, on 12 March 1947, President Truman proclaimed the

---

* Source: J. William Fulbright, *The Crippled Giant* (New York: Random-House, 1972); originally published in *The New Yorker* (8 January 1972), pp. 44-62.

doctrine that came to be recognized as the basic rationale, from the American standpoint, for the cold war. President Truman based the appeal he made to Congress for support of Greece and Turkey not primarily on the specific circumstances of those two countries at that time but on a general formulation of the American national interest which held that "totalitarian regimes imposed on free peoples, by direct or indirect aggression, undermine the foundations of international peace and hence the security of the United States." President Truman went on to say that at that moment in world history "nearly every nation must choose between alternative ways of life"— the one based on democratic institutions, like our own, and the other based on "terror and oppression," for which the model, of course, was the Soviet Union.

Most of us thought we knew how and why this great transition— from "unity of purpose and of action" to Truman's declaration of ideological warfare—had come about in so short a time. The cause was Soviet Communist aggression, limited at the outset to Stalin's subjugation of Eastern Europe but shown by Marxist-Leninist doctrine to be universal in design, aimed at nothing less than the communization of the world. American policy and opinion were profoundly influenced in the early postwar period by the thesis that George Kennan, signing himself "X," set forth in *Foreign Affairs* for July 1947, which depicted Soviet policy as relentlessly expansionist, committed by a fanatical ideology to filling "every nook and cranny available . . . in the basin of world power," and "stopping only when it meets with some unanswerable force." Warning against bluster and excessive reliance on military force, Kennan nonetheless called for an American policy of "unalterable counter force," of "firm and vigilant containment," which he anticipated would "increase enormously the strains under which Soviet policy must operate," and encourage changes within Russia leading to "either the breakup or the gradual mellowing of Soviet power."

From Korea to Berlin to Cuba to Vietnam, the Truman Doctrine governed America's response to the Communist world. Tactics changed—from "massive retaliation" to "limited war" and "counter-insurgency"—but these were variations on a classic formulation based on assumptions that few really questioned. Sustained by an inert Congress, the policy makers of the forties, fifties, and early sixties were never compelled to reexamine the premises of the Truman Doctrine, or even to defend them in constructive adversary proceedings.

Change has come not from wisdom but from disaster. The calamitous failure of American policy in Vietnam has induced on the part of scholars, journalists, and politicians a belated willingness to reexamine the basic assumptions of American postwar policy. Induced by the agitations of the present moment, this new look at old events may well result in an excess of revision, or of emotion, but the corrective is much needed if we are to profit from experience and recast our policies. It cannot be said that the assumptions underlying the Truman Doctrine were wholly false, especially for their time and place. But there is a powerful presumptive case against their subsequent universal application—the case deriving from the disaster of our policy in Asia—and it seems appropriate to look back and try to discover how and why the promise of the United Nations Charter gave way so quickly to ideological warfare between East and West.

Until fairly recently, I accepted the conventional view that the United States had acted in good faith to make the United Nations work but that the charter was undermined by the Soviet veto. In retrospect, this seems less certain, and one suspects now that, like the League of Nations before it, the United Nations was orphaned at birth. Whereas Woodrow Wilson's great creation was abandoned to skeptical Europeans, Franklin Roosevelt's project was consigned to the care of unsympathetic men of his own country. President Roosevelt died only two weeks before the opening of the meeting in San Francisco at which the United Nations was organized. Truman, as a new and inexperienced President, was naturally more dependent on his advisers than President Roosevelt had been; among these, so far as I know, none was a strong supporter of the plan for a world organization, as Cordell Hull had been. The under secretary of state, Dean Acheson, was assigned to lobby for Senate approval of the United Nations Charter, and he recalled later that "I did my duty faithfully and successfully, but always believed that the charter was impractical." And, with even greater asperity and candor, he told an interviewer in 1970, "I never thought the United Nations was worth a damn. To a lot of people it was a holy grail, and those who set store by it had the misfortune to believe their own bunk."

Disdaining the United Nations, the framers of the Truman Doctrine also nurtured an intense hostility toward communism and the Soviet Union. Stalin, of course, did much to earn this hostility, with his paranoiac suspiciousness, the imposition of Soviet domination in Eastern Europe, and the use of Western Communist parties as instruments of Soviet policy. All this is well known. Less well known, far more puzzling, and also more pertinent to our position in the world today is the eagerness with which we seized upon postwar

Soviet provocations and plunged into the cold war. If it be granted that Stalin started the cold war, it must also be recognized that the Truman Administration seemed to welcome it.

By early 1947—a year and a half after the founding of the United Nations—the assumptions of the cold war were all but unchallenged within the United States government. It was *assumed* that the object of Soviet policy was the communization of the world; if Soviet behavior in Europe and northern China were not proof enough, the design was spelled out in the writings of Lenin and Marx, which our policy makers chose to read not as a body of political philosophy but as the field manual of Soviet strategy. It is true, of course, that by 1947, with the United States virtually disarmed and Western Europe in a condition of economic paralysis, the Soviet Union might plausibly have tried to take over Western Europe through the manipulation of Communist parties, through military intimidation, through economic strangulation, and possibly even through direct military action. The fact that Stalin could have done this, and might well have tried but for timely American counteraction through the Marshall Plan and the formation of NATO, was quickly and uncritically taken as proof of a design for unlimited conquest comparable to that of Nazi Germany. Neither in the executive branch of our government nor in Congress were more than a few, isolated voices raised to suggest the possibility that Soviet policy in Europe might be motivated by morbid fears for the security of the Soviet Union rather than by a design for world conquest. Virtually no one in a position of power was receptive to the hypothesis that Soviet truculence reflected weakness rather than strength, intensified by memories of 1919, when the Western powers had intervened in an effort—however halfhearted—to strangle the Bolshevik "monster" in its cradle. Our own policy was formed without the benefit of constructive adversary proceedings. A few brave individuals, like former Vice President Henry Wallace, offered dissenting counsel—and paid dearly for it.

When Great Britain informed the United States in February 1947 that it was no longer able to provide military support for Greece, the American government was ready with a policy and a world view. The latter was an early version of the domino theory. Knowing, as we thought we did, that Russian support for Communist insurgents in Greece was part of a grand design for the takeover first of Greece, then of Turkey, the Middle East, and so forth, we were not content simply to assume the British role of providing arms to a beleaguered government; instead, we chose to issue a declaration of ideological warfare in the form of the Truman Doctrine. It may well be true that the grand phrases were motivated in part by a desire to arouse this nation's combative spirit, and so to build congressional support for the funds involved, but it is also true—at least, according to Joseph Jones, the State Department official who drafted President Truman's appeal to Congress, under Acheson's direction—that the new policy was conceived not just as a practical measure to bolster the Greeks and Turks but as a historic summons of the United States to world leadership. "*All* barriers to bold action were indeed down," as Jones has written. Among the State Department policy makers, Jones reports, it was felt that "a new chapter in world history had opened, and they were the most privileged of men, participants in a drama such as rarely occurs even in the long life of a great nation."

The Truman Doctrine, which may have made sense for its time and place, was followed by the Marshall Plan and NATO, which surely did make sense for their time and place. But as a charter for twenty-five years of global ideological warfare and unilateral military intervention against Communist insurgencies the Truman Doctrine has a different set of implications altogether. It represents a view of communism, of the world, and of our role in the world that has had much to do with the disaster of our policy in Asia. Even in the country to which it was first applied, President Truman's basic formulation—that "we shall not realize our objectives . . . unless we are willing to help free peoples to maintain their free institutions"—has been reduced to a mockery. But who remembers now (surely not Mr. Agnew) that the Truman Doctrine was initially designed to preserve democracy in Greece?

Acheson, who prided himself on being a realist, may not have taken all that ideological claptrap seriously, but his successors Dulles and Rusk certainly did, and they framed their policies accordingly. Whatever merit the Truman Doctrine may have had in the circumstances of early postwar Europe, the bond with reality became more and more strained as the doctrine came to be applied at times and in places increasingly remote from the Greek civil war. Operating on a set of assumptions that defined reality for them—that as a social system communism was deeply immoral, that as a political movement it was a conspiracy for world conquest—our leaders became liberated from the normal rules of evidence and inference when it came to dealing with communism. After all, who ever heard of giving the devil a fair shake? Since we know what he has in mind, it is pedantry to split hairs over what he is actually doing.

Political pressures at home intensified the virulence of the anti-Communist ideology. In retrospect, the surprise Democratic victory in the election of 1948 was probably a misfortune for the country. The Republicans, frustrated and enraged by their fifth successive defeat, became desperate in their search for a winning issue. They found their issue in the threat of communism, at home and abroad, and they seized upon it with uncommon ferocity. They blamed the Truman Administration for Chiang Kai-shek's defeat in the Chinese civil war; they attacked President Truman for the bloody stalemate in Korea, although they had strongly supported his initial commitment; and they tolerated and in many cases encouraged Senator Joseph R. McCarthy's attacks on reputable, and even eminent, Americans. Every American President since that time has been under intense pressure to demonstrate his anti-Communist orthodoxy.

More by far than any other factor, the anti-communism of the Truman Doctrine has been the guiding spirit of American foreign policy since the Second World War. Stalin and Mao Tse-tung and even Ho Chi Minh replaced Hitler in our minds as the sources of all evil in the world. We came to see the hand of "Moscow communism" in every disruption that occurred anywhere. First, there was the conception of communism as an international conspiracy—as an octopus with its body in Moscow and its tentacles reaching out to the farthest corners of the world. Later, after the Sino-Soviet break, sophisticated foreign policy analysts disavowed the conspiracy thesis, but at the same time they disavowed it they said things that showed that the faith lingered on. Secretary Rusk and his associates professed to be scornful of the conspiracy thesis, but still they defended the Vietnam war with references to a world "cut in two by Asian communism," the only difference between the earlier view and the later one being that where once we had seen one octopus we now saw two.

If you accepted the premise, the rest followed. If Moscow and Peking represented centers of great power implacably hostile to the United States, and if every local crisis, from Cuba to the Congo to Vietnam, had the Communist mark upon it, then it followed logically that every crisis posed a threat to the security of the United States. The effect of the anti-Communist ideology was to spare us the task of taking cognizance of the specific facts of specific situations. Our "faith" liberated us, like the believers of old, from the requirements of empirical thinking, from the necessity of observing and evaluating the actual behavior of the nations and leaders with whom we were dealing. Like medieval theologians, we had a philosophy that explained everything to us in advance, and everything that did not fit could be readily identified as a fraud or a lie or an illusion. The fact that in some respects the behavior of the Soviet Union and of China and North Vietnam lived up to our ideological expectations made it all the easier to ignore the instances in which it did not. What we are now, belatedly, discovering is not that the Communist states have never really been hostile to us but that they have been neither consistent nor united in hostility to us; that their hostility has by no means been wholly unprovoked; and that they have been willing from time to time to do business or come to terms with us. Our ideological blinders concealed these instances from us, robbing us of useful information and of promising opportunities. The perniciousness of the anti-Communist ideology of the Truman Doctrine arises not from any patent falsehood but from its distortion and simplification of reality, from its universalization and its elevation to the status of a revealed truth.

Psychologists tell us that there is often a great difference between what one person says and what another hears, or, in variation of the old adage, that the evil may be in the ear of the hearer. When Khrushchev said, "We will bury you," Americans heard the statement as a threat of nuclear war and were outraged accordingly. The matter was raised when Chairman Khrushchev visited the United States in 1959, and he replied with some anger that he had been talking about economic competition. "I am deeply concerned over these conscious distortions of my thoughts," he said. "I've never mentioned any rockets."

We will never know, of course, but it is possible that an opportunity for a stable peace was lost during the years of Khrushchev's power. As we look back now on the many things he said regarding peaceful coexistence, the words have a different ring. At the time, we did not believe them: at best, they were Communist propaganda; at worst, outright lies. I recalled recently, for example, the visit of Chairman Khrushchev to the Senate Foreign Relations Committee on 16 September 1959. Suggesting that we lay aside the polemics of the past, Mr. Khrushchev said:

> We must face the future more and have wisdom enough to secure peace for our countries and for the whole world. We have always had great respect for the American people. We have also been somewhat envious of your achievements in the economic field, and for that reason we are doing our best to try to catch up with you in that field, to compete with you, and when we do catch up to move further ahead. I should say that future generations would be grateful to us

if we managed to switch our efforts from stockpiling and perfecting weapons and concentrated those efforts fully on competition in the economic field.

Now, in retrospect, one wonders: why were we so sure that Khrushchev didn't mean what he said about peace? The answer lies in part, I believe, in our anti-Communist obsession—in the distortions it created in our perception of Soviet behavior, and in the extraordinary sense of threat we experienced when the Russians proclaimed their desire to catch up and overtake us economically. In our own national value system, competition has always been prized; why, then, should we have been so alarmed by a challenge to compete? Perhaps our national tendency to extol competition rather than cooperation as a social virtue and our preoccupation with our own primacy—with being the "biggest," the "greatest" nation—suggest an underlying lack of confidence in ourselves, a supposition that unless we are "number one" we will be nothing: worthless and despised, and deservedly so. I am convinced that the real reason we squandered $20 billion or more getting men to the moon in the decade of the sixties was our fear of something like horrible humiliation if the Russians got men there first. All this suggests that slogans about competition and our own primacy in that competition are largely hot air—sincerely believed, no doubt, but nonetheless masking an exaggerated fear of failure, which, in turn, lends a quality of desperation to our competitive endeavors. One detects this cast of mind in President Johnson's determination that he would not be "the first American President to lose a war," and also in President Nixon's specter of America as "a pitiful, helpless giant."

This kind of thinking robs a nation's policy makers of objectivity and drives them to irresponsible behavior. The distortion of priorities involved in going to the moon is a relatively benign example. The perpetuation of the Vietnam War is the most terrible and fateful manifestation of the determination to prove that we are "number one." Assistant Secretary of Defense for International Security Affairs John T. McNaughton, as quoted in the Pentagon Papers, measured the American interest in Vietnam and found that "to permit the people of South Vietnam to enjoy a better, freer way of life" accounted for a mere 10 percent and "to avoid a humiliating U.S. defeat" for up to 70 percent. McNaughton's statistical metaphor suggests a nation in thrall to fear; it suggests a policy-making elite unable to distinguish between the national interest and their own personal pride.

Perhaps if we had been less proud and less fearful, we would have responded in a more positive way to the earthy, unorthodox

Khrushchev. Whatever his faults and excesses, Khrushchev is recognized in retrospect as the Communist leader who repudiated the Marxist dogma of the "inevitability" of war between Socialist and capitalist states. Understanding the insanity of war with nuclear weapons, Khrushchev became the advocate of "goulash" communism, of peaceful economic competition with the West. During his period in office, some amenities were restored in East-West relations; the Berlin issue was stirred up but finally defused; and, most important, the limited-nuclear-test-ban treaty was concluded. These were solid achievements, though meager in proportion to mankind's need for peace, and meager, too, it now appears, in proportion to the opportunity that may then have existed. One wonders how much more might have been accomplished—particularly in the field of disarmament—if Americans had not still been caught up in the prideful, fearful spirit of the Truman Doctrine.

Even the crises look different in retrospect, especially when one takes into account the internal workings of the Communist world. A leading British authority on Soviet affairs, Victor Zorza, has traced the beginning of the Vietnam War to a "fatal misreading" by President Kennedy of Khrushchev's endorsement of "wars of national liberation." The Kennedy Administration interpreted Khrushchev's statement as a declaration that the Soviet Union intended to sponsor subversion, guerrilla warfare, and rebellion all over the world. Accordingly, the Administration attached enormous significance to Soviet material support for the Laotian Communists, as if the issue in that remote and backward land were directly pertinent to the world balance of power. It was judged that Khrushchev must be shown that he could not get away with it. We had taught Stalin that "direct" aggression did not pay; now we must teach Khrushchev—and the Chinese—that "indirect" aggression did not pay. In Zorza's view, Khrushchev's talk of "wars of national liberation" was not a serious plan for worldwide subversion but a response to Communist China, whose leaders were then accusing Khrushchev of selling out the cause of revolution and making a deal with the United States.

In the spirit of the Truman Doctrine, the Kennedy Administration read the Soviet endorsement of "wars of national liberation" as a direct challenge to the United States. Speaking of the Soviet Union and China, President Kennedy said in his first State of the Union Message, "We must never be lulled into believing that either power has yielded its ambitions for world domination—ambitions which they forcefully restated only a short time ago." I do not recall these words for purposes of reproach; they represented an assessment of

Communist intentions that most of us shared at that time, an assessment that had been held by every Administration and most members of Congress since the Second World War, an assessment that had scarcely—if at all—been brought up for critical examination in the executive branch, in congressional committees, in the proliferating "think tanks," or in the universities. Perhaps no better assessment could have been made on the basis of the information available at that time, but I doubt it. I think it more likely that we simply chose to ignore evidence that did not fit our preconceptions, or—as is more often the case—when the facts lent themselves to several possible interpretations we chose to seize upon the one with which we were most familiar: the Communist drive for world domination.

In the amplified form it acquired during the Johnson years, the conception of "wars of national liberation" as part of the Communist design for world domination became the basic rationale for the Vietnam War. All the other excuses—defending freedom, honoring our "commitments," demonstrating America's resolution—are secondary in importance and are easily shown to be fallacious and contradictory. But no one can *prove* that Mao Tse-tung and Brezhnev and Kosygin— or Khrushchev, for that matter—have not harbored secret ambitions to conquer the world. Who can prove that the desire or the intention was never in their minds? The truly remarkable thing about this cold war psychology is the totally illogical transfer of the burden of proof from those who make charges to those who question them. In this frame of reference, Communists are guilty until proved innocent—or simply by definition. The cold warriors, instead of having to say how they knew that Vietnam was part of a plan for the communization of the world, so manipulated the terms of public discussion as to be able to demand that the skeptics prove that it was not. If the skeptics could not, then the war must go on—to end it would be recklessly risking the national security. We come to the ultimate illogic: war is the course of prudence and sobriety until the case for peace is proved under impossible rules of evidence—or until the enemy surrenders.

Rational men cannot deal with each other on this basis. Recognizing their inability to know with anything like certainty what is going on in other men's minds, they do not try to deal with others on the basis of their presumed intentions. Instead, rational men respond to others on the basis of their actual, observable behavior, and they place the burden of proof where it belongs—on those who assert and accuse rather than on those who question or deny. The departure from these elementary rules for the ascertainment of truth is the essence of the cold war way of thinking; its weakened but still formidable hold on our minds is indicative of the surviving tyranny of the Truman Doctrine.

In a decade's perspective—and without the blinders of the Truman Doctrine—it even seems possible that the Cuban missile crisis of 1962 was not so enormous a crisis as it then seemed. Khrushchev in the early sixties was engaged in an internal struggle with the Soviet military, who, not unlike our own generals, were constantly lobbying for more funds for ever more colossal weapons systems. Khrushchev had been cutting back on conventional forces and, largely for purposes of appeasing his unhappy generals, was talking a great deal about the power of Soviet missiles. President Kennedy, however, was applying pressure from another direction: unnerved by Khrushchev's endorsement of "wars of national liberation," he was undertaking to build up American conventional forces at the same time that he was greatly expanding the American nuclear-missile force, even though by this time the United States had an enormous strategic superiority. Khrushchev's effort to resist the pressures from his generals was, of course, undermined by the American buildup. It exposed him to pressures within the Kremlin from a hostile coalition of thwarted generals and politicians who opposed his de-Stalinization policies. In the view of a number of specialists in the Soviet field, the placement of missiles in Cuba was motivated largely, if not primarily, by Khrushchev's need to deal with these domestic pressures; it was meant to close or narrow the Soviet "missile gap" in relation to the United States without forcing Khrushchev to concentrate all available resources on a ruinous arms race.

Lacking an expert knowledge of my own on these matters, I commend this interpretation of Khrushchev's purpose not as necessarily true but as highly plausible. As far as I know, however, none of the American officials who participated in the decisions relating to the Cuban missile crisis seriously considered the possibility that Khrushchev might be acting defensively or in response to domestic pressures. It was universally assumed that the installation of Soviet missiles in Cuba was an aggressive strategic move against the United States—that, and nothing more. Assuming Khrushchev's aggressive intent, we imposed on the Soviet Union a resounding defeat, for which Khrushchev was naturally held responsible. In this way, we helped to strengthen the military and political conservatives within the Soviet Union, who were to overthrow Khrushchev two years later. If we had been willing to consider the possibility that Khrushchev was acting on internal considerations, we would still have wished to secure the removal of the missiles from Cuba, but it might have been accomplished by means less embarrassing to Khrushchev, such as a *quid pro quo* under which we would have removed our Jupiter missiles from Turkey.

Khrushchev had paid dearly for his "softness on capitalism" in an earlier encounter with President Eisenhower. After his visit to the United States in 1959, Khrushchev apparently tried to persuade his skeptical, hard-line colleagues that Americans were not such monsters as they supposed and that President Eisenhower was a reasonable man. This heretical theory—heretical from the Soviet point of view—was shot out of the sky along with the American U-2 spy plane in May 1960. When President Eisenhower subsequently declined the opportunity Khrushchev offered him to disclaim personal responsibility, Khrushchev felt compelled to break up the Paris summit meeting. The U-2 incident was later cited by Khrushchev himself as a critical moment in his loss of power at home. It shattered his plans for President Eisenhower to pay a visit to the Soviet Union—for which, it is said, he had already had a golf course secretly constructed in the Crimea.

There were, of course, other factors in Khrushchev's fall, and perhaps more important ones; nor is it suggested that his intentions toward the West were necessarily benevolent. The point that must emerge, however—more for the sake of the future than for history's sake—is that if we had not been wearing ideological blinders, if our judgment had not been clouded by fear and hostility, we might have perceived in Khrushchev a world statesman with whom constructive business could be done. When he fell, his successors put an end to de-Stalinization, began the military buildup that has brought the Soviet Union to a rough strategic parity with the United States, and greatly stepped up their aid to Communist forces in Vietnam.

While our response to Soviet communism has been marked by hostility, tensions, and fear, our response to communism in Asia has been marked by all these and, in addition, by a profound sense of injury and betrayal. Russia never was a country for which we had much affection anyway; it was the bleak and terrible land of the czars, which, when it went to the Communist devils, was merely trading one tyranny for another. But China had a special place in our hearts. We had favored her with our merchants and missionaries and our "open door" policy; we had even given back the Boxer indemnity so that Chinese students could study in America. In the Second World War, we fought shoulder to shoulder with "free"

29

China; we were filled with admiration for its fighting Generalissimo Chiang Kai-shek, and utterly charmed by his Wellesley-educated wife.

When the Chinese darlings of our patronizing hearts went to Communist perdition, we could only assume that they had been sold or betrayed into bondage. It was inconceivable that our star pupils in the East could actually have willed this calamity; it had to be the work of Chinese traitors, abetted by disloyal Americans, joined in an unholy alliance to sell out China to those quintessential bad people the Russians. A white paper on China was issued in 1949, and Secretary of State Acheson's letter of transmittal recounted accurately the intense but futile American effort to salvage a Kuomintang regime whose officials and soldiers had "sunk into corruption, into a scramble for place and power, and into reliance on the United States to win the war for them and to preserve their own domestic supremacy." Then, having exonerated the United States from responsibility for the loss of China, Secretary Acheson wrote:

> The heart of China is in Communist hands. The Communist leaders have forsworn their Chinese heritage and have publicly announced their subservience to a foreign power, Russia, which during the last 50 years, under czars and Communists alike, has been most assiduous in its efforts to extend its control in the Far East. . . . The foreign domination has been masked behind the facade of a vast crusading movement which apparently has seemed to many Chinese to be wholly indigenous and national. . . .
>
> However tragic may be the immediate future of China and however ruthlessly a major portion of this great people may be exploited by a party in the interest of a foreign imperialism, ultimately the profound civilization and the democratic individualism of China will reassert themselves and she will throw off the foreign yoke. I consider that we should encourage all developments in China which now and in the future work toward this end.

In these words, the United States government enunciated what became its Truman Doctrine for Asia. By the end of 1950, we were at war with China in Korea, but even then our belief in Moscow's control of the "Communist conspiracy" or our sentimental unwillingness to believe that China of its own free will would make war on the United States, or some combination of the two, made it difficult for us to believe that the Chinese Communists had intervened in Korea for reasons directly related to their own national interest. The fact that General MacArthur's sweep to the Yalu was bringing American ground forces within striking distance of China's industrial heartland in Manchuria was not at that time widely thought to be a factor in China's intervention in the war. The view of Dean Rusk, then the assistant secretary of state for Far Eastern affairs, was that "the peace and security of China are being sacrificed to the ambitions of the Communist conspiracy," and that "China has been driven by foreign masters into an adventure of foreign aggression which cuts across the most fundamental national interests of the Chinese people." Mr. Rusk went on to say, "We do not recognize the authorities in Peiping for what they pretend to be. The Peiping regime may be a colonial Russian government—a Slavic Manchukuo on a larger scale. It is not the government of China."

* * *

The sudden reversal of American policy toward China in 1971 necessarily invites our attention back to the basic causes of these two decades of conflict between the United States and the Communist countries of Asia. In the course of these two decades, we have engaged in armed conflict with all three of these countries—with Communist China, North Korea, and North Vietnam—but we have never fought a war with the Soviet Union, which is the only Communist power capable of posing a direct strategic threat to the United States. Although it was assumed from the outset of the cold war that our real strategic interests lay in Europe rather than in Asia, it has been in Asia that we have thought it necessary to fight two wars to enforce the Truman Doctrine. Looking back, one is bound to ask whether these conflicts were inescapable. Having avoided war in the region we judged more important, and with the power we judged the greater threat, why have we found it necessary to fight in Asia, at such enormous cost in lives and money and in the internal cohesion of our own society? Is it possible that if Mao Tse-tung and Ho Chi Minh had not borne the title of "Communist" but otherwise had done exactly what they have done in their two countries, we would have accepted their victories over their domestic rivals and lived with them in peace? I think it quite possible that we would have come to terms with both. Apart from the North Korean invasion of South Korea, which was a direct violation of the United Nations Charter, the Communist countries of Asia have done nothing that has threatened the security of the United States and little, if anything, that has impaired our legitimate interests. We intervened in the Chinese and Vietnamese civil wars only because the stronger side in each case was the Communist side and we assumed that, as Communists, they were parties to a conspiracy for world domination, and were therefore our enemies. We intervened against them not for what they *did* but for what they *were* and for what we assumed to be their purpose.

* * *

The anti-Communist spirit that governed our relations with China after the Second World War also shaped—and distorted—our involvement in Vietnam. Our interest in China's civil war, though tragic in consequence, was attenuated and limited in time. Vietnam was less fortunate. In a test application of the new science of "counterinsurgency," it has been subjected to prolonged, though inconclusive, devastation. But for the American intervention, the Vietnamese civil war would have ended long ago—at infinitely less cost in lives, money, and property—in a nationalist Communist victory under the leadership of Ho Chi Minh.

In retrospect, it is difficult to understand how we could have accepted the "loss" of China but not the "loss" of the small, undeveloped countries on China's southern border. Only in the context of the assumptions of the Truman Doctrine could the Vietnamese war ever have been rationalized as having something to do with American security or American interests. Looking through our anti-Communist prism, we saw Ho Chi Minh not as a Vietnamese nationalist who was also a Communist but as a spear-carrier for the international Communist conspiracy, the driving force for a "world cut in two by Asian communism." The Johnson Administration, as Mr. Johnson's memoirs show clearly, believed itself to be acting on President Truman's doctrine that "totalitarian regimes imposed on free peoples, by direct or indirect aggression, undermine the foundations of international peace and hence the security of the United States." President Johnson and his advisers believed this despite a set of facts that did not fit the formula: the fact that the issue was not between a "free people" and a "totalitarian regime" but between rival totalitarian regimes; the fact that the war was not one of international aggression, "direct" or otherwise, but an anti-colonial war and then a civil war; and the fact that, in any case, the country was too small and the issue too indigenous to Vietnam to pose anything resembling a threat to "the foundations of international peace," much less to "the security of the United States." In practice, the issue had resolved itself into a corruption of the Truman Doctrine—into the fear of a "humiliating" defeat at the hands of Communists. It was not so much that we needed to win, or that there was anything for us to win, as that our leaders felt—for reasons of prestige abroad and political standing at home—that they could not afford to "lose." President

Johnson said soon after he took office, "I am not going to be the President who saw Southeast Asia go the way China went."

The notion that a country is "lost" or "gone" when it becomes Communist is a peculiarly revealing one. How can we have "lost" a country unless it was ours to begin with—unless it was some part of an unacknowledged American imperium? To my eye, China under Mao is in the same place on the map that it was in the days of Chiang. Where, then, has it "gone"? To the moon? Or to the devil? The "lost" and "gone" concept is indicative of a virulent sanctimonious-ness that is only now beginning to abate. In October 1971, members of the Senate gave President Tito of Yugoslavia a cordial reception at an afternoon tea. In September 1959, a similar reception was held for Chairman Khrushchev, but one senator refused to sit in the room with him—for fear, apparently, of ideological contamination. As the President now moves toward lifting the "quarantine" of China, as we recognize at long last that there really still is a China, Communist though it may be, the tragic irrationality of the Vietnam War is thrown once again into high relief. All that bloodletting—not just for ourselves but for the Vietnamese—could have been avoided by an awareness that communism is not a contagious disease but a political movement and a way of organizing a society.

*   *   *

As with China under Mao Tse-tung, we might have got along tolerably well—maybe even quite well—with a unified, independent Vietnam under Ho Chi Minh if our leaders' minds had not been hopelessly locked in by the imprisoning theory of the international Communist conspiracy. Ho was an authentic Vietnamese patriot, revered by his countrymen. He had led the resistance to the Japanese within Vietnam and had welcomed the allies as liberators. His unwillingness to submit to foreign domination was clear—or should have been clear—from the outset. But if the evidence of Ho Chi Minh's Vietnamese nationalism ever reached the American policy makers, it certainly did not persuade them. Acting Secretary of State Acheson instructed an American diplomat in Hanoi in December 1946, "Keep in mind Ho's clear record as agent international communism." In February 1947, by which time the war between France and the Vietminh was well under way, Secretary of State Marshall conceded, in another cable, that colonial empires were rapidly becoming a thing of the past but, as to Vietnam,

> We do not lose sight fact that Ho Chi Minh has direct Communist connections, and it should be obvious that we are not interested in seeing colonial empire administrations

33

supplanted by philosophy and political organizations emanating from and controlled by Kremlin.

General Marshall's words were prophetic of what became a guiding principle—or, more accurately, a guiding aberration—of American foreign policy for at least two decades: where Communists were involved, the United States would depart from its traditional anti-colonialism and support the imperial power. Assuming as we did that Communists by definition were agents of an international conspiracy, we further assumed that a Communist leader could not be an authentic patriot no matter what he said or did. If the choice was to be—as we then rationalized it—between the old imperialism of the West and the new imperialism of the Kremlin, we would side with the former. Where possible, we told ourselves, we would support or nurture "third forces"—genuine independence movements that were neither colonialist nor Communist—and where such movements existed, as in India, we did support and welcome independence. Where they did not exist, as in Vietnam and Cuba and the Dominican Republic, we intervened, making these countries the great crisis areas of postwar American foreign policy and, in the process, earning for the United States the reputation of foremost imperialist power.

The role is one to which we are unsuited by temperament and tradition. Until a generation ago, America was regarded throughout the world—and deservedly so—as the one great nation that was authentically anti-imperialist. It was Woodrow Wilson who introduced into international relations the revolutionary principle of "justice to all peoples and nationalities, and their right to live on equal terms of liberty and safety with one another, whether they be strong or weak." Perhaps it was a utopian dream, but Americans meant it at the time, and the world believed we meant it, and we had plans for realizing it: first the Covenant of the League of Nations and then the United Nations Charter, both purporting to introduce the rule of law into international relations, both purporting to supplant the old imperialist anarchy with the principle of trusteeship for the weak and the poor, both purporting to supplant the old balance of power with a new community of power.

The dismay and disillusion that have overtaken so many of us in America are the result, I believe, of our departure from these traditional American values. The corrosive, consuming fear of communism has driven us into a role in the world which suits us badly and which we deeply dislike. I think that the American people have sensed this all along and are moving now to an active, conscious awareness of their own real preferences. It is no easy matter for us to knock over the household gods we have been taught for a generation to worship, but I think the American people have all along had an uneasy awareness that the dictators and warlords with whom we have been in league for so long are not really our kind of people. I suspect, too, that if Khrushchev and Mao and Ho had not had the name of "Communist" we might have recognized them as men we could respect: tough and sometimes ruthless, but patriots nonetheless; committed to an ideology we would not want for ourselves, but also committed to the well-being of their own people. With China's entry into the United Nations and the President's imminent trip to Peking, we may find that we can do business with the Chinese, just as we have done with the Russians. We may even find it possible to be cordial, as we have been with the Yugoslavs. Eventually (who knows?), we may even kick over the household gods once and for all and become friends. Huck Finn, when he helped Jim escape, knew it was a sin and knew he was going to go to Hell for it, but he liked Jim, so he did it anyway.

History is filled with turning points that are not easily identified until long after the event. It seems almost inevitable that Vietnam will prove to have been a watershed in American foreign policy, but it is by no means clear what kind. Before it can represent anything of a lasting historical nature, the war, of course, will have to be ended—not just scaled down but ended, and not just for Americans but for the tortured Vietnamese as well. One assumes that it will be ended—if not by our present leaders, then by their successors— and that when at last it is, the American people will once again in their history have the opportunity and the responsibility of deciding where they want to go in the world, of deciding what kind of role they want their country to play, of deciding what kind of country they want America to be.

The Truman Doctrine, which made limited sense for a limited time in a particular place, has led us in its universalized form to disaster in Southeast Asia and demoralization at home. In view of all that has happened, it seems unlikely that we will wish to resume the anti-Communist crusade of the early postwar years. Yet it is not impossible: memories will fade, controversies may recur, pride may once again be challenged and competitive instincts aroused. The Truman Doctrine is frayed and tattered, but it is still an influence upon our policy and outlook.

I do not think we are going to return to isolationism. I will go further: I do not think there is or ever has been the slightest chance

35

of the United States returning to the isolationism of the prewar years. It will not happen because it cannot happen: we are inextricably involved with the world politically, economically, militarily, and—in case anyone cares—legally. We could not get loose if we wanted to. And no one wants to. The people who are called "neo-isolationists" are no such thing; the word is an invention of people who confuse internationalism with an intrusive American unilateralism, with a quasi-imperialism. Those of us who are accused of "neo-isolationism" are, I believe, the opposite: internationalists in the classic sense of that term—in the sense in which it was brought into American usage by Woodrow Wilson and Franklin Roosevelt. We believe in international cooperation through international institutions. We would like to try to keep the peace through the United Nations, and we would like to try to assist the poor countries through institutions like the World Bank. We do not think the United Nations is a failure; we think it has never been tried.

In the aftermath of Vietnam, it is America's option—not its "destiny," because there is no such thing—to return to the practical idealism of the United Nations Charter. It is, I believe, consistent with our national tradition and congenial to our national character, and is therefore the most natural course for us to follow. It is also the most logical, in terms of our interests and the interests of all other nations living in a diverse and crowded but interdependent world in the age of nuclear weapons.

The essence of any community—local, national, or international —is some degree of accceptance of the principle that the good of the whole must take precedence over the good of the parts. I do not believe that the United States (or any of the other big countries) has ever accepted that principle with respect to the United Nations. Like the Soviet Union and other great powers, we have treated the United Nations as an instrument of our policy, to be used when it is helpful but otherwise ignored. Orphaned at birth by the passing from the political scene of those who understood its potential real usefulness, the United Nations has never been treated as a potential world-security community—as an institution to be developed and strengthened for the long-term purpose of protecting humanity from the destructiveness of unrestrained nationalism. The immediate, short-term advantage of the leading members has invariably been given precedence over the needs of the collectivity. That is why the United Nations has not worked. There is no mystery about it, no fatal shortcoming in the charter. Our own federal government would soon collapse if the states and the people had no loyalty to it. The reason that the United Nations has not functioned as a peace-keeping organization is that its members, including the United States, have not wished it to; if they had wanted it to work, it could have—and it still can. Acheson and his colleagues were wholly justified in their expectation of the United Nations failure; their own cynicism, along with Stalin's cynicism, assured that failure.

Our shortsighted, self-serving, and sanctimonious view of the United Nations was put on vivid display in the reaction to the General Assembly's vote to take in mainland China and expel Nationalist China. Mr. Nixon expressed unctuous indignation, not at the loss of the vote but at the "shocking demonstration" of "undisguised glee" shown by the winners, especially those among the winners to whom the United States had been "quite generous"—as the President's press secretary was at pains to add. Mr. Agnew at least spared us the pomposities, denouncing the United Nations as a "paper tiger" and a "sounding board for the left," whose only value for the United States was that "it's good to be in the other guy's huddle." The Senate minority leader [Hugh Scott] was equally candid: "I think we are going to wipe off some of the smiles from the faces we saw on television during the United Nations voting." The revelations are striking. Having controlled the United Nations for many years as tightly and as easily as a big-city boss controls his party machine, we had got used to the idea that the United Nations was a place where we could work our will; Communists could delay and disrupt the proceedings and could exercise the Soviet veto in the Security Council, but they certainly were not supposed to be able to win votes. When they did, we were naturally shocked—all the more because, as one European diplomat commented, our unrestrained arm-twisting had turned the issue into a "worldwide plebiscite for or against the United States," and had thereby made it difficult for many nations to judge the question of Chinese representation on its merits. When the vote went against us nonetheless, the right-wingers among us saw that as proof of what they had always contended—that the United Nations was a nest of Red vipers.

The test of devotion to the law is not how people behave when it goes their way but how they behave when it goes against them. During these years of internal dissension over the war in Vietnam, our leaders have pointed out frequently—and correctly—that citizens, however little they may like it, have a duty to obey the law. The same principle applies on the international level. *"Pacta sunt servanda,"* the international lawyers say: "The law must be obeyed." The China vote in the General Assembly may well have been unwise, and it may have shown a certain vindictiveness toward the United States, but it was a legal vote, wholly consistent with the procedures spelled out in the charter.

The old balance-of-power system is a discredited failure, having broken down in two world wars in the twentieth century. The human race managed to survive those conflicts; it is by no means certain that it would survive another. This being the case, it is myopic to dismiss the idea of an effective world peace-keeping organization as a visionary ideal—or as anything, indeed, but an immediate, practical necessity.

With the cooperation of the major powers—and there is no reason in terms of their own national interests for them not to cooperate—the conflict in the Middle East could be resolved on the basis of the Security Council resolution of 1967, to which all the principal parties have agreed, calling for a settlement based upon, among other things, the principle of "the inadmissibility of the acquisition of territory by war." Similarly, I believe that the Security Council should have interceded to prevent war between India and Pakistan. This proved impossible largely because of the self-seeking of the great powers, each of which perceived and acted upon the situation not on its merits, and certainly not in terms of human cost, but in terms of its own shortsighted geopolitical interests. Moreover, the Security Council waited until war had actually broken out and an Indian victory seemed certain before attempting to intervene. The time for the United Nations to act on the crisis in East Pakistan was many months earlier, when the Bengalis were being brutally suppressed by the armed forces of the Pakistani government. The United Nations, it is true, is proscribed by Article 2 of the charter from intervention in "matters which are essentially within the domestic jurisdiction of any state," but Article 2 also states that "the principle shall not prejudice the application of enforcement measures" under the peace-enforcement provisions of the charter. By any reasonable standard of judgment, the mass killing of East Bengalis and the flight of 10 million refugees across the Indian border constituted a "threat to the peace" as that term is used in the charter, warranting United Nations intervention. I do not think it likely under present circumstances that the United Nations could play a mediating role in the war in Indochina, the disabling circumstance being that the belligerents, including the United States, almost certainly would not permit it. But, looking ahead to the time when the Vietnam War is finally ended, I think it would be feasible for the United Nations to oversee and police a general peace settlement, through a revived International Control Commission, and perhaps through the assignment of peace-keeping forces.

When a conflict presents what Article 39 of the charter calls a "threat to the peace, breach of the peace, or act of aggression," it makes no sense to leave the issue to the caprices of the belligerents. I have never understood why it is so widely regarded as outrageous or immoral for external parties to impose a solution to a dangerous conflict. Under the United Nations Charter, the Security Council has full authority—possibly even an obligation—to impose a settlement upon warring parties that fail to make peace on their own. The very premise of the charter is that warring nations can no longer be permitted immunity from a world police power. As far as the United States is concerned, it is worth recalling that the United Nations Charter is a valid and binding obligation upon us, ratified as a treaty with the advice and consent of the Senate. And as far as the parties to various conflicts are concerned—Arabs and Israelis, Indians and Pakistanis—it needs to be recognized that they, too, are signatories to the charter and are therefore obligated, under Article 25, "to accept and carry out the decisions of the Security Council in accordance with the present Charter."

In this century of conflict, the United States led in the conception and formulation of plans for an international peace-keeping organization. We did not invent the idea, nor have we been its only proponents, but without our leadership the ideal embodied in the Covenant of the League of Nations and the United Nations Charter would not have attained even the meager degree of realization it has attained. It is this idea of world organization—rather than our democratic ideology, or our capitalist economy, or our power and the responsibilities it is supposed to have thrust upon us—that entitles the United States to claim to have made a valuable and unique contribution to the progress of international relations. Coming as we did on the international scene as a new and inexperienced participant, with a special historical experience that had sheltered us from the normal pressures of world politics, we Americans pursued our conception of a rational world order with uncritical optimism and excessive fervor. As a consequence, the first encounter with disappointment, in the form of Stalin and his ambitions in Eastern Europe, sent us reeling back from Wilsonian idealism. And from the practical idealism of the United Nations Charter we reverted to the unrealistic "realism" of the Truman Doctrine in its universalized application. We made the conversion from Wilson to Machiavelli with zeal.

At no point, of course, did the leading architects of Vietnam or the Bay of Pigs or the participants in the Cuban missile crisis conceive of themselves as power brokers pure and simple. Having themselves been reared in the tenets of Wilson-Roosevelt internationalism, and having lived through the disaster of appeasement in the interwar years, they came to regard themselves as "tough-minded idealists," as "realists with vision," and, above all, as practitioners of collective security against aggression. What the United Nations could not do the United States could and would do, with allies if possible, alone if necessary. We, after all, were the ones who bore the burden of the "responsibilities of power." It was up to us, if all else failed, to curb aggression at its outset, to accept whatever sacrifices had to be made in order to defend the "free world" against the new Communist predator. We, in effect, were the successors to an enfeebled United Nations, and were forced by fate and circumstance to endure the glory and agony of power.

In this heady frame of reference, Vietnam and its consequences might be conceived as the ripe harvest of the American era of romantic "realism." Primarily, no doubt, because of its military failures, the war in Vietnam has brought many Americans to an awareness of the sham idealism of the "responsibilities of power," and of the inadequacies of the new "realism" once it is stripped of its romantic façade. Many young Americans, and some older ones, are appalled not only by the horrors of the Vietnam War but by the deterministic philosophy, espoused by the intellectuals who came into government in the sixties, of a permanent, purposeless struggle for power and advantage. We seem to be discovering once again that without a moral purpose and frame of reference there can be no such thing as "advantage."

America may be coming near to the closing of a circle. Having begun the postwar period with the idealism of the United Nations Charter, we retreated in disillusion to the "realism" of the cold war, to the Truman Doctrine and its consummation in Vietnam, easing the transition by telling ourselves that we were not really abandoning the old values at all but simply applying them in more practical ways. Now, having failed most dismally and shockingly, we are beginning to cast about for a new set of values. The American people, if not their leaders, have come near to recognizing the failure of romantic, aggressive "realism," although a new idealism has yet to take its place. Perhaps we will settle for an old idealism—the one we conceived and commended to the world but have never tried.

U.S. POWER IN TRANSITION *

Charles Burton Marshall

Charles Burton Marshall postulates that, in the twentieth century, American foreign policy has been dominated by efforts to institutionalize peace. These efforts follow from premises about the nature of peace that have been part of the national outlook since the founding of the nation, namely that concord is the natural situation and conflict an aberration. Since World War II, however, the United States has endured in a state of tension with the Soviet Union. Marshall contends that the United States has never renounced its fundamental goal of quickly achieving permanent peace, and that America imputes to the Soviet Union the same operating principle. But the U.S.S.R. does not share this vision, he argues, and the loss of U.S. strategic ascendancy portends serious consequences for the West.

The key words in my assigned topic are of ancient origin. The gloating serpent whispered "power!" after persuading Eve to eat Adam out of house and home. Adam spoke to Eve of "transition" on receiving the eviction notice. General affairs—"transiting" ever since—have been unceasingly concerned with capacity to achieve intended results—a point emphatically true regarding that aspect of endeavor called international politics. I neither deplore nor celebrate the circumstance, and I have no reform to suggest. I aim to ponder problems of matching capabilities to purposes in U.S. foreign policy in our time, citing only so much of the past as has a present bearing.

I

As of three dozen or so years ago, the recovery stimulated by Franklin D. Roosevelt's New Deal was evident more in intangible matters than in computable aspects of the economy. General confidence had rallied appreciably from blows suffered in the Great Depression, but unemployment remained stubborn, and investment still languished. Then World War II brought a prodigious turn. Levels of production theretofore undreamed of were achieved in manufacturing and agriculture, notwithstanding huge diversions of manpower into military service. Inventiveness flourished. Social mobility upwards was stimulated as never before. Yet inflation was minimal. Palpable dangers posed by unequivocal foes solidified national unity. What-

---

* Source: An address delivered at Texas A&M University, where the author was visiting centennial professor in the spring semester of 1976.

41

ever the imperfections in detail, in gross terms everything worked. Great military campaigns progressed to success as planned. Puissant enemies were beaten into absolute capitulation. The capability of policy to achieve wonders, given will, seemed amply confirmed.

At war's end, the nation's martial establishment, attuned to victory, was unrivaled in respect of air power, naval capabilities, and logistical versatility. In prodigious new nuclear technology, the country had a monopoly for the short term and a headstart for the longer. The country's economic resources—inhering in abundant maritime transport, a vastly improved and enlarged capital plant, great volumes of food in production and reserve, and a capacious financial structure affording the United States a position as virtually the sole source of credit in the trading world—were even more impressive. Favorable material circumstances were matched by relatively undamaged civic morale attuned to and expectant of success.

Such assets amounted to great sources of power, but how they were to be used was not at once apparent, for the extent of ruin and need left in the wake of hostilities had not yet been guessed. For the time being, high policy was preoccupied with plans to institutionalize perpetual peace. The sources of that aspiration are worth pondering because of their pertinence to present questions of national policy.

Antecedents could be found in American thought at the time of the nation's founding. Optimistic spirits sensed the advent of a happy epoch, unprecedented in the annals of organized societies. Their expectations were summed up in a phrase still found on our dollar bills—*novus ordo seclorum*—"a new order of the ages." Unique opportunities were assumed for the nation, which would mold the future by the mere fact of eschewing power. Its irresistible example would point a way of escape from vicissitudes everywhere.

For the time being, that outlook was counterbalanced by a more sober one, exemplified in Alexander Hamilton's supposition that the venture into independence involved abandoning the shelter of subordination and choosing instead to experience "a common portion of the vicissitudes and calamities which have fallen to the lot of nations." In the early 1800s, however, the optimistic outlook became unequivocally ascendant.

The Americans' situation following European military retraction from the environs incident to the Napoleonic epoch seemed to confirm the assumption of specialness. Confident in the safety afforded by remoteness from theaters of strategic competition, the prevailing American attitude became to regard peace and war as disjoined slabs of reality. Peace was the inherent condition. War was a breakdown, a deviancy. Strategy was a mode of thought and action called for in the deplorable interruptions but put out of mind under normal conditions.

The young Abraham Lincoln epitomized the mood in a boast of national invulnerability: "All the armies of Europe, Asia, and Africa combined, with all the treasure of the earth (our own excepted) in their military chest, with a Bonaparte for a commander, could not by force take a drink from the Ohio or make a track on the Blue Ridge in a trial of a thousand years."[1] It became easy to ascribe the privilege of being able to think that way not just to transient good luck but to some distinguishing popular virtue. Cause and effect became reversed. Americans' exemption from peripheral anxiety was assumed to be due to their manner of thought, rather than vice versa. Thus, by a corollary, other peoples in every continent could achieve a like measure of safety by adopting and adhering to nonstrategic norms in the mode of Americans.

According to an insight in F. S. Northedge's thoughtful essay on peace and war in *The Encyclopedia of Philosophy*,[2] people who assume concord and peace to be normal and inherent conditions and who regard conflict and war as breakdowns and abnormalities are logically cast as abolitionists of war. The Americans' operational code—meaning a collection of postulates and perceptions, which, though not necessarily subscribed to unanimously, provide a frame of reference for general discussion—reflected that approach. To be more specific—the American code was that of "soft" abolitionists of war. Such people assume the sources of conflict to be relatively superficial and readily rectifiable. In that view, the thing to do in order to ensure peace is to prevent breakdowns, and the way to go about the task is through improved communications, more cultural interchange, closer understanding, enhanced cooperation, expanded commerce, better procedures, and proliferating institutions.

The stamp of that approach has marked multiple projects of U.S. policy dating back to the peace conferences at The Hague in 1899 and 1907, President Taft's arbitration treaties in 1910, William Jennings Bryan's network of conciliation conventions in 1913–14, and the Kellogg-Briand pact for wholesale renunciation of war in 1928. More to the point, such a set of premises underlay U.S. initiatives, incident to the twentieth century's two global wars, for universalizing the

---

[1] Alfred J. Beveridge, *Abraham Lincoln, 1809-1855* (Boston: Houghton, Mifflin, 1928), pp. 227-228.

[2] F. S. Northedge, "Peace, War, and Philosophy," *The Encyclopedia of Philosophy*, vol. 6 (New York: Crowell, Collier and Macmillan, 1967), pp. 63-67.

Americans' coded norms through a world organization to the end of forestalling recurrences of such deplorable interruptions of normal tranquillity. Woodrow Wilson's explanation of his envisioned non-strategic world of nonstrategic nations in league together invoked the United States as the paradigm. In his interpretations, the great globe was to be assimilated to the United States rather than vice versa. In similar vein, Franklin D. Roosevelt interpreted the projected re-embodiment of a world organization as a device for relegating stra-tegic considerations—such as balance of power, spheres of influence, and alliances—to the unhappy past. Such is how he put the matter in addressing Congress on this return from the Yalta Conference in 1945.

That second venture is the one more relevant here. The efficacy of the resulting institution—the United Nations—as an instrumental-ity for peace has been moot all along. Believers have made their case by adding up hypothetical wars that did not occur; skeptics, by listing the ones that did. For the time being, by whatever logic, the United Nations' pacificatory utility is at discount. To some observers, the organization appears misnamed and might be designated more appro-priately the "Diverse Nations," the "Fretful Nations," or the "Divided Nations." One of the country's most faithful liberal publications has gone so far as to call it "a barbarous parliament" without "even a pretense to world authority."[3] Yet one must try to understand the high hopes once vested in the United Nations by Roosevelt and many millions of others.

The hopes reflected in part a discernment of our enemies personi-fied in Hitler. Like Kaiser Wilhelm II a generation before, but more so and with deeper conviction, Hitler and his malign movement drew upon generations of German scriveners whose romantic militarist ideas—in the manner of Friedrich Nietzsche, who said, "Let men be formed for war and women for the recreation of the warrior," and added, "Everything else is fatuous"—celebrated conflict as normal and humanly fulfilling and despised concord as decadent, debilitating, and deformative. It was easy to link hopes for permanent peace with the defeat of adversaries perceived as epitomizing the very inverse of our norms.

A second element involved discernment of our anti-Axis ally—namely the Soviet Union—marked, as the United States also was marked, to emerge from the war with enhanced scope and importance. In his zeal to coax that ally into collaboration in fostering peace

---

[3] Paul Johnson, "The Barbarous Parliament," *The New Republic* (20 December 1975), p. 10.

through the United Nations, President Roosevelt discounted Soviet ambition and disregarded Soviet querulousness and suspiciousness. His appreciation dwelt instead on what he took to be a shared concern to abolish war.

The Soviet Union then professed, as it still zealously professes, such a goal. Here, however, a distinction is called for. The Soviet approach may appropriately be called "hard" abolitionary. The causes of war are discerned as knotted into the very fabric of societies. The remedy, supposedly imposed by historic necessity, is seen to lie in a complete redoing—in conformity with Soviet prescriptions—of human awareness and relationships. Peace thus becomes a goal for a remote notional tomorrow. The asserted goal serves meanwhile, as a rationale for unremitting, though opportunistic, animosity toward every outlook and interest not in conformity with the Soviet image of affairs. The view is coupled with assertions of exclusive legitimacy, linked to the claim of historic necessity.

A contest in policy ranging the so-called superpowers as adversaries soon, and perhaps inevitably, arose from the opposed versions of peace and divergent images of the future. On this side, recognition of the fact of conflicted purposes did not come at any one moment or over any one issue. The idea that government—emphatically this one—operates with the instant and prescribed unanimity of a football huddle is a fancy entertained by revisionist historians. In that gradually unfolding phase, the United States for the first time in its national experience began to take account of strategic factors as a continuing and settled requirement while under the formalities of peace. For the first time, the United States provided itself with continuing peacetime institutions for intelligence, planning, and coordinated action to give coherence to the effort.

II

I must explain what I mean by a strategic approach to peace. I do so with considerable affirmation. For as far back as I can remember having judgments in such matters, I have shared that approach and have regarded schemes to ensure peace by abolishing war to be visionary and unhelpful. Instead of assuming the inherence of concord and peace and the aberrance of conflict and war, the approach regards them as variables across a continuum of reality. Peace as a fact of life issues from a breakdown of war, just as war as a fact of life comes from a breakdown of peace. The two are but distinguishable conditions produced by differing combinations of similar factors. Other things being equal, it is well to value peace and to eschew war—no argument about that—but the one is achieved and the other avoided by attention to, rather than disregard for, considerations that bear on the conduct of war.

In that view of things, policy is carried on in awareness of adversariness. To say that is not to portray policy as everlastingly scheming hostilities. The contingency of war, however, does remain ever in the background. Policy makers bear in mind a cluster of ideas concerning hypothetical combat—its scope, the range of participants, the presumptive theaters of action, the types and numbers of forces and weapons, the environments of operations, the targets, the duration, the consequences measured in material damage wrought on the respective sides, the impact on civil and military will to persevere, and the final outcome. Components of matching importance are estimates of the putative adversary's perceptions concerning all these matters and concerning this side's perceptions—including this side's perceptions of adversary perceptions—and so on, in multiple reciprocation.

Such mental pictures having to do with the making of hypothetical war are integral to preserving actual peace, for the counterpoised sets of concepts, however imperfect, give clues for calculating the threshold of hostilities and therefore bear on gauging leeway for pressing issues or determining when to temporize or back away. Thus, their interrelation is a key to strategic equilibrium and stability or their opposites.

Three sorts of relationship between such counterpoised evaluations are possible.

Situation A. The side that would probably prevail in the event of war is identifiable. Each side is so aware and discerns the other side's awareness. The strategic estimates are congruent. In confrontations, the constraints on the two sides are disproportionate, but the probability of war is low.

Situation B. In event of war, neither side could be sure of prevailing. Each side so discerns the matter and is aware of the other side's estimate. The strategic estimates are congruent. In confrontations the constraints on the two sides are about equal, and the probability of war is slight.

Situation C. Each side assumes the advantages of Situation A tilt its way, or one side so assumes while the other thinks the relationship is Situation B. Their strategic evaluations are discrepant. The danger of war is heightened.

At the outset, the strategic relationship between the so-called superpowers was that described as Situation A, with the United States in the advantaged position—thanks to the combination of intangible and material assets—civil, military, and economic—accruing from its intrinsic position and from the manner of its pursuit and achievement of victory. The United States undertook to extend that advantage vicariously to certain other countries likely in the absence of such support to become subject to Soviet intimidation. The scope of such undertakings was added to after the Communist takeover in continental China.

A term relevant to all those undertakings is "commitment," which has numerous interrelated meanings. One meaning is inner resolve to take certain action in a contingent event. Another meaning is the utterance of such resolve in the form of a pledge designed to affect others' wills and expectations, whether to encourage reciprocal resolve or to forestall adverse actions. A third sense is the actual engaging of resources to substantiate resolve or to redeem a pledge. What the United States undertook was a vast array of strategic commitments in all senses of the term. The essence of commitment in the sense of a pledge intended to affect the outlooks and actions of others, friendly or otherwise, is credibility. That quality hinges on discerned balance between resolve and palpable resources. Imbalance between them is expressible as "overcommitment."

Because my theme is analytic rather than narrative, I leave it for others' memories to fill in the variousness of the nation's endeavors both in entering upon commitments and in striving to maintain their credibility by demonstrating resolve and generating and expending resources, the particulars of the frustrations experienced in a dozen or so years of distant combat in Korea and Southeast Asia, and the tenacious and skillful countermeasures undertaken on the other side. What I wish to stress, notwithstanding the huge range of the pertinent commitments, is the provisionary character of the United States adaptation to a strategic perspective on peace.

How can an operational code which postulates concord and peace as inherent and readily ensurable conditions come to terms with an antithetic set of norms and aims supported by great resources over a wide scope? That problem in the logic of policy had not risen in connection with the challenges posed by rampant adversaries in the two global wars, for the Central Powers and the Axis in their turns could be coped with as transient dangers. The issue presented by the Soviet rulership was of a different order. Here—to quote George Kennan's famous "Mr. X" article of 1947—was a regime "under no ideological compulsion to accomplish its purposes in a hurry" and in a position "to afford to be patient and to look forward to a duel of infinite duration." [4]

Contending against such opposition would necessitate willingness to persevere interminably. Generating such a will would logically entail abandoning any assumption about peace as a bestowed condition and conflict as a deviancy. Instead of making a logical substitution of premises, U.S. policy makers in the main accepted a strategic approach to peace as a supplement to the established preconceptions, and doing so involved premising the Soviet Union's malleability.

Thus, however wishfully and inconsistently, Kennan's cited article attributed to the United States a "power to increase enormously the strains under which Soviet policy must operate, to force upon the Kremlin a far greater degree of moderation and circumspection than it has had to observe in recent years, and in this way to promote tendencies which must eventually find their outlet in either the breakup or the gradual mellowing of Soviet power." [5] With similarly large hope and meager evidence, President Truman's enunciation of the Truman Doctrine held out a prospect of eventual Soviet cooperation in efforts for "peaceful development of nations, free of coercion." [6] Thus also, Secretary of State Dean Acheson's appeal for Senate approval of the North Atlantic Treaty portrayed it as a device for forwarding the United Nations Charter's promise of a world made gentle by universal devotion to peace.[7] President Eisenhower in April 1953 likewise professed to anticipate that happy development "within the foreseeable future," [8] and at American University a decade later President Kennedy all but announced its advent.[9] Two years thence, President Johnson's explication of deepening involvement in Vietnam dwelt upon hopes of gaining Communist collaboration in realizing "a very old dream . . . of a world where disputes are settled by law and reason." [10]

The examples are multiple. No theme has run more persistently through U.S. policy pronouncements over three decades than anticipation of dissipating the cold war by conversion of the opposition.

---

[4] George F. Kennan (pseudonym, "Mr. X"), "The Sources of Soviet Conduct," *Foreign Affairs* (July 1947), p. 574.

[5] Ibid., p. 582.

[6] *Department of State Bulletin* (23 March 1947), p. 536.

[7] Ibid. (27 March 1949), p. 388.

[8] Ibid. (27 April 1953), p. 599.

[9] Ibid. (1 July 1963), p. 2.

[10] Ibid. (26 April 1965), p. 609.

Such was the ultimate purpose repeatedly invoked in maintaining credibility for a multiplicity of external assurances. According to the question-begging postulate, the Soviet Union—denied opportunities for meddling and expanding its sway—must sometime, and not too distantly, come to recognize the futility of its goals. Chastened by frustration, the adversary would come to resemble Roosevelt's perception of Stalin at Yalta—gruff, rough, but basically amenable. Thus, a world strategy was contrived in the hope of realizing a nonstrategic world.

Besides being desirable, an aim in foreign policy should be feasible. By that criterion, the aim of converting the adversary was dubious. Soviet attitudes and actions were, as they are still, integrally related to the exclusionary claim of being an instrumentality of historic necessity. That claim was, and remains, the regime's rationale for holding onto unaccountable power within its own domain, and the regime's continuity on an alternative basis is scarcely imaginable. The same concept is basic to the regime's asserted prerogative, given explicit form in the so-called Brezhnev doctrine, as enforcer of doctrinal rectitude among all Communist regimes. The postulate of historic necessity underlies assertions, in the so-called doctrine of national liberation wars, concerning exclusive legitimacy for use of force conducing to Communist advantage within remnant colonial areas and among the newer dependencies, wherever located.

Cleaving to its doctrinal base, while taking care to avoid direct involvement in combat against the United States, the Soviet Union would direct its efforts to vitiating the U.S. commitments designed to contain and transform it. In the Soviet version of a desired condition in succession to the cold war, the United States would resemble what must have been Stalin's perception of Roosevelt at Yalta—fatigued, distracted, strategically improvident, disposed to discount the relevance of ideology, solicitous of Soviet good will, hugely anxious for agreement, and not likely to counter Soviet claims and ambitions with anything more formidable than pro forma grumbling. In that anticipation, prolonged efforts to maintain the credibility of U.S. commitments would eventually serve to wear down the will for persevering, and reciprocally, the United States diverse allies would come to discount the reliability of U.S. pledges and accordingly seek to hedge their futures.

The two irreconcilable versions of a sequel provide a basis on which to reckon the results and the prospects now that it has become general practice—dating from President Nixon's announcement four years ago of an end to the era of confrontation and the advent of

49

an epoch of negotiation in superpower relations—to use the past tense in referring to the cold war.

III

China figures in the background of that supposed shift from animosity to amity. Understanding the China factor calls for putting out of mind a media-nurtured fancy attributing unique sapiency to the rulership in that most profuse and highly ethnocentric society—a regime with its proportionate share of fallibility in gauging external probabilities.

A challenge to Soviet primacy was implicit from the time of Communist accession in China. The Peking regime accentuated the division by its refusal to conform in the Eastern European satellites' obsequious fashion on being bidden to echo the Soviet regime's post-humous repudiation of Stalin. Subsequent Chinese efforts to displace the Soviet Union at the apex of the Marxist-Leninist realm—like Peking's overreaching scheme for a new international organization to rival and then to supplant the United Nations—did not prosper. The Chinese regime was surely alert to implications of the Soviet Union's military action in 1968 to punish and overcome doctrinal deviancy in Czechoslovakia and of the rationale for that action in the Brezhnev doctrine. A rapid tripling of Soviet troop strength abutting China, underlined by incidents of border warfare, heightened Chinese anxieties. In consequence, the regime was stimulated, as never before, to cultivate external connections.

Peking's pose of disdain for the United Nations, persisted in since the truculent visit and the stern rebuff of late 1950, was now abandoned. A hint, given in the form of quiet thanks to certain governments for perennial support of motions to seat the Chinese Communists in place of the Nationalist regime ensconced on insular Formosa, soon led to the desired opening of the United Nations' doors. In an age-old practice of playing off adversaries against each other, Peking next sought an opening to the one country with material capabilities to deter a Soviet attack. The Ping-Pong initiative was launched. One thing led to another, and a penultimate step toward normalization of relations with the United States came with the Nixon journey to Peking in early 1972.

The event prompted the Soviet rulership to court President Nixon and Henry Kissinger in earnest. The primary intent was to prevent the incipient China connection from maturing into something akin to an alliance. An auxiliary aspiration was to garner bonus effects in the form of subsidized preferential access to the benefits of U.S.

inventiveness and productivity—and thereby also to cater to an American preconception which links commerce and peace. The culmination, portrayed as marking an epochal transformation, came in the Nixon-Kissinger mission to Moscow in mid-1972.

The idea of an ameliorative turn in U.S.–Soviet relations was no novelty. Twenty-one such junctures had occurred since 1933, a dozen of them since the onset of the cold war. Mr. Nixon's portrayal of the transformation, moreover, was characteristically hyperbolic, for negotiations between the United States and the Soviet Union had been going on for thirty-nine years, except for brief gaps during Stalin's final phase in the early 1950s and after the U-2 bungle in 1960, and a ruling-out of further dangerous clashes of purpose exceeded anyone's power of foretelling. Thus, it would have been easy to discount the occasion, but to have done so would have been wrong. In plain fact, the volume and variety of U.S.-Soviet agreements produced in the following phase—touching on such diverse matters as cultural interchange, commercial accommodation, technological transference, symbolic collaboration in space, political concord, and the strategic equation—surpassed by far all theretofore achieved in U.S.-Soviet relations. One is hard put to find their match in the annals of diplomacy. Change is unquestionable. Whether the sum of those accomplishments really constitutes a mutation—that is, whether the United States and the Soviet Union have truly entered into concord—is a different question.

An index is the undertaking for constant collaboration to preserve peace in crisis situations, wherever occurring, entered into on the occasion of President Nixon's 1972 Moscow visit and elaborated during Brezhnev's return Washington visit a year later. These pertinent matters are known. After making the pledges, the Soviet Union in 1973 secretly provisioned the Yom Kippur attacks on Israel, took initiatives toward direct intervention following a shift of impetus against its clients, successfully urged on the petroleum embargo by Arab oil-producing states, and strove, though unsuccessfully, to get that venture in economic warfare prolonged. Despite having signed on as guarantor of the 1973 Paris accords on Vietnam, the Soviet Union in 1974–75 abetted the North Vietnamese in scrapping those accords and overrunning South Vietnam. More recently, in the Angola instance, the Soviet Union, scorning our secretary of state's entreaties, has vindicated doctrinal assertions of special prerogatives in so-called national liberation wars.

Without venturing to predict other examples to follow, one must ask whether the demonstrated gap between apparent promise and actual performance results from perfidy, fickleness, caprice, or what. The answer is obvious. The word "peace" continues to have not merely different but indeed quite antithetic meaning when used by the two governments. Negotiation can scarcely bridge such divergence. The universe of discourse—that shared grasp of meanings and values—basic to all effective international accords, just as it is to all other contractual relationships if they are to be relied on, is lacking.

The Soviet rulership is fully aware of the discrepancy in meaning and turns it to advantage. Meanwhile, U.S. policy, to its own detriment, prefers to avert notice. The United States portrayal dwells upon concord, however superficial or ambiguous, and mutes differences, however basic and obvious. Euphemism—meaning abundant use of words of good omen to make things seem better than warranted in reality—is brought into play. An underlying postulate is simple to a point of simplism. War is paired with disagreement, peace with agreement. Agreement is a product of negotiation. Hence negotiation equates with peace. As long as negotiation proceeds, peace is being generated. The process itself is what counts. That version yearns for negotiated agreements as good per se, irrespective of content.

In light of that basic divergence, which our policy articulators are wont to ignore or to deemphasize, it is appropriate now to consider sketchily the alterations in strategic position since the onset of the cold war. Some elements of U.S. strength, notably general productivity and potential for invention, have endured remarkably. Other components of our one-time strategic ascendancy were inherently temporary phenomena of the immediate postwar situation and have, as was inevitable, disappeared. Others could have been maintained perhaps but were suffered to slip away. On balance, the nation's once patent strategic ascendancy and the benefits which it conferred on us and others are gone, but what endures is that no combination of nations capable of coping with Soviet strategic pressures is feasible without U.S. participation.

A significant loss—let us hope not an irreversible one—pertains to the factor of civil morale. Damage done to the government's credibility on the home scene, partly though not wholly in consequence of actions undertaken to preserve credibility abroad, makes it far more difficult than it once was to achieve that meshing between tangible and intangible factors of strength so essential to coherence in the conduct of policy. Confidence in the efficacy of policy seems to have dwindled. Once-evocative words and phrases have lost their power to arouse, and aims long cherished and fostered in external affairs have come under widespread doubt. A sag in confidence in collective institutions, exemplified in the United Nations, is one example. National self-determination, once valued as a goal conducive to harmony and justice, is invoked by rampant terrorism and provides watchwords for both sides in multiple international antagonisms. Developmental aid is suspected of encouraging transitions from poverty to pauperism. Rather than being devices for strengthening security, our alliances come under suspicion as ways of burdening the country with unnecessary obligations and entrapping it in unwarranted risks. I am not asserting these thoughts, but only noting them as ideas characterizing a public mood of being oversold and let down.

Subjective as it is, much of that mood may well prove evanescent. A more tangible consideration with potentially irreversible effects pertains to the strategic equation. The points I wish to make about it hark back to the Cuban missile crisis of fourteen years ago. At that juncture our magistrates were loath to push the advantage accruing from the strategic balance, decisively in our favor, as it then stood. The outcome, though I concede it could have been worse, was improvident from our standpoint in leaving Communist power ensconced and implicitly legitimized in a nearby position—a consequence for which a full reckoning is still ahead. More pertinently, those in charge of U.S. policy, seeming abashed for having had strategic superiority and having brought it to bear even in inadequate measure, were disposed to let that advantage begin to slip away in hope of finding the Soviet adversary inclined to settle for a strategic stalemate in the configurations of what I have depicted as Situation B.

That spirit underlay the endeavor for strategic arms limitation talks broached soon after Lyndon Johnson's full-term election, later shelved as inopportune in view of the Soviet invasion of Czechoslovakia in 1968, but then renewed soon after Richard Nixon's succession to office. The asymmetry of premises reflected in the respective negotiating positions in the resulting complex deliberations—called SALT—covering more than six years is tremendously significant.

The American effort has been guided by the following postulates: A war between the nuclear-armed superpowers would surely bring on mutual annihilation and mark an end to civilized existence. At such a level of conflict, winning is obsolete. There can be only losers. Thus, in superpower terms, a war-winning capability is no longer feasible. Diplomatic settlements must henceforth be disjoined from ratios of strategic strength. The overriding concern must be to avoid war.

53

The Soviet approach does not replicate those premises or even the terms expressing them—such as "second-strike capability," "mutual assured destruction," or "strategic balance." Its opposed premises in like order are these: A war between the superpowers would not necessarily produce mutual annihilation or mark an end to civilized existence. Winning and losing have not been abolished. A war-winning capability is still a cogent concept and probably an achievable object. Diplomatic settlements neither will not can be disjoined from the interplay of perceived strategic capabilities. An inherent concern of policy must be to prevail. That aim—which cannot be disjoined from the image of war—is achieved by manifesting a preponderance of forces and the will to bring them to bear.

The United States has been striving to codify Situation B. Far from reciprocating that intention, the Soviet Union's ambition is expressible as Situation A with the Soviet Union replacing the United States as the advantaged side. Here again, as in respect of the documented agreements about fostering peace, the premises entertained and the goals sought by the respective sides are antithetic. Reconciling such mutually exclusive positions is beyond what negotiations can accomplish. Notwithstanding the optimistic appraisals made by spokesmen for U.S. policy, the point just made is not contradicted by what has been accomplished at Vladivostok and since.[11] In a metaphoric analogue from football, the overappraisal is as if agreement on the dimensions of the field of contest and the number of authorized players were to be construed as writing off a whole season as a tie.

IV

The nub of the predicament toward which present trends are carrying the United States is drastic imbalance of threat. With war implausible in the American perception but plausible in the Soviet perception—and with each side cognizant of how the opposite side sees the matter—the intimidatory contingency of war would be an instrument of power at the Soviet side's exclusive disposal. Deterrence then would operate in one direction only. The disproportionate psychological effect would thenceforth count determinatively in every transaction. In recurring contests of purpose, those representing the United States would be reduced to making threats to wring their hands again if the Soviet Union did not desist from pressing to have its own way. Eventually—with existing trends prolonged—this nation

---

[11] The joint communiqué issued after this meeting appears in Part Two of this volume.

would face an inexorable choice either to precipitate war under grave disadvantage or to accommodate permanently to a resolute adversary's designs.

Some tend to rule out such an eventuality as having been rendered impossible by contemporary developments in the destructive potential of weapon systems. Two questions attributed to Secretary of State Kissinger are in that spirit: ". . . what in the name of God is strategic superiority? . . . What do you do with it? . . ." For both queries, the Soviet Union surely knows the answers and can be counted on to manifest them not necessarily in literal combat but in pressing its advantage issue by issue while fastening the habit of capitulation on others, including preeminently the United States. Such is the thrust of Foreign Minister Andre Gromyko's recent observation that "the forces of peace . . . now have a visibly increased preponderance and may be in position to lay down the direction of international politics." [12]

The advantages of having Situation A with the United States ascendant are presumably irretrievable. Thus, the critical question becomes whether the nation can disenthrall itself and rally its will, so as to maintain its end of a strategic balance and foreclose the Soviet Union from achieving a determinative strategic preponderance.

The case for continuing in the present course, as that case is expounded on intimate occasions by our chief policy exponents, is cast in the fatalistic mood of Oswald Spengler's *Decline of the West*, complementing the dogmatic claim of historic necessity put forth on the other side. We have had our brief day of ascendancy. The Soviet Union is now the "comer" in terms of power. Those are asserted to be the facts. Thought and action must reconcile to them. Accordingly, our course is not to contest but to proffer inducements in hope of persuading the Soviet hierarchs that more is to be gained by their taking time and abiding by the usages of negotiation than by unilateral pushiness. Anyway—so the argument concludes—the American people's distaste for any course entailing risk leaves no alternative.

That last point could be right. The wise Charles E. Bohlen came to a similar view in his memoirs: "Unhappily, the United States is not ready for the continuous struggle of wills and never-ending diplomatic crises that we face with the Soviet Union. . . . It is therefore pertinent to ask whether the United States is capable of leading the free world. . . . There is doubt that as a people we possess the discipline

---

[12] "Détente in Check," *The Economist* (7 February 1976), p. 9.

and patience to prevail." [13] I incline to concur, and so I am not optimistic on the question whether the nation will disenthrall itself. The apparently prevailing general mood is to renounce the cold war by declaring it to have been unconstitutional. That mood does not give promise of a good outcome.

Yet one cannot know for sure without a thorough test, to which the combination of public euphemism and esoteric fatalism is an obstacle. Our magistrates should recognize and make known the adverseness of strategic trends and the threats they pose to what we have and are, or at least should be. Thus informed, the nation might properly consider what needs to be done and see whether it can resolve its will accordingly. If it is unable to do so, then the nation can in full awareness come to terms with the implications of Spengler's observation: "World politics destroys those countries that are not up to it." [14]

U.S. FOREIGN POLICY:
THE SEARCH FOR FOCUS *

Zbigniew Brzezinski

Zbigniew Brzezinski discerns two opposing positions in America concerning foreign policy: one sees the world dominated by national political relationships, and the other is oriented toward global issues. Both endorse the notion that the United States must remain internationally active. Brzezinski believes that a new global politics, focusing on equality, has emerged, and this makes reliance on traditional strategies among competing nation-states increasingly irrelevant. The new situation calls for adopting a synergistic policy that embraces the central concerns of both outlooks.

America was thrust into the world some thirty years ago. That jolting experience generated in America a degree of unity concerning foreign affairs unusual for a democratic and pluralist society. Largely as a consequence of that shock, America's foreign policy came to enjoy

---

[13] Charles E. Bohlen, *Witness to History, 1929-1969* (New York: Norton, 1973), p. 540.

[14] Oswald Spengler, *Aphorisms* (Chicago: Henry Regnery Co., 1967), p. 120.

* Source: *Foreign Affairs* (July 1973), pp. 708-727.

for a quarter of a century the advantage of broad popular support and of a seeming sense of direction.

Throughout much of that time, America's involvement in world affairs was characterized by an increasingly activist internationalism, by an idealistic optimism, and by a strong dose of populist Manichaeanism. The activist internationalism was in part a reaction to widely shared guilt feelings about America's earlier rejection of the League of Nations, and—as if to erase the past—America now became the most active promoter of international undertakings. The idealistic optimism combined a strong faith in the eventual emergence of a world of united nations with an unprecedented degree of popular willingness to share America's bounty with others. The populist Manichaeanism reflected the propensity of the masses to demonize foreign affairs, a tendency easily reinforced by the realities of Hitlerism and then of Stalinism.

Both World War II and the subsequent cold war gave America's involvement in world affairs a clear focus. The objectives of foreign policy were relatively easy to define, and they could be imbued with high moral content. To be sure, periodic frustrations in the conduct of the cold war prompted different Presidents to define their policies and priorities in varying terms, but the essential character of America's involvement remained unchanged. President Roosevelt focused public hopes on the "four freedoms," but the frustrations of Yalta— a case of unsuccessful *Realpolitik* at variance with the prevailing idealism—led not long afterward to President Truman's call for the containment of Stalinism and for the reconstruction of Europe. The frustrations of the Korean War in turn led to President Eisenhower's "Crusade for Freedom," including even the goal of liberating Eastern Europe (and thus repudiating Yalta). U.S. passivity in the face of the East European upheavals of 1956, and then the crisis of confidence produced by the launching of the Sputnik, led President Kennedy to articulate a doctrine of heroic universalism, combining strong anti-communism with a rhetoric of compassion for the poorer nations, but he and even more his successor, President Johnson, soon became the prisoners of the Vietnam War. By the time President Nixon assumed office the American consensus on foreign affairs was a thing of the past.

It would be premature to conclude from the foregoing that it was the Vietnam War that blurred America's vision and shattered its agreed perceptions on foreign affairs. That the change may be the product of more complex forces, and that consequently the Vietnam War was more of a catalyst than a cause, is suggested by a remarkable study of America's posture in foreign affairs, published in the early 1950s. Its author, having systematically collated data concerning foreign affairs—presidential messages, party platforms, election results, frequency of foreign treaties, naval expenditures, armed expeditions, wars, annexations, diplomatic warnings—argued that since 1776 America's relationship with the world has been characterized by alternating cycles of "extroversion" and "introversion." He concluded, with remarkable prescience, that "in view of America's past record, and of the presumed role of 'internal factors' in promoting the introvert-extrovert rhythm—it seems logical to expect America to retreat, to some extent at least, from so much world involvement, and perhaps to do so sometime in the 1960s." [1]

It is appropriate to begin our analysis by recalling this forecast, for it reinforces the proposition that the present change in America's mood may represent something deeper than a reaction to the war in Vietnam. The change that has taken place—cultural, political and social—is doubtless far-reaching. One senses it in the new generational values, especially in the dislike for "power politics" and in the widespread ambivalence about existing U.S. foreign commitments; in the mood in Congress, especially in regard to foreign involvements, including even altruistic ones such as foreign aid; and in the waning of the internationalist Eastern foreign affairs élite. "Come home, America" on the Democratic side and economic protectionism on the Republican side may thus reflect another fundamental shift, a new cycle in America's alternating relationship with the world.

II

There are many obvious parallels between the current change in American mood and earlier shifts from extroversion to introversion. Yet, in a more basic sense, these parallels are misleading. Neither on the objective plane nor on the subjective plane is the real choice today between internationalism and isolationism. Indeed, it is hard to define the practical meaning of these terms in the context of contemporary conditions.

---

[1] Frank L. Klingberg, "The Historical Alternation of Moods in American Foreign Policy," *World Politics* (January 1952). His phases are as follows:

Introversion	Extroversion
1776-1798	1798-1824
1824-1844	1844-1871
1871-1891	1891-1919
1919-1940	1940-

It is to be noted that the phases of extroversion have lasted about 27-28 years, and hence the last phase of extroversion should have ended around 1968, according to Klingberg's analysis.

On the objective level, the situation in which the United States finds itself is quite unlike that of the earlier cycles of introspection. In the area of economics, the United States is now the leading international investor both in the less-developed and in the advanced industrial economies, with returns on these investments representing for some major U.S. enterprises the critical source of their margins of profit. This outward thrust of U.S. business and capital makes the United States very vulnerable to any new wave of protectionism, and it does create a powerful constituency with an enormous vested interest against any return to "introversion."

A related major historical change—one that has also transpired since World War II—involves the transformation of the resource-autarkic American economy into an increasingly resource-dependent economy. Some experts have estimated that the United States is already dependent on imports for twenty-six out of some thirty-six basic raw materials consumed by its industrial economy; and this dependence is growing most dramatically, but by no means exclusively, in the energy field. This shift is imposing a mounting fiscal drain on the U.S. economy (with mineral imports costing $8 billion in 1970 and likely to cost about $31 billion by 1985) and it also heightens the U.S. stake in a stable and uninterrupted flow of international trade. As a consequence, America finds itself so deeply involved in the world economy, a condition reinforced by its special monetary role, that on the economic plane the concept of isolationism becomes at worst a suicidal policy and at best an irrelevance.

America's growing economic interdependence with the world economy is reinforced by social dynamics, involving massive growth in tourism, in the number of Americans studying abroad and of foreigners here, in communications in general—in all of which the United States is the pacesetter. This process creates further links, transforming America's relationship with the world from one which in the past could enjoy the alternatives of isolationism or internationalism into one in which only the forms and degrees of interdependence are the issue.

In international politics, America's options have been similarly transformed. In the past, the United States could exercise the luxury of choice between abstinence and involvement. Today, despite the debates over the desirability of the continued U.S. military presence in Europe, most Americans see their security tied closely to the continued independence and stability of Europe and Japan. The debate about troop levels is over the best means to enhance that interdependence, not on the question of its reality or even desirability. More generally, nuclear weapons have so transformed the nature of security that sudden shifts in the political-security balance are viewed as dangerous to all parties, even competing ones, and this creates interdependence even among rivals.

The question of subjective attitudes is more complicated, though it is revealing to note that those who favor policies of protectionism or of America's withdrawal from its various security-political engagements object to being described as isolationists and insist that the policies they advocate involve a higher and more responsible form of internationalism. Moreover, many vocal critics of American intervention abroad tend to be strongly opposed to American economic isolationism and to favor instead continued and even expanded American involvement in various forms of international cooperation. Overtones of old-fashioned isolationism, none the less, do make themselves heard, most notably within American labor concerned with the export of American jobs abroad by American multinational corporations and by the similar impact of foreign imports on employment. But here, too, the attitude is not a consistent one. Labor also tends to be strongly in favor of continued U.S. political and security engagements abroad—it is semi-isolationist at most.

Isolationism on the level of policy thus tends to be a partial view and not a coherent all-embracing doctrine. Even its adherents accept the proposition that at least in some respects the United States should remain actively engaged in the world, and in that sense they partake of a residual though vague consensus that the world is becoming an interdependent entity, from which there is no complete withdrawal. A broad and undefined notion of global interdependence seems to represent the general principle which most Americans share.[2]

This underlying consensus, however, is vague. It lacks a sharp focus defining, as was the case in the past, the character and thrust of America's relationship to the world. Moreover, the shared notion of global interdependence is given philosophical and political substance in significantly divergent ways by two contending schools of thought which today represent the principal lines of division among the concerned and articulate public. The outlook of these two contending

---

[2] An attempt to quantify the attitude of the U.S. public has been made in *State of the Nation*, ed. by W. Watts and L. A. Free (New York, 1973), and it suggests surprising stability during the last decade. Between the years 1964 and 1972 the percentage of Americans whose views could be described as completely isolationist or as predominantly isolationist has increased from 8 to 9 percent; of those whose views are mixed, from 27 to 35 percent. A considerable majority thus holds to an internationalist perspective, with which in part presumably some of those with "mixed" views also identify.

schools—each of which initially starts with the same basic premise of global interdependence—may be best capsulated by the terms "power realism" and "planetary humanism."

The power realists, generally more conservative in their values, tend to be preoccupied with the more traditional concerns of international affairs, particularly with such issues as strategy, the relationship of forces, the balance of power, diplomacy and monetary policy; they attach a very high value to stability, both as a concept and as a norm. They may often disagree on prescriptions and priorities (with the spectrum within the school neatly personalized by the contrasting positions of a George Ball and a John Connally), but they do hold a basic view in common in that they see the world as still dominated by *international* politics.

In contrast, the planetary humanists tend to think of the globe more as *a unit* beset by certain common problems. When attempting to translate into policy their basic predispositions, they tend to concentrate on such matters as ecology, nutrition, development, social justice and equality, or limits to growth. (An able example is Lester Brown's *World Without Borders,* but the range here, too, is wide, going beyond former Senator Eugene McCarthy to reach at one extreme some of the New Left writers). There are thus overtones in the above division of the older debate in America between "realists" and "idealists," but the differences are important: the new power realists accept more and more the notion of political interdependence, and their concern with stability preempts to some extent the idealists' earlier preoccupation with peace. Planetary humanists, unlike their predecessors the idealists, are much more concerned with social change—rather than peace—in a world which they see as beset by dynamically mounting socioeconomic crises, and their remedies focus on sociopolitical reforms. Many of them decry stability and accept the desirability in some cases even of violent change.

The former tend to be older, and hence an element of generational conflict is doubtless involved here (providing a parallel to Klingberg's cycles). This generational variance in perspectives is in large measure a consequence of the historical discontinuity experienced lately by American society. The thrust of any society into a new age for which established generalizations are lacking creates a situation of uncertainty and division ably expressed by novelist Hermann Hesse, whose writings have been sensitive to historical change:

> Human life is reduced to real suffering, to hell, only when two ages, two cultures and religions overlap. . . . There are

61

times when a whole generation is caught in this way between two ages, two modes of life, with the consequence that it loses all power to understand itself and has no standard, no security, no simple acquiescence.

Much of what has happened in America during the last decade and a half fits that evocative statement. It is no exaggeration to state that America has lately experienced—probably more so than any other contemporary society—a true cultural revolution. In the short time span of slightly more than a decade the United States has undergone a significant change in its social values, racial relations, sexual mores, and esthetic and artistic standards; all of that is bound to produce especially sharp generational gaps, including disagreements about America's role in the world.

Uncertainty about America's world role has been intensified by the almost simultaneous waning within American society of the relatively cohesive Eastern elite which hitherto has served as the source of both inspiration and leadership for America's more focused post-World War II engagement in world affairs. The disintegration of this group, its loss of self-confidence, its generational splits, go hand in hand with the appearance in American society of new groups aspiring to leadership. These groups, reflecting new economic interests and located in the Far West and Middle West, have supplied some of the personnel for the new Nixon team, but unlike their predecessors, they still lack—with some obvious exceptions—a cohesive and comprehensive world view. The result has been a further blurring of focus.

Even the extremes, whose narrow vision usually makes for a clarity of focus, are today ambivalent. The Right, traditionally primitive in its anticommunism but now thrown off balance by Nixon's flexibility toward the Communist world, is flirting with nationalism and protectionism; it is, however, unwilling to break with the President, who so far has successfully straddled the issue of protectionism vs. internationalism. The New Left, demoralized by its failures, offers mainly slogans as guides to foreign policy, while its social base, resting largely on the highly conformist intellectual world of university students and professors and some left-liberal social and media circles in New York, is too fluid to provide the jumping-off point for a serious claim to power. Outside of a small circle of true believers, *The National Review* and *The New York Review of Books* are read more for provocation than for policy guidance.

Despite this division and confusion, the power realists and the planetary humanists still remain in fundamental agreement that global interdependence—regardless of whether priority is given to political security or to social well-being—is the inescapable reality of our time. But this underlying agreement merely refutes the proposition that introversion is a viable and appealing choice. By itself, it does not provide a relevant policy focus for America's relationship with the world.

III

America is thus not turning inward, but its vision is unclear. President Nixon's foreign policy is a response to this condition of ambiguity as well as a reflection of it. As a response, it has been effective and occasionally brilliant; as a reflection it remains beset by a basic conceptual difficulty. Richard Nixon, who prides himself on his pragmatism, has perceived more sharply than many of his contemporaries—certainly more clearly than his rivals—the nature of the changed circumstances in which America finds itself. He sees— in part correctly—his foreign policy as a realistic response to world-wide and domestic changes. Recognizing the ambivalence at home, he has striven to fashion a policy that would gradually reduce America's commitments abroad while shaping what he and his associates have occasionally called "the new structure of peace." It is, by and large, a policy much in keeping with the evolution of his own views; in that sense, Nixon—though obviously the beneficiary of able advice from his Special Assistant [Henry A. Kissinger]—is to a greater extent the conceptual architect of his Administration's policy than any other U.S. President since Wilson (a point rarely conceded by his critics, who prefer to deny Nixon any credit).[3]

The extraordinary concentration of foreign policy making in the White House, particularly in the hands of the President and his special assistant, is due in part to the highly personal conceptual leadership which Nixon has provided. But the concentration is also very much the consequence of the basic thrust of the President's policy, which has put the highest priority on restructuring adversary relationships in the light of the perceived new power realities. The handling of adversary relationships is not suited to an institutionally implemented and openly articulated foreign policy; on the contrary, its very focus requires secrecy, surprise, maneuver, and even some deception.

---

[3] Instructive in this respect are his *Foreign Affairs* article of October 1967 which foreshadows the changed China policy, his acceptance speech of 1968 which pointed to the need for reshaping alliance relationships, and his Guam interview of early 1969, which spelled out the broad framework for the policies of subsequent years.

The basic conceptual framework of Nixon's foreign policy involves essentially a traditional balance-of-power approach, but more Bismarckian than Metternichian (as James Chace in *A World Elsewhere* has aptly pointed out). Unlike the static Metternichian balance, resting on a conservative ideological uniformity, the Bismarckian balance was based on movement and flexibility, on taking by surprise both friends and enemies alike. This is why the role of secret diplomacy under Nixon has risen to such heights; this is why the organizational setup requires such concentration of decision making and the exclusion of institutionalized bureaucracies both from the action of foreign policy and from the making of foreign policy. In effect, we have a merger here of an operating mechanism, a personal proclivity, and a foreign policy concept.

During the first four years—outside of seeking to end the Vietnam War—Nixon has concentrated on manipulating the new U.S.-Chinese-Soviet triangle. The fruits of this manipulation have been the partial codification of the cold war and the transformation of it from a "game" in which each side played by its own rules and kept its own score into one in which at least the rules are becoming more common. Moreover, the centrality of the arms race in the U.S.-Soviet competition has been somewhat reduced and, as a consequence, the competition has shifted to other areas, where the United States has an advantage. In addition, the normalization of relations with China has in all probability reduced Soviet freedom of action against its former ally while putting a higher premium in Moscow on American-Soviet accommodation. At the same time, American-Soviet agreements have begun to create a web of relationships that may gradually serve to reduce the intensity of their competitive relationship, and the President has wisely (though not necessarily accurately) emphasized that the improvement in American-Chinese relations has not been aimed at the Soviet Union.

The above has been accompanied by intensified efforts to shift the distribution of alliance burdens from the United States to both Western Europe and Japan, including the drastic economic measures adopted in 1971 and again in 1973. The result has been both strain and tension—but all of that has also been in keeping with the dynamic Bismarckian-Nixonian balance of power, involving neither permanent enemies nor friends. Since this policy has been responsive to the widespread feeling at home that America has been doing too much on its own, the President's approach has had the special merit of neutralizing the opposition both of many of Nixon's liberal critics—who essentially welcomed his moves toward China and the U.S.S.R., even if not sharing their underlying philosophy—and of his more conservative supporters, who have been increasingly concerned by the adverse U.S. balance of payments.

Nixon's foreign policy has thus involved an admirably intelligent application of the power-realists approach, skillfully adapted to prevailing domestic circumstances. The proof of its skill is to be found in the fact that, despite profound domestic divisions, the President's foreign policy by and large has not been the object of a major national debate. Even those who reject its underlying premises and its priorities grudgingly concede its successes.

None the less, President Nixon's foreign policy is open to several criticisms, on the operational level as well as on the broader level of historical pertinence. More specifically, three issues deserve critical consideration: the first pertains to the implicit indifference on the part of the Administration to the problems of the less-developed nations; the second criticism relates to the Administration's handling of alliance relationships; the third concerns the question of the historical relevance of the balance-of-power approach to world affairs in the 1970s.

The problem of the less-developed nations is the moral problem of our time. Given America's traditions, that dimension of the problem alone should make it an important one. Moreover, almost every index indicates that the problems of backwardness and poverty are becoming more acute: World Bank studies on the distribution of income, UNESCO studies on international education, and FAO studies of agricultural development, all agree that the gap is widening. Unlike industrial development in the nineteenth century, when objective change, by and large, was more rapid than subjective change, today subjective change is much more rapid than objective change. Access to literacy, circulation of newspapers, the impact of mass communications, increased political participation are more rapidly transforming the way people think than economic growth is transforming the way people live. The consequence is a heightened awareness of global inequality and an increased determination to erase it. Intensified social strife and global animosity are bound to be the consequence of mankind's failure to tackle the problem of global inequality.

The Administration has also been defective in its handling of alliance relationships. Though not isolationist, the Administration has certainly been unilateralist in dealing with problems affecting American-European and American-Japanese relations. As a result, Japan feels isolated and betrayed; resentment of American policies is on the rise in Canada; American relations with Europe have been by and large in a state of drift. The Japanese suspect that the United States is today assigning a higher priority to American-Chinese relations than to American-Japanese relations. Europeans are uneasy about America's longer-range intentions in Europe, and are baffled by America's willingness to deal directly with the Soviet Union while dragging its feet on such subjects as broader East-West talks and the recognition of the present European territorial arrangements (with the United States remaining the only major power in the world not to have recognized the Oder-Neisse Line). Recent monetary difficulties have intensified the political malaise, in part because the United States has relied more on a unilateralist tactical approach than on the development of a broader and longer-range strategic policy.

Third, one may wonder whether the balance-of-power approach provides an adequate response to a world dominated by rapid change, by sharpening social disparities and by a widespread resentment of inequality. It has often been noted that the principal powers engaged in the balance-of-power game are of a highly asymmetrical character: the United States and the Soviet Union are reasonably well-matched militarily but are certainly not matched economically; Japan and Europe are the economic peers of the United States and/or Russia but they are certainly not military peers. China may be becoming a peer in certain military dimensions, but it is not likely to be an economic peer for quite some time. The search for balance among these five may thus prove to be elusive.

Moreover, there is the more basic question concerning the adequacy of the power-realist approach as a tool for a comprehensive understanding of our historical condition. The power realists have a strong case when they argue that the downgrading of national might, of diplomacy, and of the more traditional tools of international behavior could jeopardize the chances for peace by prompting international instability. They are also right when they argue that an exclusive concentration on the planetary issues, though morally much more appealing, ignores the reality of a world of nation-states, of a world of national rivalries, of national armies and of ideological hostilities. Even if not isolationist in spirit, planetary humanism can be charged with being in many ways escapist in essence.

Yet those who emphasize planetary humanism have a powerful argument when they warn that to ignore the longer-range threat is to invite within a mere decade or two a situation of global anarchy, of the fragmentation of social and political institutions, of the collapse of the very stability to which the power realists attach such a high value. Moreover, the balance which the power realists advocate, is based primarily on convenience and not on principle. It implies no fidelity to common goals and no shared definition of common concepts. In a rapidly changing world, such a balance could at some point become inconvenient to those whom the United States has considered as its allies, especially after the treatment meted out to them by the United States in 1971. Thus, the notion of no permanent enemies or friends could become contagious, rebounding against the United States sooner than one thinks.

Moreover, on the more immediate, domestic plane, the planetary humanists can rightly assert that an essentially Machiavellian foreign policy is incapable of tapping the moral resources of the American people. Indeed, by alienating a significant portion of the American people, it contributes to further domestic division. With moral considerations becoming a more compelling force than ever before, and given America's traditional world role, it also weakens America on the international scene. A morally indifferent America is automatically a weaker America; an amoral America is also likely to become a lonely America.[4]

IV

The difficulty of articulating acceptable priorities for the United States, a difficulty already enormous because of the domestic split between the two major contending schools of thought, is compounded by the transformation which foreign affairs have undergone in the years since World War II. In brief, that transformation involves a shift from international politics, in which the political, security, and economic sectors have been relatively compartmentalized, to a new global politics, in which political, security, and economic issues are intermeshed and in which the distinction between the domestic and the foreign aspects is becoming increasingly blurred.

For much of the cold war, foreign affairs were preeminent in the thinking of American statesmen, with security issues dominant. Today, the situation is rather different. The politics of interdependence—largely the consequence of America's economic and social intimacy with Western Europe and Japan—are beginning to overshadow the politics of confrontation with the Communist world, and

---

[4] It is noteworthy also that either the isolation of America (brought on by obsessive application of the balance-of-power approach) or an escapist America (prompting global insecurity and perhaps even precipitating nuclear proliferation) could only prompt an increasingly conservative America, more and more preoccupied with its own well-being and security. Thus, the domestic political dynamics of both the power-realistic approach and of the planetary-humanist approach point in the same direction.

a major aspect of this is the close linkage between economic and political issues. That linkage, in turn, works to render irrelevant the former distinctions between domestic and foreign policy. The blurring of these dividing lines may well preclude altogether a return to the conceptual clarity about the world, and about America's place in it, which Americans enjoyed during the preceding several decades. That clarity was largely a crisis phenomenon, the product of unprecedented global polarization. In a world of overlapping interests, such clarity of focus simply cannot be replicated.

None the less, even within this more complex setting, one can affirm certain basic priorities for American policy toward the rest of the world. The overt definition of such priorities—and the resulting debate over them—may help eventually to create a new sense of direction for America's global engagement, an engagement which— it has been argued here—most Americans are prepared to accept as an inescapable reality. Some of these priorities are not new, but they need to be restated; some do involve new emphasis.

Despite the partial codification of the competitive relationship prevailing between the United States and the U.S.S.R., the problem of security remains, as a legacy of the past, a high-priority item. For one thing, the danger of war has not disappeared entirely, though war as an act of policy has become a luxury which only the poor and the backward nonnuclear nations can now afford. Indeed, the possibility of an accidental war may now be higher than in the past, given the extraordinary complexity and abundance of modern weapons. To reduce this danger, efforts to codify and expand the developing U.S.-Soviet arms control arrangements must be continued. In any case, one hopes that the Soviet side has a coequal interest in the avoidance of accidental war. The vigorous pursuit of SALT II is the logical conclusion.

In addition, there is reason to be concerned that at some point the Soviet leaders may be tempted to try to exploit a claimed or imagined margin of superiority in the weaponry of mass destruction, to extract, under the threat of war, significant and one-sided political gains. How to avoid this essentially incalculable political, even psychological, threat is difficult to analyze, for that threat is meaningful only in the degree to which asymmetry of power is perceived by the threatened side as being of significance. Still, sheer prudence requires the maintenance of a security posture which by itself reduces the likelihood that the Soviet leaders could at some point conclude that the moment is ripe for the extraction of political gains through the generation of a severe atmosphere of crisis. In addition to obvious security precautions, expansion of U.S. relations with China, including even some form of aid designed to create greater stability in the Sino-Soviet nuclear standoff (such as transfer to China of sophisticated communications systems), is also a contribution to the shaping of a more stable U.S.-Soviet relationship, in addition to the more cooperative initiatives which are already under way in trade and science.

These initiatives, especially if conducted on a broad front, including in them both the Soviet Union and the East European countries, are likely to promote the subtle process of philosophical reconciliation with the Communist elites, ending the increasingly irrelevant doctrinal civil war which has divided the West for more than a hundred years. This process, to be sure, will be slow; moreover, reversals in it are to be expected, especially as the more conservative, neo-Stalinist elements stage occasional counteroffensives designed to make certain the East-West links leave the Soviet and East European peoples ideologically uncontaminated. Such elements are even likely to intensify at home their efforts at ideological-political controls. However, a broadly based process of intensified peaceful East-West engagement, going beyond the purely economic aspects, will almost imperceptibly chip away at the more outmoded edges of the Communist doctrinal edifice, thereby strengthening the pressures for East-West accommodation.

How to deal with the Communist world remains a key problem for U.S. foreign policy but it may no longer represent the central problem. The power realists, moreover, have been dealing with it effectively and—as Nixon has shown—not without some success in making the competitive U.S.-Soviet relationship more stable. But the other two major problems confronting U.S. policy—namely, that of the less-developed countries and that of alliance relationships among the advanced countries—cannot be effectively tackled on the basis of the power-realist approach. The condition of the less-developed countries, indeed of the planet as a whole, requires greater concentration on the issues raised by planetary humanists, while the question of alliance relationships calls for a creative blend of both approaches.

This blend is needed because of the transformation which international affairs are undergoing—a transformation which introduces novel elements even as the old ones still remain partially operative. We noted earlier the appearance of the new global politics, which makes the older international politics increasingly irrelevant as the organizing-conceptual framework for dealing with world affairs. These emerging global politics are yet to acquire a clear-cut character:

they might become the politics of growing global responsibility and interdependence—or they might become characterized more and more by anarchy, social fragmentation, and intensified racial, ethnic, and ideological conflicts, with even the older international rivalries resurfacing in a new form. The desperate problem of the less-developed nations is central here, but an important issue at stake also is the very character of social and political organization in the more advanced states.

Modern society is thrusting into a new age, the character of which we do not still fully understand. Material wealth is creating a strange spiritual emptiness in some of the more advanced industrial societies, while scientific developments pose an ominous threat to the integrity of the human being himself by raising the specter of human malleability through social engineering. There is thus a growing need for more sustained reflection on the condition of modern man and for a mutual learning process among the societies that are in the forefront of the technetronic revolution. It is doubtful that an effective response to this internal problem—not to speak of external relations among advanced industrial countries—can be mounted on the basis of a single society, however rich or powerful.

It is to this newer and enormously complex task that American policy will have to address itself, and in so doing seek to respond to the central concerns both of the power realists and of the planetary humanists. Realism and the lessons of the past show clearly that the United States alone cannot mount the needed response, that the process of shaping a more stable and socially progressive world calls for a wider effort among those who share both certain philosophical assumptions and the needed resources. This condition imposes a special obligation, in the first instance, on the United States, Western Europe, and Japan to shape their policies with broader concerns in mind than the dictates of national interest alone. Unless these advanced sectors of the world move toward greater and more active collaboration there is a high probability that the fragile global economy and the barely emerging sense of global community will be shattered, pitching the world back into international animosities, fragmenting the world economy and intensifying the social strains within both the advanced and the developing countries.

Closer cooperation among the advanced industrial societies, which share certain political values in common, would help to create a stable core for global politics, on the basis of which a more sustained response to the traditional threats of war, or to the new danger of social fragmentation brought about by poverty, or to the broader image of collapse of the global eco-system, can be undertaken. The Atlantic concept was a creative response to the problems of the cold war era. Today, the Atlantic framework is too narrow to encompass the multitude of challenges—and opportunities—that confront the international community. It is a recognition of this reality to propose that without closer American-European-Japanese cooperation the major problems of today cannot be effectively tackled, and that *the active promotion of such trilateral cooperation must now become the central priority of U.S. policy.*

This means nothing less than deliberate, closer, and more institutionalized political consultation among these three power centers. Without such consultations, formal proclamations, including even a "new Atlantic Charter," are likely to lack substance. These consultations, designed to develop common policies with regard to the various problems confronting the global community, must be *ab initio* on the basis of trilateral parity. It simply is not enough, and psychologically wrong, to strengthen Atlantic ties and *then* invite Japan to come in—an approach which the Administration seems to be favoring, judging from Henry Kissinger's important and thoughtful speech of April 1973 on U.S.-European relations. Moreover, in President Nixon's State of the World Message for 1973, Japan was accused of a "free ride" on the Japan-U.S. Security Treaty; such affirmations can only exacerbate the already strained U.S.-Japanese relationship. (Indeed, it is time that Japan be given more public credit for its accommodation to various recent U.S. economic and political desiderata.) In any case, Japan must be included in any new initiative from the very start, and not only "ultimately."

More specifically, implementation of a decision to seek closer consultative relationships could take several forms, all of them initially modest and far short of anything resembling an alliance or formal community. First of all, to stimulate a greater degree of shared political perspective among the governmental bodies of the three units, to promote the practice of regular and ever more formal political consultation, and to develop common political planning with regard to problems or areas of mutual interest, it would be desirable: (1) to adopt as a matter of regular practice the holding of annual trilateral cabinet meetings, somewhat on the model of the U.S.-Japanese cabinet meetings. In the trilateral setting, this could involve the Common Market countries as well as the Japanese and American sides; in addition, perhaps regular meetings of the respective heads of government might also be scheduled on a less frequent basis; (2) to reinforce the above with a standing secretariat, particularly with a common policy planning and review staff, in part as back-up for the above and in part as a stimulant to the emergence and crystallization of common perspectives and policies; (3) to promote consultations in a larger framework, involving states outside the formal confines of the "cooperative triangle," with more frequent meetings of the foreign ministers of the Organization for Economic Cooperation and Development both to review common political problems and to work out joint responses to the problems of development in the Third World; (4) to hold regular three-way meetings of the respective parliamentarians, on as wide a party basis as possible.

The important point to bear in mind with regard to the foregoing proposals is that movement toward a community of the developed nations involves a long and gradual process, the pursuit of which has to be deliberate. Articulation of this very concept as the desirable goal would represent by itself a step in that direction, even though it must be recognized that the word "community" involves at best a distant objective. None the less, out of such consultations, there may eventually emerge a wider consensus—though not necessarily coordinated policies—on the specifics of political collaboration, on global security and on relations with the Communist world, as well as a more enduring response to the monetary and trade difficulties that have already strained Atlantic and Pacific relations. Free trade has been the underlying principle of world economics during the last two and a half decades, but the imbalances that have lately developed have posed the threat of new trade wars under the banner of protectionism. Closer trilateral consultations may facilitate the emergence of a third and healthier alternative, involving more deliberate periodic adjustments, reinforced by new monetary institutions.

Such a trilateral relationship also rests upon the linkage of security concerns that bind the United States, Europe, and Japan. Such a linkage already exists, and will most likely become more apparent with the passage of time. The Chinese are developing a policy toward Western Europe to encourage West European integration as a counterweight to the Soviet presence in Europe. Their attitude toward the upcoming conference on European security has already been made felt in this regard. Further, they continue to encourage any stirrings of independence within the East European Soviet bloc. A coordinated response to the Chinese-Russian rivalry as it affects Europe is a matter of simple realism. The interests of the West Europeans, in turn, overlap those of the Japanese in the Middle East as a result of their common dependence on oil, and, consequently, in such strategic areas as the Straits of Malacca and the Indian Ocean. Such security considerations cannot easily be divorced from those economic interests that are vital to their well-being; and it is not desirable, particularly as America reduces its global role, for the United States to assume unilaterally the overarching security needs of its major allies.

Doubtless, many obstacles to such trilateral cooperation will have to be overcome. Some Europeans may resent an approach which seems to place Atlantic relations on a par with Pacific relations and suspect that it represents essentially an American effort to shift onto European shoulders some of the imbalances in U.S.-Japanese relations. Some Japanese may feel that the initiative reflects a desire to entangle them in an expanded NATO. These fears are real, even though they are not justified. For good historical and cultural reasons, Atlantic relations will remain for some time to come of a different order than Pacific links, while trade and monetary problems between the United States and Japan have already had such a major impact on Atlantic relations that they simply cannot be compartmentalized. To acknowledge this reality, and to postulate the need for a wider political response on the above matters, as well as on the broader global problems, is not, however, to extend the framework of NATO to the Pacific, but to respond jointly to joint concerns. Thus rather than refute, the above fears highlight the need for more sustained trilateral consultations and additional trilateral links.

The adoption of these objectives would entail some operational consequences for the way in which policy is made and executed in Washington. A secretive and highly personal foreign policy, heavily reliant on maneuver and surprise, is admirably suited to handling adversary relationships. It is bound to have a short life, and the longer it lasts, the more likely it is to backfire, since it is inadequate for dealing with the complex problems involving U.S.-Japanese-European relations. Recent Japanese reactions, including the cancellation of Emperor Hirohito's trip to the United States, indicate that a secretive unilateralism is contagious. Trilateral relations, be they monetary, trade or security, must be nurtured by stable and extensive negotiations and reinforced by further institutional growth. The recovery of the State Department and of the Treasury are thus the operational requirements of the broader strategy outlined above.

The very process of seeking to shape a community of the developed nations would inescapably involve a greater degree of consultation concerning the major longer-range problems of global politics, most notably that of backwardness and poverty in the Third World, a concern uppermost in the minds of the planetary humanists. It is to be expected that in the next two or three decades we will witness an intensified crisis in the Third World, brought about by the twin impacts of demographic growth and the spread of education. Both will make global inequality even more intolerable at a time when equality is becoming the most powerful moral imperative of our time, thus paralleling the appeal of the concept of liberty during the nineteenth century.

This quest for equality is already being felt both within societies and on a global scale; it is, therefore, essential that the richer nations develop more comprehensive, more cooperative, and more planned policies toward the poorer parts of the world. They must further increase the participation by all of the advanced countries in institutions designed to improve the lot of the Third World (for example, Japan might usefully participate as a member of the Latin American Development Bank, and Europe and America might participate in other regional activities of this sort as well). One of the frequent objections to the concept of the community of the developed nations is that it will be "a rich man's club," insensitive to the problems of the Third World. Yet it is difficult to see how the monumental problems which the Third World confronts can be resolved unless advanced countries do cooperate in generating a major response. Social stability and progress are not going to be achieved if the three most powerful units of the world are pushed by their internal and external dynamics into increasing protectionism as well as other economic conflicts.

Similarly, objections have been made that closer trilateral cooperation as the central goal of U.S. policy runs counter to the aim of improving relations with the Communist world. Yet that improvement is not likely to be attained in a setting which is unstable and thus feeds the residual revolutionary aspirations of the Communist leaders. A cooperative component, embracing the richest and the most powerful countries, seriously seeking to develop common policies designed to promote more rapid growth in the Third World, is hence more likely to develop enduring and constructive relations with the Communist states than individual policies of détente, often competitively pursued.

Indeed, a gradually emerging community of the developed nations will be in a better position to pursue true détente, the aim of which is not an artificially compartmentalized globe, fundamentally in conflict with basic global dynamics, but a world in which spheres of exclusive predominance fade. Just as American hegemony in Latin America must decline—and the United States is beginning to accept that reality—and just as a Japanese coprosperity sphere in

Asia is not compatible with Asian nationalisms, so Soviet predominance in Eastern Europe will have to be gradually replaced by an Eastern Europe that—though retaining some links with the U.S.S.R. —is part of a wider European association.

The policy outlined above would involve a building-block approach toward the goal of creating a global community that is stable and progressive. By being responsive to the central concerns of the power realists and of the planetary humanists—both of whom recognize the reality of global interdependence though they define its priorities differently—it might also lead to greater clarity in America's global engagement.

CHOICES *

Stanley Hoffmann

Stanley Hoffmann argues that the world has become exceedingly complicated as the primacy of strictly defense issues has declined. Policy choices are more difficult now because the decision-making process no longer follows from a simple formula—such as bipolar dominance of world affairs by the U.S. and U.S.S.R.—but rather necessitates consideration of the prerequisites underlying policy actions. Hoffmann examines possible foundations for foreign policy in the areas of structures for global relationships, styles of international conduct, and arrangements of the policy-making apparatus.

Discussing the [Nixon] Administration's world view is an exercise in frustration. Its leaders are superb at telling us what they have saved us from and what they are not aiming at (such as "a classical balance of power"). But the inflation which affects the length of the yearly "state of the world" messages, along with the price of all goods, seems almost designed to blur the focus and the main directions of the policy and to preserve deliberate unpredictability and momentary improvisation.

We are told about a lower profile, a world of pluralism and consensus, shared responsibilities, the reduction of differences with our ex-adversaries, and the preservation of our old alliances. The new emphasis suggests quite rightly that the age of grandiose blueprints

* Source: *Foreign Policy*, no. 12 (Fall 1973), pp. 3-35.

is over and that the creation of a peaceful set of relationships in a world of extreme heterogeneity can only result from complex processes—to go back to Kennan's familiar distinction, it is a matter of gardening not engineering. But gardeners know what kind of a garden they want and how to feed, prune, and shape different plants in order to get it. The ritual, incantatory assertion of our search for a "stable structure of peace" tells us very little of substance. At most, it indicates a vague, sound set of "philosophic" hunches, which neither amount to a genuine "fresh vision" nor account for all those tactical moves, or omissions, that are in flat contradiction with the stated goals.

For there is a growing tension between the sensible, if vague, features of the "stable structure" indefatigably mentioned in each report and the methods that consist of either shock tactics or top-level summitry; "process" requires not only a sense of direction but also regularity and deep-rooted consensus—at home and abroad—on the way. So far, the Administration's acts are a mix of bold "breakthroughs" that have removed obsolescent obstacles to a new international order and brusque or brutal blows that contradict the pious renunciation of "maneuvering for marginal advantages over others" and the sanctimonious statements of concern for their principles and national interests. And the Administration's words are a mix of formulas for a transition from a past described in cartoonlike ways to a mysterious idyllic future—and obfuscation.

The effort to examine critically the premises of our official policy is further complicated by the change in the international system. It is partly a change in the realities, partly a change in our perceptions. For twenty years, we both observed and assumed three characteristics: bipolarity, nationalism, and the primacy of foreign policy.

A basic element of this system was the security dilemma. Like the thought of hanging, it concentrated the mind (the scholar's as well as the statesman's). It ordered the priorities. It explained the emphasis on strategic issues, especially nuclear weapons and arms control; it accounted for the fascination with the Third World, seen as a potentially decisive stake in the superpowers' contest; above all, it "disciplined" domestic politics (and the external by-products of domestic economic policies) by subordinating internal affairs to the single objective of survival (or independence). It really was to a large extent, and to an even larger one was perceived as, a war-in-peacetime.

Today, we observe and perceive bewildering complexity—probably with the same margin of exaggeration, but this time in the opposite direction. Three new characteristics are being stressed:

- There is (pardon the jargon) asymmetrical multipolarity—which means not only (1) that there are other important players besides the two superpowers, despite the vast gap between these two and all others, but also (2) that there are other influential components of power besides military might, and (3) that the international system is far more fragmented than when the cold war appeared to command its whole structure.

- Attention has moved from the new state actors in the Third World to the transnational forces and organizations, such as the so-called multinational corporations, which have emerged as important actors, "represent a principle of organization foreign to the nation-state system," [1] and either operate primarily among or originate from the more advanced nations.

- Analysts often now tend to see domestic interests or bureaucratic "games" as imposing their priorities on, or determining the outcomes of, foreign policy.

At the root, there is the displacement of the security dilemma; the move from a world dominated by a single chessboard—the strategic-diplomatic one (which either eclipsed or controlled all others)—to a world dispersed into a variety of chessboards. This is partly the result of the nuclear stalemate (which has somewhat neutralized the strategic chessboard and reduced, if not its fundamental importance, at least its daily saliency), partly the product of economic and social processes and scientific invention in a world obsessed by the quest for economic growth.

This very complexity explains why the answer to the Administration's obscure homilies cannot be simple inspirational designs. Before any grand alternative can be offered, or before any "next steps" on the many familiar issues of the current foreign policy agenda can be proposed, one must examine what might be called the prerequisites to any policy action, or the choices for policy planning, had "policy planning" not become discredited by a combination of misuse and nonuse. The purpose of this essay is to discuss nine such choices. Three can be called *strategic;* they both describe and prescribe (the two tend to be inextricably tied) the dynamics of the coming international system. Three can be termed *tactical;* they concern the role which the United States ought to play and the way of playing it. Three are *organizational;* they deal with the manner in

---

[1] Samuel P. Huntington, "Transnational Organizations in World Politics," *World Politics*, vol. 25, no. 3 (April 1973), p. 368.

which the U.S. "foreign policy machine" ought to be arranged. Clearly, the choices are largely interdependent. My purpose is not to provide full answers but only to discuss the alternatives. Sometimes, it will be obvious that the answer is "neither," sometimes "both," sometimes one of the alternatives against the other. To revert to the earlier metaphor: the strategic choices concern the ideal garden; the tactical ones, the gardener's acts; the organizational ones, his tools. But the metaphor breaks down in one vital respect: the gardener himself is a part—a major part—of the garden, and his vision of the ideal garden is itself largely shaped by the place he assigns to himself, among the trees and flowers.

Strategic Choices: "State of War" or Global Society?

The first, and probably most important, of these is a choice between *classiques* and *modernes*. This is a debate that (gently) rages almost exclusively among scholars. And yet, just as Molière's Mr. Jourdain spoke in prose without knowing it, policy makers implicitly choose between these two alternative conceptions of world dynamics. . . . I am referring to the discussion between those who believe that international relations will remain a "state of war," dominated by security concerns even if, for a while, these seem less urgent than before (the most essential may not be the most pressing), and those who believe that world politics will become more like domestic politics—a complex set of processes with no inherent essence, no dominant concern determined once and for all by the structure of the milieu.

The classical approach—what could be called the Thucydides-Clausewitz-Aron conception—emphasizes the state as the main actor in world affairs. Even when it acknowledges the unprecedented costs of an unrestrained use of force, it stresses the continuing difference between politics among armed actors without any common superior or legitimacy and the internal politics of actors restrained either by common values or by the superior force of the state. The modernists point to the stability of the nuclear balance and to the inhibition of large-scale force by the nuclear peril. They show the collapse of the old distinction between state acts and the moves of private forces (trans- or sub-national). They show the artificiality of the distinction between domestic and foreign affairs. In their view, the old specificity of interstate relations has been abolished. With bureaucratic coalitions across borders, with transnational actors destroying the economic and financial autonomy of states, with the increasingly obvious irrelevance of military power to most of the goals pursued by states, especially in the realm of resources and markets, international affairs will, as in domestic societies, turn into a host of problems of management, bargaining, pressures resulting in trade-offs, games of skill (and perhaps of chicken) rather than fights. There may be no world state, but there will be more world institutions, and sovereignty will mean little; there may not be substantive common values, but there will be common concerns and procedural values. Already, in the academic community, those who study strategy and arms control are quite separate, in assumptions and language, from those who apply economic analysis to international relations.

This debate has wide-ranging implications. First it involves two very different bets about the future. The *modernes* make a kind of Comte-like bet about the pacification of the world through industrialization (or maybe it is a Kantian bet on harmony brought about by fear and greed: by the increasing irrationality of modern war and the unbreakable interdependence of trade). In such a view, we are moving towards a "world without borders," and force is likely to be relegated to domestic breakdowns and a few extreme cases, especially among poor nations where old "tribal" hatreds still rage. The classicists remain skeptical and point to the proliferation of conventional, if not nuclear, weaponry, to the increasing economic importance of war industries among advanced nations, and to the domestic functions of armies in countless states governed or dominated by the military. They add that economic "interdependence" in a world of states remains highly uneven and that even pseudosovereigns who feel threatened by more powerful states or transnational agents still have the power to destroy the tenuous networks of functional solidarity or the capacity to exploit the domestic strains of others. Thus, there is both a risk of uncontrollable regression into the traditional violent conflict inherent in the structure of the international milieu and a risk of weakening the countervailing forces through economic mismanagement and unrestrained competition for scarce goods. At bottom, this is a debate between undaunted heirs of the Enlightenment, convinced that the processes of science and technology will make common interests prevail over separate ones, and those who remember Rousseau's metaphor of the stag hunt (in a competition for scarce goods, the separate interest of each hunter prevails over the common interest).

Secondly, this is a choice between two different conceptions of the nature of the competition among nations. One remains that of a contest which, at the moment of truth, becomes again a zero-sum game. To be sure, as Thomas Schelling in particular has shown, in a nuclear world, strategic opponents have mixed, rather than purely antagonistic, interests. But even prenuclear analysts and practitioners of power politics recognized that in a modern international system the main players had mixed interests and could, at times, find ways for all of them to make (some) gains. What is distinctive is the view that the moment may always come when the gain which *I* am after will be perceived by all of *you* as an unacceptable loss. In other words, the classical approach, while making some allowance for the consequences of nuclear weapons, still sees a balance-of-power approach to international affairs as the best way of moderating the competition; and, while recognizing that the actual use of force on the chessboards of economic interdependence may be irrelevant, it sees nothing absurd in the resort to threats, blackmail, or shock tactics there.

The other approach, however, stresses the solidarity of economic variables, the irrelevance not only of force but, increasingly, of borders to economic phenomena, and also that of the stag hunt metaphor: here states are often more interested in absolute (domestic) gains than in comparative advantages. Thus, the balance-of-power model is declared inapplicable: meaningless on the new chessboards, invalidated by nuclear weapons on the old one. And although it cannot be said that the *modernes* offer any normative model of their own, it is Ernst Haas's notion of "upgrading the common interest" and the neofunctionalist analysis of regional integration, which seems their inspiration.

Thirdly, the choice of conceptions entails a policy choice for the United States. A "classical" bet about the future suggests concentrating on the key strategic relationships: with the Soviet Union and with China, of course, but also with the other nuclear or potential nuclear powers. It implies that priority must be given to the settlement of those disputes that could result in large-scale war and to the arms race. The alternative approach does not provide quite as much policy guidance. While its main thrust is the consolidation of interdependence, it points out the increasing dispersion of economic power—both among states and between states and transnational organizations—and indeed suggests that the best way of hastening the transcendence of the old "state of war" may be to strengthen processes in which states play only a limited part.

The policy differences become most acute in regard to the "linkage" between security and other interests. Classical partisans of *Realpolitik* see nothing wrong in using the security relationship as a lever, in order to obtain concessions or redress their country's weaknesses on the other chessboards. The "modern" school tends to favor trade-offs or linkages between economic chessboards (again, as in the theory—and occasionally the practice—of European integration); but it excommunicates any attempt at bringing the blackmail tactics of the security realm into the other "issue-areas." Here, one can best observe that the choice of conceptions is not merely an analytic, but also partly a normative, choice. The classicists say in effect that, since the essence of international politics is untransformed, to behave as if the essence had changed or were changing is foolish. This may be true but leaves no other alternative for the future than the eternal return of the past. The *modernes* tell us that we ought to take advantage of those forces of change that make old divisions, contests, and concepts obsolete. This is indeed desirable except if it implies that one should act as if the millennium had arrived. There is no more difficult yet necessary intellectual problem than to try to arrive, not at a choice between the two alternatives, but at a synthesis—especially between the hard realism of one and the implicit idealism of the other.

A look at the "linkage" scene tells us, on the one hand, that security issues *have* remained essential for the states. It is Western Europe's military insecurity and its nations' different reactions to it which have slowed down and continue to slow down not only the "strategico-diplomatic" unification but also the economic integration of the half continent. It is the protection provided by the United States through the security treaty which has allowed Japan to become the "economic animal" admired or deplored all over the world. All Western attempts to use the Soviet Union's and Eastern Europe's need or greed for Western technology in order to obtain concessions in the realm of European security or in the arms race have proven futile. In other words, as the classicists have assumed, "linkage" works among allies huddled together against a peril—to the advantage of the strongest—but not among adversaries. On the other hand, as the *modernes* are warning us, any attempt by the stronger to use its military predominance in order to extract exorbitant economic concessions from its allies—in other words any deliberate playing of "balance of power" politics across the chessboards—could very easily backfire on all the chessboards, and lead both to chaos on the economic ones and to greater insecurity on the strategic ones. This suggests that, however valid or profound the classicists' insights remain about the persistence of force as the *ultima ratio* of world politics, or of the state as the power of last resort, or about the purely marginal importance of nonnational actors (many of which turn out to be quite national after all), a world of nuclear weapons and of problems that cannot be managed within national borders needs something *beyond* the classical conception. For the game which it describes had no other goal than its own perpetuation (or its resurrection after breakdowns), whereas today's game must aim both at the avoidance of such a breakdown and at the resolution of the problems which the traditional game can only either exacerbate or, at best (as Mr. John W. Dean III would say), "contain." This need for a synthesis applies to all nations. But it is essential for the United States, as one of the two nuclear superpowers, the world's most powerful economy (still), and the nation whose money (however battered) remains the principal transnational reserve currency.

Strategic Choices: Which Triangle?

A second choice has also been much debated, although less in academia than in the foreign policy establishment. Again, it involves both a judgment about the future and an American decision about priorities. It is the choice between pursuing a balance-of-power approach and seeking a community of advanced industrial societies; in geopolitical terms, it is a choice between two triangles: Washington-Moscow-Peking and Washington-Tokyo-whatever capital may represent Western Europe. It could be seen as a political translation of the two conceptual alternatives described above, but things are not quite so simple.

The balance-of-power approach is what the first Nixon Administration practiced. It is based on a postulate: as in the classical conception, it is the primacy, in world affairs, of "high politics" between the key military powers—the United States and its two main adversaries. (Here, trade is clearly treated as a tool, designed to affect the behavior of the Soviet Union in particular, and to give Moscow incentives for moderation, indeed for agreeing to codify great-power rules of conduct.) Should—in the absence of a common legitimacy—something like a pragmatic code of behavior develop between them, the world would be manageable. The improvement of relations among adversaries, the reduction of security anxieties (if not necessarily of forces), certainly does not make it unnecessary for Washington to maintain its alliances; for only the strength which they give to the United States, making it both a European and an Asian power, allows for the neo-Bismarckian tour de force of manipulating *all* relationships: a feat neither Moscow nor Peking can perform, due to their own antagonism. But it is no longer necessary for the United States to subordinate its economic relations with its allies to the imperative of survival. In other words, the direction of the "linkage" can now be reversed; as long as our "security dilemma" was as acute as our allies' we had to accept certain economic disadvantages in return for their military subordination; now, we can exploit their security needs for economic redress. Clearly, the lever for acting on and changing the world is the great-powers policy.

The alternative, suggested by a large segment of the pre-Nixon foreign policy elite, emphasizes on the contrary that "the active promotion of . . . trilateral cooperation" between the United States, Japan, and Western Europe "must now become the central priority of U.S. policy." It suggests that, while the security problem that is at the heart of the other approach "remains, as a legacy of the past, a high-priority item," [2] the main issues of the future are those which the *modernes* keep pointing out. For the solution of those problems, China's importance is purely marginal, and the Soviet Union remains outside the mainstream of the world economy. Moreover, hidden behind this formulation, one finds, as another cold war legacy, the conviction that the Russians' interest in intense cooperation with the "advanced nations" is tactical at best, that their willingness to play by the same rules as these nations is dubious, and that a real change in their behavior will be obtained, not through early and direct efforts at accommodation, but at the end of a long process in which they will be confronted with a successful "trilateral" organization of the non-Communist world. (Shades of "situations of strength.") This alternative can be seen as a way both of giving to the generalized insight of the *modernes* a specific political thrust (not all *modernes* are "trilateralists") and of adding to this insight a dash of "classical" concern for security relations.

Some interesting paradoxes are entangled in this debate. The first one concerns the connection between these alternatives and the earlier ones. The "balance of power" approach practiced by the Nixon Administration consisted of applying some of the "classical" techniques of *Realpolitik*, not only to the still primarily "strategico-diplomatic" relations with Moscow and Peking, and to the dampening of those conflicts in which the three adversaries could get involved—that is, on the terrain for which these tools were devised—but also to the economic and monetary relations among allies, to which they are quite unfit; so that, unfortunately, the very policies that succeed in restoring self-restraint and moderation on the traditional chessboard threaten to breed antagonisms on the new ones and to

---

[2] Zbigniew Brzezinski, "U.S. Foreign Policy: The Search for Focus," *Foreign Affairs*, vol. 51, no. 4 (July 1973), pp. 723, 720 [pp. 71 and 68 of this volume].

bring about the formation of competing blocs precisely in those realms where "balancing" would be absurd.[3] On the other hand, the "community of advanced nations," for all its "modern" casting and concern for "global interdependence," rests on the hypothesis of continuing relations of rather intense hostility between the United States and the Communist powers on the traditional chessboard. Indeed, if security is to remain one of the cements of the trilateral edifice, it is almost necessary for the great powers' détentes not to go too far. Thus, the synthesis which this conception appears to have achieved between the modern and the classical views turns out to be based on a questionable and fragile postulate.

Secondly, even though both alternatives are concerned with security, and both pretend to provide long-range "stable structures of peace," neither has a great deal to say about one of the issues that will be most complex and troublesome in the future: the global and regional management of force in a world of multiple arms races, in which violence across borders is the last resort not only of states but of frustrated groups and individuals, in which weapons of mass destruction may become cheaper to produce and easier to deliver, in which the resort to force can still often appear as a rational means toward political ends, in which the buildup of force may, even more often, be an end in itself (as in the "action-reaction" mad momentum of arms races, or for status and prestige reasons, or for the domestic consolidation of military cliques). On this score, both approaches lapse into vague generalities and short-term suggestions; indeed, both are inhibited by what they have, despite everything else, in common: their way of seeing the security problem as fundamentally a U.S.-Soviet one, to be either solved by direct negotiation or managed by a combination of direct discussions and "trilateral" impact. Neither approach faces the issue of nuclear proliferation. The second seems to assume that "trilateral" honey and continuing East-West tensions may make such a spread unnecessary; the balance-of-power approach dodges the problem of how to prevent the great powers' détente from becoming an incentive to proliferation.

Thirdly, both concepts have one other point in common: they are attempts at maintaining American primacy, although in different fashions. The balance-of-power approach tries to do so in two ways. It emphasizes the traditional chessboard, on which "bipolarity" persists (even the acceptance of "sufficiency" and the results of SALT I leave the United States with an appreciable advantage in the number

---

[3] I have discussed this in more detail in "Weighing the Balance of Power," *Foreign Affairs*, vol. 50, no. 4 (July 1972), pp. 618-643.

of deliverable warheads and in the qualitative race)—whereas the United States's relative predominance on the other chessboards is shrinking. This policy also tries to exploit the military advantage of the United States on the other chessboards, through the linkage discussed above. In the "trilateral" approach, American primacy is less explicit. But is it not clear that "common policy planning" would give a great advantage to the one power that has, for almost thirty years, developed the practices, tools, positions, and lingo of globalism? The West Europeans remain mired in the mud of integration, the Japanese wrapped in a mix of defensiveness and economic specialization, and both are still accustomed to leaving major chunks of "high politics" to their Protector. Is it not clear that the "linkage of security concerns that bind the United States, Europe and Japan"[4] works to Washington's advantage? In that edifice, the United States would be the central part, the other two the wings.

Like so many past American great debates, this one turns out to be not quite so great after all: it is all in the family—two ways of preserving pride of place. Also, as in other great debates, both alternatives are somewhat inadequate. The Administration—either because it became aware of the fallacies of a "balance of power" model in the world of the 1970s or because it wanted to steal its critics' thunder— recently came up with an attempted synthesis. Several passages of Dr. Kissinger's speech on Europe, on 23 April 1973, sounded like a loan (or a theft) from George Ball; and the 1973 "state of the world" message repeats, almost stridently, that "there is no higher objective than the strengthening of our partnerships." One can easily see the tactical function of such a shift. For instance, in the case of our relations with Western Europe, adding the balance-of-power approach (with its double emphasis on superpower diplomacy and on economic quasi-warfare) *and* the call for a new Atlantic Charter, that is, combining and applying the two yardsticks of great-power primacy and trilateral "common enterprise," results in neatly boxing in the Europeans, who are being told that their unity or autonomy is "not an end in itself." This amounts to *Realpolitik* in a trilateral framework; it provides a smooth justification for the linkage of issues.

And yet, such a synthesis of the two main ways of assuring American predominance is inherently artificial. The friendlier the triangle Washington–Moscow–Peking, the less willing Western Europe and Japan will be to tailor everything to their security relations with us; and it is difficult for us to demand from them a continuing will-

---

[4] Brzezinski, "U.S. Foreign Policy," p. 725 [p. 72 of this volume].

ingness to subordinate economic to military issues while *we* repudiate any further subordination of that sort. The attempted synthesis merely combines the flaws of both approaches. The first one assumes that the great-power relationship (quite correctly seen as essential from the viewpoint of world peace) somehow controls or shapes all the others. In reality, each chessboard has its own rules, and the impact which diplomatic and strategic détente is likely to have elsewhere may well make the application of balance-of-power methods there even more questionable. The other approach assumes that the trilateral relationship is impervious to the changes that affect the other triangle and that, as the hold of security fears weakens, the sense of common interests—which was always far more assumed by us than by our allies, even in the cold war years—will keep growing; the opposite is rather obvious. While Washington pursues ever more actively peaceful engagement with its ex-enemies and global competition with its allies and manifests an interest, if not in dropping its commitment to their defense, at least in limiting the strategic implications thereof, the West Europeans and the Japanese will become less willing to remain on America's orbit, and more eager to assure their own kinds of accommodation with or security from the Communist powers. They may not desire or achieve strong self-assertion, but they will seek autonomy. Thus, both approaches are exercises in nostalgia. I have written elsewhere that Mr. Kennan's obsession was 1914, while Mr. Acheson's was 1938.[5] Mr. Kissinger's inspiration remains the 1880s, and Mr. Brzezinski's the 1950s.

Strategic Choices: North vs. South

The two preceding approaches have a last thing in common: while both assert that it is not so, they have very little to say about the less-developed nations. Both tell us to concentrate on our relations with "the North" (although it is not the same North). To be sure, the central balance which has been the main focus of the Nixon Administration includes China, a huge underdeveloped nation, once feared as a potential leader of the Third World in the days when the late Marshal Lin-Piao was being totally misread. But the very purpose of catching China into the great powers' net is to give it a stake in the kind of world order that we are trying to build, to dissuade it from becoming the champion of the poor against the rich, to discon-

---

[5] Stanley Hoffmann, "After the Creation, or the Watch and the Arrow," *International Journal*, vol. 27, no. 2 (Spring 1973),

nect it from the potentially subversive and to make it play the cold game of states rather than serve the burning cause of revolution. Both approaches assume—once more in somewhat different ways— the growing irrelevance of the Third World as a collective force in world affairs. The balance-of-power approach, while aware of "the element of consensus,"[6] has very little to contribute to the solution of any of the problems which affect the less-developed countries. Indeed, it assumes that as the competition between the great powers abates, their interest in the Third World as a possible source of "marginal advantages" will also diminish, and the capacity of the poorer nations to stir up troubles among the great powers by playing one off against the other will crumble. "Decoupling" between the great powers and the others is seen as a necessary part of the "stable structure." Moreover, one worries about the Third World only insofar as one fears its continuing, or indeed increasing, potential for harm with respect to oil. And one of the reactions is to try to make sure that our chief ex-adversaries will refrain from exploiting our possible troubles: if we cannot "decouple," they should.

The advocates of a "community of advanced nations" are full of pious statements about how "the problem of the less-developed nations is the moral problem of our time."[7] But their answer makes one wonder whether they do not subscribe to Acheson's nasty distinction between moral problems and real ones. For they clearly assume that the solution of the Third World's problems depends on the advanced nations "generating a major response" in concert: should the rich succeed in defining their common plan, the poor would have to accept their leadership. It is sometimes hinted that such a joint effort would indeed thwart attempts by less-developed nations to exploit their own advantages through common fronts (for instance in oil), and could extend to a joint policing of vital sea lanes. What the rich would offer the poor in exchange is far from clear. Increased participation "by all of the advanced countries in institutions designed to improve the lot of the Third World" is a bizarre bait to the less advanced, and arguments about their interests in unimpeded development of their resources by "cosmocorps" may also appear as somewhat less than disinterested to them. (Moreover, some of the advanced nations—namely, our allies—may see in our appeal for a common front a clever way for us to gain access to their *chasses gardées* and to cut in on their special deals.)

[6] *U.S. Foreign Policy for the 1970s: Shaping a Durable Peace*, p. 232 [excerpts from this report appear at the beginning of part one of this volume].

[7] Brzezinski, "U.S. Foreign Policy," pp. 717, 726 [pp. 65, 73-74 of this volume].

Once again, good ideas are being carried too far, and the American pendulum does not know how to stop in the middle. Having (often for the wrong reasons) exaggerated the importance of the "South" yesterday is no reason to forget it today. The need to avoid absurd military entanglements; the fear that bungled interventions in the muddy domestic affairs of Third World countries could all too easily strengthen isolationist drives at home; a hunch that internal turmoil may be better for Third World nations than the social status quo preferred by the West; disillusionment with the effects of foreign aid and the mechanistic theories of "nation-building"; the belief that the network of transnational private organizations is sufficiently strong and indeed (as in the case of oil) more apt to allow for the preservation of mutually beneficial links of capital and trade, even while interstate relations are being decoupled (both from the Third World and from private links); these are some of the causes of the new wisdom. But it is empirically and normatively unsound. Empirically, it does not take into sufficient account the difference between the strategic-diplomatic chessboard, on which decoupling makes sense, and the other ones. There, the competition for influence among the major actors (not only our ex-adversaries but our half-friends) will continue and, even (or especially) if we cross our arms, they are likely to keep trying to score points and register presence among the less-developed. Moreover, on these chessboards, power is spread both more widely than on the strategic one and quite unevenly. Some of the less-developed nations enjoy a monopolistic or oligopolistic position over resources essential to the rich, whom they can oblige to "recouple." And the nonstrategic chessboards, even when some of the players are private enterprises, are all at least half-politicized. The international economy is only partly "private," both because the companies of the rich deal with the states of the poor and because the former play too important a role in the economic strategies of their parent states and have too many connections with the political systems of their parent countries for any decoupling between them and their own governments to be carried very far. Also, there is an ultimate interdependence of all the chessboards; even if the poor cannot create a serious and direct military threat to the two "triangles," they have ways of affecting, by their behavior, the international monetary and trade systems, which in turn, if out of order, can affect the security relationships among the major actors. Conversely, the less-developed countries may become adept at exploiting these actors' fears of military instability for economic and political advantage. In other words, the capacity of the big ones to deal with the Third World on their terms may be highly overrated.

Normatively, everyone recognizes that the goal must be "creating a global community that is stable and progressive," as Brzezinski puts it, and that even if the central nuclear balance remains secure, a world of partial jungles or large-scale nonmilitary disasters and break-downs would be neither stable nor progressive. Both weaponry and economic interdependence have changed the requirements for a mod-erate world system and pushed them far beyond the requirement in the past; that is, the mere avoidance of total violence among the great. Gradually, the problems of economic management which are the central functions of the modern nation-state (and are increasingly less ably performed by it) will have to be at least partly dealt with on the world (or regional) plane. Even if in many respects a concern for efficiency suggests *initiatives* by the advanced nations, *solutions* will almost invariably require the full participation of the less advanced, if only because many of their problems—from population to genocide, from industrialization to pollution—cannot be decoupled from the world of the rich. At any rate, nothing could backfire more dis-astrously than a division of world politics along degrees of develop-ment, whether a common front of the underdeveloped emerges from a confrontation with a coalition of "advanced nations," or as a reaction to "benign neglect." A manageable world requires the fragmentation of the highly heterogeneous Third World into its different compo-nents, issue by issue; either overt decoupling or promoting a bloc of advanced nations would have the opposite effect. Already, in the discussions on the seabed, one can see how damaging for world order an artificial coalition of underdeveloped countries—which throws together coastal, landlocked, and shelflocked states despite their diver-gent interests—could be. And, as C. Fred Bergsten has shown in this journal,[8] it is particularly in America's self-interest to "renew U.S. cooperation with the Third World," if only for self-protection. There is another reason as well. Neither of the two triangles can really mobilize for world order purposes the reservoir of American idealism. Brzezinski is right, of course, when he says that a Machiavellian foreign policy is "incapable of tapping the moral resources of the American people." But a "trilateral" policy that would appeal only to the skills of the professionals in diplomacy, academia, business, and the media would deepen the gap which, in all of the advanced countries, exists between an indifferent or indignant "next generation"

---

[8] C. Fred Bergsten, "The Threat from the Third World," *Foreign Policy*, no. 11 (Summer 1973), pp. 102-124.

and the interconnected managers of what Péguy once called the established disorder.

None of this suggests, of course, that we reject the two North-oriented policies only in order to follow a "Southern" strategy. Nobody has come forth with any very convincing blueprint of that sort. Moreover, those who believe in giving priority, at least for the long run, to the concerns of the less-advanced nations have often failed to deal seriously with the problems internal to the two "Northern" triangles or minimized the huge differences and conflicts among the less-developed, or tended to see in multilateral undertakings or international organizations a panacea, whereas they are all too often escapes, alibis, or simply forums in which familiar political contests continue. However, the kind of world we should want would do more than bring our ex-adversaries out of their quarantines, and allow the advanced nations to pursue harmoniously their restless business. It would also make room for the kind of global planning which only a handful of insufficiently political utopians or functionalists have advocated, with little impact. This will require not permanent alignments but permanent bargaining with shifting and overlapping coalitions.

Tactical Choices: Primacy vs. Modesty

There are evident connections between one's strategic choice—one's view of how the world should be structured—and one's tactical choice—one's view of how one's own nation should act. The second of the three strategic sets of choices, as we have seen, did not in any way question America's primacy. Official statements remain, to be sure, politely ambiguous. Actually, there are moments of candor: "the Nixon doctrine represented a new definition of American leadership, not abandonment of that leadership," said the last state of the world message; and Kissinger in his 23 April speech pointed out that "the United States has global interests and responsibilities; our European allies have regional interests." There is no real retreat of American power; there is a skillful attempt at redistributing burdens in such a way that primacy could be maintained at less cost and less strain. The advantages are obvious—if the attempt succeeds. But so are the disadvantages. Primacy continues to require costly presence wherever "redistribution" appears impossible or would be a euphemism for collapse. . . . Direct control means tension at home, but reliance on others to do one's job means both uncertainty (will they be able to do it?) and external tension (will they take our advice, if our grip is looser?). Primacy through control requires the kinds of organizational talents that Americans possess in abundance; indirect primacy demands psychological skills which are far less in evidence. Moreover, the preservation of primacy in areas of slippage may entail sudden attempts at regaining the upper hand, which breed resentments even if they succeed for a while—and such resentments throw into doubt the long-term possibility of what might be called primacy-with-the-complicity-of-others (I am thinking here not only of "Nixon shocks" against Japan or Western Europe but also of bombings in Indochina). Basically, the Nixon-Kissinger approach has a built-in contradiction. Redistribution requires, in others, an aptitude and willingness to bear more costs and responsibilities, but the preservation of primacy requires that they do not become too self-reliant: they ought to get stronger, but not get ideas.

The alternative, based on the conception of a multipolar world with a stable central military balance, is gloomier about American skills and the enthusiasm of others for playing our game, yet more optimistic about trusting pluralism and about the convergence of essential interests, even (perhaps especially) without American attempts at pulling all the strings. I advocated such devolution several years ago in *Gulliver's Troubles*. So has, recently, Robert Osgood, in *Retreat from Empire?* with persuasive arguments and pervasive skepticism. The advantages, of course, are exactly the reverse of the flaws of primacy. We would be relieved from playing Atlas and others would be rescued from the frustrations, humiliations, narrowing of vision, self-doubts, and petulance which dependence breeds. We would become, in effect, more responsible by being less intoxicated by world responsibility; and others would become more responsible by having to deal with world (and not just parochial) issues on their own.

The disadvantages have until now, and not surprisingly, appeared far greater to the policy makers. Dependence is self-fulfilling and self-perpetuating; to let go might create vacuums which rivals would fill, or heady displays of immature independence which would lead to nuclear proliferation or upset the networks of fragile relationships woven over the past twenty-five years. For devolution to be smooth, rather than destabilizing, one may need the same kinds of psychological skills and diplomatic subtlety as for indirect primacy. Moreover, all bureaucracies are better at incremental tinkering with instrumentalities, such as alliances, whose worth has been sanctified by time, than at the kinds of mutation which genuine devolution would imply. Last but not least, those who denounce the domestic strains of continuing primacy do not always realize the international

91

costs of devolution. It could seriously worsen the balance-of-payments crisis (a West European military entity would undoubtedly want to buy less of its weaponry in the United States and compete even more with us in the sale of arms abroad). It might also encourage the somewhat short-sighted neo-isolationism according to which the United States basically needs nothing more than physical security. Its advocates forget not only that major powers always want more from the world than safety but also that the management of inter-dependence, indeed the needs of even as relatively self-sufficient an economy as that of the United States, will oblige the major powers to contribute more to the world than complacency.

To conclude: each alternative has its problems. The question is neither to find a synthesis (which is hard to conceive) nor to invent a third approach but to decide which of the two has the flaws that can be most successfully limited or overcome. My own answer has not changed.

Tactical Choices: Self-Interest vs. World Ideals

Here, I am less concerned with asking *"What* should our role be?" than with asking *"How* should we assert our interests?" Again, two answers are being suggested. One might be termed an American imitation of Gaullism, or rather of the Gaullist style (for one often forgets that this style was at the service of a long-term vision of a moderate, multipolar world order). It consists in the strong assertion of American self-interest, rather narrowly defined. The alternative interprets U.S. national interest more broadly, identifies it with the promotion of "a more peaceful and just world order,"[9] and asserts that the style of action ought to match this goal, rather than draw attention to selfish U.S. needs or demands. Obviously, there is a tie to the previous tactical choice. It would take a singularly imaginative or perverse (and risk-taking) statesman who would use the shock tactics of Gaullism on behalf of devolution in the hope of knocking the dependents out of their slumber. On the other hand, policies of primacy can be pursued either through such tactics or in the loftier style of global idealism (the advocates of a "community of developed nations" blame the present foreign policy not only for its choice of the wrong triangle but also for its addiction to maneuver, secrecy, surprise, and unilateralism—as if the latter, at least, had begun in 1969).

[9] Seyom Brown, "The Changing Essence of Power," *Foreign Affairs*, vol. 51, no. 2 (January 1973), p. 295.

Whether one calls it neo-Gaullism or the aggressive defense of self-interest, such a style has few overt champions—however many practitioners or admirers there may be. Its dangers are obvious; one remembers how Kissinger, at the end of 1971, had to glue together some of the crockery broken by [John] Connally. And yet, breaking it, getting everyone to holler for repairs, and having Uncle Sam provide the glue, had been among the objects of the exercise. If such tactics are so appealing—whether they take the form of deliberate, not-so-benign neglect (as in the current downward float of the dollar), or the form which Pierre Hassner had christened "malignant attention"—it is because they serve a number of functions. They exploit the domestic mood of impatience with foreign entanglements, yet in such a way as to legitimize continuing external involvement, rather than retrenchment; for being tough on others (especially one's allies) combines psychic satisfaction with activism. They help Washington regain a liberty of maneuver which the huge, chained giant had almost lost in the last years of the 1960s, while others, under its protection, were busy exploiting their own margin of freedom. Thus, such tactics show a determination to liberate oneself from the shackles which "world responsibility" had imposed on the United States alone. They also combine the will to resort exactly to the same practices as everyone else with the ambition of continuing primacy: since the others too must be concerned with keeping the world manageable, yet can hardly make it so without us, why should we behave in any special way? Finally, in enforcing the new definition of primacy, the Gaullist style combines the attempt to force others to carry more burdens, the hope that the shocks will teach them our new unwillingness to let them get away with such fringe benefits of dependence as payments surpluses, special trade deals, and low military budgets and the intuition that such treatment will not make them less dependent on us objectively, however much we hurt their feelings.

This raises precisely the most important question. Such tactics are merely irritating when used by a lesser power, whose capacity to disrupt world order is limited and which calculates quite rightly that the protecting giant will not let his annoyance interfere with his interests. But are these methods appropriate when used by the superpower? In the international jungle, can the lion imitate the mosquito? The lion is indeed the pace-setter; others are at least as likely to pattern their behavior after his as to cower when he roars. We used to denounce Gaullism as a contagious disease; what irony if the virus should have spread only to Washington. Hence the plea for an alternative mode of conduct, for "a providential statesmanship" that realizes the special responsibility of the most powerful and richest nation, appeals to the "deep strain of idealism," and defines the national interest as community-building, the downplaying of force or threats, the resort to "stable and extensive negotiations" and "institutional growth." [10] Only if we adopt such a stance will we be in a position to demand of others that they continue to grant us certain privileges.

And yet there are problems with the idealistic style. Abroad, it could breed sour misunderstandings between our good conscience, and other nations' readiness to suspect in our stance a clever disguise of crass interests (the Gaullist style has the merit of its defects: brutality leaves no dark corners, no ambiguity about motives). It could also encourage allies and dependents to exploit American meekness-for-world-order either by playing the familiar blackmail of weakness so often performed by Saigon . . . or so as to preserve their own special advantages, such as the vast remnants of Japanese protectionism or the complexities of EEC's Common Agricultural Policy. Concerns for world order must be spread wide, and even though there is a special "shaping role" of the United States, there is also a danger of others using Washington as a huge procrustean bed.

Domestically, it is just as risky to ignore the strain of xenophobia exasperated by battle fatigue . . . as to let the pool of idealism evaporate. In this realm as in others, Pascal was right: he who wants to play the angel plays the brute. The Administration has, with some virtuosity, disguised a policy of primacy as a request for rehabilitation: it has presented its demands on others as a mere claim for "reciprocity." It has anchored in many people's minds the rather biased view that Japan, as President Nixon's foreign policy message put it, "enjoyed the special advantage that her reliance on the United States for her security freed resources" for becoming "a major economic power and competitor" and for imbalancing her trade with us; or the view that the U.S. role in the Bretton Woods system, which deprived us of the right to change the value of the dollar, had allowed others to accumulate huge surpluses (as if they had been so eager to collect dollars and feed both their inflations and the acquisition of their firms by U.S. enterprises).

It will be difficult, in the future, to give up such embattled self-righteousness, and to show that there has been vastly more "reciprocity" than we assert, without appearing soft, or a bleeding heart, or a bad citizen who believes that the United States can compete

---

[10] Brown, "The Changing Essence of Power," pp. 295, 297; Brzezinski, "U.S. Foreign Policy," p. 726 [p. 73 of this volume].

"with one hand tied behind its back." What is needed here is neither a clear choice in favor of one of the alternatives nor a synthesis (one cannot synthesize water and oil), but a careful limited borrowing from the first so as to mitigate the weaknesses of the second in the hope of avoiding the sanctimoniousness of both.

Tactical Choices: Domestic vs. External Priorities

The reassertion of domestic priorities can be observed all over the world. Partly, it reacts against the double impact of the cold war on domestic affairs—their subordination to external "necessities" and the limits imposed on the internal freedom of maneuver among parties or factions to the benefit of those which stood within the cold war consensus. It is also a reaction against the new international relations of interdependence, a reawakened determination to try to push on others the burden of eliminating one's own troubles—for instance, to oblige one's competitors to restore the U.S. balance-of-payments equilibrium, rather than resorting to painful, domestic measures. Unemployment at home is a greater concern than the possibility of a recession abroad; increasing one's exports by forcing others to adjust their currencies is better than having to take the unpopular and uncertain steps that might restore American competitiveness. Partly, the tyranny of domestic pressures merely reflects the increase in the number of actors in world affairs, many of which, poor and needy, or rich and dependent on raw materials or energy or markets, tend to look at the world as a quarry, not a duty.

Clearly, no U.S. foreign policy could afford to neglect the domestic base. On issues such as troops in Western Europe and the continuing quest for freer trade, the erosion of internal support has already gone quite far. The Gaullist style, as we have seen, is in part a reaction to and a "cooptation" of the new mood of rebellion against the old priority to foreign affairs. It aims not only at shoring up external primacy but also at satisfying domestic interests. The new international monetary policy, born in 1971, aims less at correcting the basic trouble of the international monetary system—America's freedom to accumulate balance-of-payments deficits—than at obliging others to curtail their exports to the United States, thus meeting some of U.S. labor's objections to the consequences of free trade. At the same time, the search for a trade surplus that would allow the United States to keep investing its capital abroad satisfies those business interests that look toward expansion in foreign markets; and the new toughness in trade negotiations with Western Europe and Japan aims

95

at destroying real or imaginary barriers to American exports of agricultural products or high technology. The request for "burden-sharing" with NATO also caters to the new mercantilism.

The problem, here, is once again the risk of contagion. (Should the United States chief competitors succeed in curbing their inflation, will they remain as willing as they have been so far to revalue their currencies, facilitate U.S. imports, and limit their exports?) There are other perils as well. Domestic pressures and moods are multiple and contradictory; a policy that seeks to respond to them could easily lose any coherence (already now one can observe some signs of this —we indict the European Community's Common Agricultural Policy and preferential arrangements in the name of free trade, but we arrange "voluntary" limitations of Japanese textile or steel exports and embargo exports of soybeans). Moreover, invariably, the domestic voices to which policy makers listen tend to be the voices of special interests, greed, resentment, and envy, for they speak both louder and far more clearly (and are politically more potent) than the often mumbling voices of idealism. Everywhere, farm lobbies are more influential than Peace Corps supporters.

And yet a return to external priorities is easier to advocate than to pursue. This is due partly to the lack of any agreement on what these priorities should be, as our exploration of earlier alternatives has shown. Also, the deliberate choice of any one of these would probably satisfy some domestic interests only by making others unhappy or fearful. But some choice will have to be made. The present course—which tries to combine balance-of-power and trilateralism, shock tactics and a distant concern for "stable structures," U.S. primacy and more-responsibilities-for-others, domestic grievances and priority to "a new positive vision of the world"—is so riddled with tensions and contradictions, so permanently threatened with disintegrating or capsizing, that it depends almost exclusively on the skill of the handful of men who conceive, negotiate, and enforce it. Juggling a bagful of balls while walking a tightrope can be a great performance; but it cannot be institutionalized. What will be needed, after the artists have returned to the tent or to the road, will be the definition of a coherent set of external priorities, and, correspondingly, an elaborate attempt at mobilizing those domestic interests and emotions to which these priorities appeal, and at neutralizing those pressures and moods which they ignore, reject, or anger. For such a task, the U.S. foreign policy machine will have to be properly organized.

Organizational Choices: Long vs. Short Range*

Modern government—not just in the United States—seems to be able to deal best only with the urgent. This is, of course, of the essence of any bureaucracy, as Professor Kissinger wrote for many years. It is particularly true in democratic polities, obliged to respond to sudden shifts in opinion or often ephemeral problems. But one could also argue that, in foreign policy, anything but a concern for the short run would be dysfunctional from the viewpoint of state machinery. For the myopic manipulation of crises and issues, even when they are created by the activities of the new, nonstate actors in world politics, such as cosmopolitan corporations or transnational terrorists, tends to perpetuate the state-centered condition of international affairs: this is precisely what the machinery is good at.

Nothing is more obvious, however, than the need for long-range reflection and action. One could assert that in security matters statesmen can advance only one step at a time and that a worldwide set of controlled security relations can only emerge gradually. It is enough that each step taken be the right one. However, even if it is, long-term thinking might have helped devise a "righter" one (the ABM has been contained just in time, but was MIRV really necessary?). The pattern of "correct" short-term thinking here has consisted essentially in trying to drag back into the barn wild horses that one had let escape. Moreover, on most of the newer chessboards of world affairs, a crisis approach can be not merely second-best but outright bad. Measures taken once they can no longer be postponed may be highly detrimental to international cooperation, such as those of August 1971. And while policy makers may be right in saying that no set of institutions can be repaired à froid (that is, while it is time), to wait until they have collapsed does not seem the best way of building new ones—it may well be the moment when antagonisms are sharpest. The inter- and trans-national economy that has developed across the Atlantic and the Pacific and in particular the huge amounts of capital in search of maximum profit have undermined the autonomy of national economic policy so thoroughly that a short-term or crisis approach allows the governments only to draw belated consequences from their impotence and to try to limit the wreckage and thus give themselves some respite until the next onslaught. Finally, the short-range atavism of bureaucracies prevents a timely approach to

---

* Editor's note: Two of the organizational choices in Professor Hoffmann's original article—dealing with centralization vs. decentralization and split vs. integrated policy—are not included in this excerpt.

a host of problems which only a handful of experts denounce as major potential headaches. By the time bargaining begins, interests have crystallized, frenzy may have set in, and alignments that have very little to do with the issue may be entrenched. This has been the world's experience with environmental problems, the oceans, and oil.

In world affairs, as in domestic societies in the earlier parts of this century, the concern for stability or moderation now requires a shift from a system in which the management of interdependence was sought through the observance by states of a set of rules (such as those of GATT or Bretton Woods), to a system in which joint management will be required, through international institutions, the pooling of sovereignties, and the coordination of policies and goals. Rules prescribing to states what to do and not to do are no longer enough; yet the governments responsible to their publics remain unwilling to let, for instance, indicators determine automatically when they would have to eliminate their payments surpluses or deficits. Whether one considers the regime of the oceans or the future international monetary system, one sees no way of avoiding the establishment of international organizations with considerable powers either of administration or even of policy making (for instance, for the creation of a truly international reserve instrument).

Resistance to such a change is partly due to the paradox that long-term thinking about almost any important issue in world affairs takes one "beyond the nation-state," or at least beyond autonomous nation-states. Even if one does not believe that transnationalism is the wave of the future, its expansion creates problems for the states that can only be solved by joint management; but the horizon of every bureaucracy remains parochial (this—especially at a time of strong domestic priorities—is a far more potent obstacle to European integration than is usually acknowledged). Long-term thinking and action do indeed run into domestic obstacles. It is not only the bureaucracy's inertia but also the momentum of domestic interests and pressures that demands immediate intervention by the state itself when things go wrong and suspects technocratic plots behind all schemes for long-range planning. For these tend to increase the distance between domestic producers or consumers, and inter-, supra-, or trans-national decision makers and to make the latter look at the world as a single unit rather than as "us vs. them." Thus, the built-in unresponsiveness of any bureaucracy to the next headaches after the current ones is buttressed by the tension which exists between the highly resilient domestic legitimacy of the nation-state (reinforced rather than weakened by the government's increasing role in welfare) and its inadequacy to cope with major issues. All of these require a *fuite-en-avant;* yet the states' feet are leaden.

Before 1969, no writer criticized more acidly the U.S. foreign policy machine for its inability to put the important ahead of the urgent than Henry Kissinger. In office, he has not been too modest about celebrating his Administration's "profound enterprise" and "philosophical, as well as . . . practical reorientation of our foreign policy." However, one of the weaknesses of the balance-of-power approach is that, being all process, it tells one nothing about substantive undertakings and relies on mechanisms (essentially unilateral shocks and interstate negotiations) that may be inappropriate to twentieth century issues. One of the problems with the call for a "new Atlantic Charter" is that while it correctly sees the danger of a series of irritating, disconnected, short-term negotiations aimed at shoring up the old alliances, it really has nothing better to offer by way of an overarching, long-term, joint political directive than a list of common *problems* and a set of promises of good mutual *behavior* (something that is far more significant in U.S.-Soviet relations than in interallied ones). Paradoxically enough, the monopolization of foreign policy by the NSC staff under Kissinger may have made effective long-term planning more rather than less difficult. For when he leaves, he will probably take with him whatever capacity for long-range thought and action that exists within the U.S. government. . . .[11]

AMERICA'S PRINCIPLED ROLE IN WORLD AFFAIRS: A REALISTIC POLICY OF PEACE AND FREEDOM *

Melvin R. Laird

A former congressman and secretary of defense, Melvin R. Laird, sees the future world role of the United States as still a dominant one in terms of military and nonmilitary power. He notes the importance, however, of establishing broad, idealistic purposes for U.S. foreign policy in order to gain the public consensus necessary to sustain this dominant role. Historically, the principles of peace and freedom have

---

[11] The champions of the "advanced nations" concept are concerned about the distant future, but theirs is the wrong concept.

---

* Source: Written especially for this volume by Melvin R. Laird.

served this purpose, and Laird believes these principles are still valid. He argues that recent policies aimed at producing short-term adjustments in superpower relations should be refocused toward achieving long-term U.S. objectives.

After the U.S. foreign policy reversals of the 1960s, which were caused in large measure by an indiscriminate overreach and a crucial lack of public understanding and support, the last two Administrations have set about building a new "structure" for peace. Though the image of this policy has been architectural, its constructs have been more modest than those of the 1950s and 1960s. A sense of finitude was, perhaps, inevitable. The rhetoric of the past eight years has boasted no ambitious plans for alliances around the globe. Gone are the elaborate notions of U.S. involvement in counterinsurgency warfare. Crises pitting Moscow and Washington against each other in blindman's buff also occur less frequently. The Mideast conflict of 1973, when the superpowers staggered to the brink of direct confrontation, was accounted a failure for the main thrust of U.S. policy in the 1970s, which sought to continue our traditional dedication to global freedom with less militance than during the previous twenty years. A most fitting epitaph for the October 1973 Middle East War, a crisis that seriously threatened American security interests, lay in the one-paragraph admission by Secretary of State Henry Kissinger, in London in December 1973, that perhaps the United States did not exercise enough initiative for peace *before* the Arab-Israeli conflict occurred. A more strenuous peace policy might better have served vital national interests.

From the earliest National Security Council meetings of 1969, international conciliation was among the foremost topics of discussion. In Vietnam, this conciliatory mood took the form of an integrated policy, involving the gradual withdrawal of U.S. forces, the assumption of responsibility by Saigon for its own defense ("Vietnamization"), and the conduct of secret negotiations to end the war. The Middle East was not slighted in this peace policy, at least not during 1969–71: after bilateral negotiations with the U.S.S.R. reached an impasse in 1969, direct American initiatives with Israel and the Arab states led to the cease-fire of August 1970 as well as the peace plans of Secretary of State William Rogers. Efforts such as these obviously required that superpower relations be adjusted drastically from continuous confrontation to cooperation and mutually advantageous accommodations. In my view, such accommodations were not always advantageous to the United States (more of this later), but they did indicate the strength of efforts to buttress the so-called structure of peace during the early 1970s. Moscow and Peking, as well as Washington, were seen as founders of a stable global edifice, based on accommodation without appeasement.

Efforts at building this structure of peace have not been completed, and may never be. The ongoing process of politics never leads to a static utopia. New aspirants for "architectural" awards constantly appear. Yet a notable calm has settled on the United States, resulting partly from the fact that U.S. military personnel have not been engaged in combat since early 1973. No draft calls disturb ordinary life. No campus riots against far-off foreign involvements disrupt formal learning. No casualty, missing-in-action, or prisoner-of-war counts create anxiety. And, because transient controversies no longer alienate them, some of America's better intellects now spend more time debating long-term issues, such as nuclear proliferation and the role of national values in foreign policy. Now, there is a good deal of intelligent debate over specific policies, such as the latitude to be allowed the Soviet Union in the name of détente, and few thoughtful Americans can long for a return to the furor of the Vietnam War or the strong ideological passions of the 1960s and early 1970s.

Under seemingly ideal conditions of peace and calm, America is searching for a new foreign policy consensus, with greater government accountability. Unlike the period when the cold war era originated, no sense of crisis pervades our relations with our allies or the Soviet Union. Some might even hope for a crisis to galvanize American resolve, but if such a resolve were dependent on a crisis, it could easily be dissipated by a relaxation of tension or by a new emergency that did not fit the original design. Instead of relying on ephemeral events for domestic unity in foreign affairs, I think it wiser to depend on traditional principles of conduct, the historic role and mission of the United States in world affairs as a dominant force for peace and freedom. Such principles have a greater chance for public acceptance and endurance against the passage of time.

II

As a member of Congress elected for nine terms, I criticized the Americanization of the Vietnam War and advocated a strategy of initiative rather than response to enhance our global posture. Then, as secretary of defense, I had to win support from Congress for the de-Americanization of Vietnam through the initiation of novel assistance measures. From these two dissimilar vantage points, I can attest to the crucial importance of approaching first-things-first in American foreign policy: our activity in international affairs can have credibility only if the legitimacy of our national security decisions is recognized by the nation at large. We must establish principled priorities, providing above all for the safety and survival of the United States, because only such priorities can give a direction to our foreign policy that commands comprehension, evaluation, and popular consent. Only by deciding what role we would like to play in the world can we determine whether specific steps are in the proper direction.

Given the existing world situation, still partly determined by the cold war but much more fluid than before, the role choices facing America at its Bicentennial are relatively clear. During the third quarter of this century, the United States was the dominant world force. The question facing us is whether we will choose to continue as one of the dominant world forces.

The United States emerged from World War II with its power greatly enhanced, the unchallenged leader of a large portion of humanity. Over the past three decades, this impressive global influence has declined relative to other nations, as was inevitable in a world of shifting power. The worst material and psychological damage of the war was inflicted upon European nations and Japan, and its repair under our leadership and with our help has narrowed the gap between the United States and these countries. Similarly, the Soviet Union has recovered from its wartime desolation, China has emerged from Japanese occupation and from revolution, and many nations have achieved independence from the wreckage of prewar empires. The world has become less lopsided in its distribution of power. Too frequently, this situation is described as undesirable from the American standpoint. We tend to forget that the reconstruction of Europe and Japan, and the call for independence of colonial possessions were primary American goals, designed to create a more just and stable world order and to enhance peace and freedom.

The United States never desired a monopoly of world power, and it is debatable how long our power actually was supreme. President John F. Kennedy in his inaugural address exhorted the American people to sacrifice, and he pledged a nearly unlimited commitment of our resources on behalf of freedom, implying that the United States possessed unfathomable might. Yet, even at that time, many questioned the validity and reasoning behind such an indiscriminate and pervasive assertion of power. It is true that we can no longer decisively influence any situation we choose, but it is questionable whether the American people ever truly wanted hegemony over the world.

Although the United States may not be able to affect every situation decisively, in the balance we are still a dominant force in the world. Our economy is the largest by far of all nations, and our military posture is the most powerful (though certain trends seem to be running against us and require corrective action soon). Our way of life is extremely attractive, even if many nations do not wish to imitate us. More often than not, other nations look to the United States for world leadership, not only because we are powerful but also because we are a free society.

Although military might is an essential component of American power, it certainly does not follow that we should concentrate only on military force to continue our global leadership. The United States has no militaristic tradition and does not glory in things martial. Consistent with America's tradition, all the components of international power from the most to the least tangible should be developed to the maximum in support of our world role. Indeed, what I noted in the 1968 *Republican Papers* about urgent American domestic problems applies just as well to our foreign policy today: "the sheer complexity and diversity of our manifold ills require arrangements different from those attempted in the past, arrangements that will unleash all the forces in our society, public and private, that are capable of contributing to the solutions we seek."

Some might reply that the indispensability of U.S. influence in the world is too self-evident to need to be argued. The necessity for global leadership may well be apparent to those most involved in foreign affairs, though even among knowledgeable analysts some interesting arguments for neoisolationism and strategic disengagement have been made. Unlike domestic policy, however, foreign policy seems to make only a sporadic impact on most of the public over the long term. Headlines and telecasts bring the world into nearly every home but usually in terms of disparate, ephemeral events. If the public grants longer term support to foreign policy, this constancy must center on basic principles of conduct rather than specific issues.

Making special problems rather than general roles the focus of public debate on foreign policy tends to endow them with an overwhelming force that moves them beyond any moral evaluation. Hence, it often happens that choices must be based on urgent questions of the day, in which no range of choices, and thus no room for debate, may be perceived. Bureaucracies, interest groups, and political parties favor such situations in order to avoid accountability for making wrong decisions. By asserting that the nuclear equation between the United States and the Soviet Union is the commanding international issue of our time, for example, Washington and Moscow tend to become the loci of our foreign policy. It has been stated by proponents of détente, of course, that the policy of easing tensions between Moscow and Washington cannot be applied in all international situations. Yet sometimes it is difficult to find what *principles* should limit the application of détente. If obsession with communism during the early postwar era had its limitations when projected across the totality of American world interests, so have the more recent, overly advertised centerpieces of learned opinion on foreign policy.

III

Seeking to maintain power for its own sake is incompatible with the American tradition. If anything, our history has tended to be suspicious of power, favoring instead the ideal of individual liberty. This suspicion has extended to foreign affairs, as a number of students of international relations have noted, often with contradictory applications to U.S. policy. Can the idea of the "free world," for example, be applied both to the European democracies and to certain dictatorships that are defending their right to self-determination against aggression? Is it that considerations of power alone dominate policy in regard to the latter, while *freedom* may be properly applied only to democracies? Or may we use *freedom*, in different ways, both for internal liberty and for national independence?

The United States has sound reasons for choosing to remain a dominant force in the world. Perhaps this year more than most has been an occasion for introspection and reflection about its international future. Certain paradoxes about America have emerged: it is a new nation by some measures, yet old in terms of political continuity; we feel a kinship with the founding fathers and the ideas they expressed, yet few Americans had relatives in this country at the dawn of its independence two hundred years ago. Throughout our history, whether our lineage is traced back to the Revolution or to Ellis Island, we Americans have believed in peace and freedom as powerful international as well as domestic ideals. Within our borders, issues relating to domestic tranquility and individual freedom have dominated domestic politics. In foreign relations, the achievement of these goals is much more elusive, and we have learned through bitter experience not to assume our national ideals prevail beyond our shores and not to confuse institutionalized domestic politics with a much less structured international environment.

There is a certain ambiguity in espousing *both* peace and freedom. Ideally, U.S. policy should promote both, but reality will not always allow both. The quest for peace may have to be delayed in order to defend freedom, and we should be prepared for this defense. More tragically, we may have to choose between governments—too few of which are truly free—so that we encourage the stability necessary for free development, both internal and external. In the 1920s and 1930s, it should be recalled, global instability prepared the way for the most powerful dictatorships ever seen. We can reject authoritarianism in any form while recognizing that some dictatorships are surely worse than others and that an unstable world can bring greater grief than we can now imagine.

To implement our basic goals of peace and freedom, the U.S. position on certain issues must be clarified. We should reaffirm our traditional commitments to the spread of liberty, peaceful commerce, representative institutions, and national self-determination, though we cannot thereby avoid making painful choices between alternatives that involve some compromise. The United States has gone to war in the past to protect national interests and long-range peace. Circumstances may necessitate dealing with governments that are less than totally free or peaceful. If we have a clear view of the policies toward which we ultimately aspire, however, America will be less likely to make expediency the rule rather than the exception in conducting foreign affairs within a complicated international system.

IV

In the last decade, U.S. foreign policy has won a number of diplomatic triumphs. A mere list of those since 1969 belies the very complicated study and action that went into these important contributions toward a more stable international order. The Middle East cease-fire in 1970, the quadripartite agreement on Berlin in 1971, the opening to Peking in 1972, the Moscow summit and SALT accords of 1972, the second U.S.–U.S.S.R. summit meeting and agreement on the prevention of nuclear war in 1973, the Vietnam truce accords of 1973, the Vladivostok declaration in 1974, and the Middle East disengagement agreements of 1974 and 1975 constitute major landmarks in U.S. diplomacy during this decade. Ingenious, conciliatory activity such as this can only be described as prodigious.

As a counterpart to this diplomacy, under the formula of "peace through strength," U.S. defense strategy has sought ways to maintain a military lead over the Soviet Union, still our most powerful potential adversary, while at the same time providing some capability for lesser contingencies within the constraints of the post-Vietnam period. Although we could hardly fault the wisdom behind it, the flexible response strategy of the Kennedy and Johnson years was unsuited to circumstances in which the public consensus had been weakened by the Vietnam War. Hence, in our strategy of realistic deterrence in the early 1970s, plans that would involve U.S. military personnel in combat abroad were curtailed in favor of improved, more realistic concepts of nuclear deterrence, conventional warfare technology, and security assistance.

In addition to our triumphs over the past decade, there have also been reverses, traceable to the absence of a coherent foundation for U.S. foreign policy. Long-term objectives for this policy were unclear. Pursuing peace—or a structure of peace—was its main theme, but often expressed in a rhetoric devoid of definition. How would the historical American devotion to the spread of freedom comport with a policy that strove for peace, or at least détente, with adversaries of freedom as we know it? Was this peace at any price? If not at any price, then at what price—South Vietnam, Israel, Eastern Europe, Taiwan, the dissidents in the Soviet Union, the non-Communist forces in Africa? How were the areas of very real conflict in Southeast Asia and the Middle East to be brought under the aegis of détente with the Soviet Union? Most important, perhaps, how was the strong suggestion of expediency in our foreign policy to be made compatible with values comprehensible and acceptable to the American public?

Lacking any well-articulated, long-term vision beyond the negative goal of avoiding nuclear war, U.S. foreign policy became preoccupied with short-term tactics and theatrics aimed at balancing global power relationships. Juggling crises became the order of the day. The most active centers of national security were the emergency task forces put together overnight in the National Security Council and the Department of State. The result was a peculiar, and paradoxical, situation: lacking a comprehensive policy, the country became excessively concerned with so-called global conceptions of security, to the detriment of specific nations and groups. It was not realized that these summarily handled situations were important *in themselves* because we had no scale on which to weigh their ramifications. The point of our policies frequently became obscured because they possessed no guiding content. And, not paying enough attention to America's role and basic goals, our government did not always choose appropriate means to protect American interests. When a policy lacks the principles to evaluate the means of its realization, that policy is deficient in both practice and principle: the damage possible from expedient, shortsighted international operations cannot easily be assessed, and the remedies may not be applied until too late.

Several times during the decade, the supreme American interests of encouraging self-determination and free governments were not pursued. At the time, other interests appeared more important, but the fallacy of the short-term approach became apparent. Vietnam was our major defense policy involvement of the past decade and perhaps the most trying international conflict in this nation's history. The debate over the origins and purposes of this war is not finished, and this is no place to enter into such a complex subject. The termination of American involvement and the conclusion of the Vietnam War, however, deserve scrutiny. To end the direct role of the United States in Vietnam, a plan of gradual disengagement was implemented in early 1969 with increasing defense burdens falling on the South Vietnamese. After this policy of Vietnamization was well under way, the United States and North Vietnam concluded an accord: the United States would withdraw completely, and the North Vietnamese would stand aside so that South Vietnam and the Provisional Government might negotiate peace in South Vietnam. In other words, North Vietnam became a party to guaranteeing peace in South Vietnam, with the clear understanding that there was and would continue to be a separate South Vietnam. After these accords were signed, however, the United States did not take appropriate action through its détente partners, the Soviet Union and the People's Republic of China, to stem violations by both North Vietnam and the Provisional Government, equipped by the U.S.S.R. and China. The strenuous efforts necessary to make the two Communist giants agree to restrict weapon flows were never undertaken. The problem of excessive arms shipments, intended to deliver a knockout blow against a regional adversary, has plagued us in the Middle East as well.

Rather than pursuing American aims of peace and freedom in Southeast Asia, South Vietnam became something of an embarrassment as relations between the United States and the Communist nations evolved after 1972. Yet, even if our whole involvement with ground forces in Vietnam was questionable from the first, America's convenient neglect of its solemn pledge to guarantee the security of South Vietnam cannot be excused. No long-term goal was served by ignoring the enforcement of the Vietnam accords. The United States gained no permanent favor, in the eyes of either its friends or its adversaries, by shrugging off arms build-ups prior to the North Vietnamese offensive of 1975. The issue did not revolve around the question of whether to rush emergency aid to Saigon in the spring of 1975, or around Congress's reluctance to continue supporting a cause that the Administration claimed was doomed anyway. Critical moments were missed when, by our silence, we condoned new preparations for Hanoi's attack on the South. It would be small wonder if, in other areas of the world, U.S. security guarantees might be seen as decreasingly reliable, not because we are not powerful when we choose to be, but because we lack consistent long-term principles.

Some of our other negotiations with adversaries also revealed the problems resulting from the lack of widely understood principles of conduct and accountability to guide us in novel situations. One key area of negotiation involved the strategic arms limitation talks (SALT). Accomplishments in this area include ABM control and additional measures to enhance communications between Washington and Moscow. One would be hard-pressed, however, to name the long-term aims of the United States in SALT except to avoid nuclear war (which was pledged by the United States and the U.S.S.R. in a separate statement of principles in 1973) and to advance the somewhat nebulous cause of détente (though few ever argued that the mere presence of nuclear weapons was the prime cause of tensions between the U.S. and U.S.S.R.). Short-term expediencies dominated the final stages of the SALT I agreements in 1972, when the urge to get an agreement at any cost became the chief end.

Now we are facing another instance of linking our long-term objectives to short-term trends in domestic and international politics. For much of America's history, an interest in Cuba and the Caribbean has been central to U.S. foreign policy. This concern, though perhaps not always expressed in the most persuasive manner to our friends in Latin America, has been based on the most vital of interests, that involving the physical security of the United States. In the wake of Vietnam and Watergate, and in part motivated by détente with the Soviet Union, there has been a noticeable relaxation of America's vigil toward the growing Soviet control of Cuba's economy, military establishment, politics, and secret police. Some members of Congress not only have urged a new rapprochement with Fidel Castro but also have so intimidated our intelligence apparatus that it may well be unable to counter the Soviet Union's efforts to capture states through graduated internal subversion. In addition, the Cubans have been encouraged by Moscow to become engaged in Angola and elsewhere, but Congress has voted against an appropriate U.S. response. The national hangover from Vietnam and Watergate is understandable and will pass, but will our historic dedication to freedom remain?

V

Since World War II, the United States has achieved many foreign policy triumphs in which we can take pride. NATO is a notable example. Many of these accomplishments occurred when we took an expansive view of our world role in light of our abiding belief in peace and freedom, with the solid support of an informed public opinion. The efforts undertaken were not solely military. To be sure, such actions as the Berlin airlift, the aid to Greece against Communist aggression, and the defense of South Korea required armed capability for the pursuit of basic goals. Efforts such as the Marshall Plan and President Kennedy's vision of inter-American cooperation were equally impressive programs, showing a national purpose to build peace and freedom through nonmilitary power.

In the rush of complex actions on the world stage, we have lost the sense that certain permanent concepts survive momentary trials. We have become overly absorbed with the immediate. The problems we deal with are always current, of course, but they need not be approached from only short-run or expedient viewpoints. Such approaches find us too often in the position either of reacting to situations or of initiating actions aimed at ameliorating crises, without considering underlying causes. Too often, our policies appear directionless and difficult to evaluate because there is no standard against which they can be measured—by our allies, our friends, our adversaries, or even ourselves.

Events of recent years, good and bad for U.S. interests, show clearly the need for a strong, principled foreign policy, dedicated to peace and freedom—whatever its difficulties and ambiguities. The American people expect it, our allies call for it, and our adversaries would respect it. Such an idealistic policy is eminently realistic. For most Americans, the vagaries of power politics hold little appeal and make little sense. I share their suspicion that so-called *Realpolitik* is merely an excuse by a lazy elite for not doing its homework in the difficult field of ethical choice, which steadfastly accents the priority of peace and freedom among our foreign policy goals.

PART TWO
DETENTE

2

BASIC AGREEMENTS ON DETENTE

Between 1972 and 1974, the United States entered joint agreements with the Soviet Union and the People's Republic of China in an effort to begin continuous détente relations with the two Communist superpowers. Among these agreements were three central instruments on strategic arms limitations with the U.S.S.R. In May 1972, a treaty limiting the development of antiballistic missile systems (ABM) and an interim agreement restricting offensive strategic nuclear systems were signed. Interpretations of these agreements were submitted by Secretary of State William P. Rogers. An understanding between the United States and the Soviet Union reached at Vladivostok in November 1974 committed both nations to limiting strategic delivery vehicles and missiles equipped with MIRVs (multiple independently-targetable reentry vehicles).

The United States and the U.S.S.R. also delineated, during 1972–73, understandings for their evolving détente relationship. The first specifies basic principles to guide this relationship during the long process of its implementation; it pledges both nations to peaceful coexistence and expanded contacts. By a second agreement reached in June 1973, both states assume specific responsibilities for checking nuclear war.

Even before the major détente understandings with the Soviet Union, the United States and the People's Republic of China issued a joint communiqué in Shanghai in February 1972 giving some broad directions for improved relations between Washington and Peking. In this statement, the first such declaration made by the two countries, each party delineates its views and indicates areas of agreement and disagreement.

BASIC PRINCIPLES OF RELATIONS BETWEEN THE UNITED STATES OF AMERICA AND THE UNION OF SOVIET SOCIALIST REPUBLICS, 29 MAY 1972 *

The United States of America and the Union of Soviet Socialist Republics,

Guided by their obligations under the Charter of the United Nations and by a desire to strengthen peaceful relations with each other and to place these relations on the firmest possible basis,

Aware of the need to make every effort to remove the threat of war and to create conditions which promote the reduction of tensions in the world and the strengthening of universal security and international cooperation,

Believing that the improvement of U.S.-Soviet relations and their mutually advantageous development in such areas as economics, science, and culture will meet these objectives and contribute to better mutual understanding and businesslike cooperation, without in any way prejudicing the interests of third countries,

Conscious that these objectives reflect the interests of the peoples of both countries,

Have agreed as follows:

First. They will proceed from the common determination that in the nuclear age there is no alternative to conducting their mutual relations on the basis of peaceful coexistence. Differences in ideology and in the social systems of the United States and the U.S.S.R. are not obstacles to the bilateral development of normal relations based on the principles of sovereignty, equality, noninterference in internal affairs and mutual advantage.

Second. The United States and the U.S.S.R. attach major importance to preventing the development of situations capable of causing a dangerous exacerbation of their relations. Therefore, they will do their utmost to avoid military confrontations and to prevent the outbreak of nuclear war. They will always exercise restraint in their mutual relations and will be prepared to negotiate and settle differences by peaceful means. Discussions and negotiations on outstanding issues will be conducted in a spirit of reciprocity, mutual accommodation, and mutual benefit.

---

* Source: *Department of State Bulletin,* vol. 66, no. 1722 (26 June 1972), pp. 898-899.

Both sides recognize that efforts to obtain unilateral advantage at the expense of the other, directly or indirectly, are inconsistent with these objectives. The prerequisites for maintaining and strengthening peaceful relations between the United States and the U.S.S.R. are the recognition of the security interests of the parties based on the principle of equality and the renunciation of the use or threat of force.

Third. The United States and the U.S.S.R. have a special responsibility, as do other countries which are permanent members of the United Nations Security Council, to do everything in their power so that conflicts or situations will not arise which would serve to increase international tensions. Accordingly, they will seek to promote conditions in which all countries will live in peace and security and will not be subject to outside interference in their internal affairs.

Fourth. The United States and the U.S.S.R. intend to widen the juridical basis of their mutual relations and to exert the necessary efforts so that bilateral agreements which they have concluded and multilateral treaties and agreements to which they are jointly parties are faithfully implemented.

Fifth. The United States and the U.S.S.R. reaffirm their readiness to continue the practice of exchanging views on problems of mutual interest and, when necessary, to conduct such exchanges at the highest level, including meetings between leaders of the two countries.

The two governments welcome and will facilitate an increase in productive contacts between representatives of the legislative bodies of the two countries.

Sixth. The parties will continue their efforts to limit armaments on a bilateral as well as on a multilateral basis. They will continue to make special efforts to limit strategic armaments. Whenever possible, they will conclude concrete agreements aimed at achieving these purposes.

The United States and the U.S.S.R. regard as the ultimate objective of their efforts the achievement of general and complete disarmament and the establishment of an effective system of international security in accordance with the purposes and principles of the United Nations.

Seventh. The United States and the U.S.S.R. regard commercial and economic ties as an important and necessary element in the strengthening of their bilateral relations and thus will actively promote the growth of such ties. They will facilitate cooperation between the relevant organizations and enterprises of the two countries and the conclusion of appropriate agreements and contracts, including long-term ones.

The two countries will contribute to the improvement of maritime and air communications between them.

Eighth. The two sides consider it timely and useful to develop mutual contacts and cooperation in the fields of science and technology. Where suitable, the United States and the U.S.S.R. will conclude appropriate agreements dealing with concrete cooperation in these fields.

Ninth. The two sides reaffirm their intention to deepen cultural ties with one another and to encourage fuller familiarization with each other's cultural values. They will promote improved conditions for cultural exchanges and tourism.

Tenth. The United States and the U.S.S.R. will seek to ensure that their ties and cooperation in all the above-mentioned fields and in any others in their mutual interest are built on a firm and long-term basis. To give a permanent character to these efforts, they will establish in all fields where this is feasible joint commissions or other joint bodies.

Eleventh. The United States and the U.S.S.R. make no claim for themselves and would not recognize the claims of anyone else to any special rights or advantages in world affairs. They recognize the sovereign equality of all states.

The development of U.S.-Soviet relations is not directed against third countries and their interests.

Twelfth. The basic principles set forth in this document do not affect any obligations with respect to other countries earlier assumed by the United States and the U.S.S.R.

Moscow, *May 29, 1972*

For the United States
of America:

RICHARD NIXON

*President of the United
States of America*

For the Union of Soviet
Socialist Republics:

LEONID I. BREZHNEV

*General Secretary of the
Central Committee, CPSU*

TREATY BETWEEN THE UNITED STATES OF AMERICA AND THE UNION OF SOVIET SOCIALIST REPUBLICS ON THE LIMITATION OF ANTIBALLISTIC MISSILE SYSTEMS, 26 MAY 1972 *

The United States of America and the Union of Soviet Socialist Republics, hereinafter referred to as the parties,

Proceeding from the premise that nuclear war would have devastating consequences for all mankind,

Considering that effective measures to limit antiballistic missile systems would be a substantial factor in curbing the race in strategic offensive arms and would lead to a decrease in the risk of outbreak of war involving nuclear weapons,

Proceeding from the premise that the limitation of antiballistic missile systems, as well as certain agreed measures with respect to the limitation of strategic offensive arms, would contribute to the creation of more favorable conditions for further negotiations on limiting strategic arms,

Mindful of their obligations under Article VI of the Treaty on the Nonproliferation of Nuclear Weapons,

Declaring their intention to achieve at the earliest possible date the cessation of the nuclear arms race and to take effective measures toward reductions in strategic arms, nuclear disarmament, and general and complete disarmament,

Desiring to contribute to the relaxation of international tension and the strengthening of trust between states,

Have agreed as follows:

ARTICLE I

1. Each party undertakes to limit antiballistic missile (ABM) systems and to adopt other measures in accordance with the provisions of this treaty.

2. Each party undertakes not to deploy ABM systems for a defense of the territory of its country and not to provide a base for such a defense, and not to deploy ABM systems for defense of an individual region except as provided for in Article III of this treaty.

ARTICLE II

1. For the purposes of this treaty, an ABM system is a system to counter strategic ballistic missiles or their elements in flight trajectory, currently consisting of:

---

* Source: *Department of State Bulletin*, vol. 66, no. 1722 (26 June 1972), pp. 918-920.

(a) ABM interceptor missiles, which are interceptor missiles constructed and deployed for an ABM role, or of a type tested in an ABM mode;

(b) ABM launchers, which are launchers constructed and deployed for launching ABM interceptor missiles; and

(c) ABM radars, which are radars constructed and deployed for an ABM role, or of a type tested in an ABM mode.

2. The ABM system components listed in paragraph one of this article include those which are:

(a) operational;
(b) under construction;
(c) undergoing testing;
(d) undergoing overhaul, repair, or conversion; or
(e) mothballed.

ARTICLE III

Each party undertakes not to deploy ABM systems or their components except that:

(a) within one ABM system deployment area having a radius of 150 kilometers and centered on the party's national capital, a party may deploy: (1) no more than 100 ABM launchers and no more than 100 ABM interceptor missiles at launch sites, and (2) ABM radars within no more than six ABM radar complexes, the area of each complex being circular and having a diameter of no more than three kilometers; and

(b) within one ABM system deployment area having a radius of 150 kilometers and containing ICBM [intercontinental ballistic missile] silo launchers, a party may deploy: (1) no more than 100 ABM launchers and no more than 100 ABM interceptor missiles at launch sites, (2) two large phased-array ABM radars comparable in potential to corresponding ABM radars operational or under construction on the date of signature of the treaty in an ABM system deployment area containing ICBM silo launchers, and (3) no more than eighteen ABM radars each having a potential less than the potential of the smaller of the above-mentioned two large phased-array ABM radars.

ARTICLE IV

The limitations provided for in Article III shall not apply to ABM systems or their components used for development or testing, and located within current or additionally agreed test ranges. Each party may have no more than a total of fifteen ABM launchers at test ranges.

ARTICLE V

1. Each party undertakes not to develop, test, or deploy ABM systems or components which are sea-based, air-based, space-based, or mobile land-based.

2. Each party undertakes not to develop, test, or deploy ABM launchers for launching more than one ABM interceptor missile at a time from each launcher, nor to modify deployed launchers to provide them with such a capability, nor to develop, test, or deploy automatic or semi-automatic or other similar systems for rapid reload of ABM launchers.

ARTICLE VI

To enhance assurance of the effectiveness of the limitations on ABM systems and their components provided by this treaty, each party undertakes:

(a) not to give missiles, launchers, or radars, other than ABM interceptor missiles, ABM launchers, or ABM radars, capabilities to counter strategic ballistic missiles or their elements in flight trajectory, and not to test them in an ABM mode; and

(b) not to deploy in the future radars for early warning of strategic ballistic missile attack except at locations along the periphery of its national territory and oriented outward.

ARTICLE VII

Subject to the provisions of this treaty, modernization and replacement of ABM systems or their components may be carried out.

ARTICLE VIII

ABM systems or their components in excess of the numbers or outside the areas specified in this treaty, as well as ABM systems or their components prohibited by this treaty, shall be destroyed or dismantled under agreed procedures within the shortest possible agreed period of time.

ARTICLE IX

To assure the viability and effectiveness of this treaty, each party undertakes not to transfer to other states, and not to deploy outside its national territory, ABM systems or their components limited by this treaty.

119

ARTICLE X

Each party undertakes not to assume any international obligations which would conflict with this treaty.

ARTICLE XI

The parties undertake to continue active negotiations for limitations on strategic offensive arms.

ARTICLE XII

1. For the purpose of providing assurance of compliance with the provisions of this treaty, each party shall use national technical means of verification at its disposal in a manner consistent with generally recognized principles of international law.

2. Each party undertakes not to interfere with the national technical means of verification of the other party operating in accordance with paragraph one of this article.

3. Each party undertakes not to use deliberate concealment measures which impede verification by national technical means of compliance with the provisions of this treaty. This obligation shall not require changes in current construction, assembly, conversion, or overhaul practices.

ARTICLE XIII

1. To promote the objectives and implementation of the provisions of this treaty, the parties shall establish promptly a Standing Consultative Commission, within the framework of which they will:

(a) consider questions concerning compliance with the obligations assumed and related situations which may be considered ambiguous;

(b) provide on a voluntary basis such information as either party considers necessary to assure confidence in compliance with the obligations assumed;

(c) consider questions involving unintended interference with national technical means of verification;

(d) consider possible changes in the strategic situation which have a bearing on the provisions of this treaty;

(e) agree upon procedures and dates for destruction or dismantling of ABM systems or their components in cases provided for by the provisions of this treaty;

(f) consider, as appropriate, possible proposals for further increasing the viability of this treaty, including proposals for amendments in accordance with the provisions of this treaty;

(g) consider, as appropriate, proposals for further measures aimed at limiting strategic arms.

2. The parties through consultation shall establish, and may amend as appropriate, regulations for the Standing Consultative Commission governing procedures, composition, and other relevant matters.

ARTICLE XIV

1. Each party may propose amendments to this treaty. Agreed amendments shall enter into force in accordance with the procedures governing the entry into force of this treaty.

2. Five years after entry into force of this treaty, and at five-year intervals thereafter, the parties shall together conduct a review of this treaty.

ARTICLE XV

1. This treaty shall be of unlimited duration.

2. Each party shall, in exercising its national sovereignty, have the right to withdraw from this treaty if it decides that extraordinary events related to the subject matter of this treaty have jeopardized its supreme interests. It shall give notice of its decision to the other party six months prior to withdrawal from the treaty. Such notice shall include a statement of the extraordinary events the notifying party regards as having jeopardized its supreme interests.

ARTICLE XVI

1. This treaty shall be subject to ratification in accordance with the constitutional procedures of each party. The treaty shall enter into force on the day of the exchange of instruments of ratification.

2. This treaty shall be registered pursuant to Article 102 of the Charter of the United Nations.

Done at Moscow on 26 May 1972, in two copies, each in the English and Russian languages, both texts being equally authentic.

For the United States
of America:

RICHARD NIXON

*President of the United
States of America*

For the Union of Soviet
Socialist Republics:

LEONID I. BREZHNEV

*General Secretary of the
Central Committee, CPSU*

INTERIM AGREEMENT BETWEEN THE UNITED STATES OF AMERICA AND THE UNION OF SOVIET SOCIALIST REPUBLICS ON CERTAIN MEASURES WITH RESPECT TO THE LIMITATION OF STRATEGIC OFFENSIVE ARMS, 26 MAY 1972 *

The United States of America and the Union of Soviet Socialist Republics, hereinafter referred to as the parties,

Convinced that the Treaty on the Limitation of Antiballistic Missile Systems and this Interim Agreement on Certain Measures with Respect to the Limitations of Strategic Offensive Arms will contribute to the creation of more favorable conditions for active negotiations on limiting strategic arms as well as to the relaxation of international tension and the strengthening of trust between states,

Taking into account the relationship between strategic offensive and defensive arms,

Mindful of their obligations under Article VI of the Treaty on the Nonproliferation of Nuclear Weapons,

Have agreed as follows:

ARTICLE I

The parties undertake not to start construction of additional fixed land-based intercontinental ballistic missile (ICBM) launchers after 1 July 1972.

ARTICLE II

The parties undertake not to convert land-based launchers for light ICBMs, or for ICBMs of older types deployed prior to 1964, into land-based launchers for heavy ICBMs of types deployed after that time.

ARTICLE III

The parties undertake to limit submarine-launched ballistic missile (SLBM) launchers and modern ballistic missile submarines to the numbers operational and under construction on the date of signature of this Interim Agreement, and in addition to launchers and submarines constructed under procedures established by the parties as replacements for an equal number of ICBM launchers of older types deployed prior to 1964 or for launchers on older submarines.

---

* Source: Ibid., pp. 920-921.

ARTICLE IV

Subject to the provisions of this Interim Agreement, modernization and replacement of strategic offensive ballistic missiles and launchers covered by this Interim Agreement may be undertaken.

ARTICLE V

1. For the purpose of providing assurance of compliance with the provisions of this Interim Agreement, each party shall use national technical means of verification at its disposal in a manner consistent with generally recognized principles of international law.

2. Each party undertakes not to interfere with the national technical means of verification of the other party operating in accordance with paragraph one of this article.

3. Each party undertakes not to use deliberate concealment measures which impede verification by national technical means of compliance with the provisions of this Interim Agreement. This obligation shall not require changes in current construction, assembly, conversion, or overhaul practices.

ARTICLE VI

To promote the objectives and implementation of the provisions of this Interim Agreement, the parties shall use the Standing Consultative Commission established under Article XIII of the Treaty on the Limitation of Antiballistic Missile Systems in accordance with the provisions of that article.

ARTICLE VII

The parties undertake to continue active negotiations for limitations on strategic offensive arms. The obligations provided for in this Interim Agreement shall not prejudice the scope or terms of the limitations on strategic offensive arms which may be worked out in the course of further negotiations.

ARTICLE VIII

1. This Interim Agreement shall enter into force upon exchange of written notices of acceptance by each party, which exchange shall take place simultaneously with the exchange of instruments of ratification of the Treaty on the Limitation of Antiballistic Missile Systems.

2. This Interim Agreement shall remain in force for a period of five years unless replaced earlier by an agreement on more complete measures limiting strategic offensive arms. It is the objective of the parties to conduct active follow-on negotiations with the aim of concluding such an agreement as soon as possible.

3. Each party shall, in exercising its national sovereignty, have the right to withdraw from this Interim Agreement if it decides that extraordinary events related to the subject matter of this Interim Agreement have jeopardized its supreme interests. It shall give notice of its decision to the other party six months prior to withdrawal from this Interim Agreement. Such notice shall include a statement of the extraordinary events the notifying party regards as having jeopardized its supreme interests.

Done at Moscow on 26 May 1972, in two copies, each in the English and Russian languages, both texts being equally authentic.

For the United States
of America:

RICHARD NIXON

*President of the United
States of America*

For the Union of Soviet
Socialist Republics:

LEONID I. BREZHNEV

*General Secretary of the
Central Committee, CPSU*

PROTOCOL TO THE INTERIM AGREEMENT BETWEEN THE UNITED STATES OF AMERICA AND THE UNION OF SOVIET SOCIALIST REPUBLICS ON CERTAIN MEASURES WITH RESPECT TO THE LIMITATION OF STRATEGIC OFFENSIVE ARMS, 26 MAY 1972 *

The United States of America and the Union of Soviet Socialist Republics, hereinafter referred to as the parties,

Having agreed on certain limitations relating to submarine-launched ballistic missile launchers and modern ballistic missile submarines, and to replacement procedures, in the Interim Agreement,

Have agreed as follows:

The parties understand that, under Article III of the Interim Agreement, for the period during which that agreement remains in force:

The U.S. may have no more than 710 ballistic missile launchers on submarines (SLBMs) and no more than forty-four modern ballistic missile submarines. The Soviet Union may have no more than 950 ballistic missile launchers on submarines and no more than sixty-two modern ballistic missile submarines.

---

* Source: Ibid., p. 921.

Additional ballistic missile launchers on submarines up to the above-mentioned levels, in the United States—over 656 ballistic missile launchers on nuclear-powered submarines, and in the U.S.S.R. —over 740 ballistic missile launchers on nuclear-powered submarines, operational and under construction, may become operational as replacements for equal numbers of ballistic missile launchers of older types deployed prior to 1964 or of ballistic missile launchers on older submarines.

The deployment of modern SLBMs on any submarine, regardless of type, will be counted against the total level of SLBMs permitted for the U.S. and the U.S.S.R.

The protocol shall be considered an integral part of the Interim Agreement.

Done at Moscow this twenty-sixth day of May 1972.

For the United States of America:	For the Union of Soviet Socialist Republics:
RICHARD NIXON	LEONID I. BREZHNEV
President of the United States of America	*General Secretary of the Central Committee, CPSU*

REPORT OF SECRETARY OF STATE WILLIAM P. ROGERS ON THE STRATEGIC ARMS LIMITATIONS AGREEMENTS, 10 JUNE 1972 *

ABM Treaty

*   *   *

C. Verification and Consultation. (1) *Verification.* Article XII relates to verification of compliance with the treaty's provisions, which is to be accomplished by national technical means. Paragraph one states that each party will use national technical means of verification at its disposal in a manner consistent with generally recognized principles of international law for purposes of providing assurance of compliance with provisions of the treaty. It does not require changes from current operating practices and procedures with respect to systems which will be used as national technical means of verification.

---

* Source: *Department of State Bulletin*, vol. 67, no. 1723 (3 July 1972), pp. 7–14.

The second paragraph of this article provides that each party agrees not to interfere with the national technical means of verification of the other which are operating in accordance with paragraph one of the article. This provision would, for example, prohibit interference with a satellite in orbit used for verification of the treaty.

Paragraph three contains an agreement not to use deliberate concealment measures which impede verification by national technical means. This paragraph expressly permits continuation of current construction, assembly, conversion and overhaul practices.

(2) *Standing Consultative Commission.* Article XIII provides that the parties shall establish promptly a Standing Consultative Commission (hereafter referred to as the commission) to promote the objectives and to facilitate the implementation of the ABM Treaty. The parties have further agreed to use the commission to promote the objectives and implementation of the Interim Agreement. (See Article VI of the Interim Agreement.) The commission will provide a consulting framework within which the parties may consider various matters relating to the treaty and the Interim Agreement. The parties may also consider these matters in other channels.

A principal function of the commission will be to consider questions of compliance with the obligations assumed under this treaty and the Interim Agreement and also related situations which may be considered ambiguous. Each party may voluntarily provide through the commission information it considers necessary to assure confidence in compliance. Thus one party might raise a question of compliance based on information gathered by national technical means of verification and the other party could provide information to clarify the matter.

Attention was called above to the provisions in Article XII prohibiting intentional interference with national technical means of verification operating in accordance with its provisions. The commission is charged by Article XIII with the responsibility to consider any questions of interference with such means. The commission may also consider questions of concealment impeding verification by national means. The commission may consider changes in the general strategic situation which have a bearing on the provisions of the treaty. Related to this is the commission's authority to consider proposals to further increase the viability of the treaty—such as agreed interpretations after the treaty has entered into force—and to consider proposals for amendment of the treaty. (Amendments to the treaty would have to be ratified pursuant to Articles XIV and XVI.) The commission may also consider other appropriate measures, not specifically enumerated in Article XIII, aimed at further limiting strategic arms. Finally, through the commission the parties are to agree on procedures and dates for the implementation of Article VIII concerning destruction or dismantling of ABM systems or ABM components. (For corresponding responsibility of the commission under the Interim Agreement, see section C of the discussion thereof.)

The second paragraph of Article XIII provides for the establishment of regulations for the commission governing procedures, composition and other relevant matters. Such matters can be worked out early in the follow-on negotiations. Meanwhile, any consultation desired by either side under these articles can be carried out by the delegations during such negotiations or, when they are not in session, through other diplomatic channels.

The commission is intended as a means to facilitate the implementation of the agreements and would not replace follow-on negotiations or use of other diplomatic channels.

D. Duration, Withdrawal and Further Negotiations. Article XV provides that the treaty shall be of unlimited duration but contains a withdrawal clause of the type that has become standard in postwar arms control treaties. This clause provides that each party, in exercising its national sovereignty, shall have the right to withdraw from the treaty if it decides that extraordinary events related to the subject matter of the treaty have jeopardized its supreme interests. Notice of such decision is to be given to the other party six months prior to withdrawal from the treaty. Such notice is required to include a statement of the extraordinary events involved.

In this connection, the United States has stressed the unique relationship between limitations on offensive and defensive strategic arms. This interrelationship lends extraordinary importance to the undertaking in Article XI "to continue active negotiations for limitations on strategic offensive arms."

The special importance we attach to this relationship was reflected in the following formal statement relating to Article XI, which was made by the head of the United States delegation on 9 May 1972:

> The U.S. delegation has stressed the importance the U.S. government attaches to achieving agreement on more complete limitations on strategic offensive arms, following agreement on an ABM Treaty and on an Interim Agreement on certain measures with respect to the limitation of strategic offensive arms. The U.S. delegation believes that an objective of the follow-on negotiations should be to con-

strain and reduce on a long-term basis threats to the survivability of our respective strategic retaliatory forces. The U.S.S.R. delegation has also indicated that the objectives of SALT would remain unfulfilled without the achievement of an agreement providing for more complete limitations on strategic offensive arms. Both sides recognize that the initial agreements would be steps toward the achievement of more complete limitations on strategic arms. If an agreement providing for more complete strategic offensive arms limitations were not achieved within five years, U.S. supreme interests could be jeopardized. Should that occur, it would constitute a basis for withdrawal from the ABM Treaty. The U.S. does not wish to see such a situation occur, nor do we believe that the U.S.S.R. does. It is because we wish to prevent such a situation that we emphasize the importance the U.S. government attaches to achievement of more complete limitations on strategic offensive arms. The U.S. executive will inform the Congress, in connection with congressional consideration of the ABM Treaty and the Interim Agreement, of this statement of the U.S. position.

E. Other Provisions. Article XIV deals with amendments and review. Paragraph one provides that the parties may propose amendments to the treaty. Agreed amendments shall enter into force upon exchange of instruments of ratification. The second paragraph of Article XIV provides for formal review of the treaty by the parties at five-year intervals. Paragraph two does not preclude agreement on proposed amendments of the treaty during the first five years, or between formal reviews thereafter; it simply reflects recognition of the possibility of changes in the strategic relationship and the development of new strategic systems. These questions are also within the purview of the Standing Consultative Commission.

Article XVI and the final paragraph of the treaty contain standard provisions on entry into force, registration pursuant to the United Nations Charter, and equal authenticity of the English and Russian language texts.

Interim Agreement and Protocol

The Interim Agreement between the United States of America and the Union of Soviet Socialist Republics on Certain Measures with respect to the Limitation of Strategic Offensive Arms (Interim Agreement), including a protocol which is integral thereto, was signed on 26 May 1972. The Interim Agreement consists of a preamble and eight operative articles. In the course of the negotiations, agreement was reached on a number of interpretive matters related to the Interim Agreement. Enclosure three contains agreed interpretations and certain noteworthy unilateral statements.

This agreement provides for a restriction of five years on strategic offensive missile launcher deployments pending negotiation of more complete limitations on strategic offensive arms. The main effects of the Interim Agreement will be that:

- the aggregate number of fixed, land-based ICBM launchers and SLBM launchers will be limited;
- starting construction of additional fixed, land-based ICBM launchers is prohibited;
- the number of launchers for modern heavy ICBMs, such as the Soviet SS-9, will be limited to that number currently operational and under construction;
- ceilings will be placed on the number of SLBM launchers and modern ballistic missile submarines operational on each side; and
- up to the agreed ceilings, deployment of additional SLBM launchers above a specified number for each party requires an offsetting reduction of ICBM launchers of older types or SLBM launchers on older ballistic missile submarines.

In the first paragraph of the preamble of the agreement the parties express the conviction that the ABM Treaty and the Interim Agreement will contribute to the creation of more favorable conditions for active negotiation on limiting strategic arms and will improve international relations. In the second paragraph the parties acknowledge the relationship between strategic offensive and defensive arms, and in the third they acknowledge their obligations under Article VI of the Nonproliferation Treaty to pursue disarmament negotiations.

A. ICBM Launchers. Article I of the Interim Agreement prohibits starting construction of additional fixed land-based ICBM launchers. While the text of Article I prescribes 1 July 1972 as the freeze date, the United States and the Soviet Union understand that, pending ratification and acceptance of the agreements, neither will take any action that will be prohibited thereby, in the absence of notification by either signatory of its intention not to proceed with ratification or approval.

This construction freeze covers all fixed land-based ICBM launchers, both silo and soft-pad, but does not include test and training ICBM launchers or mobile land-based ICBM launchers. Test and training launchers are, however, subject to other constraints. The United States has made clear to the Soviets that we would consider the deployment of operational land-mobile ICBM launchers during the period of the Interim Agreement to be inconsistent with the objectives of the agreement. The parties have agreed that the term ICBM includes any land-based strategic ballistic missile capable of ranges in excess of the shortest distance between the northeastern border of the continental United States and the northwestern border of the continental Soviet Union. Launchers for fractional orbital bombardment systems are considered to be ICBM launchers.

On 26 May 1972, the United States had 1,054 operational, land-based ICBM launchers and none under construction; on that date, the Soviet Union had a total of land-based ICBM launchers operational and under active construction estimated to be about 1,618. (ICBM launchers for testing and training purposes are excluded in each case.) Under the freeze, the Soviet Union may complete construction of ICBM launchers under active construction on 26 May 1972. While the Interim Agreement remains in effect, neither party may start new construction (nor resume previously suspended construction) of fixed ICBM launchers except test and training launchers.

B. Heavy ICBM Launchers. Article II provides that the parties shall not convert land-based launchers for light, or older heavy, ICBMs into land-based launchers for modern heavy ICBMs, such as the Soviet SS-9. All currently operational ICBMs other than the SS-9 are either "light" (the United States Minuteman and the Soviet SS-11 and SS-13) or "older" ICBM launchers of types first deployed prior to 1964 (the United States Titan and the Soviet SS-7 and SS-8).

Article II would thus prohibit the conversion of a launcher for an SS-7, SS-8, SS-11, or SS-13 ICBM into a launcher for an SS-9 or any new modern heavy ICBM, and would similarly prohibit the conversion of a launcher for a Minuteman or Titan into a launcher for a modern heavy ICBM. The parties agree that in the process of modernization and replacement the dimensions of land-based ICBM silo launchers will not be significantly increased, and that this means that any increase will not be greater than 10–15 percent of the present dimensions. The United States has also made clear that it would consider any ICBM having a volume significantly greater than that of the largest light ICBM now operational on either side (which is the Soviet SS-11) to be a heavy ICBM.

C. SLBM Launchers and Modern Ballistic Missile Submarines.
Article III limits SLBM launchers and modern ballistic missile submarines to the numbers operational and under construction on 26 May 1972.

In addition, Article III and the protocol permit launchers and submarines beyond 740 SLBM launchers on nuclear-powered submarines for the Soviet Union and 656 SLBM launchers on nuclear-powered submarines for the United States, subject to two constraints. First, additional SLBM launchers may become operational only as replacements for an equal number of ICBM launchers of types first deployed prior to 1964, or for launchers on older nuclear-powered submarines or for modern SLBM launchers on any type of submarine. Second, such substitution may not result in:

- the Soviet Union having operational more than sixty-two modern ballistic missile submarines or more than 950 SLBM launchers, including all SLBM launchers on nuclear-powered submarines and all modern SLBM launchers on any type of submarine;

- the United States having operational more than forty-four modern ballistic missile submarines or more than 710 SLBM launchers.

Construction of replacement SLBM launchers up to the limits under the protocol would require the dismantling or destruction, under agreed procedures, of an equal number of ICBM launchers of older types or of SLBM launchers on nuclear-powered submarines. Moreover, modern SLBM launchers deployed on any type of submarine would count against the total ceiling on SLBM launchers. Dismantling or destruction would be required to commence no later than the date on which sea trials of a replacement ballistic missile submarine begin and to be completed in the shortest possible agreed period of time. Thus the Soviets will have to begin dismantling older ICBM or SLBM launchers no later than when the 741st SLBM launcher on a nuclear-powered submarine enters sea trials. Dismantling or destruction, as well as timely notification thereof, are to be carried out in accordance with procedures to be agreed upon in the Standing Consultative Commission.

D. Test and Training Launchers.
The parties agree that the number of test and training launchers for ICBMs and SLBMs, including

"modern heavy" ICBMs, shall not be increased significantly above the current number of test and training launchers for such missiles. It is understood that construction or conversion of ICBM launchers at test ranges shall be undertaken only for the purposes of testing and training. It is also understood that ICBM launchers for test and training purposes may be constructed at operational sites.

E. Modernization and Replacement. Article IV provides that, subject to the provisions of the Interim Agreement, modernization and replacement of strategic ballistic missiles and launchers covered by the Interim Agreement may be undertaken. The conversion of current United States ICBM launchers to handle Minuteman III missiles, the conversion of current submarine launchers to handle Poseidon missiles, and the construction of new submarines as replacements for older submarines, are not prohibited by the agreement.

F. Other Provisions. Article V of the Interim Agreement contains the same provisions on verification as appear in Article XII of the ABM Treaty. Verification will be carried out by national technical means operating in accordance with generally recognized principles of international law. Interference with, or deliberate concealment from, such means is prohibited. Neither party is required to change its current practices of construction, assembly, conversion, or overhaul.

Article VI provides that in order to promote the objectives and implementation of the Interim Agreement, the parties shall use the Standing Consultative Commission to be established pursuant to Article XIII of the ABM Treaty.

In Article VII the parties agree to continue active negotiation for limitations on strategic offensive arms. This article also provides that the terms of this Interim Agreement will not prejudice the scope and terms of the limitations on strategic offensive arms which may be worked out in the subsequent negotiations. It is expected that these subsequent negotiations will start in the near future.

The first paragraph of Article VIII of the Interim Agreement provides that it shall enter into force upon the exchange of written notices of acceptance, simultaneously with the exchange of instruments of ratification of the ABM Treaty.

Paragraph two of Article VIII provides that the Interim Agreement shall remain in effect for five years, unless earlier replaced by agreement on more complete measures limiting strategic offensive arms.

The third paragraph of this Article provides each party with a right, parallel to that contained in paragraph two of Article XV of the ABM Treaty, to withdraw upon six months' notice if such party decides its supreme interests have been jeopardized by extraordinary events related to the subject matter of the Interim Agreement.

Conclusion

I believe the treaty limiting antiballistic missile systems, together with the accompanying Interim Agreement and its protocol constraining strategic offensive arms, constitute the most important step in arms limitation ever taken by this country. In these agreements, the two most powerful nations on earth are adopting measures designed to curb the deployment of strategic arms.

The parties have protected their vital interests during the careful negotiation and elaboration of these agreements. We did not agree to anything adversely affecting the national interests of our allies, who were regularly consulted during the negotiations. The Congress has been kept closely informed throughout the negotiations. Ambassador Smith and other delegation members conducted a total of thirty executive session briefings for congressional committees.

These agreements should help to improve Soviet-American relations and preserve and strengthen international security and world order. The entry into force of these measures should significantly advance the cause of peace in the world, and I hope that they can be brought into force as soon as practicable.

Respectfully submitted,

WILLIAM P. ROGERS

Agreed Interpretations: Initialed Statements

The texts of the statements set out below were agreed upon and initialed by the heads of the delegations on 26 May 1972.

ABM Treaty. [A] The parties understand that, in addition to the ABM radars which may be deployed in accordance with subparagraph (a) of Article III of the treaty, those non-phased-array ABM radars operational on the date of signature of the treaty within the ABM system deployment area for defense of the national capital may be retained.

[B] The parties understand that the potential (the product of mean emitted power in watts and antenna area in square meters) of

133

the smaller of the two large phased-array ABM radars referred to in subparagraph (b) of Article III of the treaty is considered for purposes of the treaty to be 3 million.

[C] The parties understand that the center of the ABM system deployment area centered on the national capital and the center of the ABM system deployment area containing ICBM silo launchers for each party shall be separated by no less than 1,300 kilometers.

[D] The parties agree not to deploy phased-array radars having a potential (the product of mean emitted power in watts and antenna area in square meters) exceeding 3 million, except as provided for in Articles III, IV, and VI of the treaty, or except for the purposes of tracking objects in outer space or for use as national technical means of verification.

[E] In order to insure fulfillment of the obligation not to deploy ABM systems and their components except as provided in Article III of the treaty, the parties agree that in the event ABM systems based on other physical principles and including components capable of substituting for ABM interceptor missiles, ABM launchers, or ABM radars are created in the future, specific limitations on such systems and their components would be subject to discussion in accordance with Article XIII and agreement in accordance with Article XIV of the treaty.

[F] The parties understand that Article V of the treaty includes obligations not to develop, test, or deploy ABM interceptor missiles for the delivery by each ABM interceptor missile of more than one independently guided warhead.

[G] The parties understand that Article IX of the treaty includes the obligation of the United States and the U.S.S.R. not to provide to other states technical descriptions or blueprints specially worked out for the construction of ABM systems and their components limited by the treaty.

Interim Agreement. [H] The parties understand that land-based ICBM launchers referred to in the Interim Agreement are understood to be launchers for strategic ballistic missiles capable of ranges in excess of the shortest distance between the northeastern border of the continental United States and the northwestern border of the continental U.S.S.R.

[I] The parties understand that fixed land-based ICBM launchers under active construction as of the date of signature of the Interim Agreement may be completed.

[J] The parties understand that in the process of modernization and replacement the dimensions of land-based ICBM silo launchers will not be significantly increased.

[K] The parties understand that dismantling or destruction of ICBM launchers of older types deployed prior to 1964 and ballistic missile launchers on older submarines being replaced by new SLBM launchers on modern submarines will be initiated at the time of the beginning of sea trials of a replacement submarine, and will be completed in the shortest possible agreed period of time. Such dismantling or destruction, and timely notification thereof, will be accomplished under procedures to be agreed in the Standing Consultative Commission.

[L] The parties understand that during the period of the Interim Agreement there shall be no significant increase in the number of ICBM or SLBM test and training launchers, or in the number of such launchers for modern land-based heavy ICBMs. The parties further understand that construction or conversion of ICBM launchers at test ranges shall be undertaken only for purposes of testing and training.

Agreed Interpretations: Common Understandings

Common understanding of the parties on the following matters was reached during the negotiations:

A. Increase in ICBM Silo Dimensions. Ambassador Smith made the following statement on 26 May 1972: "The parties agree that the term 'significantly increased' means that an increase will not be greater than 10–15 percent of the present dimensions of land-based ICBM silo launchers."

Minister Semenov replied that this statement corresponded to the Soviet understanding.

B. Location of ICBM Defenses. The U.S. delegation made the following statement on 26 May 1972: "Article III of the ABM Treaty provides for each side one ABM system deployment area centered on its national capital and one ABM system deployment area containing ICBM silo launchers. The two sides have registered agreement on the following statement: 'The parties understand that the center of the ABM system deployment area centered on the national capital and the center of the ABM system deployment area containing ICBM silo launchers for each party shall be separated by no less than 1,300 kilometers.' In this connection, the U.S. side notes that its ABM system deployment area for defense of ICBM silo launchers, located west of the Mississippi River, will be centered in the Grand Forks ICBM silo launcher deployment area." (See Initialed Statement [C].)

C. ABM Test Ranges. The U.S. delegation made the following statement on 26 April 1972: "Article IV of the ABM Treaty provides that 'the limitations provided for in Article III shall not apply to ABM systems or their components used for development or testing, and located within current or additionally agreed test ranges.' We believe it would be useful to assure that there is no misunderstanding as to current ABM test ranges. It is our understanding that ABM test ranges encompass the area within which ABM components are located for test purposes. The current U.S. ABM test ranges are at White Sands, New Mexico, and at Kwajalein Atoll, and the current Soviet ABM test range is near Sary Shagan in Kazakhstan. We consider that non-phased-array radars of types used for range safety or instrumentation purposes may be located outside of ABM test ranges. We interpret the reference in Article IV to 'additionally agreed test ranges' to mean that ABM components will not be located at any other test ranges without prior agreement between our governments that there will be such additional ABM test ranges."

On 5 May 1972, the Soviet delegation stated that there was a common understanding on what ABM test ranges were, that the use of the types of non-ABM radars for range safety or instrumentation was not limited under the treaty, that the reference in Article IV to "additionally agreed" test ranges was sufficiently clear, and that national means permitted identifying current test ranges.

D. Mobile ABM Systems. On 28 January 1972, the U.S. delegation made the following statement: "Article V(1) of the joint draft text of the ABM Treaty includes an undertaking not to develop, test, or deploy mobile land-based ABM systems and their components. On 5 May 1971, the U.S. side indicated that, in its view, a prohibition on deployment of mobile ABM systems and components would rule out the deployment of ABM launchers and radars which were not permanent fixed types. At that time, we asked for the Soviet view of this interpretation. Does the Soviet side agree with the U.S. side's interpretation put forward on 5 May 1971?"

On 13 April 1972, the Soviet delegation said there is a general common understanding on this matter.

E. Standing Consultative Commission. Ambassador Smith made the following statement on 24 May 1972: "The United States proposes that the sides agree that, with regard to initial implementation of the ABM Treaty's Article XIII on the Standing Consultative Commission (SCC) and of the consultation articles to the Interim Agreement on offensive arms and the Accidents Agreement,[1] agreement establishing the SCC will be worked out early in the follow-on SALT negotiations; until that is completed, the following arrangements will prevail: when SALT is in session, any consultation desired by either side under these articles can be carried out by the two SALT delegations; when SALT is not in session, *ad hoc* arrangements for any desired consultations under these articles may be made through diplomatic channels."

Minister Semenov replied that, on an *ad referendum* basis, he could agree that the U.S. statement corresponded to the Soviet understanding.

F. Standstill. On 6 May 1972, Minister Semenov made the following statement: "In an effort to accommodate the wishes of the U.S. side, the Soviet delegation is prepared to proceed on the basis that the two sides will in fact observe the obligations of both the Interim Agreement and the ABM Treaty beginning from the date of signature of these two documents."

In reply, the U.S. delegation made the following statement on 20 May 1972: "The U.S. agrees in principle with the Soviet statement made on 6 May concerning observance of obligations beginning from date of signature but we would like to make clear our understanding that this means that, pending ratification and acceptance, neither side would take any action prohibited by the agreements after they had entered into force. This understanding would continue to apply in the absence of notification by either signatory of its intention not to proceed with ratification or approval."

The Soviet delegation indicated agreement with the U.S. statement.

---

[1] See Article 7 of Agreement to Reduce the Risk of Outbreak of Nuclear War between the United States of America and the Union of Soviet Socialist Republics, signed 30 September 1971. . . .

Unilateral Statements

(a) The following noteworthy unilateral statements were made during the negotiations by the United States delegation:

A. Withdrawal from the ABM Treaty. On 9 May 1972, Ambassador Smith made the following statement: "The U.S. delegation has stressed the importance the U.S. government attaches to achieving agreement on more complete limitations on strategic offensive arms, following agreement on an ABM Treaty and on an Interim Agreement on certain measures with respect to the limitation of strategic offensive arms. The U.S. delegation believes that an objective of the follow-on negotiations should be to constrain and reduce on a long-term basis threats to the survivability of our respective strategic retaliatory forces. The U.S.S.R. delegation has also indicated that the objectives of SALT would remain unfulfilled without the achievement of an agreement providing for more complete limitations on strategic offensive arms. Both sides recognize that the initial agreements would be steps toward the achievement of more complete limitations on strategic arms. If an agreement providing for more complete strategic offensive arms limitations were not achieved within five years, U.S. supreme interests could be jeopardized. Should that occur, it would constitute a basis for withdrawal from the ABM Treaty. The U.S. does not wish to see such a situation occur, nor do we believe that the U.S.S.R. does. It is because we wish to prevent such a situation that we emphasize the importance the U.S. government attaches to achievement of more complete limitations on strategic offensive arms. The U.S. executive will inform the Congress, in connection with congressional consideration of the ABM Treaty and the Interim Agreement of this statement of the U.S. position."

B. Land-Mobile ICBM Launchers. The U.S. delegation made the following statement on 20 May 1972: "In connection with the important subject of land-mobile ICBM launchers, in the interest of concluding the Interim Agreement the U.S. delegation now withdraws its proposal that Article I or an agreed statement explicitly prohibit the deployment of mobile land-based ICBM launchers. I have been instructed to inform you that, while agreeing to defer the question of limitation of operational land-mobile ICBM launchers to the subsequent negotiations on more complete limitations on strategic offensive arms, the U.S. would consider the deployment of operational land-mobile ICBM launchers during the period of the Interim Agreement as inconsistent with the objectives of that agreement."

BASIC AGREEMENTS ON DETENTE

C. Covered Facilities. The U.S. delegation made the following statement on 20 May 1972: "I wish to emphasize the importance that the United States attaches to the provisions of Article V, including in particular their application to fitting out or berthing submarines."

D. "Heavy" ICBMs. The U.S. delegation made the following statement on 26 May 1972: "The U.S. delegation regrets that the Soviet delegation has not been willing to agree on a common definition of a heavy missile. Under these circumstances, the U.S. delegation believes it necessary to state the following: The United States would consider any ICBM having a volume significantly greater than that of the largest light ICBM now operational on either side to be a heavy ICBM. The U.S. proceeds on the premise that the Soviet side will give due account to this consideration."

E. Tested in ABM Mode. On 7 April 1972, the U.S. delegation made the following statement: "Article II of the joint draft text uses the term 'tested in an ABM mode,' in defining ABM components, and Article VI includes certain obligations concerning such testing. We believe that the sides should have a common understanding of this phrase. First, we would note that the testing provisions of the ABM Treaty are intended to apply to testing which occurs after the date of signature of the treaty, and not to any testing which may have occurred in the past. Next, we would amplify the remarks we have made on this subject during the previous Helsinki phase by setting forth the objectives which govern the U.S. view on the subject, namely, while prohibiting testing of non-ABM components for ABM purposes: not to prevent testing of ABM components, and not to prevent testing of non-ABM components for non-ABM purposes. To clarify our interpretation of 'tested in an ABM mode,' we note that we would consider a launcher, missile, or radar to be 'tested in an ABM mode' if, for example, any of the following events occur: (1) a launcher is used to launch an ABM interceptor missile, (2) an interceptor missile is flight tested against a target vehicle which has a flight trajectory with characteristics of a strategic ballistic missile flight trajectory, or is flight tested in conjunction with the test of an ABM interceptor missile or an ABM radar at the same test range, or is flight tested to an altitude inconsistent with interception of targets against which air defenses are deployed, (3) a radar makes measurements on a cooperative target vehicle of the kind referred to in item (2) above during the reentry portion of its trajectory or makes measurements in conjunction with the test of an ABM interceptor missile or an ABM radar at the same test range. Radars used for purposes such as range safety or instrumentation would be exempt from application of these criteria."

F. No-Transfer Article of ABM Treaty. On 18 April 1972, the U.S. delegation made the following statement: "In regard to this Article [IX], I have a brief and I believe self-explanatory statement to make. The U.S. side wishes to make clear that the provisions of this article do not set a precedent for whatever provision may be considered for a Treaty on Limiting Strategic Offensive Arms. The question of transfer of strategic offensive arms is a far more complex issue, which may require a different solution."

G. No Increase in Defense of Early Warning Radars. On 28 July 1970, the U.S. delegation made the following statement: "Since Hen House radars [Soviet ballistic missile early warning radars] can detect and track ballistic missile warheads at great distances, they have a significant ABM potential. Accordingly, the United States would regard any increase in the defenses of such radars by surface-to-air missiles as inconsistent with an agreement."

*   *   *

The following noteworthy unilateral statement was made by the delegation of the U.S.S.R. and is shown here with the U.S. reply:

On 17 May 1972, Minister Semenov made the following unilateral "Statement of the Soviet Side": "Taking into account that modern ballistic missile submarines are presently in the possession of not only the U.S., but also of its NATO allies, the Soviet Union agrees that for the period of effectiveness of the Interim 'Freeze' Agreement the United States and its NATO allies have up to fifty such submarines with a total of up to 800 ballistic launchers thereon (including forty-one U.S. submarines with 656 ballistic missile launchers). However, if during the period of effectiveness of the agreement U.S. allies in NATO should increase the number of their modern submarines to exceed the numbers of submarines they would have operational or under construction on the date of signature of the agreement, the Soviet Union will have the right to a corresponding increase in the number of its submarines. In the opinion of the Soviet side, the solution of the question of modern ballistic missile submarines provided for in the Interim Agreement only partially compensates for the strategic imbalance in the deployment of the nuclear-powered missile submarines of the U.S.S.R. and the United States. Therefore, the Soviet side believes that this whole question, and above all the question of liquidating the American missile submarine bases outside the United States, will be appropriately resolved in the course of follow-on negotiations."

On 24 May, Ambassador Smith made the following reply to Minister Semenov: "The United States side has studied the 'statement made by the Soviet side' of 17 May concerning compensation for submarine basing and SLBM submarines belonging to third countries. The United States does not accept the validity of the considerations in that statement."

On 26 May Minister Semenov repeated the unilateral statement made on 17 May. Ambassador Smith also repeated the U.S. rejection on 26 May.

JOINT U.S.-CHINESE COMMUNIQUE
ISSUED AT SHANGHAI, 27 FEBRUARY 1972 *

President Richard Nixon of the United States of America visited the People's Republic of China at the invitation of Premier Chou En-lai of the People's Republic of China from 21 February to 28 February 1972. Accompanying the President were Mrs. Nixon, U.S. Secretary of State William Rogers, Assistant to the President Dr. Henry Kissinger, and other American officials.

President Nixon met with Chairman Mao Tse-tung of the Communist Party of China on 21 February. The two leaders had a serious and frank exchange of views on Sino-U.S. relations and world affairs.

During the visit, extensive, earnest, and frank discussions were held between President Nixon and Premier Chou En-lai on the normalization of relations between the United States of America and the People's Republic of China, as well as on other matters of interest to both sides. In addition, Secretary of State William Rogers and Foreign Minister Chi Peng-fei held talks in the same spirit.

President Nixon and his party visited Peking and viewed cultural, industrial, and agricultural sites, and they also toured Hangchow and Shanghai where, continuing discussions with Chinese leaders, they viewed similar places of interest.

The leaders of the People's Republic of China and the United States of America found it beneficial to have this opportunity, after

---

* *Department of State Bulletin*, vol. 66, no. 1708 (20 March 1972), pp. 435-438.

so many years without contact, to present candidly to one another their views on a variety of issues. They reviewed the international situation in which important changes and great upheavals are taking place and expounded their respective positions and attitudes.

The U.S. side stated: Peace in Asia and peace in the world require efforts both to reduce immediate tensions and to eliminate the basic causes of conflict. The United States will work for a just and secure peace: just, because it fulfills the aspirations of peoples and nations for freedom and progress; secure, because it removes the danger of foreign aggression. The United States supports individual freedom and social progress for all the peoples of the world, free of outside pressure or intervention. The United States believes that the effort to reduce tensions is served by improving communication between countries that have different ideologies so as to lessen the risks of confrontation through accident, miscalculation, or misunderstanding. Countries should treat each other with mutual respect and be willing to compete peacefully, letting performance be the ultimate judge. No country should claim infallibility, and each country should be prepared to reexamine its own attitudes for the common good. The United States stressed that the peoples of Indochina should be allowed to determine their destiny without outside intervention; its constant primary objective has been a negotiated solution; the eight-point proposal put forward by the Republic of Vietnam and the United States on 27 January 1972 represents a basis for the attainment of that objective; in the absence of a negotiated settlement the United States envisages the ultimate withdrawal of all U.S. forces from the region consistent with the aim of self-determination for each country of Indochina. The United States will maintain its close ties with and support for the Republic of Korea; the United States will support efforts of the Republic of Korea to seek a relaxation of tension and increased communication in the Korean peninsula. The United States places the highest value on its friendly relations with Japan; it will continue to develop the existing close bonds. Consistent with the United Nations Security Council Resolution of 21 December 1971, the United States favors the continuation of the ceasefire between India and Pakistan and the withdrawal of all military forces to within their own territories and to their own sides of the ceasefire line in Jammu and Kashmir; the United States supports the right of the peoples of South Asia to shape their own future in peace, free of military threat, and without having the area become the subject of great power rivalry.

The Chinese side stated: Wherever there is oppression, there is resistance. Countries want independence, nations want liberation, and the people want revolution—this has become the irresistible trend of history. All nations, big or small, should be equal; big nations should not bully the small, and strong nations should not bully the weak. China will never be a superpower, and it opposes hegemony and power politics of any kind. The Chinese side stated that it firmly supports the struggles of all the oppressed peoples and nations for freedom and liberation and the peoples of all countries have the right to choose their social systems according to their own wishes and the right to safeguard the independence, sovereignty, and territorial integrity of their own countries and oppose foreign aggression, interference, control, and subversion. All foreign troops should be withdrawn to their own countries.

The Chinese side expressed its firm support to the peoples of Vietnam, Laos, and Cambodia in their efforts for the attainment of their goal and its firm support to the seven-point proposal of the Provisional Revolutionary Government of the Republic of South Vietnam and the elaboration of February this year on the two key problems in the proposal, and to the Joint Declaration of the Summit Conference of the Indochinese Peoples. It firmly supports the eight-point program for the peaceful unification of Korea put forward by the government of the Democratic People's Republic of Korea on 12 April 1971 and the stand for the abolition of the "UN Commission for the Unification and Rehabilitation of Korea." It firmly opposes the revival and outward expansion of Japanese militarism and firmly supports the Japanese people's desire to build an independent, democratic, peaceful, and neutral Japan. It firmly maintains that India and Pakistan should, in accordance with the United Nations resolutions on the India-Pakistan question, immediately withdraw all their forces to their respective territories and to their own sides of the ceasefire line in Jammu and Kashmir and firmly supports the Pakistan government and people in their struggle to preserve their independence and sovereignty and the people of Jammu and Kashmir in their struggle for the right of self-determination.

There are essential differences between China and the United States in their social systems and foreign policies. However, the two sides agreed that countries, regardless of their social systems, should conduct their relations on the principles of respect for the sovereignty and territorial integrity of all states, nonaggression against other states, noninterference in the internal affairs of other states, equality and mutual benefit, and peaceful coexistence. International disputes

143

should be settled on this basis, without resorting to the use or threat of force. The United States and the People's Republic of China are prepared to apply these principles to their mutual relations.

With these principles of international relations in mind, the two sides stated that:

- progress toward the normalization of relations between China and the United States is in the interests of all countries;

- both wish to reduce the danger of international military conflict;

- neither should seek hegemony in the Asia-Pacific region and each is opposed to efforts by any other country or group of countries to establish such hegemony; and

- neither is prepared to negotiate on behalf of any third party or to enter into agreements or understandings with the other directed at other states.

Both sides are of the view that it would be against the interests of the peoples of the world for any major country to collude with another against other countries, or for major countries to divide up the world into spheres of interest.

The two sides reviewed the long-standing serious disputes between China and the United States. The Chinese side reaffirmed its position: The Taiwan question is the crucial question obstructing the normalization of relations between China and the United States; the government of the People's Republic of China is the sole legal government of China; Taiwan is a province of China which has long been returned to the motherland; the liberation of Taiwan is China's internal affair in which no other country has the right to interfere; and all U.S. forces and military installations must be withdrawn from Taiwan. The Chinese government firmly opposes any activities which aim at the creation of "one China, one Taiwan," "one China, two governments," "two Chinas," and an "independent Taiwan" or advocate that "the status of Taiwan remains to be determined."

The U.S. side declared: The United States acknowledges that all Chinese on either side of the Taiwan Strait maintain there is but one China and that Taiwan is a part of China. The United States government does not challenge that position. It reaffirms its interest in a peaceful settlement of the Taiwan question by the Chinese themselves. With this prospect in mind, it affirms the ultimate objective of the withdrawal of all U.S. forces and military installations from Taiwan. In the meantime, it will progressively reduce its forces and military installations on Taiwan as the tension in the area diminishes.

The two sides agreed that it is desirable to broaden the understanding between the two peoples. To this end, they discussed specific areas in such fields as science, technology, culture, sports, and journalism, in which people-to-people contacts and exchanges would be mutually beneficial. Each side undertakes to facilitate the further development of such contacts and exchanges.

Both sides view bilateral trade as another area from which mutual benefit can be derived, and agreed that economic relations based on equality and mutual benefit are in the interest of the peoples of the two countries. They agree to facilitate the progressive development of trade between their two countries.

The two sides agreed that they will stay in contact through various channels, including the sending of a senior U.S. representative to Peking from time to time for concrete consultations to further the normalization of relations between the two countries and continue to exchange views on issues of common interest.

The two sides expressed the hope that the gains achieved during this visit would open up new prospects for the relations between the two countries. They believe that the normalization of relations between the two countries not only is in the interest of the Chinese and American peoples but also contributes to the relaxation of tension in Asia and the world.

AGREEMENT BETWEEN THE UNITED STATES OF AMERICA AND THE UNION OF SOVIET SOCIALIST REPUBLICS ON THE PREVENTION OF NUCLEAR WAR, 22 JUNE 1973 *

The United States of America and the Union of Soviet Socialist Republics, hereinafter referred to as the parties,

Guided by the objectives of strengthening world peace and international security,

Conscious that nuclear war would have devastating consequences for mankind,

Proceeding from the desire to bring about conditions in which the danger of an outbreak of nuclear war anywhere in the world would be reduced and ultimately eliminated,

---

* Source: *Department of State Bulletin*, vol. 69, no. 1778 (23 July 1973), pp. 160-161.

145

Proceeding from their obligations under the Charter of the United Nations regarding the maintenance of peace, refraining from the threat or use of force, and the avoidance of war, and in conformity with the agreements to which either party has subscribed,

Proceeding from the Basic Principles of Relations between the United States of America and the Union of Soviet Socialist Republics signed in Moscow on 29 May 1972,

Reaffirming that the development of relations between the United States of America and the Union of Soviet Socialist Republics is not directed against other countries and their interests,

Have agreed as follows:

ARTICLE I

The United States and the Soviet Union agree that an objective of their policies is to remove the danger of nuclear war and of the use of nuclear weapons.

Accordingly, the parties agree that they will act in such a manner as to prevent the development of situations capable of causing a dangerous exacerbation of their relations, as to avoid military confrontations, and as to exclude the outbreak of nuclear war between them and between either of the parties and other countries.

ARTICLE II

The parties agree, in accordance with Article I and to realize the objective stated in that article, to proceed from the premise that each party will refrain from the threat or use of force against the other party, against the allies of the other party and against other countries, in circumstances which may endanger international peace and security. The parties agree that they will be guided by these considerations in the formulation of their foreign policies and in their actions in the field of international relations.

ARTICLE III

The parties undertake to develop their relations with each other and with other countries in a way consistent with the purposes of this agreement.

ARTICLE IV

If at any time relations between the parties or between either party and other countries appear to involve the risk of a nuclear conflict, or if relations between countries not parties to this agreement appear to involve the risk of nuclear war between the United States of America and the Union of Soviet Socialist Republics or between either party and other countries, the United States and the Soviet Union, acting in accordance with the provisions of this agreement, shall immediately enter into urgent consultations with each other and make every effort to avert this risk.

ARTICLE V

Each party shall be free to inform the Security Council of the United Nations, the Secretary General of the United Nations and the governments of allied or other countries of the progress and outcome of consultations initiated in accordance with Article IV of this agreement.

ARTICLE VI

Nothing in this agreement shall affect or impair:

(a) the inherent right of individual or collective self-defense as envisaged by Article 51 of the Charter of the United Nations,

(b) the provisions of the Charter of the United Nations, including those relating to the maintenance or restoration of international peace and security, and

(c) the obligations undertaken by either party towards its allies or other countries in treaties, agreements, and other appropriate documents.

ARTICLE VII

This agreement shall be of unlimited duration.

ARTICLE VIII

This agreement shall enter into force upon signature.

Done at Washington on 22 June 1973, in two copies, each in the English and Russian languages, both texts being equally authentic.

For the United States
of America:

RICHARD NIXON

*President of the United
States of America*

For the Union of Soviet
Socialist Republics:

LEONID I. BREZHNEV

*General Secretary of the
Central Committee, CPSU*

JOINT U.S.-SOVIET STATEMENT AND AGREEMENT
ISSUED AT VLADIVOSTOK, 24 NOVEMBER 1974 *

Joint U.S.-Soviet Statement

During their working meeting in the area of Vladivostok on 23–24 November 1974, the President of the United States of America Gerald R. Ford, and General Secretary of the Central Committee of the CPSU L. I. Brezhnev discussed in detail the question of further limitations of strategic offensive arms.

They reaffirmed the great significance that both the United States and the U.S.S.R. attach to the limitation of strategic offensive arms. They are convinced that a long-term agreement on this question would be a significant contribution to improving relations between the United States and the U.S.S.R. to reducing the danger of war and to enhancing world peace. Having noted the value of previous agreements on this question, including the Interim Agreement of 26 May 1972, they reaffirm the intention to conclude a new agreement on the limitation of strategic offensive arms, to last through 1985.

As a result of the exchange of views on the substance of such a new agreement, the President of the United States of America and the General Secretary of the Central Committee of the CPSU concluded that favorable prospects exist for completing the work on this agreement in 1975.

Agreement was reached that further negotiations will be based on the following provisions:

1. The new agreement will incorporate the relevant provisions of the Interim Agreement of 26 May 1972, which will remain in force until October 1977.

2. The new agreement will cover the period from October 1977 through 31 December 1985.

3. Based on the principle of equality and equal security, the new agreement will include the following limitations:

a. Both sides will be entitled to have a certain agreed aggregate number of strategic delivery vehicles;

b. Both sides will be entitled to have a certain agreed aggregate number of ICBMs and SLBMs [intercontinental ballistic missiles; submarine-launched ballistic missiles] equipped with multiple independently targetable warheads (MIRVs).

---

* Source: *Department of State Bulletin*, vol. 71, no. 1852 (23 December 1974), pp. 879-881.

4. The new agreement will include a provision for further negotiations beginning no later than 1980–81 on the question of further limitations and possible reductions of strategic arms in the period after 1985.

5. Negotiations between the delegations of the United States and U.S.S.R. to work out the new agreement incorporating the foregoing points will resume in Geneva in January 1975.

Joint U.S.-Soviet Communiqué

In accordance with the previously announced agreement, a working meeting between the President of the United States of America, Gerald R. Ford, and the General Secretary of the Central Committee of the Communist Party of the Soviet Union, L. I. Brezhnev, took place in the area of Vladivostok on 23 and 24 November 1974. Taking part in the talks were the secretary of state of the United States of America and assistant to the President for national security affairs, Henry A. Kissinger, and member of the Politburo of the Central Committee of the CPSU and minister of foreign affairs of the U.S.S.R., A. A. Gromyko.

They discussed a broad range of questions dealing with American-Soviet relations and the current international situation.

Also taking part in the talks were:

On the American side, Walter J. Stoessel, Jr., ambassador of the U.S. to the U.S.S.R.; Helmut Sonnenfeldt, counselor of the Department of State; Arthur A. Hartman, assistant secretary of state for European affairs; Lieutenant General Brent Scowcroft, deputy assistant to the President for national security affairs; and William Hyland, official of the Department of State.

On the Soviet side, A. F. Dobrynin, ambassador of the U.S.S.R. to the U.S.; A. M. Aleksandrov, assistant to the general secretary of the Central Committee of the CPSU; and G. M. Korniyenko, member of the collegium of the Ministry of Foreign Affairs of the U.S.S.R.

I

The United States of America and the Soviet Union reaffirmed their determination to develop further their relations in the direction defined by the fundamental joint decisions and basic treaties and agreements concluded between the two states in recent years.

They are convinced that the course of American-Soviet relations, directed towards strengthening world peace, deepening the relaxation of international tensions, and expanding mutually beneficial cooperation of states with different social systems meets the vital interests of the peoples of both states and other peoples.

Both sides consider that based on the agreements reached between them important results have been achieved in fundamentally reshaping American-Soviet relations on the basis of peaceful coexistence and equal security. These results are a solid foundation for progress in reshaping Soviet-American relations.

Accordingly, they intend to continue, without a loss in momentum, to expand the scale and intensity of their cooperative efforts in all spheres as set forth in the agreements they have signed so that the process of improving relations between the United States and the U.S.S.R. will continue without interruption and will become irreversible.

Mutual determination was expressed to carry out strictly and fully the mutual obligations undertaken by the United States and the U.S.S.R. in accordance with the treaties and agreements concluded between them.

II

Special consideration was given in the course of the talks to a pivotal aspect of Soviet-American relations: measures to eliminate the threat of war and to halt the arms race.

Both sides reaffirm that the agreements reached between the United States and the U.S.S.R. on the prevention of nuclear war and the limitation of strategic arms are a good beginning in the process of creating guarantees against the outbreak of nuclear conflict and war in general. They expressed their deep belief in the necessity of promoting this process and expressed their hope that other states would contribute to it as well. For their part the United States and the U.S.S.R. will continue to exert vigorous efforts to achieve this historic task.

A joint statement on the question of limiting strategic offensive arms is being released separately.

Both sides stressed once again the importance and necessity of a serious effort aimed at preventing the dangers connected with the spread of nuclear weapons in the world. In this connection they stressed the importance of increasing the effectiveness of the Treaty on the Nonproliferation of Nuclear Weapons.

It was noted that, in accordance with previous agreements, initial contacts were established between representatives of the United States and of the U.S.S.R. on questions related to underground nuclear explosions for peaceful purposes, to measures to overcome the dangers of the use of environmental modification techniques for military purposes, as well as measures dealing with the most dangerous lethal means of chemical warfare. It was agreed to continue an active search for mutually acceptable solutions of these questions.

III

In the course of the meeting an exchange of views was held on a number of international issues: special attention was given to negotiations already in progress in which the two sides are participants and which are designed to remove existing sources of tension and to bring about the strengthening of international security and world peace.

Having reviewed the situation at the Conference on Security and Cooperation in Europe, both sides concluded that there is a possibility for its early successful conclusion. They proceed from the assumption that the results achieved in the course of the conference will permit its conclusion at the highest level and thus be commensurate with its importance in ensuring the peaceful future of Europe.

The United States and the U.S.S.R. also attach high importance to the negotiations on mutual reduction of forces and armaments and associated measures in Central Europe. They agree to contribute actively to the search for mutually acceptable solutions on the basis of the principle of undiminished security for any of the parties and the prevention of unilateral military advantages.

Having discussed the situation existing in the Eastern Mediterranean, both sides state their firm support for the independence, sovereignty, and territorial integrity of Cyprus and will make every effort in this direction. They consider that a just settlement of the Cyprus question must be based on the strict implementation of the resolutions adopted by the Security Council and the General Assembly of the United Nations regarding Cyprus.

In the course of the exchange of views on the Middle East both sides expressed their concern with regard to the dangerous situation in that region. They reaffirmed their intention to make every effort to promote a solution of the key issues of a just and lasting peace in that area on the basis of the United Nations Resolution 338, taking into account the legitimate interests of all the peoples of the area, including the Palestinian people, and respect for the right to independent existence of all states in the area.

The sides believe that the Geneva Conference should play an important part in the establishment of a just and lasting peace in the Middle East, and should resume its work as soon as possible.

IV

The state of relations was reviewed in the field of commercial, economic, scientific, and technical ties between the United States and the U.S.S.R. Both sides confirmed the great importance which further progress in these fields would have for Soviet-American relations, and expressed their firm intention to continue the broadening and deepening of mutually advantageous cooperation.

The two sides emphasized the special importance accorded by them to the development on a long-term basis of commercial and economic cooperation, including mutually beneficial large-scale projects. They believe that such commercial and economic cooperation will serve the cause of increasing the stability of Soviet-American relations.

Both sides noted with satisfaction the progress in the implementation of agreements and in the development of ties and cooperation between the United States and the U.S.S.R. in the fields of science, technology, and culture. They are convinced that the continued expansion of such cooperation will benefit the peoples of both countries and will be an important contribution to the solution of world-wide scientific and technical problems.

The talks were held in an atmosphere of frankness and mutual understanding, reflecting the constructive desire of both sides to strengthen and develop further the peaceful cooperative relationship between the United States and the U.S.S.R. and to ensure progress in the solution of outstanding international problems in the interests of preserving and strengthening peace.

The results of the talks provided a convincing demonstration of the practical value of Soviet-American summit meetings and their exceptional importance in the shaping of a new relationship between the United States of America and the Soviet Union.

President Ford reaffirmed the invitation to L. I. Brezhnev to pay an official visit to the United States in 1975. The exact date of the visit will be agreed upon later.

For the United States of America:

GERALD R. FORD

President of the United States of America

24 November 1974

For the Union of Soviet Socialist Republics:

LEONID I. BREZHNEV

General Secretary of the Central Committee, CPSU

3

DETENTE: TWO STATEMENTS

**DETENTE WITH THE SOVIET UNION:
THE REALITY OF COMPETITION AND THE
IMPERATIVE OF COOPERATION ***

Henry A. Kissinger

In this statement (prepared for testimony before the U.S. Senate Committee on Foreign Relations on 19 September 1974), Secretary of State Henry A. Kissinger presents a rationale for the Nixon Administration's policy of pursuing détente with the Soviet Union. Kissinger contends that the maintenance of a peaceful international order requires a constructive relationship between the two principal superpowers: given the vast nuclear power both possess, there seems little choice. Because significant, deeply rooted differences separate the United States and the U.S.S.R., the object of détente policy is to modify present competition with the long-term aim of creating a more cooperative relationship between the two nations. Kissinger argues that by engaging in a wide spectrum of negotiations embracing many issues, progress will be fostered toward the goal of the Soviet Union's accepting the need for accommodation and restraint, a prerequisite for establishing a constructive relationship. The late 1960s and early 1970s proved an ideal period in which to embrace this policy, and Kissinger outlines the improvements in relations that have been achieved as well as the pitfalls that must be avoided.

---

* Source: *Department of State Bulletin* (14 October 1974), pp. 505-519.

153

I. The Challenge

Since the dawn of the nuclear age the world's fears of holocaust and its hopes for peace have turned on the relationship between the United States and the Soviet Union.

Throughout history men have sought peace but suffered war; all too often, deliberate decisions or miscalculations have brought violence and destruction to a world yearning for tranquillity. Tragic as the consequences of violence may have been in the past, the issue of peace and war takes on unprecedented urgency when, for the first time in history, two nations have the capacity to destroy mankind. In the nuclear age, as President Eisenhower pointed out two decades ago, "there is no longer any alternative to peace."

The destructiveness of modern weapons defines the necessity of the task; deep differences in philosophy and interests between the United States and the Soviet Union point up its difficulty. These differences do not spring from misunderstanding or personalities or transitory factors:

- They are rooted in history and in the way the two countries have developed.

- They are nourished by conflicting values and opposing ideologies.

- They are expressed in diverging national interests that produce political and military competition.

- They are influenced by allies and friends whose association we value and whose interests we will not sacrifice.

Paradox confuses our perception of the problem of peaceful coexistence: if peace is pursued to the exclusion of any other goal, other values will be compromised and perhaps lost; but if unconstrained rivalry leads to nuclear conflict, these values, along with everything else, will be destroyed in the resulting holocaust. However competitive they may be at some levels of their relationship, both major nuclear powers must base their policies on the premise that neither can expect to impose its will on the other without running an intolerable risk. The challenge of our time is to reconcile the reality of competition with the imperative of coexistence.

There can be no peaceful international order without a constructive relationship between the United States and the Soviet Union. There will be no international stability unless both the Soviet Union and the United States conduct themselves with restraint and unless they use their enormous power for the benefit of mankind.

Thus we must be clear at the outset on what the term "détente" entails. It is the search for a more constructive relationship with the Soviet Union reflecting the realities I have outlined. It is a continuing process, not a final condition that has been or can be realized at any one specific point in time. And it has been pursued by successive American leaders, though the means have varied as have world conditions.

Some fundamental principles guide this policy:

- The United States cannot base its policy solely on Moscow's good intentions. But neither can we insist that all forward movement must await a convergence of American and Soviet purposes. We seek, regardless of Soviet intentions, to serve peace through a systematic resistance to pressure and conciliatory responses to moderate behavior.

- We must oppose aggressive actions and irresponsible behavior. But we must not seek confrontations lightly.

- We must maintain a strong national defense while recognizing that in the nuclear age the relationship between military strength and politically usable power is the most complex in all history.

- Where the age-old antagonism between freedom and tyranny is concerned, we are not neutral. But other imperatives impose limits on our ability to produce internal changes in foreign countries. Consciousness of our limits is recognition of the necessity of peace—not moral callousness. The preservation of human life and human society are moral values, too.

- We must be mature enough to recognize that to be stable a relationship must provide advantages to both sides and that the most constructive international relationships are those in which both parties perceive an element of gain. Moscow will benefit from certain measures, just as we will from others. The balance cannot be struck on each issue every day, but only over the whole range of relations and over a period of time.

II. The Course of Soviet-American Relations

In the first two decades of the postwar period U.S.-Soviet relations were characterized by many fits and starts. Some encouraging developments followed the Cuban missile crisis of 1962, for example. But at the end of the decade the invasion of Czechoslovakia brought progress to a halt and threw a deepening shadow over East-West relations.

During those difficult days some were tempted to conclude that antagonism was the central feature of the relationship and that U.S. policy—even while the Vietnam agony raised questions about the readiness of the American people to sustain a policy of confrontation—had to be geared to this grim reality. Others recommended a basic change of policy; there was a barrage of demands to hold an immediate summit to establish a better atmosphere, to launch the SALT talks [Strategic Arms Limitation Talks], and to end the decades-old trade discrimination against the Soviet Union, which was widely criticized as anachronistic, futile, and counterproductive.

These two approaches reflected the extremes of the debate that had dominated most of the postwar period; they also revealed deep-seated differences between the American and the Soviet reactions to the process of international relations.

For many Americans, tensions and enmity in international relations are anomalies, the cause of which is attributed either to deliberate malice or to misunderstanding. Malice is to be combated by force, or at least isolation; misunderstanding is to be removed by the strenuous exercise of good will. Communist states, on the other hand, regard tensions as inevitable by-products of a struggle between opposing social systems.

Most Americans perceive relations between states as either friendly or hostile, both defined in nearly absolute terms. Soviet foreign policy, by comparison, is conducted in a gray area heavily influenced by the Soviet conception of the balance of forces. Thus Soviet diplomacy is never free of tactical pressures or adjustments, and it is never determined in isolation from the prevailing military balance. For Moscow, East-West contacts and negotiations are in part designed to promote Soviet influence abroad, especially in Western Europe—and to gain formal acceptance of those elements of the status quo most agreeable to Moscow.

The issue, however, is not whether peace and stability serve Soviet purposes, but whether they serve our own. Indeed, to the extent that our attention focuses largely on Soviet intentions we create a latent vulnerability. If détente can be justified only by a basic change in Soviet motivation, the temptation becomes overwhelming to base U.S.-Soviet relations not on realistic appraisal but on tenuous hopes: a change in Soviet tone is taken as a sign of a basic change of philosophy. Atmosphere is confused with substance. Policy oscillates between poles of suspicion and euphoria.

Neither extreme is realistic, and both are dangerous. The hopeful view ignores that we and the Soviets are bound to compete for the foreseeable future. The pessimistic view ignores that we have some parallel interests and that we are compelled to coexist. Détente encourages an environment in which competitors can regulate and restrain their differences and ultimately move from competition to cooperation.

A. American Goals. America's aspiration for the kind of political environment we now call détente is not new.

The effort to achieve a more constructive relationship with the Soviet Union is not made in the name of any one administration or one party or for any one period of time. It expresses the continuing desire of the vast majority of the American people for an easing of international tensions and their expectation that any responsible government will strive for peace. No aspect of our policies, domestic or foreign, enjoys more consistent bipartisan support. No aspect is more in the interest of mankind.

In the postwar period, repeated efforts were made to improve our relationship with Moscow. The spirits of Geneva, Camp David, and Glassboro were evanescent moments in a quarter century otherwise marked by tensions and by sporadic confrontation. What is new in the current period of relaxation of tensions is its duration, the scope of the relationship which has evolved, and the continuity and intensity of consultation which it has produced.

A number of factors have produced this change in the international environment. By the end of the sixties and the beginning of the seventies the time was propitious—no matter what administration was in office in the United States—for a major attempt to improve U.S.-Soviet relations. Contradictory tendencies contested for preeminence in Soviet policy; events could have tipped the scales either toward increased aggressiveness or toward conciliation.

- The fragmentation in the Communist world in the 1960s challenged the leading position of the U.S.S.R. and its claim to be the arbiter of orthodoxy. The U.S.S.R. could have reacted by adopting a more aggressive attitude toward the capitalist world in order to assert its militant vigilance; instead, the changing situation and U.S. policy seem to have encouraged Soviet leaders to cooperate in at least a temporary lessening of tension with the West.

- The prospect of achieving a military position of near parity with the United States in strategic forces could have tempted Moscow

157

to use its expanding military capability to strive more determinedly for expansion; in fact, it tempered the militancy of some of its actions and sought to stabilize at least some aspects of the military competition through negotiations.

- The very real economic problems of the U.S.S.R. and Eastern Europe could have reinforced autarkic policies and the tendency to create a closed system; in actuality, the Soviet Union and its allies have come closer to acknowledging the reality of an interdependent world economy.

- Finally, when faced with the hopes of its own people for greater well-being, the Soviet government could have continued to stimulate the suspicions of the cold war to further isolate Soviet society: in fact, it chose—however inadequately and slowly—to seek to calm its public opinion by joining in a relaxation of tensions.

For the United States the choice was clear: To provide as many incentives as possible for those actions by the Soviet Union most conducive to peace and individual well-being and to overcome the swings between illusionary optimism and harsh antagonism that had characterized most of the postwar period. We could capitalize on the tentative beginnings made in the sixties by taking advantage of the compelling new conditions of the seventies.

We sought to explore every avenue toward an honorable and just accommodation while remaining determined not to settle for mere atmospherics. We relied on a balance of mutual interests rather than Soviet intentions. When challenged—such as in the Middle East, the Caribbean, or Berlin—we always responded firmly. And when Soviet policy moved toward conciliation, we sought to turn what may have started as a tactical maneuver into a durable pattern of conduct.

Our approach proceeds from the conviction that, in moving forward across a wide spectrum of negotiations, progress in one area adds momentum to progress in other areas. If we succeed, then no agreement stands alone as an isolated accomplishment vulnerable to the next crisis. We did not invent the interrelationship between issues expressed in the so-called linkage concept; it was a reality because of the range of problems and areas in which the interests of the United States and the Soviet Union impinge on each other. We have looked for progress in a series of agreements settling specific political issues, and we have sought to relate these to a new standard of international conduct appropriate to the dangers of the nuclear age. By acquiring a stake in this network of relationships with the West, the Soviet Union may become more conscious of what it would lose by a return to confrontation. Indeed, it is our hope that it will develop a self-interest in fostering the entire process of relaxation of tensions.

B. The Global Necessities. In the late 1940s, this nation engaged in a great debate about the role it would play in the postwar world. We forged a bipartisan consensus on which our policies were built for more than two decades. By the end of the 1960s, the international environment which molded that consensus had been transformed. What in the fifties had seemed a solid bloc of adversaries had fragmented into competing centers of power and doctrines; old allies had gained new strength and self-assurance; scores of new nations had emerged and formed blocs of their own; and all nations were being swept up in a technology that was compressing the planet and deepening our mutual dependence.

Then as now, it was clear that the international structure formed in the immediate postwar period was in fundamental flux and that a new international system was emerging. America's historic opportunity was to help shape a new set of international relationships—more pluralistic, less dominated by military power, less susceptible to confrontation, more open to genuine cooperation among the free and diverse elements of the globe. This new, more positive international environment is possible only if all the major powers—and especially the world's strongest nuclear powers—anchor their policies in the principles of moderation and restraint. They no longer have the power to dominate; they do have the capacity to thwart. They cannot build the new international structure alone; they can make its realization impossible by their rivalry.

Détente is all the more important because of what the creation of a new set of international relations demands of us with respect to other countries and areas. President Ford has assigned the highest priority to maintaining the vitality of our partnerships in Europe, Asia, and Latin America. Our security ties with our allies are essential, but we also believe that recognition of the interdependence of the contemporary world requires cooperation in many other fields. Cooperation becomes more difficult if the United States is perceived by allied public opinion as an obstacle to peace and if public debate is polarized on the issue of whether friendship with the United States is inconsistent with East-West reconciliation.

One important area for invigorated cooperative action is economic policy. The international economic system has been severely tested. The Middle East war demonstrated dramatically the integral relationship between economics and politics. Clearly, whatever the state of our relations with the U.S.S.R., the international economic agenda must be addressed. But the task would be infinitely more complex if we proceeded in a cold war environment.

International economic problems cut across political dividing lines. All nations, regardless of ideology, face the problems of energy and economic growth, feeding burgeoning populations, regulating the use of the oceans, and preserving the environment.

At a minimum, easing international tensions allows the West to devote more intellectual and material resources to these problems. As security concerns recede, humane concerns come again to the fore. International organizations take on greater significance and responsibility, less obstructed by cold war antagonisms. The climate of lessened tensions even opens prospects for broader collaboration between East and West. It is significant that some of these global issues—such as energy, cooperation in science and health, and the protection of the environment—have already reached the U.S.-Soviet agenda.

In the present period, mankind may be menaced as much by international economic and political chaos as by the danger of war. Avoiding either hazard demands a cooperative world structure for which improved East-West relations are essential.

III. The Evolution of Détente—The Balance of Risks and Incentives

The course of détente has not been smooth or even. As late as 1969, Soviet-American relations were ambiguous and uncertain. To be sure, negotiations on Berlin and SALT had begun. But the tendency toward confrontation appeared dominant.

We were challenged by Soviet conduct in the Middle East ceasefire of August 1970, during the Syrian invasion of Jordan in September 1970, on the question of a possible Soviet submarine base in Cuba, in actions around Berlin, and during the Indo-Pakistani war. Soviet policy seemed directed toward fashioning a détente in bilateral relations with our Western European allies, while challenging the United States.

We demonstrated then, and stand ready to do so again, that America will not yield to pressure or the threat of force. We made clear then, as we do today, that détente cannot be pursued selectively in one area or toward one group of countries only. For us détente is indivisible.

Finally, a breakthrough was made in 1971 on several fronts—in the Berlin settlement, in the SALT talks, in other arms control negotiations—that generated the process of détente. It consists of these elements: An elaboration of principles; political discussions to solve outstanding issues and to reach cooperative agreements; economic relations; and arms control negotiations, particularly those concerning strategic arms.

A. The Elaboration of Principles.

Cooperative relations, in our view, must be more than a series of isolated agreements. They must reflect an acceptance of mutual obligations and of the need for accommodation and restraint.

To set forth principles of behavior in formal documents is hardly to guarantee their observance. But they are reference points against which to judge actions and set goals.

The first of the series of documents is the statement of principles signed in Moscow in 1972. It affirms: (1) the necessity of avoiding confrontation; (2) the imperative of mutual restraint; (3) the rejection of attempts to exploit tensions to gain unilateral advantages; (4) the renunciation of claims of special influence in the world; and (5) the willingness, on this new basis, to coexist peacefully and build a firm long-term relationship.

An Agreement on the Prevention of Nuclear War based on these principles was signed in 1973. It affirms that the objective of the policies of the United States and the U.S.S.R. is to remove the danger of nuclear conflict and the use of nuclear weapons. But it emphasizes that this objective presupposes the renunciation of *any* war or threat of war by the two nuclear superpowers not only against each other but also against allies or third countries. In other words, the principle of restraint is not confined to relations between the United States and the U.S.S.R.; it is explicitly extended to include *all* countries.

These statements of principles are not an American concession; indeed, we have been affirming them unilaterally for two decades. Nor are they a legal contract; rather, they are an aspiration and a yardstick by which we assess Soviet behavior. We have never intended to "rely" on Soviet compliance with every principle; we do seek to elaborate standards of conduct which the Soviet Union would violate only to its cost. And if over the long term the more durable relationship takes hold, the basic principles will give it definition, structure, and hope.

B. Political Dialogue and Cooperative Agreements. One of the features of the current phase of U.S.-Soviet relations is the unprecedented consultation between leaders, either face to face or through diplomatic channels.

Although consultation has reached a level of candor and frequency without precedent, we know that consultation does not guarantee that policies are compatible. It does provide a mechanism for the resolution of differences before they escalate to the point of public confrontation and commit the prestige of both sides.

The channel between the leaders of the two nations has proved its worth in many crises; it reduces the risk that either side might feel driven to act or to react on the basis of incomplete or confusing information. The channel of communication has continued without interruption under President Ford.

But crisis management is not an end in itself. The more fundamental goal is the elaboration of a political relationship which in time will make crises less likely to arise.

It was difficult in the past to speak of a U.S.-Soviet bilateral relationship in any normal sense of the phrase. Trade was negligible. Contacts between various institutions and between the peoples of the two countries were at best sporadic. There were no cooperative efforts in science and technology. Cultural exchange was modest. As a result, there was no tangible inducement toward cooperation and no penalty for aggressive behavior. Today, by joining our efforts even in such seemingly apolitical fields as medical research or environmental protection, we and the Soviets can benefit not only our two peoples but all mankind; in addition, we generate incentives for restraint.

Since 1972 we have concluded agreements on a common effort against cancer, on research to protect the environment, on studying the use of the ocean's resources, on the use of atomic energy for peaceful purposes, on studying methods for conserving energy, on examining construction techniques for regions subject to earthquakes, and on devising new transportation methods. Other bilateral areas for cooperation include an agreement on preventing incidents at sea, an agreement to exchange information and research methods in agriculture, and the training of astronauts for the Soviet-U.S. rendezvous-and-docking mission planned for 1975.

Each project must be judged by the concrete benefits it brings. But in their sum—in their exchange of information and people as well as in their establishment of joint mechanisms—they also constitute a commitment in both countries to work together across a broad spectrum.

C. The Economic Component. During the period of the cold war, economic contact between ourselves and the U.S.S.R. was virtually nonexistent. Even then, many argued that improved economic relations might mitigate international tensions; in fact, there were several congressional resolutions to that effect. But recurrent crises prevented any sustained progress.

The period of confrontation should have left little doubt, however, that economic boycott would not transform the Soviet system or impose upon it a conciliatory foreign policy. The U.S.S.R. was quite prepared to maintain heavy military outlays and to concentrate on capital growth by using the resources of the Communist world alone. Moreover, it proved impossible to mount an airtight boycott in practice since, over time, most if not all the other major industrial countries became involved in trade with the East.

The question, then, became how trade and economic contact—in which the Soviet Union is obviously interested—could serve the purposes of peace. On the one hand, economic relations cannot be separated from the political context. Clearly, we cannot be asked to reward hostile conduct with economic benefits, even if in the process we deny ourselves some commercially profitable opportunities. On the other hand, when political relations begin to normalize, it is difficult to explain why economic relations should not be normalized as well.

We have approached the question of economic relations with deliberation and circumspection and as an act of policy, not primarily of commercial opportunity. As political relations have improved on a broad basis, economic issues have been dealt with on a comparably broad front. A series of interlocking economic agreements with the U.S.S.R. has been negotiated side by side with the political progress already noted. The twenty-five-year-old lend-lease debt was settled; the reciprocal extension of most-favored-nation (MFN) treatment was negotiated, together with safeguards against the possible disruption of our markets and a series of practical arrangements to facilitate the conduct of business in the U.S.S.R. by American firms; our government credit facilities were made available for trade with the U.S.S.R.; and a maritime agreement regulating the carriage of goods has been signed.

These were all primarily regulatory agreements conferring no immediate benefits on the Soviet Union but serving as blueprints for an expanded economic relationship if the political improvement continued.

This approach commanded widespread domestic approval. It was considered a natural outgrowth of political progress. At no time were issues regarding Soviet domestic political practices raised. Indeed, not until *after* the 1972 agreements was the Soviet domestic order invoked as a reason for arresting or reversing the progress so painstakingly achieved. This sudden ex post facto form of linkage raises serious questions:

- For the Soviet Union, it casts doubt on our reliability as a negotiating partner.

- The significance of trade, originally envisaged as only one ingredient of a complex and evolving relationship, is inflated out of all proportion.

- The hoped-for results of policy become transformed into preconditions for any policy at all.

We recognize the depth and validity of the moral concerns expressed by those who oppose, or put conditions on, expanded trade with the U.S.S.R. But a sense of proportion must be maintained about the leverage our economic relations give us with the U.S.S.R.:

- Denial of economic relations cannot by itself achieve what it failed to do when it was part of a determined policy of political and military confrontation.

- The economic bargaining ability of most-favored-nation status is marginal. MFN grants no special privilege to the U.S.S.R.; in fact it is a misnomer, since we have such agreements with over 100 countries. To enact it would be to remove a discriminatory holdover of the days of the cold war. To continue to deny it is more a political than an economic act.

- Trade benefits are not a one-way street; the laws of mutual advantage operate, or there will be no trade.

- The technology that flows to the U.S.S.R. as a result of expanded U.S.-Soviet trade may have a few indirect uses for military production. But with our continuing restrictions on strategic exports, we can maintain adequate controls—and we intend to do so. Moreover, the same technology has been available to the U.S.S.R. and will be increasingly so from other non-Communist sources. Boycott denies us a means of influence and possible commercial gain; it does not deprive the U.S.S.R. of technology.

- The actual and potential flow of credits from the United States represents a tiny fraction of the capital available to the U.S.S.R.

domestically and elsewhere, including Western Europe and Japan. But it does allow us to exercise some influence through our ability to control the scope of trade relationships.

- Over time, trade and investment may leaven the autarkic tendencies of the Soviet system, invite gradual association of the Soviet economy with the world economy, and foster a degree of interdependence that adds an element of stability to the political equation.

D. The Strategic Relationship. We cannot expect to relax international tensions or achieve a more stable international system should the two strongest nuclear powers conduct an unrestrained strategic arms race. Thus, perhaps the single most important component of our policy toward the Soviet Union is the effort to limit strategic weapons competition.

The competition in which we now find ourselves is historically unique:

- Each side has the capacity to destroy civilization as we know it.

- Failure to maintain equivalence could jeopardize not only our freedom but our very survival.

- The lead time for technological innovation is so long, yet the pace of change so relentless, that the arms race and strategic policy itself are in danger of being driven by technological necessity.

- When nuclear arsenals reach levels involving thousands of launchers and over 10,000 warheads, and when the characteristics of the weapons of the two sides are so incommensurable, it becomes difficult to determine what combination of numbers of strategic weapons and performance capabilities would give one side a militarily and politically useful superiority. At a minimum, clear changes in the strategic balance can be achieved only by efforts so enormous and by increments so large that the very attempt would be highly destabilizing.

- The prospect of a decisive military advantage, even if theoretically possible, is politically intolerable; neither side will passively permit a massive shift in the nuclear balance. Therefore the probable outcome of each succeeding round of competition is the restoration of a strategic equilibrium, but at increasingly higher levels of forces.

165

- The arms race is driven by political as well as military factors. While a decisive advantage is hard to calculate, the *appearance* of inferiority—whatever its actual significance—can have serious political consequences. With weapons that are unlikely to be used and for which there is no operational experience, the psychological impact can be crucial. Thus each side has a high incentive to achieve not only the reality but the appearance of equality. In a very real sense each side shapes the military establishment of the other.

If we are driven to it, the United States will sustain an arms race. Indeed, it is likely that the United States would emerge from such a competition with an edge over the Soviet Union in most significant categories of strategic arms. But the political or military benefit which would flow from such a situation would remain elusive. Indeed, after such an evolution it might well be that *both* sides would be worse off than before the race began. The enormous destructiveness of weapons and the uncertainties regarding their effects combine to make the massive use of such weapons increasingly incredible.

The Soviet Union must realize that the overall relationship with the United States will be less stable if strategic balance is sought through unrestrained competitive programs. Sustaining the buildup requires exhortations by both sides that in time may prove incompatible with restrained international conduct. The very fact of a strategic arms race has a high potential for feeding attitudes of hostility and suspicion on both sides, transforming the fears of those who demand more weapons into self-fulfilling prophecies.

The American people can be asked to bear the cost and political instability of a race which is doomed to stalemate only if it is clear that every effort has been made to prevent it. That is why every President since Eisenhower has pursued negotiations for the limitation of strategic arms while maintaining the military programs essential to strategic balance.

There are more subtle strategic reasons for our interest in SALT. Our supreme strategic purpose is the prevention of nuclear conflict through the maintenance of sufficient political and strategic power. Estimates of what constitutes "sufficiency" have been contentious. Our judgments have changed with our experience in deploying these weapons and as the Soviets expanded their own nuclear forces. When in the late 1960s it became apparent that the Soviet Union, for practical purposes, had achieved a kind of rough parity with the United States, we adopted the current strategic doctrine.

We determined that stability required strategic forces invulnerable to attack, thus removing the incentive on either side to strike first. Reality reinforced doctrine. As technology advanced, it became apparent that neither side *could* realistically expect to develop a credible disarming capability against the other except through efforts so gigantic as to represent a major threat to political stability.

One result of our doctrine was basing our strategic planning on the assumption that in the unlikely event of nuclear attack, the President should have a wide range of options available in deciding at what level and against what targets to respond. We designed our strategic forces with a substantial measure of flexibility, so that the U.S. response need not include an attack on the aggressor's cities— thus inviting the destruction of our own—but could instead hit other targets. Translating this capability into a coherent system of planning became a novel, and as yet uncompleted, task of great complexity; but progress has been made. In our view such flexibility enhances the certainty of retaliation and thereby makes an attack less likely. Above all, it preserves the capability for human decision even in the ultimate crisis.

Another, at first seemingly paradoxical, result was a growing commitment to negotiated agreements on strategic arms. SALT became one means by which we and the Soviet Union could enhance stability by setting mutual constraints on our respective forces and by gradually reaching an understanding of the doctrinal considerations that underlie the deployment of nuclear weapons. Through SALT the two sides can reduce the suspicions and fears which fuel strategic competition. SALT, in the American conception, is a means to achieve strategic stability by methods other than the arms race.

Our specific objectives have been:

(1) To break the momentum of ever-increasing levels of armaments;

(2) To control certain qualitative aspects—particularly MIRVs [multiple independently targetable reentry vehicles];

(3) To moderate the pace of new deployments; and

(4) Ultimately, to achieve reductions in force levels.

The SALT agreements already signed represent a major contribution to strategic stability and a significant first step toward a longer term and possibly broader agreement.

When the first agreements in 1972 were signed, the future strategic picture was not bright:

- The Soviet Union was engaged in a dynamic program that had closed the numerical gap in ballistic missiles; they were deploying three types of ICBMs [intercontinental ballistic missiles], at a rate of over 200 annually, and launching on the average eight submarines a year with sixteen ballistic missiles each.

- The United States had ended its numerical buildup in the late 1960s at a level of 1,054 ICBMs and 656 SLBMs [submarine-launched ballistic missiles]. We were emphasizing technological improvements, particularly in MIRVs for the Poseidon and Minuteman missiles. Our replacement systems were intended for the late 1970s and early 1980s.

- By most reasonable measurements of strategic power, we held an important advantage, which still continues. But it was also clear that if existing trends were maintained the Soviet Union would, first, exceed our numerical levels by a considerable margin and then develop the same technologies we had already mastered.

The agreements signed in 1972 which limited antiballistic missile [ABM] defenses and froze the level of ballistic missile forces on both sides represented the essential first step toward a less volatile strategic environment.

- By limiting antiballistic missiles to very low levels of deployment, the United States and the Soviet Union removed a potential source of instability; for one side to build an extensive defense for its cities would inevitably be interpreted by the other as a step toward a first-strike capability. Before seeking a disarming capability, a potential aggressor would want to protect his population centers from incoming nuclear weapons.

- Some have alleged that the interim agreement, which expires in October 1977, penalizes the United States by permitting the Soviet Union to deploy more strategic missile launchers, both land based and sea based, than the United States. Such a view is misleading. When the agreement was signed in May 1972, the Soviet Union *already* possessed more land-based intercontinental ballistic missiles than the United States, and given the pace of its submarine construction program, over the next few years it could have built virtually twice as many nuclear ballistic missile submarines.

The interim agreement confined a dynamic Soviet ICBM program to the then-existing level; it put a ceiling on the heaviest Soviet

ICBMs, the weapons that most concern us; and it set an upper limit on the Soviet submarine-launched ballistic missile program. No American program was abandoned or curtailed. We remained free to deploy multiple warheads. No restraints were placed on bombers —a weapons system in which we have a large advantage. Indeed, the U.S. lead in missile warheads is likely to be somewhat greater at the end of this agreement than at the time of its signature.

The SALT I agreements were the first deliberate attempt by the nuclear superpowers to bring about strategic stability through negotiation. This very process is conducive to further restraint. For example, in the first round of SALT negotiations in 1970–72, both sides bitterly contested the number of ABM sites permitted by the agreement; two years later both sides gave up the right to build more than one site. In sum, we believed when we signed these agreements —and we believe now—that they had reduced the danger of nuclear war, that both sides had acquired some greater interest in restraint, and that the basis had been created for the present effort to reach a broader agreement.

The goal of the current negotiations is an agreement for a ten-year period. We had aimed at extending the interim agreement with adjustments in the numbers and new provisions aimed at dealing with the problem of MIRVs. We found, however, that our negotiation for a two- or three-year extension was constantly threatened with irrelevance by the ongoing programs of both sides that were due to be deployed at the end of or just after the period. This distorted the negotiation and, indeed, devalued its significance. We shifted to the ten-year approach because the period is long enough to cover all current and planned forces but not so long as to invite hedges that would defeat the purpose of an arms control agreement. In fact, it invites a slowing down of planned deployments; further, a period of this length will allow us to set realistic ceilings that represent more than a temporary plateau from which to launch a new cycle in the arms race. Future reductions thus become a realistic objective.

With respect to ceilings on strategic forces, we have defined our goal as essential equivalence in strategic capabilities. What constitutes equivalence involves subjective judgment. Because U.S. and Soviet forces *are* different from each other—in number and size of weapons, in technological refinement, in performance characteristics —they are difficult to compare.

Yet in the negotiations we shall, for example, have to compare heavy bombers, in which the United States is ahead, with heavy missiles, which the U.S.S.R. has emphasized. We shall have to decide whether to insist on equivalence in every category or whether to permit trade-offs in which an advantage in one category compensates for a disadvantage in another. The equation does not remain static. We shall have to relate present advantages to potential development, existing disparities to future trends. This is a difficult process, but we are confident that it can be solved.

Numerical balance is no longer enough. To achieve stability, it will be necessary to consider as well the impact of technological change in such areas as missile throw weight, multiple reentry vehicles, and missile accuracy. The difficulty is that we are dealing not only with disparate levels of forces but with disparate capabilities, MIRV technology being a conspicuous example. The rate of increase of warheads is surging far ahead of the increase in delivery vehicles. This is why the United States considers MIRV limitation an essential component of the next phase of the SALT negotiations. If we fail, the rate of technology will outstrip our capacity to design effective limitations; constantly proliferating warheads of increasing accuracy will overwhelm fixed launchers. An arms race will be virtually inevitable.

The third area for negotiations is the pace of deployments of new or more modern systems. Neither side will remain in its present position without change for another decade. The Soviets are already embarked on testing an initial deployment of a third generation of ICBMs and on a third modification of submarine-launched missiles— though the rate of deployment so far has been far short of the maximum pace of the late sixties.

For our part, we are planning to introduce the Trident system and to replace the B-52 force with the B-1; we also have the capability of improving our Minuteman ICBM system, of adding to the number as well as capability of MIRV missiles, and, if we choose, of deploying mobile systems, land based or airborne. Thus our task is to see whether the two sides can agree to slow the pace of deployment so that modernization is less likely to threaten the overall balance or trigger an excessive reaction.

Finally, a ten-year program gives us a chance to negotiate reductions. Reductions have occasionally been proposed as an alternative to ceilings; they are often seen as more desirable or at least easier to negotiate. In fact, it is a far more complicated problem. Reductions in launchers, for example, if not accompanied by restrictions on the number of warheads, will only magnify vulnerability. The fewer the aim points, the simpler it would be to calculate an attack.

At the same time, reductions will have to proceed from some baseline and must therefore be preceded by agreed ceilings—if only of an interim nature. But a ten-year program should permit the negotiation of stable ceilings resulting from the start of a process of reductions.

Détente is admittedly far from a modern equivalent to the kind of stable peace that characterized most of the nineteenth century. But it is a long step away from the bitter and aggressive spirit that has characterized so much of the postwar period. When linked to such broad and unprecedented projects as SALT, détente takes on added meaning and opens prospects of a more stable peace. SALT agreements should be seen as steps in a process leading to progressively greater stability. It is in that light that SALT and related projects will be judged by history.

IV. An Assessment of Détente

Where has the process of détente taken us so far? What are the principles that must continue to guide our course?

Major progress has been made:

- Berlin's potential as Europe's perennial flashpoint has been substantially reduced through the quadripartite agreement of 1971. The United States considers strict adherence to the agreement a major test of détente.

- We and our allies are launched on negotiations with the Warsaw Pact and other countries in the conference on European security and cooperation, a conference designed to foster East-West dialogue and cooperation.

- At the same time, NATO and the Warsaw Pact are negotiating the reduction of their forces in Central Europe.

- The honorable termination of America's direct military involvement in Indochina and the substantial lowering of regional conflict were made possible by many factors. But this achievement would have been much more difficult, if not impossible, in an era of Soviet and Chinese hostility toward the United States.

- America's principal alliances have proved their durability in a new era. Many feared that détente would undermine them. Instead, détente has helped to place our alliance ties on a more enduring basis by removing the fear that friendship with the

171

United States involved the risk of unnecessary confrontation with the U.S.S.R.

• Many incipient crises with the Soviet Union have been contained or settled without ever reaching the point of public disagreement. The world has been freer of East-West tensions and conflict than in the fifties and sixties.

• A series of bilateral cooperative agreements has turned the U.S.-Soviet relationship in a far more positive direction.

• We have achieved unprecedented agreements in arms limitation and measures to avoid accidental war.

• New possibilities for positive U.S.-Soviet cooperation have emerged on issues in which the globe is interdependent: science and technology, environment, energy.

These accomplishments do not guarantee peace. But they have served to lessen the rigidities of the past and offer hope for a better era. Despite fluctuations, a trend has been established; the character of international politics has been markedly changed.

It is too early to judge conclusively whether this change should be ascribed to tactical considerations. But in a sense, that is immaterial. For whether the change is temporary and tactical, or lasting and basic, our task is essentially the same: To transform that change into a permanent condition devoted to the purpose of a secure peace and mankind's aspiration for a better life. A tactical change sufficiently prolonged becomes a lasting transformation.

But the whole process can be jeopardized if it is taken for granted. As the cold war recedes in memory, détente can come to seem so natural that it appears safe to levy progressively greater demands on it. The temptation to combine détente with increasing pressure on the Soviet Union will grow. Such an attitude would be disastrous. We would not accept it from Moscow; Moscow will not accept it from us. We will finally wind up again with the cold war and fail to achieve either peace or any humane goal.

To be sure, the process of détente raises serious issues for many people. Let me deal with these in terms of the principles which underlie our policy.

First, if détente is to endure, both sides must benefit.

There is no question that the Soviet Union obtains benefits from détente. On what other grounds would the tough-minded members of the Politburo sustain it? But the essential point surely must be that détente serves American and world interests as well. If these coincide with some Soviet interests, this will only strengthen the durability of the process.

On the global scale, in terms of the conventional measures of power, influence, and position, our interests have not suffered—they have generally prospered. In many areas of the world, the influence and the respect we enjoy are greater than was the case for many years. It is also true that Soviet influence and presence are felt in many parts of the world. But this is a reality that would exist without détente. The record shows that détente does not deny us the opportunity to react to it and to offset it.

Our bilateral relations with the U.S.S.R. are beginning to proliferate across a broad range of activities in our societies. Many of the projects now under way are in their infancy; we have many safeguards against unequal benefits—in our laws, in the agreements themselves, and in plain common sense. Of course, there are instances where the Soviet Union has obtained some particular advantage. But we seek in each agreement or project to provide for benefits that are mutual. We attempt to make sure that there are trade-offs among the various programs that are implemented. Americans surely are the last who need fear hard bargaining or lack confidence in competition.

Second, building a new relationship with the Soviet Union does not entail any devaluation of traditional alliance relations.

Our approach to relations with the U.S.S.R has always been, and will continue to be, rooted in the belief that the cohesion of our alliances, and particularly the Atlantic alliance, is a precondition to establishing a more constructive relationship with the U.S.S.R.

Crucial, indeed unique, as may be our concern with Soviet power, we do not delude ourselves that we should deal with it alone. When we speak of Europe and Japan as representing centers of power and influence, we describe not merely an observable fact but an indispensable element in the equilibrium needed to keep the world at peace. The cooperation and partnership between us transcend formal agreements; they reflect values and traditions not soon, if ever, to be shared with our adversaries.

Inevitably, a greater sense of drama accompanies our dealings with the Soviet Union, because the central issues of war and peace cannot be other than dramatic. It was precisely a recognition of this fact and our concern that alliance relations not be taken for granted that led to the American initiative in April 1973 to put new emphasis on our traditional associations. We sought political acts of will which would transcend the technical issues at hand, symbolize our enduring goals, and thus enhance our fundamental bonds. Much has been accomplished. The complications attendant to adapting U.S.-European relations should not be confused with their basic character. We were tested in difficult conditions that do not affect our central purposes. Today relations with Europe and Japan are strong and improving. We have made progress in developing common positions on security, détente, and energy. The experience of the past year has demonstrated that there is no contradiction between vigorous, organic alliance relations and a more positive relationship with adversaries; indeed, they are mutually reinforcing.

Third, the emergence of more normal relations with the Soviet Union must not undermine our resolve to maintain our national defense.

There is a tendency in democratic societies to relax as dangers seem to recede; there is an inclination to view the maintenance of strength as incompatible with relaxation of tensions rather than its precondition. But this is primarily a question of leadership. We shall attempt to be vigilant to the dangers facing America. This administration will not be misled—or mislead—on issues of national defense. At the same time, we do not accept the proposition that we need crises to sustain our defense. A society that needs artificial crises to do what is needed for survival will soon find itself in mortal danger.

Fourth, we must know what can and cannot be achieved in changing human conditions in the East.

The question of dealing with Communist governments has troubled the American people and the Congress since 1917. There has always been a fear that by working with a government whose internal policies differ so sharply with our own we are in some manner condoning these policies or encouraging their continuation. Some argue that until there is a genuine "liberalization"—or signs of serious progress in this direction—all elements of conciliation in Soviet policy must be regarded as temporary and tactical. In that view, demands for internal changes must be the precondition for the pursuit of a relaxation of tensions with the Soviet Union.

Our view is different. We shall insist on responsible international behavior by the Soviet Union and use it as the primary index of our relationship. Beyond this we will use our influence to the maximum to alleviate suffering and to respond to humane appeals. We know what we stand for, and we shall leave no doubt about it.

Both as a government and as a people we *have* made the attitude

174

of the American people clear on countless occasions in ways that have produced results. I believe that both the executive and the Congress, each playing its proper role, have been effective. With respect to the specific issue of emigration:

- The education exit tax of 1971 is no longer being collected. We have been assured that it will not be reapplied.

- Hardship cases submitted to the Soviet Government have been given increased attention, and remedies have been forthcoming in many well-known instances.

- The volume of Jewish emigration has increased from a trickle to tens of thousands.

- And we are now moving toward an understanding that should significantly diminish the obstacles to emigration and ease the hardship of prospective emigrants.

We have accomplished much. But we cannot demand that the Soviet Union, in effect, suddenly reverse five decades of Soviet, and centuries of Russian, history. Such an attempt would be futile and at the same time hazard all that has already been achieved. Changes in Soviet society have already occurred, and more will come. But they are most likely to develop through an evolution that can best go forward in an environment of decreasing international tensions. A renewal of the cold war will hardly encourage the Soviet Union to change its emigration policies or adopt a more benevolent attitude toward dissent.

V. Agenda for the Future

Détente is a process, not a permanent achievement. The agenda is full and continuing. Obviously the main concern must be to reduce the sources of potential conflict. This requires efforts in several inter-related areas:

- The military competition in all its aspects must be subject to increasingly firm restraints by both sides.

- Political competition, especially in moments of crisis, must be guided by the principles of restraint set forth in the documents described earlier. Crises there will be, but the United States and the Soviet Union have a special obligation deriving from the unimaginable military power that they wield and represent. Exploitation of crisis situations for unilateral gain is not acceptable.

175

- Restraint in crises must be augmented by cooperation in removing the causes of crises. There have been too many instances, notably in the Middle East, which demonstrate that policies of unilateral advantage sooner or later run out of control and lead to the brink of war, if not beyond.

- The process of negotiations and consultation must be continuous and intense. But no agreement between the nuclear superpowers can be durable if made over the heads of other nations which have a stake in the outcome. We should not seek to impose peace; we can, however, see that our own actions and conduct are conducive to peace.

In the coming months we shall strive:

- To complete the negotiations for comprehensive and equitable limitations on strategic arms until at least 1985;

- To complete the multilateral negotiations on mutual force reductions in Central Europe, so that security will be enhanced for all the countries of Europe;

- To conclude the conference on European security and cooperation in a manner that promotes both security and human aspirations;

- To continue the efforts to limit the spread of nuclear weapons to additional countries without depriving those countries of the peaceful benefits of atomic energy;

- To complete ratification of the recently negotiated treaty banning underground nuclear testing by the United States and U.S.S.R. above a certain threshold;

- To begin negotiations on the recently agreed effort to overcome the possible dangers of environmental modification techniques for military purposes; and

- To resolve the longstanding attempts to cope with the dangers of chemical weaponry.

We must never forget that the process of détente depends ultimately on habits and modes of conduct that extend beyond the letter of agreements to the spirit of relations as a whole. This is why the whole process must be carefully nurtured.

In cataloging the desirable, we must take care not to jeopardize what is attainable. We must consider what alternative policies are available and what their consequences would be. And the implications of alternatives must be examined not just in terms of a single issue but for how they might affect the entire range of Soviet-American relations and the prospects for world peace.

We must assess not only individual challenges to détente but also their cumulative impact:

If we justify each agreement with Moscow only when we can show unilateral gain,

If we strive for an elusive strategic "superiority,"

If we systematically block benefits to the Soviet Union,

If we try to transform the Soviet system by pressure,

If, in short, we look for final results before we agree to any results, then we would be reviving the doctrines of liberation and massive retaliation of the 1950s. And we would do so at a time when Soviet physical power and influence on the world are greater than a quarter century ago when those policies were devised and failed. The futility of such a course is as certain as its danger.

Let there be no question, however, that Soviet actions could destroy détente as well:

If the Soviet Union uses détente to strengthen its military capacity in all fields,

If in crises it acts to sharpen tension,

If it does not contribute to progress toward stability,

If it seeks to undermine our alliances,

If it is deaf to the urgent needs of the least developed and the emerging issues of interdependence, then it in turn tempts a return to the tensions and conflicts we have made such efforts to overcome. The policy of confrontation has worked for neither of the superpowers.

We have insisted toward the Soviet Union that we cannot have the atmosphere of détente without the substance. It is equally clear that the substance of détente will disappear in an atmosphere of hostility.

We have profound differences with the Soviet Union—in our values, our methods, our vision of the future. But it is these very differences which compel any responsible administration to make a major effort to create a more constructive relationship.

We face an opportunity that was not possible twenty-five years, or even a decade, ago. If that opportunity is lost, its moment will not quickly come again. Indeed, it may not come at all.

177

As President Kennedy pointed out: "For in the final analysis our most basic common link is that we all inhabit this small planet. We all breathe the same air. We all cherish our children's future. And we are all mortal." (President Kennedy's commencement address at American University, Washington, D.C., on 10 June 1963.)

REPORT TO THE TWENTY-FIFTH CONGRESS OF THE COMMUNIST PARTY OF THE SOVIET UNION, 24 FEBRUARY 1976 *

Leonid I. Brezhnev

Leonid I. Brezhnev, general secretary of the Central Committee of the Communist Party of the Soviet Union, discusses the international objectives of the Soviet Union and emphasizes a basic goal of pursuing peace through peaceful coexistence with the United States and other Western nations. If both the U.S. and the U.S.S.R. work toward the settlement of disputes by pacific means, a sound basis for good future relations will be established. Détente, as manifested by various treaties and agreements, has created a solid political and juridical foundation for mutually beneficial cooperation, and constitutes a step toward achieving amicable, equal relations between these two nations. Brezhnev discusses additional areas where progress is needed. Yet, he also avers that these agreements will not impinge on fundamental historic realities: they will actually strengthen the inevitable growth of Socialist and Communist construction.

In the present conditions, our party's activity on the international scene is exceptionally broad and varied. In shaping our foreign policy, we now have to reckon, in one way or another, with the state of affairs in virtually every spot on the globe. But, naturally, the closest to us Communists, to our minds and hearts, is that part of the world where Communist ideals—freedom from exploitation and oppression, full power of the working people, development of Socialist democracy, flowering of culture and uplift of the well-being of the broad masses, equality and fraternity of all peoples and nationalities—are being embodied in practice. It is natural, therefore, that our party's Central Committee and the Central Committee Political Bureau have through-

* Source: Soviet Embassy Information Department, *News and Views from the U.S.S.R.* (24 February 1976), pp. 1-27.

out the period under review, as before, devoted attention first and foremost to relations with the Socialist states. There has hardly been a political bureau sitting that did not deliberate questions related to strengthening the unity and developing cooperation with the fraternal countries and consolidating our common international positions.

And these positions are growing stronger from year to year. No impartial person can deny that the Socialist countries' influence on world affairs is becoming ever stronger and deeper. That, comrades, is a great boon to mankind as a whole, to all those who aspire to freedom, equality, independence, peace, and progress.

In the Socialist countries, the past five years have seen steady progress and confident advance to developed Socialist society, to communism. Along with their further political consolidation, there has been rapid growth of social production and of their peoples' material and cultural standards.

The ties between the Socialist states are becoming ever closer with the flowering of each Socialist nation and the strengthening of their sovereignty, and elements of community are increasing in their policy, economy, and social life. There is a gradual leveling up of their development. This process of a gradual drawing together of Socialist countries is now operating quite definitely as an objective law.

Of course, much depends on the policy of the ruling parties and their ability to safeguard unity, to combat isolation and national exclusiveness, to honor the common international tasks, and to act jointly in performing them.

Thanks to their unity, solidarity, and mutual support, the Socialist countries have succeeded in fulfilling major tasks in the past five years, achieving what they had long been working for.

*   *   *

Struggle to consolidate the principles of peaceful coexistence, to assure lasting peace, to reduce, and later also to eliminate, the danger of another world war was, and remains, the main element of our policy towards the capitalist states. It may be noted that considerable progress has been achieved in this area in the past five years.

The passage from cold war, from the explosive confrontation of the two worlds, to détente was largely connected with changes in the correlation of world forces. But much effort was required for people —especially those responsible for the policy of states—to become accustomed to the thought that not brinkmanship but negotiation of disputed questions, not confrontation but peaceful cooperation, is the natural state of things.

179

A big part here was played by the fact that our party succeeded in accurately defining the main practical tasks of consolidating international security and presenting them at its Twenty-fourth Congress in the Peace Program. The very first foreign-political actions of Soviet power based on the platform of the peaceful coexistence of states with different social systems showed the peoples of the world, as Lenin put it, "the only correct way out of the difficulties, chaos, and danger of wars" (*Collected Works,* vol. 33, p. 357). Invariably mindful of this platform and acting on Lenin's behests and the half-century's experience of its foreign policy of peace, our party advanced the Peace Program at its Twenty-fourth Congress. This program showed the realistic way to end the cold war and set clear objectives in the struggle to replace the danger of wars with peaceful cooperation.

The facts have borne out the program's timeliness and realism. And though world peace is by no means guaranteed as yet, we have every reason to declare that the improvement of the international climate is convincing evidence that lasting peace is not merely a good intention, but an entirely realistic objective. And we can and must continue to work tirelessly in the name of achieving it.

*   *   *

Comrades, the turn for the better in our relations with the United States of America, the largest power of the capitalist world, has, of course, been decisive in reducing the danger of another world war and in consolidating peace. This has beyond question contributed to the improvement of the international climate in general, and that of Europe in particular. Acting in complete accord with the guidelines set by the Twenty-fourth Congress, we have devoted very great attention to the objective of improving relations with the United States.

As a result of the negotiations with U.S. President Nixon in Moscow and Washington, and later of the meetings with President Ford in Vladivostok and Helsinki, important and fundamental mutual understanding has been reached between the leaders of the Soviet Union and the United States on the necessity of developing peaceful equal relations between the two countries. This is reflected in a whole system of Soviet-U.S. treaties, agreements, and other documents. Unquestionably the most important of these are "The Basic Principles of Relations between the United States of America and the Union of Soviet Socialist Republics," the "Agreement between the United States of America and the Union of Soviet Socialist Republics on the Prevention of Nuclear War," and the series of strategic arms limitation agreements.[1] What is the main significance of these documents? Cumulatively, they have laid a solid political and juridical foundation for greater mutually beneficial cooperation between the U.S.S.R. and the U.S. in line with the principles of peaceful coexistence. To a certain extent they have lessened the danger of nuclear war. Precisely in this we see the main result of the development of Soviet-U.S. relations in the past five years.

There are good prospects for our relations with the United States in the future as well—to the extent to which they will continue to develop on this jointly created realistic basis when, given the obvious differences between the class nature of the two states and between their ideologies, there is the firm intention to settle differences and disputes not by force, not by threats or saber rattling, but by peaceful political means.

In recent years, our relations with the United States have been developing in many areas. There is a lively exchange of delegations, including parliamentary, and cultural exchanges have become more active. Many Soviet-U.S. agreements have been concluded, envisaging expansion of mutually beneficial cooperation in a variety of economic, scientific, technical, and cultural areas. Most of them have already come into force and are being put into practice with obvious benefits for both sides, and, more important still, for the mutual understanding of the Soviet and U.S. peoples.

The essentially positive development of Soviet-U.S. relations in recent years is, however, complicated by a number of serious factors. Influential forces in the United States that have no stake either in improving relations with the Soviet Union or in international détente as a whole, are trying to impair it. They portray the policy of the Soviet Union in a false light and refer to an imaginary "Soviet threat" to urge a new intensification of the arms race in the U.S. and in NATO. We may recall that there have also been attempts to interfere in our internal affairs in connection with the adoption of U.S. discriminatory measures in the field of trade. Naturally, we could not and will not suffer that sort of thing, that is not the kind of language one can use with the Soviet Union. By now, I think, this is clear to all.

It is no secret that some of the difficulties stem from those aspects of Washington policy which jeopardize the freedom and independence of peoples and constitute gross interference in their internal affairs on the side of the forces of oppression and reaction. We have opposed and will continue to oppose such actions. At the same time I want to emphasize once more that the Soviet Union is

---

1 These documents appear in Part Two of this volume.

firmly determined to follow the line of further improving Soviet-U.S. relations in strict accordance with the letter and spirit of the agreements reached and commitments taken, in the interests of both peoples and peace on earth.

*   *   *

Efforts to end the arms race and to promote disarmament are and remain—as the Peace Program requires—one of the main trends in the foreign-political activity of the Central Committee of the Communist Party of the Soviet Union and the Soviet government. Today, this objective is more vital than ever. Mankind is tired of sitting upon mountains of arms, yet the arms race spurred on by aggressive imperialist groups is becoming more intensive.

The main motive for the arms race given by its advocates is a so-called Soviet threat. They invoke this motive when they want to drag through a larger military budget, reducing allocations for social needs, and when new types of deadly weapons are being developed, and when they try to justify NATO's military activity. In fact, of course, there is no Soviet threat either in the West or in the East. It is all a monstrous lie from beginning to end. The Soviet Union has not the slightest intention of attacking anyone. The Soviet Union does not need war. The Soviet Union does not increase its military budget, and, far from reducing, is steadily augmenting allocations for improving the people's well-being. Our country is consistently and staunchly fighting for peace, and making one concrete proposal after another aimed at arms reductions and disarmament.

The Soviet Communists are proud of having undertaken the difficult but noble mission of standing in the front ranks of the fighters striving to deliver the peoples from the danger of the continuing arms race. Our party calls on all the peoples, all countries, to unite their efforts and end this perilous process. General and complete disarmament was and remains our ultimate goal in this field. At the same time, the Soviet Union is doing all it can to achieve progress along separate sections of the road leading to this goal.

An International Convention on Banning and Destroying Bacteriological Weapons, based on a project submitted by the Soviet Union and other Socialist countries, was drawn up and signed and has entered into force. In effect, it is the first real disarmament measure in the history of international relations. It envisages removal of a whole category of highly dangerous mass annihilation weapons from the military arsenals of states.

The sphere of operation of the Treaty on the Nonproliferation of Nuclear Weapons has expanded. Recently, additional large states, including the Federal Republic of Germany and Italy, have become party to it. Yet further effective measures to prevent the spread of nuclear weapons are still a most important objective. The U.S.S.R. is prepared to cooperate with other states on this score.

Let me refer specifically to the current Soviet-U.S. negotiations on further strategic arms limitation. We are holding them in an effort to effectuate the 1974 Vladivostok understanding and to prevent the opening of a new channel for the arms race, which would nullify everything achieved so far. An agreement on this issue would obviously be of very great benefit both for the future development of Soviet-U.S. relations, for greater mutual confidence, and for the consolidation of world peace. We attach the utmost importance to the whole of this problem, we have persistently and repeatedly offered the United States not to stop at just limiting the existing types of strategic weapons. We thought it possible to go further. Specifically, we suggested coming to terms on banning the development of new, still more destructive weapons systems, in particular, the new Trident submarines carrying ballistic missiles and the new strategic B-1 bombers in the United States, and similar systems in the U.S.S.R. Deplorably, these proposals were not accepted by the U.S. side.

But we have not withdrawn them, and need we say how beneficial their implementation would be for mutual confidence. Furthermore, both sides would be able to save considerable resources, and use them for productive purposes, for improving peoples' lives.

Let me add one more thing. Of late, pronouncements have been proliferating in many countries against any of the powers setting up military bases in the region of the Indian Ocean. We are in sympathy with these pronouncements. The Soviet Union has never had, and has not now, any intention whatever of building military bases in the Indian Ocean. And we call on the United States to take the same stand.

Certainly, the time will come when the inevitable association of other nuclear powers with the process of strategic arms limitation will arise on the agenda. And those which refuse would assume a grave responsibility before the peoples. On our country's initiative, the UN General Assembly has in recent years adopted a number of important resolutions on the questions of restraining the arms race and banning development and manufacture of new types of mass annihilation weapons and of new weapons systems.

The task is to have these resolutions implemented. Frankly, this is not easy to achieve, because a number of major states are still obviously reluctant to end the arms race. The opponents of détente and disarmament still dispose of considerable resources. They are highly active in different forms and from different angles. Though imperialism's possibilities for aggressive action are now considerably reduced, its nature has remained the same. This is why the peace-loving forces must be highly vigilant. Energetic action and unity of all forces of peace and goodwill are essential. Therefore, special importance attaches to the proposal supported by the vast majority of UN member-countries to convene a world disarmament conference.

Political détente needs to be backed up by military détente. The Peace Program advanced a clear aim: to reduce armed forces and armaments in Central Europe. The Vienna negotiations on this score have already been going on for more than two years. However, there has been no visible progress for only one reason: the NATO countries refuse to give up trying to use the negotiations to secure unilateral military advantages. For some reason, the West wants, even demands, concessions prejudicial to the security of the Socialist countries. Yet we have not noticed any inclination on the part of the NATO bloc to make similar concessions to the other side.

Recently, the Socialist states submitted new proposals in Vienna in an effort to get matters off the ground. For a start, we are prepared to accept a reduction of only Soviet and U.S. troops in the course of this year, while the strength of the armed forces of the other participants in the negotiations remains "frozen" and not subject to reduction until the second stage in 1977–78. We have also made perfectly concrete proposals concerning reduction by both sides of the number of tanks, nuclear-missile-carrying planes, and missile launchers along with a definite quantity of nuclear warheads for them.

Our proposals are based on the only realistic approach to preserving the existing relations of strength, in substance one of balance in the center of Europe. Their implementation will not prejudice the security of either side. And it is to be hoped that all this will win due response of the Western countries, and it will, at last, be possible to go from discussion to actual measures reducing armed forces and armaments.

The Twenty-fourth Congress set this objective: renunciation of the use and threat of force in settling questions in dispute must become the rule in international relations. Later, this principle was reflected in a number of treaties concluded by the U.S.S.R. with other countries. It is contained in the final act of the European Conference. To make the danger of war recede still further and to create favorable conditions for progress towards disarmament, we now offer to conclude a world treaty on the nonuse of force in international relations. Its participants, naturally including the nuclear powers, would undertake to refrain from using all types of weapons, including nuclear, in settling disputes that may arise between them. The Soviet Union is prepared to join other states in examining practical steps leading to the implementation of this proposal.

*   *   *

Comrades, assessing our country's international situation and world conditions, the party's Central Committee considers that further struggle for peace and the freedom and independence of the peoples first of all requires fulfillment of the following vital tasks:

- Augment the joint active contribution to the consolidation of peace by the fraternal Socialist states, while steadily strengthening their unity and expanding their all-around cooperation in building the new society.

- Work for the termination of the expanding arms race, which is endangering peace, and for transition to reducing the accumulated stockpiles of arms, to disarmament. For this purpose: (a) do everything to complete the preparation of a new Soviet-U.S. agreement on limiting and reducing strategic armaments, and conclude international treaties on universal and complete termination of nuclear weapons tests, on banning and destroying chemical weapons, on banning development of new types and systems of mass annihilation weapons, and also banning impairment of the natural environment for military or other hostile purposes; (b) launch new efforts to activate negotiations on the reduction of armed forces and armaments in Central Europe, and, following agreement on the first concrete steps in this direction, continue to deepen the military détente in the region in the subsequent years; (c) work for a switch from the present continuous growth of the military expenditures of many states to their systematic reduction; and (d) take all measures to assure the earliest possible convocation of the world disarmament conference.

- Concentrate the efforts of peace-loving states on eliminating the remaining seats of war, first and foremost on assuring a just and durable settlement in the Middle East. In connection with such a settlement the states concerned should examine the question of helping to end the arms race in the Middle East.

- Do everything to deepen international détente, to embody it in concrete forms of mutually beneficial cooperation between states.

185

Work vigorously for the full implementation of the final act of the European Conference and for greater peaceful cooperation in Europe. In accordance with the principles of peaceful coexistence continue consistently to develop relations of long-term mutually beneficial cooperation in various fields—political, economic, scientific, and cultural—with the United States, France, the Federal Republic of Germany, Britain, Italy, Canada, and also Japan and other capitalist countries.

- Work for Asian security based on joint efforts by the states of that continent.

- Consider as crucial the international task of completely eliminating all the vestiges of the system of colonial oppression, all encroachments on the equality and independence of peoples, and all seats of colonialism and racism.

- Work for removing discrimination and all artificial barriers in international trade, and eliminating all manifestations of inequality, *diktat*, and exploitation in international economic relations.

Those, comrades, are the main tasks, the attainment of which, as we see it, is essential at present in the interests of peace and the security of peoples and the progress of mankind. We consider these proposals an organic projection and development of the Peace Program advanced by our Twenty-fourth Congress, a program of further struggle for peace and international cooperation and for the freedom and independence of the peoples. We shall center our country's foreign policy on achieving these tasks, and shall cooperate in this with other peace-loving states.

Permit me to express confidence that the lofty aims of our policy on the international scene will be received with understanding and win the broad support of all the peace-loving, progressive forces and all decent people on earth.

Comrades, this is an epoch of radical social change. Socialism's positions are expanding and growing stronger. The victories of the national liberation movement are opening new horizons for countries that have won independence. The class struggle of the working people against monopoly oppression, against the exploiting order, is gaining in intensity. The scale of the revolutionary-democratic anti-imperialist movement is steadily growing. Cumulatively, all this signifies growth of the world revolutionary process.

*　　*　　*

Interimperialist rivalries and discord in the Common Market and NATO have grown sharper. The greater power of the international monopolies has made the competitive struggle still more ruthless. The governments of the capitalist countries are making repeated attempts to moderate the contradictions and come to terms on joint anticrisis measures. But the nature of imperialism is such that each endeavors to gain advantages at the expense of others, to impose its will. The differences surface in new forms, and contradictions erupt with new force.

This shows that the present crisis is unusual. Now everyone can see that one of the main myths created by reformists and bourgeois ideologists has collapsed—the myth that present-day capitalism is able to avert crisis. The instability of capitalism is becoming more and more apparent. Promises to make capitalism "sounder" and to create a "welfare society" within its framework have obviously failed. A heavy burden has fallen on the masses. The rising cost of living is inexorably reducing people's real incomes. Even according to official UN figures, more than 15 million people in the developed capitalist countries have been flung out of factories and offices, and subsist with their families on allowances. In addition, millions are compelled to work a short day or two–three days a week.

The working class retaliates in the proletarian spirit by intensifying the struggle against big capital, the main culprit of social calamities. The strike wave, which involves diverse sections of working people, has risen to the highest level of the past several decades. The strength and prestige of the working class are greater, and its role of vanguard in the struggle for the interests of working people, the true interests of the nation, has increased. A leftward shift is witnessed in the trade unions. In a number of countries, unity of action by workers' and other democratic parties is shaping steadily, and their positions are stronger.

The politico-ideological crisis of bourgeois society is more acute. It afflicts the institutions of power and bourgeois political parties, and impairs elementary ethical standards. Corruption is increasingly candid, even in the top echelons of the state machinery. The decline of spiritual culture continues, and the crime rate is rising.

It is furthest from the Communists' minds to predict an "automatic collapse" of capitalism. It still has considerable reserves. Yet the developments of recent years forcefully confirm that capitalism is a society without a future. . . .

The recent experience of the revolutionary movement provides graphic evidence that imperialism will stop at nothing, ending all pretense of being any kind of democracy, if a serious threat arises to the domination of monopoly capital and its political agents. It is prepared to trample upon the sovereignty of states and upon all legality, to say nothing of humanism. Slander, duping the public, economic blockade, sabotage, organizing hunger and dislocation, bribes and threats, terrorism, assassination of political personalities, and fascist-style pogroms—such is the armory of present-day counter-revolution, which always operates in conjunction with international imperialist reaction. But all this is ultimately doomed to failure. The cause of freedom and progress is unconquerable.

The growth of the influence of Communist parties in the capitalist world is an auspicious development of the past five years. Their numerical strength has grown by nearly 1 million, including almost 400,000 in Western Europe. People voting for Communists in parliamentary and local elections have greatly increased in numbers.

*   *   *

Now that détente has become reality, the question of how it influences the class struggle arises often in the international working-class movement, and among its opponents.

Some bourgeois leaders affect surprise and raise a howl over the solidarity of Soviet Communists, the Soviet people, with the struggle of other peoples for freedom and progress. This is either outright naïveté or, more likely, a deliberate befuddling of minds. It could not be clearer, after all, that détente and peaceful coexistence refer to interstate relations. This means mainly that disputes and conflicts between countries are not to be settled by war, by the use or threat of force. The détente does not in the slightest abolish, and cannot abolish or alter, the laws of the class struggle. None should expect that because of the détente Communists will reconcile themselves with capitalist exploitation or that monopolists become followers of the revolution. On the other hand, strict observance of the principle of noninterference in the affairs of other states and respect for their independence and sovereignty are essential conditions of détente.

We make no secret of the fact that we see détente as the way to create more favorable conditions for peaceful Socialist and Communist construction. This only confirms that socialism and peace are indissoluble. And, when we are rebuked for this, we can hardly help thinking that those who rebuke us are not sure that capitalism can survive without resort to aggression and threats of force and without encroaching on the independence and interests of other peoples.

As for the ultraleftist assertions that peaceful coexistence is the next thing to "helping capitalism" and "freezing the socio-political status quo," our reply is this: every revolution is above all a natural result of the given society's internal development. What is more, life itself has refuted the inventions about the "freezing of the status quo." Suffice it to recall the far-reaching revolutionary changes in the world in recent years.

That is how things stand with the relationship between détente and the class struggle. Faithful to the revolutionary cause, we Soviet Communists are fighting and will continue to fight for peace, that greatest of all boons for all peoples and that important condition for the progress of mankind in our time.

*   *   *

4

IS DETENTE IN
THE AMERICAN INTEREST?

**DETENTE: AN EVALUATION
BY A GROUP OF STUDENTS
OF SOVIET AND INTERNATIONAL AFFAIRS ***

*The authors of this article contend that the Soviet Union is shifting
the world balance of power in its favor through initiatives taken under
the guise of the present détente. True détente cannot exist without
internal Soviet liberalization, only this would indicate honest intentions, but cultural and political repression have increased. Various
actions concerning military force, economic relations with the West,
policies in Europe and the Middle East, and the legitimacy of subversion confirm Soviet insincerity. Détente has worked against Western interests, and the authors call upon these nations to embrace
realistic policies that could foster a genuine détente. The authors of
this article include Robert Conquest, Brian Crozier, John Erickson,
Joseph Godson, Gregory Grossman, Leopold Labedz, Bernard Lewis,
Richard Pipes, Leonard Schapiro, Edward Shils, and P. J. Vatikiotis.*

The Aims of the Soviet Foreign Policy in the Period of Détente

In the present Soviet terminology *détente*, or *peaceful coexistence*,
denotes a strategic alternative to overtly militant antagonism against
the so-called capitalist countries. It does not imply the abandonment
by the Soviet Union and its allies of conflict with the liberal Western
countries. It does not mean the cessation of the slogans about class

* Source: *Survey, a Journal of East & West Studies*, no. 91/92 (Spring/Summer
1974), pp. 1-27.

warfare and about the "ideological" conflict between the "two systems" with the aim of replacing the capitalist (democratic) system by the Communist system. The point is emphatically and repeatedly made in Soviet theoretical pronouncements intended for consumption within the Communist bloc. *Détente* means a change of methods. Head-on conflict is to yield to indirect methods of combat, using non-military means, described as "ideological": in Soviet practice this term covers subversion, propaganda, political blackmail, and intelligence operations.

Historically the first period of détente occurred in 1921 when, following the victory over the White Armies, Lenin decided that his country required a long period of consolidation of power and economic rehabilitation. At this time the Soviet Union entered into regular diplomatic relations with those "capitalist" powers which were willing to reciprocate, and engaged with them in extensive negotiations and collaboration aimed at propping-up the Soviet economy. This period came to an end around 1930 with the triumph of Stalin's one-man dictatorship and the drive for the militarization of the Soviet Union. Immediately after Stalin's death, and particularly after 1957 when Khrushchev established himself in full authority, the policy of "peaceful coexistence" was renewed. Its initial intention seems to have been twofold: to slow down the military effort of the United States, as well as to break out of the diplomatic isolation in which Stalin had placed the Soviet Union. Khrushchev's successors maintained this policy in full vigor. In addition to the original aims of détente—the expansion of the Soviet system and the enfeeblement of the liberal democracies—they had a new aim, namely the securing of Western financial aid and the technical assistance for their lagging economy.

The Soviet government expects the policy of détente to accomplish the following:

1. To weaken the Western alliance by making it appear to be unnecessary, indeed, dangerous to peace.

2. To reduce the pace of the American defense effort and to eliminate the United States presence in Europe.

3. To secure from the West financial and technological assistance which would directly enhance Soviet military power by making easier the continuous build-up of the military sector of the economy.

4. To isolate China and to counter the political consequences of the fact that the Soviet Union is involved in a hostile confrontation with both East and West.

191

5. To legitimize its domination over Eastern Europe by making it appear historically irreversible.

As theoretical writings appearing in the Soviet Union make it quite clear, the ultimate result of a carefully pursued policy of détente should be a decisive shift of the world balance of power in favor of the Soviet Union and its bloc. This shift, it is expected, will permit the Soviet Union to achieve further expansion without recourse to general war, largely by the use of methods of internal subversion and external intimidation.

It is only if this policy is frustrated and its aims are abandoned by the Soviet Union that conditions for a genuine détente may arise. Until that time, the West, while not relinquishing hope for the relaxation of international tension, must distinguish between the real targets of Soviet policy and the smokescreen used to camouflage them. A genuine policy for peace, providing a convincing promise for the future, must rest on public opinion which is aware of the realities of the international situation (including the need to preserve the Western position in the balance of power) and not on illusory slogans about "peace" and "friendship," or stern condemnation of the "cold war" —without any substantive changes in conduct by the Soviet leaders. Above all the West must not allow itself to be deluded into believing that the policy of détente is directly related to the avoidance of nuclear conflict between the United States and the Soviet Union—as both countries, for different political reasons, tend to suggest. In fact the determination to avoid nuclear conflict has characterized the policy of both the United States and the Soviet Union for many years before talk of détente became fashionable—the first striking instance was on the occasion of the Cuba confrontation of 1962, and the last one was on the occasion of the nuclear alert during the October 1973 Middle East War. There were other less striking examples.

Whilst détente does not mean the abandonment of the Soviet posture of ideological struggle, it tends to foster in the West the idea that it has to accept tacitly Soviet political practices as a necessary condition for avoiding a nuclear war. This false alternative provided in the past the underlying premise for those advocating unilateral Western disarmament. Today it is Western government spokesmen who often use this simplified dichotomy to justify an attitude of silent indifference toward victims of Soviet persecution. This can only confuse the Western public about wider political issues. Contrary to official suggestions, a defense of Solzhenitsyn or Sakharov does not in any way increase the risks of a nuclear war. The Soviet Union does not accept "ideological coexistence" and there is no reason why the West should compromise its own fundamental values and ideas. Avoiding ambiguity in this respect, also on the governmental level, can only decrease the risks of nuclear confrontation in the long run.

Détente and the Internal Evolution of the Soviet Union

One of the major points raised about détente has been whether, and in what sense, it is connected with—and should be connected with—a "liberalization" in the internal affairs of the Soviet Union and of other countries in the Soviet bloc. The question has been dramatized in particular by the amendment, through which Senator Henry Jackson, supported by large majorities in the United States Senate and House of Representatives, has sought to deny to the Soviet Union "most-favored-nation" treatment and similar trade advantages unless and until it permits the free emigration of its subjects. Although in practice, this has primarily until now revolved around the question of Jewish emigration, the amendment expresses a general principle and does not limit its application to Jews.

The Jackson Amendment and similar demands have been denounced by the Soviet Union as intervention in its internal affairs. For it is a matter which would require altering Soviet law, or at any rate, Soviet treatment of their own citizenry. But this argument, even at its own level, is false. No change of law is required, only a change of practice. The United Nations Declaration on Human Rights, though not legally binding, is an expression of international principle which is held to be generally applicable; it specifically covers the free movement of people. The Soviet Union has accepted the Declaration of Human Rights. The observance or nonobservance of these international standards should certainly be regarded as one touchstone of the reliability of Moscow's attitude to the formally accepted obligations which constitute a part of the general guarantees which the Soviet Union has undertaken to give as part of its contribution to détente.

The Jackson Amendment, and the demands made by representatives of many Western countries at the Helsinki and Geneva talks for a free exchange of people and ideas between Russia and the West, puts the problem in its clearest form. Those who defend the policy of détente in the way in which it is understood in the Soviet Union argue that international negotiations between powers are simply a matter of realistic policies to which ethical issues of this sort are irrelevant. A supplementary argument for the Soviet form of détente is that whatever the current conduct of the Soviet leadership, inter-

193

national détente will in the long run, more or less automatically, lead to an improvement in the Soviet treatment of its own citizens, if only through an increase in the standard of living.

This argument has no foundation in experience. For centuries Russia has sought (with some success) to import Western technology, but this has never had any effect on the internal nature of its regime, tsarist or Soviet. The Soviet authorities are, of course, well aware of the fact that the United States and other Western countries believe that détente will lead to a liberalization of the Soviet regime, and that is why there has been a progressive tightening-up of controls in the Soviet bloc during the period when détente has been mooted. There are certainly signs of fear inside the U.S.S.R. among the hardliners, or those who fear for their own privileges (the hack writers and venal intellectuals, for example), or the KGB officials, that the United States arguments for détente may be right: this is why Brezhnev has repeatedly been reassuring them in his speeches that détente provides the best platform for ideological warfare, and, following up words with deeds, he has been intensifying persecution of dissent.

The Soviet leadership makes no secret of the fact—and indeed states it in speech after speech and document after document—that its opposition to Western ideas and to any significant "liberalization" is total and irreconcilable. Such a persistent and unrelentingly hostile attitude is quite incompatible with any development of real progress towards genuine friendly relations between the two sides. Until genuine liberalization takes place, or at least until there are some signs of serious progress in that direction, we may unreservedly take all the other elements of "détente" in current Soviet policy as temporary and tactical. They are not evidence that the Soviet Union is inclined to reduce its hostility towards the Western countries.

The Fate of Culture in the Age of Détente

As explained above, when faced with the prospect of détente, the internal party line in the Soviet Union and Eastern Europe hardened to prevent any undesirable cultural developments which might undermine the party's ideological domination. The increasing cultural rigidity was most pronounced in the Soviet Union itself where a determined effort was made to end the phenomenon of *samizdat* and to crush the dissidents. The KGB arrested many of them: some were sent to mental prisons, some to camps with harsher sentences than were usually given to dissidents sentenced earlier. The most important of the *samizdat* journals, *The Chronicle of Current Events*, was finally hunted out of existence. "Case 24" as it was called by the KGB, culminated in the Yakir-Krasin trial during which the accused, after a year of preliminary "investigation" in prison, cooperated with their prosecutors and—broken men—"confessed" in a manner reminiscent of the infamous Moscow trials of the thirties. There was, of course, no similarity in the gravity of the charges and the accused earned themselves a reduction of the already lenient sentence by "freely" denouncing their own "misdeeds" during the press conference at which they were presented to foreign correspondents. There was, however, another ominous sign recalling the technique of the thirties: during the same press conference, the state prosecutor, Malyarov, declared that the two most prestigious Soviet dissidents, Sakharov and Solzhenitsyn, "are not immune" before Soviet law, a clear indication that they might also be arrested, which indeed is what happened to Solzhenitsyn later on.

At the same time the KGB succeeded after a five-day interrogation in breaking Solzhenitsyn's friend who had typed the manuscript of *The Gulag Archipelago*. Having disclosed the manuscript's whereabouts to the KGB, the woman was released (only to commit suicide). Solzhenitsyn and Sakharov, faced with an impending threat to themselves, appealed to Western public opinion. They denounced the increased oppression in the Soviet Union and reproached the West for its lack of moral stamina and courage in defending the universal cultural values, as well as for the short-sightedness of its policy of sacrificing freedom for the chimera of pseudo-détente. Already, during President Nixon's visit to Moscow in May 1972, Sakharov had warned that the Soviet leaders would take the new agreements as a green light for increasing internal repression, since they would assume that such repression would no longer affect Western policy towards the Soviet Union. In this they may have been mistaken, although the American Administration has indeed been attempting to dissociate its foreign policy from the question of internal Soviet rigidity. Secretary of State Kissinger and Chancellor Brandt, both refugees from Hitler, declared that they would be pursuing the same policies even if Hitler and Stalin, respectively, were still in power. It is an ironical situation in which Sakharov and Solzhenitsyn stand for the cultural values of the West, while Western statesmen are ready to sacrifice them for the sake of an unrealistic *Realpolitik* which, as Sakharov noted in this message to the American Congress, would in the end also undermine Western security.

In contrast to the political leaders' noncommital reaction, Western cultural and scientific milieus, and Western public opinion in general, have been overwhelmingly sympathetic to Sakharov and Solzhenitsyn. As the latter stated, this was the only factor which had until then prevented his arrest. The publication in the West of *The Gulag Archipelago* prompted another campaign against Solzhenitsyn, the style and vocabulary of which was not very different from the assaults of Soviet propaganda in the Stalinist period. He was soon to be expelled from the country.

The point so forcefully made by Sakharov and Solzhenitsyn, and only very rarely encountered in Western writings on détente, is the extreme importance of internal Soviet policies as an indication of the Soviet Union's future external behavior. A more liberal internal policy could be regarded as a test of the nature of Soviet political evolution. It would not be a sufficient guarantee that the Soviet Union has ceased to be expansionist, but it would constitute a necessary precondition for its evolution in this direction. Internal cultural control based on ideological mendacity (doublethink, doubletalk, and double standards) suggests that similar attitudes and methods will also be used in foreign relations, and raises the problem of Soviet reliability vis-à-vis détente. That is why the question of "free flow of ideas, information, and people" is of paramount importance in gauging the future of East-West relations. In the long run, the official attitude of the Communist countries to cultural developments is the only indication which makes possible an assessment of Western security on the political, rather than on the military plane. The West can disregard this fact only at its peril. Yet the Soviet view of détente includes both pressure to prohibit any Western criticism and the acceptance by the West of the principle that so far as the Soviet Union is concerned, the Soviet leaders are to be free to pursue the "ideological struggle." The most pungent comment on the double standards evident in the Soviet definition of détente was given in the *New York Times* (3 February 1947): "The Soviet contention clearly is that Moscow is free to tell lies about the West but the West must not tell the truth about the Soviet Union."

The Soviet formula for this is that the "free flow of ideas" must not violate "the customs and sovereignty of each country" (which means, in effect, that ideas and information are free to flow within the bounds allowed by Soviet censorship). The official Soviet idea is that international cultural relations are to be limited to innocuous state-controlled "cultural exchanges"—as if culture were a commodity which could be manipulated and exchanged.

*   *   *

The fundamental naïveté of so many political perceptions in the West is ultimately due to lack of understanding, not just of the mechanisms of the Soviet political system, but of the mentality rooted in the political culture underlying it. It is the Western lack of political comprehension which makes possible Soviet attempts at cultural exploitation of détente. The situation would indeed be laughable if it were not so tragic for the Soviet artists and writers and if it were not for the threat which it poses for the West through the extension of Soviet political influence, the infiltration of Soviet doublethink and the possible debasement of Western cultural standards. The fate of culture in the age of détente depends, in no small measure, on the steadfast attachment of the West to its own cultural standards and the avoidance of confusion which pseudo-détente could bring to them as a result of Soviet political pressure.

Détente and the Military Balance

It is generally assumed in the West that détente by its very nature reduces the need for reliance on military strength. It is thought that relaxation in international tension is the obvious occasion to reduce military establishments and to run down weapons programs. An inspection of military programs in the Soviet Union and among its allies, however, shows that they do not share this Western view. Even in simple numerical terms, détente has brought no diminution, nor even a leveling, but rather a program to expand both Soviet strategic offensive and defensive systems, as well as adding to the capacities of general purpose or "conventional" ground, sea, and air forces. Behind these military armament programs lies an extensive civil defense program, a major military training program for Soviet adolescents and a mass of well-trained reservists, continually swelled by the Soviet conscript system. In brief, there is *no* sector of Soviet military policy where expansion, diversification, and modernization cannot be observed. The growth of the Soviet Navy serves as but one example of this relentless process.

In terms of strategic offensive weapons the SALT-I agreements of 1972 served the Soviet Union handsomely, investing it with a 40 percent advantage in ICBMs—1,618 for the Soviet Union to 1,054 for the United States—and missile-launching submarines—62 to 44, over 30 percent more submarine-launched ballistic missiles—950 to 710—and a massive threefold lead over the United States in total destructive power. It was argued, nonetheless, at the time that the

United States could afford this numerical disadvantage by virtue of superiority in technology, namely the multiple independently targetable warhead (MIRV). Strategic bomber forces were not included in this initial agreement. In the twenty-one months that elapsed after the SALT-I agreement, the Soviet command steadily increased the numbers of its ICBM force to well over 1,500 and increased its submarine missile strength to some 580: numbers, however, tell only part of the story, since four *new* ICBMs with large yield have been developed; an improved version of the DELTA-class missile-carrying submarine, capable of carrying sixteen rather than twelve 4,000-mile range SLBMs is under development; and at least one of the new ICBMs is mobile. All the while ICBM plants have been modernized, facilities for testing missile engines expanded, and new "cold launch" techniques for ICBMs developed, utilizing varied diameter canisters enabling the Soviet Union to circumvent the SALT-I limitation on numbers of *missile-silos*, since they make it possible for one silo to house a range of missile types. Thus, the "numbers game" has been exploited in favor of the Soviet Union; while the other factor which it was believed at the time of SALT-I would prevent the balance of advantage from tipping in the Soviet favor, namely, United States superiority in technical innovation, has crumbled. The Soviet Union has itself developed MIRVs for its massive new ICBMs, thereby compounding the Soviet lead both in numbers and in missile throw weight (meaning more MIRVs on bigger missiles). Meanwhile, a new strategic bomber, the Backfire, is entering the Soviet arensal and adds to the strategic offensive potential (while the USAF B-1 strategic bomber is not yet in full production).

The momentum of this Soviet build-up shows no signs of relaxation. Ominous though that is in an era of détente, the Soviet conduct at the SALT-II negotiations gives much cause for uneasiness: the Soviet Union's requirement for permanent numerical advantage, coupled with the energy with which it pursues its own technological progress, could only result in consigning the United States to permanent strategic inferiority. It follows, therefore, that Soviet objectives aim at overt strategic superiority as opposed to the mere "insurance" of limited numerical advantage: "parity" no longer suffices. While the Soviet MIRV is disquieting, the most alarming element of the strategic weapons build-up is its scope and rate, with significant long-term implications. The pattern of détente based on undisputed Soviet strategic superiority has not been fully explored in the West. Existing evidence is sufficient to suggest that military superiority is incompatible with the mode of political accommodation which is what the

West thinks détente ought to be. This kind of détente could best be served if the Soviet Union accepted this conception. The crisis at the SALT-II negotiations tends to confirm that it does not.

Meanwhile, the Soviet general purpose forces have grown and continue to grow. The Soviet Navy, modern and powerfully armed with a wide range of missiles, displays its oceanic presence and presents an oceanic challenge. The Soviet Air Force modernizes and improves its tactical air power, with ultramodern aircraft, such as the Foxbat, and significantly adds to its capacity for strategic and medium-range airlift; this was shown in the recent Middle East War. It is in the European theater, however, that Soviet policies of military reinforcement expose the emptiness of the talk of political détente. Over the past five or six years, the ground forces of the Soviet Union, which from the core of the power of the Warsaw Pact countries, have undergone major improvements in combat capacity. In the past three years some nine thousand tanks have been added to the Soviet tank force, more than four thousand armored personnel carriers have been introduced into Eastern Europe, tactical air power has been improved in both quantity and quality, the number of nuclear weapons assigned to the ground forces has been increased, more than one thousand additional guns have been provided for the Soviet divisions and stocks of conventional ammunition have been augmented. A marked improvement has also taken place in the Soviet logistical system, with emphasis on serving armored and missile units. The net result is to give the Soviet command a preponderance in the European theater of at least three-to-one in armor and of more than two-to-one in tactical aircraft. And once again, in line with the SALT-II negotiations, Soviet conduct during the present (1974) talks on the reduction of forces shows no sign of yielding any element of this superiority.

Even on this brief inspection, the Soviet policy of preaching détente while increasing military strength is demonstrably the reverse of our own. More than that, however, the détente sought by the Soviet Union is viewed by that country not as the justification for accepting the prevailing military balance, but as an opportunity to spurt forward towards unchallengeable superiority.

The Economic Consequences of Détente

Some of the most uncritical attitudes generated by détente in the West are in the field of East-West trade. The understanding of its limitations and of the Soviet motives involved is quite inadequate not only among the general public but also among Western businessmen and governments. Yet such understanding is of crucial importance for a realistic view of the prospects for détente.

Soviet purposes are related to the current difficulties confronting the Soviet economy. They include the decreasing rate of growth of the GNP, the exhaustion of employable reserves of manpower, the balance-of-payments deficit and the inefficiency which is particularly apparent in agriculture and in the Soviet inability to respond to demand and to generate technical progress.

Having rejected any far-reaching economic reform which might, or might not, have raised efficiency, but which would certainly have antagonized many powerful vested interests in Soviet society, especially the party apparatus, Soviet leaders have opted for the other major course that bore some promise of countering the unfavorable trends in the economy: massive assistance from the West. This policy is all the more attractive because, while it is expected to bring large amounts of capital into the Soviet Union, the repayment is to be mainly in the very commodities that the Western-financed projects would produce. At the same time, the flow of Western technology and know-how is expected by the Soviet leaders to narrow the growing technological gap with the West and to improve Soviet export capacity. The Americans, the Japanese, and the Europeans are to build up whole industries for the Soviet Union and develop vast regions there at very little cost to the Soviet Union itself, and with minimal risk to Soviet institutions.

Contrary to widespread Western belief, the "more liberal" Soviet economic strategy abroad is quite compatible with a conservative policy at home. Indeed, this double-pronged economic strategy is an alternative to domestic economic reform which the Soviet leaders feared might jeopardize the stability of existing Soviet institutions and generate political strife. The risks to domestic political control from increased Western contacts can be minimized by police methods designed to isolate the bulk of the population from contact with the West. Past experience has shown that such contacts in the economic sphere involve only a relatively small and select group of Soviet citizens. To the extent that some risks are nevertheless present, they are counterbalanced by the promise of additional economic benefits which might assuage the growing consumer demand. They are countered prophylactically by the tightening of control over dissidence that we have witnessed in recent years. Contrary to some Western expectations, past experience shows that a more reactionary policy at home can well be combined with economic advances to the West.

The paramount Soviet target in its economic détente offensive is the gaining of large long-term credits at low interest rates (chiefly from the U.S.) in order to finance the purchase of equipment and technology for the development of oil, natural gas, and other mineral resources. Such assistance from the West may not only increase Soviet overall economic strength, but it could also enable the Soviet government to engage in military spending on a scale which would otherwise be impossible, given the competing claims of investment and consumption.

The economic détente strategy of seeking large Western credits may thus bring enormous economic advantage not only to the Soviet Union internally but also to Soviet military and foreign policies, particularly as it will tend to create groups in the West with vested interests in Soviet-derived profits and in the protection of Western loans. These groups can be politically manipulated in the free societies, while the appetite for profits among businessmen is also easily exploitable.

But it is not necessarily true that what is good for Pepsi Cola, or for the Chase Manhattan Bank (and their European equivalents), in their dealings with the Soviet Union is also good for the United States or Western Europe. Yet very little homework has been done in the West on the problems involved in close relations with the Soviet economic state monopoly. Instead of soberly assessing the disadvantages of a free enterprise system in a situation in which the Soviet state monopoly can exploit economic competition among Western firms while it makes only deals it chooses to make, many Western business leaders have shown themselves to be remarkably eager to take Soviet economic propaganda at face value. Whether the enthusiasm will survive the diminishing prospects of governmental credit guarantees following the passage of the Jackson Amendment is another question.

Not only was the shortsightedness and the bandwagon psychology of the supposedly hardheaded Western businessmen amazing; so was the small amount of public discussion in the West on the questions whether assuming the role of the Soviet Union's banker was in the national interest of the Western countries; and whether it was wise to invest in the development of Soviet resources of energy (especially after the experience with the Arab oil embargo) rather than in Western sources. At a time of inflationary pressure, is a substantial outflow of capital from the West to Communist countries desirable either politically or economically? And is it true, as advocates of détente-at-any-price never cease to proclaim, that trade promotes peace?

A realistic answer to these questions is quite different from what the Western public was led to believe in the period between President Nixon's visit to Moscow in May 1972, and Secretary Brezhnev's visit to Washington in June 1973.

The private interest of business corporations and banks is not equivalent to the national interest, much less to the interest of the West as a whole. Competition for investment in the Soviet Union and the granting of large long-term credits to it not only would divide the West, and strengthen economically, politically and militarily its most dangerous and avowed adversary, but would also reduce political options for the West in the future by making it (particularly the United States) dependent on the U.S.S.R. for a substantial amount of the energy supply and other essential goods. It would give the Soviet Union a lever on Western policy through the very fact of its indebtedness and its control over the new sources of energy on which the West would come to rely. Moreover, this Western policy may produce the opposite effect from the intended one of "intermeshing" Western and Soviet economic interests, of "Gulliverization" of the Soviet Union. Trade and investment generate friction and conflict even among friends; history provides enough examples to show that they do not ensure peace. Germany was the largest trading partner of Russia just before each of the two world wars, and the high point of Russian-Chinese trade was immediately before the break between Moscow and Peking.

Political as well as economic realism would thus dictate caution in granting credits for the export of Western technology and commodities to the Communist countries and a sober assessment of each deal (after the grain deal fiasco), together with the realization that Soviet purposes in expanding trade are as different from the Western ones as are the economic rules of the game adhered to by the two sides. So far, there is no evidence that the tough problems involved here have been generally comprehended either by businessmen, or by governments, or by the public of Western countries. Yet there is little doubt that the original euphoria over trade and credits as the miracle weapons for dealing with the Soviet Union—bringing both profits and peace—has subsided and a more realistic mood is slowly expanding in the West. The effects of the Soviet-American wheat deal and of the Arab oil embargo have not been lost on the Western, particularly the American, public. These have dampened the early enthusiasm. But the policy's premises which have generated unrealistic expectations and illusions are still operative. One example should suffice. A U.S. official very much responsible for the 1972 wheat deal, faced with a Soviet proposal to resell to the United States some of the still-undelivered grain at a much higher price than Russia had paid for it, still justified the original deal on the grounds that it "constructively helped the process of détente" and defended its "historic importance" in opening up agricultural trade with Russia. Vladimir S. Alkhimov, the Soviet trade official who offered to sell (at a much higher price) grain (originally sold to the Soviet Union at subsidized prices) which would replenish the U.S. stock diminished by exports to the U.S.S.R., made a less euphoric comment: "Look at Alaska, which we sold to you for $7 million back in 1867. That was cheap too, but you don't hear us complaining." Clearly the Soviet attitude to détente involves a rather long view of economic reciprocity.

In the meantime, the Soviet Union is trying to narrow down the technology gap by acquiring advanced American technology. The American Control Data Corporation and other firms are helping to close this gap. According to spokesmen of this firm, by spending $3 million in three years, the Soviet Union gained fifteen years in R & D. Lockheed and other aircraft firms compete for deals with the Soviet Union which will provide that country with access to the latest American jet-liner technology, design and know-how. But at the same time as the Soviet Union is negotiating the purchase of most advanced items, like the high-speed electronic computer "Cyber," Soviet technological achievements remain inaccessible to the West. The economic and technological advantages of détente are thus somewhat one-sided and in the long run this asymmetry could be dangerous.

Soviet Aims in Western Europe in the Context of Détente

As has been seen, the policy of détente was primarily envisaged by the Soviet Union in relation to the United States as having two objects in view: first to obtain American capital and technology as a means of reviving and expanding Soviet industry, and of developing essential resources, particularly oil; and secondly, to negotiate, in partnership with the only other serious nuclear power, settlements of conflicts all over the world, with the need to avoid nuclear confrontation with the United States always in mind. Détente, vis-à-vis the United States, from the Soviet point of view, is a continuation of the *old* "spheres of influence" and "hot line" policy in improved form and a *new* exploitation of American willingness, consequent upon the end of United States involvement in Vietnam, to trade with the Soviet Union.

The relationship with Western Europe is regarded quite differently by the Soviet Union. Before the dramatic change in United States policy in 1971, the aim of the Soviet Union was to obtain its capital and technological requirements from Western Europe, while Soviet propaganda was mainly directed towards encouraging economic disunity between Europe and the United States. The United States is, however, a much more attractive supplier of capital and technology than Europe, because of the EEC, of which the Soviet Union disapproves as an entity, and because expanded business relations with the EEC might act as a new temptation to certain "bloc" countries, especially Poland and Rumania, to develop their own economic ties with the EEC and to escape thereby from the Soviet stranglehold. Moreover, as far as Europe is concerned, the Soviet Union can reasonably hope to exploit to the maximum its already overwhelming preponderance and its military proximity, in order to increase its political influence—and especially so if isolationist and economic pressures inside the United States may lead to U.S. withdrawal from Europe. The Soviet Union may also hope to gain political advantage from exploiting the divisions which exist between the individual countries of the EEC and any economic and political discord between the United States and Europe.

Soviet policy regarding the European Security Conference shows that the Soviet Union hopes (vainly so far) to replace an effective defense system (NATO) by meaningless declarations and treaties which would leave Europe virtually disarmed against the Soviet Union. It also seeks to consolidate social and cultural relations in the only form acceptable to the Soviet Union: namely, state-to-state relations, in which all contacts are organized and therefore controlled by the state. If this policy were to succeed, which at present seems unlikely in view of the position taken by several European powers, this would give the Soviet Union a powerful argument for claiming to stifle all criticism of the Soviet Union in Europe—which in practice covers all objective discussion of Soviet reality, and in particular to bring about the closing down of certain wireless stations, especially Radio Liberty. This has been one of the main aims of the Soviet Union for years.

Whatever the outcome of the present MFR and "Security" talks, the policy of the Soviet Union towards Europe is likely to remain for a time radically different from its policy towards the United States. In the case of the United States the Soviet Union may well offer for some time the concession which Polyphemus offered to Outis, that of being devoured last. In Europe, where the Soviet Union hopes for an ever-increasing military preponderance, its policy aiming to increase

Soviet political influence as that of the United States declines, is likely to employ the following tactics:

(a) Clandestine subversion. [This activity is discussed below.] This has particular advantage which the Soviet Union has enjoyed for half a century—of conducting subversion and "peaceful coexistence" side-by-side, such as entertaining the British Foreign Secretary while arms are being supplied to the Provisional IRA for the purpose of killing British soldiers.

(b) A vigorous policy of misinformation, for example, through feeding false stories to press correspondents and through the recruitment of conscious or unwitting agents of influence.

(c) The exercise of pressure on scientists and university teachers by withholding of visas from those who have not been sufficiently congenial to the Soviet Union, as a warning to others.

(d) The exercise of pressure on businessmen, who are interested in trade with the Soviet Union, to use their influence to prevent unwelcome criticism.

(e) If the opportunity arises, direct political action, reinforced by military pressure. This is not difficult to imagine if one thinks of the situation already obtaining in Scandinavia, which has to live under the shadow of the vast Soviet Baltic Fleet. This danger of political pressure under cover of military preponderance would clearly increase if isolationism grows in the United States and if the present discord between the United States and Europe is not repaired.

Détente and the Middle East

The Middle East conflict is not a local dispute. If it were, it would have been resolved some time ago. As it is, however, neither side in the conflict is able to impose its will on the other.

Nor are the great powers simply "sucked into" the conflict. On the contrary, the Soviet Union has exploited the conflict for a variety of purposes. These include: (1) the neutralization and detachment of Turkey and Iran from the Western alliance; (2) the outflanking of NATO, assisted by a prolonged energy crisis, and the disruption of the EEC; (3) the acquisition of a bridge to Asia and Africa; (4) the isolation of its own Muslim subject peoples against influences from the region; and (5) the control of the route to India, which is particularly important in view of the rivalry and conflict with China.

In short, the Soviet Union is in the Middle East because of its vital interest in the confrontation with the West, that is, the United

States and Western Europe; the conflict with China; and the vast oil resources.

The arms deal concluded in September 1955 with Egypt inaugurated a period of massive Soviet military, technical, and economic assistance, which was soon extended to Syria and Iraq. During the Suez War in 1956, the Soviet Union exploited to its advantage the instant and unequivocal American opposition to the Anglo-French military action. It was thus only after President Eisenhower had publicly warned his allies of this position that the Soviets issued their threats against Britain and France. Yet the myth grew among the Arabs that the Soviet Union was responsible for the frustration of the Anglo-French venture. In the decade from 1957 to 1967, the Soviet Union used its greater military, technical, and economic assistance programs in the region (for example, arms supplies, the Aswan High Dam, increased aid to Syria and Iraq) to impose the nearly total dependence of these states in their domestic, regional, and international policies. At the same time, it sought to isolate the United States from the region, and to divide the policies of Western European states.

Although the Six Day War in 1967 ended in the defeat of Soviet clients in the Middle East, and was a blow to its military assistance policy in the region, it nonetheless produced a still greater dependence of Egypt, Syria, and Iraq on the Soviet Union for arms and economic aid. Even while the relations between these states and the Soviet Union deteriorated, the program of massive rearmament was accelerated on a greater scale.

Despite the acceptance of Secretary of State Rogers's plan, and the ending of the war of attrition on the canal in August 1970, the Soviet Union immediately took advantage of the standstill to introduce more missiles on the ceasefire line. Despite the publicized expulsion of the Soviet military advisers and technicians from Egypt in the summer of 1972, the treaties of friendship and cooperation, which were signed with Egypt and Iraq in the early seventies, provided for the continued massive infusion of Soviet arms, consultation and collaboration in regional and international policies. Military assistance to Syria was increased and accelerated.

In part, it was the Nixon-Brezhnev détente agreement in May 1972 which prompted some of the Arab clients of the Soviet Union to reconsider their relations with Moscow. By 1973, however, it was clear that détente was having no effect in reducing—on the contrary, it increased—the Soviet military activity in Iraq and Syria. Simultaneously, the Soviet Mediterranean fleet, and particularly its amphibious and air operational strengths, was greatly increased. It continued to use shore facilities in Egypt and Syria, and was complemented by a stronger presence in the Indian Ocean, where the West had been weakened by the British withdrawal from the Persian Gulf.

In the war of October 1973 it became clear that the Soviet Union had prior knowledge of the coordinated attack on Israel by Egypt and Syria. Détente, however, was not understood by the Soviet Union to mean sharing this information with its American partner, in spite of its formal obligation undertaken in the U.S.-Soviet agreement of 24 June 1973. Nor did it exert any effort in seeking a cease-fire. On the contrary, it urged, in a series of notes, the nonbelligerent Arab states to join in the fight. And for some time before that it had been encouraging them to apply the "oil weapon" against the West (later it urged them to continue the oil embargo against the United States until the moment it had been lifted).

On the third day of the war the Israelis halted the Syrian advance in the North. On the fourth day, the Soviet Union began a massive airlift of arms to Egypt and Syria; its allies, North Korea and North Vietnam, supplied pilots for the Syrian air force. Even when the imminent collapse of the Egyptian Third Army at the end of the second week of hostilities forced the Soviet Union to seek an immediate cease-fire, it did so by threatening disruption of the détente. No sooner was the cease-fire agreement worked out in Moscow with the United States Secretary of State, Dr. Kissinger, than the Soviet Union ventured a repetition of its August 1970 performance by seeking to introduce further, more sophisticated weapons into Egypt.

The importance of the Middle East, in contrast to Vietnam, in the confrontation between the United States and the Soviet Union derives from the proximity of the region to Europe and Russia. It is the meeting place of three continents, Africa, Asia, and Europe. It is a vast reservoir of oil, upon the availability of which depends the life of all the industrial countries in the West.

The Soviet Union has shown a keen appreciation of this importance. At the end of the Suez War, it made the transition from a faraway, silent spectator, to a strident agitator in the area. Its violation of the August 1970 standstill agreement on the canal revealed the complaisance of the United States, which, in turn, encouraged the steady Soviet build-up and expansion of its military presence in Egypt, Syria, and Iraq. Seen as a signal of the West's weakness, the Rogers plan led to a hardening of the Soviet-Arab line.

More recently, the Soviet Union has developed links with the

Palestine Liberation Organization, which could be used as a "destruct mechanism" of a possible peace settlement.

While the Soviet Union uses détente as an instrument for the advancement of its own policies in the Middle East, the dilemma of the United States is clear: in order to detach the Arabs from the Soviet Union, it must restrain the Israelis and press them into accepting an accommodation which can seriously weaken their security. This also means saving the Soviet Union from defeat. It will continue its policy of expansion in the region, notwithstanding détente, in spite of the alleged "end of the era of confrontation" between the superpowers and whatever the consequences of the diplomatic efforts of Dr. Kissinger to achieve peace in the Middle East. One cannot help remembering that in June 1973 Dr. Kissinger declared that the United States and the Soviet Union "will make an effort not to become *inextricably* involved in the Arab-Israeli conflict" and the two countries signed a solemn agreement to "continue to exert their efforts to promote the quickest possible settlement in the Middle East." The ink was not yet dry on this declaration when the Soviet Union began to speed up its arms deliveries to the Middle East which made possible the October War.

*   *   *

Détente in the Age of Subversion

As has been noted, détente, in Soviet eyes, is not incompatible with subversion. What the Russians understand by *détente* is consistent with what the West means by *subversion*.

In the Soviet view détente entails the *de jure* as well as the *de facto* recognition by the members of NATO and other Western countries of the permanent division of Europe on ideological lines, and the validity of the Brezhnev doctrine which "justified" Soviet military intervention in any Communist country which departs from "socialist" principles, as defined in Moscow.

In the Soviet view "subversion" is what Western countries would be doing to the Soviet Union and other Communist countries if Moscow conceded that principle of free movement of persons and ideas which is required for a genuine détente. Similarly, as understood by the Soviet Union, the cold war includes all Western activities considered by Moscow to be hostile, including any Western criticisms of the Soviet treatment of political dissidents. "Peaceful coexistence," on the other hand, is regarded in Moscow as essentially a transitory—

although possibly prolonged—phase in relations between the Soviet Union and non-Communist states pending the "final triumph of communism." During this phase, the Soviet Union reserves the right to subvert other countries, while sealing itself off from, and in other ways resisting, any exposure to non-Communist ideas and influences.

There are thus two sets of rules: on the Soviet side, a right to operate anywhere and to subvert any other country; and on the Western side, the obligation to avoid criticisms of the Soviet Union and of all countries under Soviet protection, and to abstain from communicating to those countries any ideas which their rulers think might make their citizens critical of them.

Soviet spokesmen have said repeatedly that "peaceful coexistence" implies the intensification of the struggle between the world systems. The intensification of the struggle implies, above all, more subversion in all its forms.

Détente and China

The Chinese attitude towards détente is basically determined by the Sino-Soviet conflict.

When after the Cultural Revolution China emerged from self-imposed isolation and entered the mainstream of international political life on the level of state relations, it was the result of its perception of the growing Soviet menace. It was this factor which necessitated a shift in Chinese foreign policy. This brought about restoration of diplomatic relations with those countries which had recognized China before the Cultural Revolution, efforts to win recognition from other countries, entry to the United Nations, and *rapprochement* with the United States. The Soviet invasion of Czechoslovakia and the Brezhnev Doctrine made China even more acutely sensitive about the danger of Soviet expansionism.

The shift in Chinese foreign policy has as its primary motive the reduction of this danger. This led not only to a new policy towards the United States and Japan, but also to the support of the idea of a strong, united Western Europe which would continue to tie down Soviet military forces and provide a political counterbalance to the Soviet Union on its Western flank. Hence the Chinese criticism of the Soviet détente moves in Europe (*Peking Review*, 8 February 1974):

> The Soviet Union . . . while making further military deployments in Eastern Europe, took pains to press for the heads of the European governments to meet before the end of last

year in the third stage of the conference on European security and cooperation, so as to lay what it called a "solid foundation" for European security and cooperation. It hoped in this way not only to consolidate its overlordship in Eastern Europe, but also to lull the vigilance of the West European countries, divide them and edge the United States out so it could not put the whole of Europe under its sole domination. . . . The Soviet leading clique has tried its best to advertise "relaxation" of the international situation. However, the reality of the stepped-up Soviet arms expansion and war preparations in Europe and its intensified contention with the United States in the Middle East have relentlessly exploded the détente myth. . . .

While the Chinese assert that for all their talks about détente the two superpowers are engaged in a struggle to achieve world hegemony, the Soviet press maintains that the Chinese "modified at the Tenth (Party) Congress (held in 1973) their foreign policy in such a way as to be able to use various forces, including the imperialist circles, for their struggle with the Soviet Union, the paramount obstacle on the way to Peking's hegemony" (*Mezhdunarodnaya Zhizn*, January 1974).

*　　*　　*

Given its geopolitical context and the nature of the Sino-Soviet conflict China can have either a policy of equidistance vis-à-vis the Soviet Union and the U.S., or a policy of *rapprochement* with the U.S. (with the Soviet Union being "enemy number one"). The Sino-Soviet *rapprochement*, the regular bugbear of Western analysts, is unlikely in the present state of Sino-Soviet relations, and even in the post-Maoist period, although factional struggle can be seen as offering an opportunity eventually to be exploited by the Soviet Union.

In this situation the American advances to the Soviet Union cause irritation among Chinese leaders. They look with growing concern at the Soviet-American summit meetings as Chou En-lai made clear in his speech at a banquet for President Nyerere in March 1974. They have shown their disappointment on several occasions. When Dr. Kissinger visited Peking in October 1973 not even a common communiqué was produced. Shortly afterwards the heads of the respective diplomatic missions were withdrawn from Peking and Washington. The visit of Dr. Kissinger to Moscow in March 1974 caused another painful reaction on the part of the Chinese leaders. They perceive the American détente policy vis-à-vis the Soviet Union as jeopardizing both European and Chinese security interests.

Détente and the U.S.-Europe Relations

It is not just the détente policy itself that has caused the present state of disarray in the Atlantic Alliance but it has certainly contributed to this disarray. The fact that the post-Gaullist regime in France is straining the alliance to breaking point is not sufficient explanation for it. It was the Nixon Doctrine which helped to release the forces detrimental to the Atlantic Alliance and made possible their narrow-minded nationalistic ascendancy.

At the moment, however, the problem is not how to apportion the blame—this can be left to future historians—but how the special relationship between the United States and Europe, which was and is the only realistic basis for the survival of Western civilization, can be preserved.

For that purpose it is not sufficient to concentrate on the details of day-to-day politics of the alliance, on the mechanisms of decision making, on the accommodation of national interests, on the "atmospherics" favoring or undermining such adjustments, in short, on the pragmatic side of American and European diplomacy. No less important is a wider historical context of such analysis which is concerned with the fundamental purposes of the alliance.

It is only within this context that success and failures of diplomacy can be judged. Diplomacy, however brilliant, is no substitute for policy, and policy, particularly one which stresses its "realistic" character, has to be assessed by its results. Looked upon in this way the policy of détente has very little to show in terms of either promoting Western interests or Western cohesion. Shuttle diplomacy of Dr. Kissinger may be dazzling, but just as it is difficult to see what were the actual results of the peripatetic efforts of General de Gaulle, so it is difficult to see the positive historical consequences of Dr. Kissinger's travels to implement his "grand design" for the "structure of peace." The epigones of the general try to imitate his foreign policy performance, but *où sont les neiges d'antan*? What happened to the "grand design" on "Europe from the Atlantic to the Urals"? What remained as a result of all those diplomatic tours to Russia, Latin America, Canada (*'Vive Quebec libre!'*)? Similarly, a comparison of the aims of American policy—as formulated by President Nixon and Secretary Kissinger—shows a striking contrast between promise and fulfillment, between hopes raised and the results obtained.

During the period of the implementation of this policy the balance of power has shifted against the West. Instead of a new "pentagonal balance" we have witnessed the disenchantment, to a smaller or greater degree, of Europe, China, and Japan, the three pillars on which the new "structure of peace" was supposed to rest. The American-European relations in particular are worse than ever before in the last half century. What is more, such dangerous symptoms do not elicit sufficient anxiety on either side of the Atlantic to foster initiative to improve the situation. They are smothered by the soothing perspective of détente. The dangers involved in the present drift in the Atlantic Alliance would suggest that the fundamentals of this policy should be soberly assessed and brought home to the general public. Otherwise no realistic cure for the present ills of the American-European relations can be achieved. Diplomatic or administrative palliatives would not be sufficient to have this particular world restored.

Détente: Past and Future

Détente is not a modern Soviet invention. Its tactical beginnings are to be found in Lenin's views on Bolshevik strategy and tactics in 1921. Western enthusiasts proclaimed its existence already in Khrushchev's time. But the present policy of détente emerged as a result of a United States initiative, a concomitant to America's reduction of its global commitments. It was conceived as a means which was expected to facilitate American disengagement from its confrontation with the Soviet Union, to permit a policy of balancing between Moscow and Peking (made possible by the resumption of American-Chinese relations), and to promote an increased international role for Europe and Japan.

As has been noted, the results of the détente policy in its present form do not conform to its political premises, to its proclaimed purposes, and to the expectations raised with the public at large.

The Soviet Union has deftly turned the tables and used détente to promote its own interests against the interests of the United States and of the Western countries in general, rather than accept détente as a *modus vivendi* leading to a "structure of peace." Western policies were immediately handicapped because of the illusions generated by the Western perception of détente as based on genuine relaxation and reciprocity, while the Soviet Union saw it as an opportunity to lull Western public opinion into a lack of vigilance towards the perils it was facing, to divide the West by exploiting the differences between America and Europe, in short to promote one-sidedly and vigorously its own political and strategic interests.

The experience of détente in action during the period since it was proclaimed is a string of Western disappointments, of political developments which were directly contrary to the hopes of the architects of this policy. There has been since then a general weakening of the Western position strategically, economically, and politically.

First of all, détente was presented as promising increased security for the West, that is, for both America and Europe. The SALT-I agreement was hailed as a turning point in the arms race. It was seen as a genuinely reciprocal arrangement stabilizing the strategic balance, thereby dispelling American and European anxieties about security. The acceptance of nuclear parity with the Soviet Union was interpreted as a step towards further reciprocal measures of arms control (through supplementary arrangements in SALT-II) rather than a step which put on the agenda the possibility of the Soviet Union reaching for military superiority, the American debate about the proper response to it and the highest military budgets in the peacetime history of the two countries. It is not surprising that the Western public, fed for years on the optimistic fare of détente, is puzzled and bewildered, and that the West is at a disadvantage in matters of security-spending (Soviet leaders do not have to "sell" it to their public politically). The repeated visits of Kissinger and Nixon to Moscow are not likely to affect this picture in favor of the West, as is now quite clear.

As far as Europe is concerned, the Soviet-supported Middle Eastern War resulting in the Arab oil embargo has struck a heavy blow to the NATO alliance. A combination of the détente-induced complacency and of the most shortsighted economic nationalism has seriously undermined its cohesion. For the first time the prospect of European neutralism as a first step towards the "Finlandization" of Europe has acquired reality. Politically, the Western world has reached such a point of disarray that *Time* magazine has even referred to "the West" as an obsolete concept.

It is not difficult to see that the present kind of détente policy has contributed to this outcome. The exaggerated American preoccupation with Soviet exigencies resulted in a neglect of European susceptibilities and the universal hopes generated by détente lowered the Europeans' concern about their security so much that Dr. Kissinger's "Year of Europe" turned out to be a resounding flop. Later, there was a chain reaction to the treating of allies as a nuisance and of enemies as friends. One cannot absolve the Europeans for their vacillations and the shortsightedness of their conduct. During and after the Middle East War the European "allies" indeed behaved in a most reprehensible and unallied fashion. The fact remains that American policy instead of strengthening the Atlantic community has only deepened the already existing European malaise and contributed to the weakening of the alliance.

While the Soviet Union is registering slow and intermittent, but cumulative, political gains and becoming more menacing, the West is bickering. At a time when the internal situation in many Western countries is at its most dismal since the war, when détente has clearly not brought any *quid pro quo* for all the Western concessions made for its sake, when the newly recognized East Germans are already occasionally resuming the tactics of traffic obstruction to Berlin (a problem which détente was supposed to have solved) the picture of political disunity, both within Europe and between Europe and America can only gladden the hearts of the Soviet leaders. The political illusions of détente have certainly contributed to this picture. The Soviet press is gloating with satisfaction over the mess on both sides of the Atlantic, and the Soviet leaders are only too keen to profit by the French-American quarrels. The politics of blackmail, so successfully practiced by the Arab countries, may not remain the monopoly of those countries. Détente will not preclude its application by the Soviet Union as well, once it feels that it can be used without undue risks. The Watergate paralysis in the United States and the economic beggar-my-neighbor policies of the European states may offer new opportunities to the Soviet Union. Its imperial aggrandizement is predicated on the weakening of the political will of its opponents. A genuine détente is, of course, most desirable, but in its present form détente proved to be an effective instrument in the process of weakening the West, as it has hidden from it the political and military realities of the situation and lowered the threshold of risks for the Soviet Union. It made possible the presentation in the West of political failures as successes for peace, of businessmen's fantasies about profits as rational enterprises in the interests of the state, of Western military decline as an achievement leading towards strategic stability. It is time for the West to recover its sense of reality if Western civilization is to survive. The Soviet attitude to the détente, even in its present form, is not irreversible, it may well one day be followed by a more militant posture as happened before when the Soviet Union decided that the circumstances were ripe for a change of strategy.

It is only as the end product of a well thought out and firmly executed policy, supported by public opinion aware of the issues, that a genuine détente may come. It can only be a result of the Soviet recognition of its necessity and it would certainly be welcome. No one wishes a recurrence of military confrontations which carry with them unforeseen consequences. However, détente cannot be based on illusions. It must be a two-way street. The Soviet Union must contribute to it by giving some indications that it does not intend cynically to exploit it as an opportunity to improve its ability to subvert and destroy the West. Détente will not be genuine as long as "peaceful coexistence" is for the Soviet leaders only a euphemism for a conflict by all means short of war.

An evolution of Soviet policy towards a meaningful détente would require its moving away from this position. Among the measures that can be taken as indications of such an evolution in the Soviet Union would be the following points:

1. Abandoning the "ideological war" against the West.

2. Decelerating the arms build-up.

3. Giving up the idea of military superiority in the SALT-II negotiations.

4. Providing a proof of a serious approach to détente at the talks on European security by liberalizing the movement of peoples and the flow of ideas.

5. Stopping the sabotage of the peace efforts in the Middle East.

6. Discontinuing the supply of arms to the so-called guerrilla movements and desisting from other forms of subversion.

If none of these steps is taken, Soviet assurances about détente will remain empty. If, however, some of them are taken, even gradually, it would be an indication of an evolution in the right direction. When all of them begin to be implemented it would be a sign that the Soviet Union is genuinely interested in détente and is prepared to take its place as a responsible member of the community of nations.

DETENTE OR ENTENTE? *

Richard Rosecrance

In this article, Richard Rosecrance outlines Soviet objections to détente. Although an American case against détente can also be made, both nations have strong reasons to preserve and strengthen this relationship. These countries, as well as the rest of the world, face various

* Source: Foreign Affairs (April 1975), pp. 464-481.

uncertainties in the near future, and links between nations are needed for dealing with these problems. If under these circumstances the détente relationship collapses, a rigid polarization could follow, and historical parallels indicate that such a static situation is dangerous.

The U.S.-Soviet détente is neither fully understood nor certain to endure. The sheer complexity of détente balancing—holding the Soviet Union, China, the Western allies, and Japan in a complicated network of associations with the United States which involve conflict as well as cooperation—may not last. Even if it could be sustained, some argue that American interests dictate that it should be dropped or radically modified. To others détente is an attitude, but not a policy. It represents a desirable and overdue recognition of realities in foreign policy—the need to achieve better relations with the Soviet Union and China. But it does not specify where the United States should go from there. Détente without a positive core of policy goals could jeopardize American relations with Japan and Western Europe without gaining any durable benefit from the Soviet Union. The collapse of the Soviet-American trade agreement makes it seem even less likely that the United States can use détente as a means to extract important concessions from the U.S.S.R.

Other critics contend that whatever the merits of détente policy, the political costs it imposes cannot ultimately be borne. Congress and the American public can understand and support a policy which clearly discriminates friend from foe. They can accept a policy of nonintervention and reliance upon allies. But they can neither understand nor fully support a policy which switches back and forth: now balancing for one state, now for another.

Such shifts in policy depend upon a bureaucratic mastery of the defense and foreign policy apparatus that has seldom existed in American history. Today they rest on the personal ascendancy of one man, Henry Kissinger. But even in 1975 new centers of opposition to Secretary Kissinger—on the President's staff and in the Defense Department, to say nothing of Congress—were threatening his unparalleled sway. No successor seems likely to achieve a similar primacy.

Entirely aside from its apparent structural weaknesses, the opponents of détente now note the presumed advantages which the Soviet Union may be coming to derive. Pentagon and congressional critics see the United States being lulled into a false sense of security while the U.S.S.R. makes signal advances in international power and influence. The SALT II agreement reached at Vladivostok does not allay critics' fears because it perpetuates Soviet advantages in strategic throw-weight and allows such a large number of multiple targetable reentry vehicles (MIRVs) that U.S. land-based forces are likely to be vulnerable to attack. In the economic field as well, the Soviet Union and its militant Arab allies, so it is argued, have put the industrial countries, including the United States, on the defensive. Western states are now squabbling about economic policy, and Russia has gained a significant edge militarily.

It is useful to record these negative estimates of the value and viability of the détente if only to lay the ground for counterargument. For it is this writer's view that the superpower relationship must be preserved, and that if it collapses a much greater tension and polarization in world politics will follow. At the extreme this could lead perhaps to overt conflict between America and Russia. The choices that American and Soviet decision makers face are similar to those confronted by European and American statesmen in eras past. Before World War I and immediately after World War II, critical decisions were made by European and American leaders which led directly to major periods of conflict or war. These decisions were by no means inevitable: they were the result of conscious choices, not the impartial and irresistible pressure of circumstances. The parallel is that today the world is moving toward possibly similar and equally disastrous decisions, decisions which could affect mankind for decades to come. The choice that is involved is essentially between a mixed international system in which allies and potential adversaries are held together in a network of fundamental cooperation, and a system in which lines of conflict are starkly drawn, with the United States and its allies more or less firmly on one side, and its enemies more or less firmly on the other. It is a choice between a new form of bipolarity and an ambivalent system in which neither cooperation nor conflict is permitted to dominate patterns of alignment.

The point of decision is coming nearer if only because conflicts in world politics are becoming sharper: the détente has suffered important reverses in the past eighteen months—the Soviet-American accord linking trade and a greater freedom of emigration has foundered; the Middle East War of 1973 raised important and still unanswered questions about détente's value in both Moscow and Washington. Meanwhile the oil crisis has signaled new and yet-undigested shifts in economic power, and compounded the already grave twin problems of inflation and recession throughout the world.

But equally important and in a longer term sense more critical, the political basis of Western progress and stability may be cast into question. It has frequently been observed that democratic political structures have become more fragile. They cannot abide inflation, yet neither can they tolerate the remedies which would be necessary to stop or contain it. Even more certainly, however, they may not survive a prolonged period of economic dislocation. Any sustained industrial or economic chaos would create a belt of discontent and political ferment running across Western and central Europe which could ultimately undermine the bases of internal politics forged after World War II. Depending on the choices that are made in the next several years, the basic political world of the post-World War II period could come unstuck.

II

The historical parallels for this situation are at least three in number. The first is to be found in German policy in 1890. Prior to Chancellor Otto von Bismarck's dismissal early in that year, European diplomacy had been dextrously bound up in a network of alliances and alignments that linked Germany with every major state except France. Bismarck had been particularly successful in preventing the chronic rivals, Austria and Russia, from coming to blows over Balkan real estate. The alliance ties with Austria dated back to 1879 on a bilateral basis, and they had been reaffirmed in the Triple Alliance of Germany, Austria-Hungary, and Italy. The Russians, on the other hand, had not lacked for German support and friendship. Their aims had been supported nationally by Bismarck, but the German chancellor had also been careful to sponsor an opposing coalition, including England, Austria, and Italy, to prevent Russia from actually taking military steps to realize them. In 1887, Bismarck had negotiated the Reinsurance Treaty with the tsar, to secure Russia against Austrian expansion. Bismarckian alliances were condemned as "inconsistent" because the alliance with Austria was directed against Russia, and the alliance with Russia against Austria. At the same time it was precisely the "inconsistency" of Bismarck's central position that allowed him to keep on good terms with both protagonists, and to prevent them from going to war.

After Bismarck's fall, the new German emperor and his chancellor, Caprivi, decided to drop the Russian connection. It was thought to prevent an alliance with England, and it made their link with Vienna much more difficult. It was simpler to eliminate the inconsistency and take sides in world politics. As it turned out, of course, England was not ready to be one of Germany's formal allies. She was willing to cooperate only on limited bases in particular parts of the world. When this was proved, it was already too late for Berlin to reverse its course: Russia had already allied with France, commencing a new process of polarization in European politics.

The polarization was not yet complete, however. England remained unconnected with the Triple Alliance or with its Franco-Russian adversary. Nor were the British ready to join one against the other. In 1904, in Lord Lansdowne's ministry, the British concluded a colonial entente with the French which was supposed to alleviate the friction over Egypt and Morocco. But the entente was not a general alliance, nor was it directed against Germany. Lansdowne had treated overtures from Germany and France evenhandedly. He had worked together with Germany in Venezuela, and the prospect of a more far-reaching accommodation with Berlin had not been ruled out. The defeat of France's ally, Russia, by Japan in 1905 made the reconciliation with France still less attractive, and France's own obeisance before German pressure in that same year cast doubt on its solidity as a useful makeweight in world politics. Lansdowne's understanding with the French was based on previous British policy: it was limited; it operated in specific areas of the world; it was not intended to circumscribe British freedom of action.

But Sir Edward Grey, Lansdowne's successor at the Foreign Office, began in 1906 to treat the French entente as if it were a fixed and general article of British policy, almost as if it were an alliance.[1] Grey did not seek to keep on good terms with both France and Germany. The Germans also ceased trying to lure England into their net. They sought rather to build a continental position which was unassailable.[2] Once again, consistency was chosen at the expense of general cooperation, and the European international system became finally polarized into two camps: Triple Alliance and Triple Entente. World War I followed shortly thereafter.

But the most salient blunder in modern international relations occurred after World War II when Russia and America lurched into a cold war that neither wanted or could easily afford. President Roosevelt knew that the United States would never fight the U.S.S.R. over the Soviet position in Eastern Europe; intermittently, he understood how important the East European buffer was to Premier Stalin.

---

[1] I am indebted here to recent research in Grey's papers by Mr. Alan Alexandroff.

[2] Fritz Fischer argues: "Up to 1911 Germany had not succeeded in adopting Britain's policy of concluding compromises with her competitors, for she had equated moderation with an inferiority incompatible with the world power status which was her aim." *Germany's Aims in the First World War* (New York: W. W. Norton, 1967), p. 24.

Yet he and President Truman allowed themselves to be trapped into a policy that made conflict with the Soviet Union inevitable. It was not possible for the United States to meddle in the Soviet sphere of occupation and still maintain Russian friendship.

Similarly, Stalin made egregious errors in his relations with the Western powers. He did not realize that Roosevelt's offers of friendship were genuine, and that in any event the American leader was not in a position really to oppose Soviet policy in Eastern Europe. The very abrasiveness in Soviet dealings with Western statesmen after 1945 actually made easier the creation of the strong group of anti-Communist nations that it was in the Russian interest to avoid. Here the issue was not that of choosing between two possible partners, but of maintaining tolerable relations where interests were partly opposed but also partly harmonious. Bismarck had maintained good relations with Russia in similar circumstances in the 1880s. In 1945, however, rather than live with the ambiguity, both Russians and Americans lapsed into more "consistent" modes of diplomacy. The result was the cold war, and an ensuing series of major crises in world politics.

III

Today similar temptations beset the two major powers. The American case against superpower détente is well known and needs only brief restatement here. Critics claim that the United States has gained little and lost much from its "special relationship" with the U.S.S.R. In the Middle East crisis of 1973, it is contended, the Soviet Union did little to restrain its clients, but then threatened to intervene to save them from Israeli counteroffensives. Despite American efforts to pledge Moscow to a "hands-off" position, the Soviet resupply of the Arabs took place at the first sign of an Arab deficiency. Only after the Soviet effort was in full swing did America reluctantly begin to aid Israel. Americans ponder the value of détente in managing crises if on each occasion the Soviets still threaten unilateral intervention.

In economic terms, it is held, the Soviet Union only seeks high technological inputs from the United States and other industrial countries, not a stable trading relationship with two-way advantages. Even in the agricultural field, the Soviet Union will use its access to Western food markets merely to supplement harvests, buying episodically and with little warning.

In the military realm, congressional and Pentagon specialists fear not only Moscow's strategic rearmament but also the growing power of its conventional land and sea forces. The Soviet threat to the central region in Europe is greater now than it was five years ago, and

Western, particularly American, strength has declined.[3] The Soviet Navy is not growing in size, but is definitely increasing in capability. The danger it poses to U.S. carrier forces has considerably increased.[4] The Soviets, it is argued, will use their growing might to gain political influence in Europe, the Middle East, and the Indian Ocean.

Finally, the Soviets are seen as encouraging the militant oil producers to take advantage of the economic troubles of the West. Growing talk of counteraction against Arab states—whether it be political, economic or military—has downplayed the Soviet role. Yet the more U.S. leaders think about intervention, the more surely they must consider Soviet involvement.

In short, the opposition to détente in America—while diverse and inconsistent from one group to another—must be rated today as strong. One could well imagine developments that would make it predominant in the next few years.

IV

It is not generally recognized, however, that the Russian case against détente is fully as strong as the American one. For many reasons it is a pity that the Soviet Union is such a closed society. If we knew more about opposition in Soviet bureaucratic and political circles to Brezhnev's policy, perhaps some Americans would see it in a more favorable light. In any event, from a variety of Soviet bureaucratic perspectives it could be argued that many of the supposed advantages to the U.S.S.R. of the détente policy have not in fact accrued. America did not remain in a state of post-Vietnam paralysis after 1972. The revulsion against the war and things military did not lead to a drastic cut in the U.S. defense budget. The weakness of U.S. foreign policy in Europe was not as great as the Russians had thought it might be. Russia's *Westpolitik* was a successful reciprocation of Willy Brandt's *Ostpolitik*, but it did not lead to European political weakness nor to a favorable environment for the reception of Soviet policy. In the Vienna mutual and balanced force reduction negotiations, the Europeans, not the United States, have pressed for tough negotiating stances. In the Conference on Security and Cooperation in Europe, the Europeans, more than the Americans, were unwilling to concede on political and economic issues unless the

---

3 *The Military Balance, 1974-75* points out: "In 1962 the American land, sea and air forces in Europe totalled 434,000; now the figure is around 300,000. There were 26 Soviet divisions in Eastern Europe in 1967; now there are 31." (London: International Institute for Strategic Studies, 1974), p. 101.

4 U.S. Department of Defense, *Annual Defense Department Report, FY 1975* (4 March 1974), pp. 11-12.

Soviet Union would yield important concessions in the field of information and cultural exchange. Far from softening up European populaces for more far-reaching Soviet gestures, a limit to the rapprochement appeared to have been drawn.

In the Middle East the United States rebounded with vigor after October 1973. The Russians lost leverage with Egypt and Syria and had little in Tel Aviv. Secretary Kissinger, on the other hand, maintained and increased his influence on both sides. At minimum the October War showed that the Arabs might win battles, but that they could not force Israel to withdraw from the territories occupied in 1967. This meant that a solution could only be found diplomatically. Kissinger was in a unique position to negotiate the beginnings of such a settlement. The American reconciliation with Egypt even improved his negotiating position with Israel: Tel Aviv could no longer take American support for granted. His position was also enhanced by his style of negotiation: taking a leaf from Bismarck's book, he refused to take sides. He knew that opposite numbers cannot simply be "forced" to agree. The art of gaining diplomatic acceptance depends upon a subtle mixture of constraint and volition. Whatever the realistic pressures, a statesman has to be persuaded to reach an accommodation, if it is to endure. This policy was in direct contradiction to that used previously in dealing with the militant Arab world; it was also in sharp contrast to the cold-war diplomacy of 1945–47. From the Soviet standpoint, therefore, American foreign policy success in the Middle East was completely unprecedented. Brezhnev's doctrines of U.S. weakness and passivity had not prepared the Russians for such an outcome.

Equally important, though the U.S. military position might seem weak to Americans, it looked formidable to the Russians. To be sure, the U.S.S.R. gained important advantages in the 1972 SALT negotiations. The Soviets were building launchers, the Americans were not. The former had to be persuaded to stop. At the same time, the United States was into the full rush of its MIRV (and follow-on MaRV [maneuverable, independently targetable reentry vehicles]) technology. In numbers of warheads and in accuracy, Washington remained far ahead of Moscow. It was not until the announcement of four new Soviet missiles (three initially equipped with MIRVs) in August 1973 that it began to appear that the Russians would catch up.

The failure to reach agreement on limitations on MIRVed missiles in June 1974, and the relatively high levels (1,320) set for such missiles in November, however, did not leave the United States in an inferior position. Both larger and more accurate warheads (the

Mk 12A and a terminally guided MaRV) were in prospect for Minuteman III.[5] Either or both will permit the 550 advanced Minuteman missiles to pose a hard-target threat to a substantial portion of the Soviet land-based missile force. With terminal guidance it will not be long before U.S. CEPs (circular error probable) fall to less than 700 feet. With a 200-kiloton warhead, such accuracies will permit target overpressures of well beyond the 300 pounds per square inch needed to destroy many current ICBM silos.[6]

The superior accuracy of present and prospective U.S. missiles over systems the Soviets have in prospect also has an important bearing on the effectiveness of warheads deployed against a single target or a cluster of targets.[7] American accuracies may more than counterbalance Russian superiority in throw-weight for some time to come, so that by 1980 U.S. first-strike capabilities against Soviet land-based missiles may be considerably greater than corresponding Soviet capabilities against the American fixed-base force.

The 1974 Vladivostok agreement between the U.S.S.R. and the United States, while placing rather high limits on MIRVed missiles, in no way constrains the research and development race in sophisticated warhead technology, mobile intercontinental ballistic missiles, and antisubmarine warfare. Any such competition will almost certainly underscore American advantages, not only putting some Soviet systems under constraint or pressure but also demonstrating American prowess before the rest of the world. Very accurate missiles,

---

[5] Ibid., pp. 52-55.

[6] Dr. Kosta Tsipis in *Offensive Missiles*, Stockholm Paper No. 5, Stockholm International Peace Research Institute (1974), develops a measure of the lethality of U.S. and Soviet warheads. If the United States adds terminal guidance and doubles the yield of Poseidon and Minuteman III warheads, "the total (kiloton) value of the U.S. arsenal will rise to over 110,000, that is, to a value five times more than the Soviet nuclear arsenal could possibly have by 1981-82, and high enough to threaten the Soviet silos with assured destruction" (p. 27).

[7] These conclusions are reinforced by recent revelations concerning the "fratricide" effect which limits the number of reentry vehicles which can be deployed against a single target in rapid succession. The detonation of the first warhead may disable subsequent ones before the latter can hit the target. In addition, when a number of incoming warheads are targeted on a relatively dense cluster of ICBM silos, their explosions cause crater debris, shock waves and nuclear clouds which reduce accuracy and penetration of subsequent warheads. This makes U.S. Minuteman fields particularly difficult to attack. The answer to this problem appears to be higher accuracy, so that no more than one reliable reentry vehicle need be allocated to a single target. U.S. Congress, Senate, Committee on Armed Services, Testimony of Secretary of the Air Force John McLucas, *FY 1975 Authorization for Military Procurement, Research and Development, etc.,* Part 2. *Authorizations*, 7, 19, and 22 February 1974, p. 317. This issue is extensively reviewed in Lt. Col. J. J. McGlinchey and Dr. Jacob W. Seelig, "Why ICBMs Can Survive," *Air Force* magazine (September 1974), pp. 82-85.

higher-yield warheads, maneuverable reentry vehicles are only some of the innovations that will follow from the reopening of the Pandora's box of American technological wizardry. Despite the U.S.-Soviet *aide-mémoire* of December 1974 and the offer to negotiate lower ceilings on MIRVed missiles, the completion of currently planned U.S. deployments and force improvement programs at levels below the agreed ceiling will put considerable pressure on Soviet systems.

The détente can be attacked from other Soviet standpoints. In the traditional Soviet lexicon the strength of adversary coalitions has been roughly assessed in terms of their cohesion. This is not a surprising criterion because it is one the U.S.S.R. uses in its relations with Eastern Europe. A cohesive Soviet bloc, from Moscow's standpoint, is *ipso facto* a strong bloc. Conversely, a Western alliance in disarray is automatically weaker: it is both more vulnerable to Soviet pressure and more open to Soviet blandishments. These assessments are made independently of the basic strength of the component units of the alliance. On the other hand, while it is true that American relationships with traditional allies are somewhat looser than they were ten years ago, it is also true (except in raw materials) that the strength of U.S. allies has grown greatly over the last ten years, certainly in economic and to some degree even in military technological fields. Thus the Soviet Union now faces a stronger alliance than it did previously, if one that is less tightly knit. Where previously the Soviets encountered a single American-allied response, now there are several. But in certain areas British, French, and even Japanese objections may be harder to deal with than American ones.

In other words, détente, by drawing the United States slightly closer to the Soviet Union, has not simplified the U.S.S.R.'s negotiating task. Because of greater independence within U.S. alliances, American assent is no longer the assent of the developed world. Even after U.S. concurrence, Paris, Bonn, London, and Tokyo must still be dealt with. If détente is to be fully implemented, Moscow should even want a more cohesive Western alliance, if only to be sure that its tentative agreements with the United States will be endorsed by other powerful states.

A final thorn in Moscow's side is the U.S. connection with Peking. The American rapprochement with Russia's major enemy is hardly likely to make American policy more consistent with Soviet aims. Of course, long-term normalization of the Sino-Soviet relationship is not entirely out of the question. But neither the Soviets nor the Chinese appear willing to make the fundamental concessions that would make that possible. The Chinese assert their independence at every point. If the current regime will not accept dictation from Moscow, their successors seem even less likely to do so. They will not give up their nuclear weapons; nor will they concede Chinese territory. The Russians, on the other hand, are likely to demand far-reaching concessions for any accommodation. China's very power and independence will lead the Soviet Union to insist upon the most formal and complete coordination of all policies from Moscow. Nothing short of this will assure Russian leaders that China would not use an accommodation to further its own divisive policies. The Russians view China as an "apostate" power which must make no small obeisance to be admitted back among the "faithful." Thus the terms for a resumption of normal relations between them will be very stiff. There is little evidence that any Chinese regime would be willing to pay them.

But if the Sino-Soviet split is a relatively dependable reference point in interstate relations, the United States gains major advantages. Secretary Kissinger, like Bismarck, is in the position of being "honest broker" between them. Kissinger formally declines such a role. He told James Reston recently: "The current policy for the United States is to take account of what exists and to conduct a policy of meticulous honesty with both of them, so that neither believes we are trying to use one against the other." [8] It remains true, however, that Washington has approached Moscow through Peking. Just as Bismarck's Dual Alliance with Austria in 1879 made possible the Three Emperors' Alliance in 1881, so it is that good American relations with China make the Soviet Union more pliable. Only after the China visit in 1972 could Kissinger and Nixon have expected such a profitable reception in Russia.

It could even be argued that the solidity of the Chinese military position on the Soviet border, tying up 1,000,000 Soviet troops, had some useful implications for European defense. In Secretary Schlesinger's fiscal 1975 posture statement it is noted that the West may be able to counter a Warsaw Pact mobilized threat to central Europe of 80 to 90 divisions if NATO continues and expands its force-improvement programs. But it could not hope to cope with the threat of up to 130 divisions that would result from a transfer of Soviet troops from the eastern regions of the Soviet Union. Since the Soviet Union has to be concerned with the Chinese theater, however, NATO can effectively concentrate upon meeting the designated threat of 80

---

[8] *The New York Times* (13 October 1974).

to 90 divisions.[9] This means that Chinese forces are an essential analytical ingredient in European defense. As long as Sino-American ties remain tolerable, Russia faces complications if it exerts pressure on either front. Some experts have recently speculated that if Russia sought to attack China or to eliminate Chinese nuclear capabilities, it could not be certain that Chinese nuclear weapons might not be replenished from the American arsenal,[10] adding additional uncertainties to the Soviet calculus.

V

With such pervasive reasons on both Soviet and American parts for distrust of détente, it may seem surprising that it has lasted this long. There is certainly nothing automatic in its continuance, nor has it become an accepted article of policy in either Washington or Moscow. Important political and bureaucratic groups in each capital almost certainly oppose it. On the other hand, there are overriding claims in its favor. One very important consideration is that international politics would become a much more unpredictable arena if America and Russia were not frequently able to coordinate their policies. And policy coordination, at least episodically, has become possible because the Soviet Union has begun to recognize that it derives important benefits from the existing international situation which might be jeopardized by radical adventures.

The Soviet Union and the United States are now at the summit of the international power and status pyramid. Both are conscious that there are forces and nations in world politics that are rising to challenge their ascendancy. China and Japan, the Arab nations, Iran, Brazil, and even India, to say nothing of the states of Western Europe, may be much more powerful relative to the superpowers ten years from now than they are at present.

In years past, Russia probably believed that forces producing domestic unrest or revolution would greatly improve her international position while harming that of the United States, the apostle of the *status quo*. Today, it is no longer clear that Moscow calculates that it would be the beneficiary of domestic chaos. Domestic progress and economic growth seem to be the *sine qua non* of political stability in Eastern Europe. If this growth should falter, or if local Communist regimes sought to deny their citizens a better life in economic and social terms, the pattern of Polish resistance might be repeated in a

---

[9] *Defense Report*, p. 89.

[10] International Institute for Strategic Studies, *Strategic Survey 1973* (May 1974), p. 69.

variety of contexts. As the Czechoslovakian example in 1968 showed, these developments would produce political currents and eddies in the Soviet Union itself.

A total disruption of international trade and a severing of economic relations with the West could have grave effects, particularly in Eastern Europe where trade with non-Communist industrial countries has helped to make a better life possible. Indeed, it has been the development of East European economies, partly through Western technological cooperation and trade, which has sustained the momentum of the Communist bloc in its competition with the West. The drive to true "modernity," as many Communist leaders are now beginning to recognize, cannot be sustained in isolation from the rest of the world.[11]

From an opposite point of view, it is no longer unequivocally clear (if indeed it ever was) that it is in Moscow's interest to have local Communist parties triumph in Western states. In the aftermath of World War II and the vacuum of power which resulted, the Soviet Union organized the countries of Eastern Europe through the device of military occupation. Where Soviet troops did not penetrate, as in Yugoslavia, Moscow did not have dependable or controlling influence. Even where Russian troops were present, as in Rumania, the longer term evolution of the regime could not be predicted. The fact is that the Soviet Union bought control only through military power, and even that control is not absolute. It is therefore questionable whether governmental coalitions including Communists, where Moscow has no military presence, would represent unalloyed boons. Coalitions tend to co-opt local Communists, to make them work within the system. That they would call the tune politically is far from transparent.

But even if Communists were to dominate a government, the independence of European Communist parties has been amply demonstrated in a series of episodes since 1956. These unruly parties would not be a dependable instrument of Russian will. They might even contribute to what has probably been one of Moscow's greatest head-

---

[11] It is significant that in the leading industrial sectors, East European dependence upon imports from the West has been very marked. The Joint Economic Committee study on *Soviet Economic Prospects for the Seventies* observes: "The degree of dependence in fact is considerably greater than the share of the West in total East European imports would indicate. The industries dominating East European growth are leading the way in imports from the West." U.S. Congress, Joint Committee Print, 93d Congress, 27 June 1973, p. 39. Statistical information for all countries but Bulgaria indicates that if Western trade were cut off, East European development would be considerably affected.

aches and fears—the need to commit itself to support regimes which de facto it does not control. Cuba was a major lesson to Russian policy makers in this regard, and they may not want to repeat the experience.

Ultimately, of course, such evolutions would look problematical from Moscow's viewpoint because Western responses could well be unpredictable or severe. Khrushchev's policy was to challenge the West, to take risks, to probe for weak spots. But he did not add much to Russian power and influence. He neither improved the Soviet position in Europe nor in the developing world. He did not prevent China from leaving the bloc. He did not gain an edge over the United States technologically or militarily. Nor did his domestic schemes solve the problem of agriculture, or production of a wide variety of sophisticated industrial goods. Rather, he provoked a Western response that greatly fueled the arms race, provided major counter-challenges in Berlin and Cuba and kept the Soviet Union off-balance. Khrushchev, in this respect, can be held responsible for Kennedy's anti-Communist "world policy."

It is an important question whether the Russians now wish to press a maximum international offensive against the West. They might urge their more militant Arab clients either to reimpose the oil embargo or to raise the price greatly; they might put more pressure on in certain domestic contexts. But the ensuing Western and American response could not be foretold: how much industrial chaos would Western countries accept *without* intervening militarily in the Middle East? And if they did intervene, would the Russians have improved their position? They would then face the alternative either of accepting the local success, and a large-scale and perhaps permanent Western presence in the Middle East, or of very high risk opposition to Western forces. Neither could possibly be attractive to Moscow.

The policy of maximum pressure and "adventurism" also has other defects. During Khrushchev's rule, the Soviets' challenge to Western governments kept them in the position of international "pariahs." Russia was distrusted by many, including some of its titular allies. It was not in a position to forge useful contacts with capitalist economies. The current Russian leadership, in contrast, has sought to stress the Soviet Union's responsible international role, and for the first time Russia has in effect been admitted to a Western system of international relations. Its initiatives are no longer immediately and categorically rejected. Its advice and help are sometimes sought. It has a certain standing in the international community. The long-term goal of recognition and acceptance by Western nations has in effect been achieved.

From a Western point of view, such gains may seem ephemeral, but to Soviet leaders accustomed to backwardness, isolation, and exclusion from international contacts, they are of first importance. One should remember that the Soviet Union is a "new nation" unused to patterns of Western diplomacy and initially incapable of participating in them. Russia's international policy, originally based on a rather vulgar Marxism, was crude. In its Communist lexicon other nations would favor it only if it was in their manifest economic and military interest to do so. If cooperation was not given automatically on the basis of such interests, the only leverage the U.S.S.R. had was through the threat of force and the building of substantial military power. In this sense, after World War II the Soviet Union had "power" in international relations, but it did not possess "influence." For the attainment of "influence" depended upon a strict disciplining of power, and a rather complete avoidance of threat and bluster in world politics. It depended in short on "responsibility" and the development of a more or less predictable policy in international politics. Crises could not be staged from year to year, if the Soviet Union hoped to gain cooperation and help from Western and non-Communist regimes.

Today the Soviet Union faces the choice between crude power and responsible influence in world politics. The attempt to use the former will surely undermine the latter. Since this dilemma is coming to be understood in Moscow, there is reason to believe that Russia's "revolutionary" policy may well be nearing an end. Henceforth it seems likely that Russian gains will be sought through marginal increments in its own domestic political, economic, and military position, and through ties with other nations that do not commit it to crisis intervention. If gains are not sought in this marginalist fashion, the ultimate achievement of modernity in the Soviet Union itself may be jeopardized.

VI

Détente has other important foundations. The pattern of international change today is anarchic. Economic trends, the exhaustion of critical raw materials, the spread of nuclear weaponry, the rapid mobilization of domestic crisis all mean that nations have to react to a much more bewildering and dynamically changing international and domestic environment. Givens of yesteryear are dubious today. . . . There are fissures in the Soviet bloc as well. Rumania has achieved and continues to express a distinctive and independent position in foreign relations. As Czechoslovakia showed in 1968, the placidity of East European Communist regimes is marred by deep currents of unrest. If these rise to the surface, Communist leadership in several countries, not least Yugoslavia, would be affected. Nationality problems continue, along with desires throughout the Soviet orbit for a much greater degree of personal and political freedom, and for access to the Western storehouse of ideas, and industrial and consumer goods. The very "slablike" solidity of Communist governments means that there are few political safety valves for the outlet of discontent. Domestic crises within communism are thus extremely serious, imperiling the regime itself. The Russians have not forgotten that the most unregenerate and thoroughgoing autocracy of the tsars ultimately collapsed of its own weight. International connections with Western states may not prevent domestic change, but they may very well mitigate the advantage which capitalist powers might otherwise seek to gain in such circumstances. Here the Russians clearly bear in mind the danger of interventionist precedents set after World War I.

Trends in the international economy also hold dangers for the Soviet Union. Despite large apparent reserves of oil and natural gas, Russia in recent years has become more dependent upon Middle Eastern sources of supply, and it has coincidentally reduced its fuel and energy exports to Eastern Europe. This paradox is explained by the fact that the new reserves in the northern part of Western Siberia are exceedingly difficult to develop. Thus far, Soviet and East European technology and resources have been inadequate to the task. Western help seems absolutely required if substantial production is to be realized. A measure of Soviet incapacity in this realm is the fact that Moscow has actually been increasing exploratory efforts in the European regions and offshore where new finds are likely to be high-cost. Coal presents equivalent problems. Even if it can be extracted, Siberian coal will be difficult to use because of a completely inadequate transport system. Thus the U.S.S.R. has tried to make expensive energy sources in the western regions do additional service, so far with little success.[12] But if the Soviet bloc must import more oil, increases in the price of Middle Eastern crude will have growing significance for Moscow and an even more dynamic impact upon Eastern Europe.

The West, however, should not take comfort from Soviet energy dilemmas, for the world industrial system, capitalist as well as Soviet, may be nearing a crisis created by temporary or permanent limits to

---

[12] For a definitive review of Soviet energy problems see Marianna Slocum, "Soviet Energy: An Internal Assessment," *Technology Review* (October-November 1974).

expansion and welfare. The availability of food, oil, and raw materials may be less than that needed by Communist and Western states in the next decade. The West is vulnerable on oil, and the Communist states may be becoming increasingly vulnerable on both food and oil. Only a sharing of total world supplies of both items may ultimately suffice.

The spread of nuclear technology and ultimately weaponry also provides new justifications for cooperation with the West and the United States. The nuclear Nonproliferation Treaty has failed to prevent the dissemination of such technology. And even where the treaty remains formally in force, nations may develop their nuclear power programs to a point where a weapons option can be taken up in short order. India's "peaceful" detonation will certainly not slow down the nuclear arms acquisition process in the Middle East and South Asia, and it seems to be providing an additional spur to Japanese and Australian efforts in the general nuclear field. No new nuclear decisions can be expected in the next few years, but the process of industrial and technological familiarization with nuclear techniques will, if anything, accelerate.[13] Meanwhile, existing nuclear forces in China and France, and perhaps also in the United Kingdom and India, will become less vulnerable and more sophisticated.

If and when major nuclear capabilities are possessed by five, seven, or more powers, the international strategic environment will undergo important transformations. It is seldom understood that deterrence was a fundamentally bipolar doctrine, requiring clear identification of an attacker and depending upon the possession of relatively modest retaliatory capabilities. As long as each of the two superpowers had only to retaliate against the other, deterrent requirements were not onerous. When China became the fifth nuclear power, however, the retaliatory requirements of "assured destruction" capabilities against "any combination of attackers" became much more stringent. If Indian targets are eventually to be added to superpower lists, the task will become still more difficult.

The development of new nuclear powers raises deterrent requirements because it increases the population that any global deterrent power must be able to hold at risk. It also heightens the deterrent threshold in another way: the size of the aggressive coalition that might seek to launch a disarming attack against a single power is now at least potentially greater. For multilateral deterrence, one wants relatively equal, invulnerable forces. But since at least the first-genera-

---

[13] George Quester takes a slightly more optimistic view in "Can Proliferation Now Be Stopped?" *Foreign Affairs* (October 1974), pp. 77-97.

tion capacities of new nuclear states will be much smaller than those of established powers and also vulnerable to attack, neither of the conditions is likely to be met.

Entirely aside from global deterrent problems, nuclear rivals may possess local first-strike capabilities. China's nuclear force may deter an attack by Delhi on Peking, but the converse may not be true. In much the same way a fledgling nuclear force in Pakistan might be vulnerable to Indian attack while India would not have to worry about a first strike from Karachi. In the Middle East, two-sided vulnerabilities could exist. The inability of conventional capabilities to force a resolution of the Arab-Israeli conflict will tend to encourage the development of nuclear capabilities in the region. With adequate intelligence, however, victory in a local nuclear war could depend upon who struck first.

Failures of deterrence in such cases could place enormous strain on the general structure of peace in world politics. A small client of one superpower might act, relying on its major power guarantor to prevent counteraction by its opposite number. If, on the other hand, the United States and the Soviet Union agreed to act together, the local aggressor might be inhibited from either the threat or the use of nuclear weapons. Indeed, it may even be possible that some such minimal superpower cooperation will be forced by manifest and rising deterrent instabilities in the next decades.

VII

In nineteenth-century international relations, the pattern of peace or war was largely determined by the state of relations among Germany, Russia, and England. When despite their differences, basic agreement was obtained, war could not take place. The Austrians were dependent upon Germany, and the French could not act without an ally. When the three great powers fell out, however, no recombination or alignment would prevent war. War actually occurred when each of the three began to treat its combination with a lesser power as decisive, ruling out a more general accommodation in world politics. Britain and Russia began listening to France, while Germany gave all its attention to Austria. In this respect, the role of allies as a conflictual factor in world politics has not been sufficiently stressed.

After World War II, the United States and Russia initially made conservative choices, preferring known associates and probable outcomes to the "leap in the dark" that would have been involved in an attempt at general reconciliation in world politics. Today, the interests of allies or associates might also take precedence. In the

Middle East, it is now possible that either or both sides will take matters into its own hands—the Israelis militarily, the Arabs through the use of the oil weapon. Israeli action would be strongly resisted by the Soviet Union. It would be difficult for it to tolerate another Arab defeat. The United States and Western Europe, however, could scarcely acquiesce in another application of oil sanctions. If either superpower yielded to such temptations, however, the contemporary system of international relations would be overthrown.

But in the longer term the détente will not be maintained simply by avoiding entanglement in the disputes of allies or clients. The European system of international relations ultimately collapsed when there was no one who understood its complexities to run it, as did Bismarck. In the final quarter of the twentieth century, the world cannot tolerate dependence upon the bureaucratic skill or diplomatic prescience of a single statesman to perform a similar sleight of hand. Some new institutional and political structures may have to be developed to ensure that legerdemain is not the only policy instrument.

As nuclear weapons spread and the economic disruption of industrial economies proceeds, nothing short of a partial Soviet-American entente will provide the necessary structure in which present destabilizing currents can be contained. Such an entente, of course, could not be a condominium, nor could it deal with all important issues. It should not prevent even closer Sino-American relations. It would not substitute for NATO, a European defense system, or from the Soviet point of view, for the Warsaw Pact. It clearly could not hope to regulate the world's economic and financial system, in which the United States and the Soviet Union are important but by no means dominant participants. It could not be used as a means of repressing the poorer, less satisfied fraction of the globe in hopes of maintaining a permanent inequity in the division of world wealth. Above all, it could not repeat Grey's error: of forging ties with one nation or group at the expense of another, and thereby creating a new polarization in world politics.

A policy of significantly strengthening American-Soviet links, however, should now be embarked upon. Without its opposite number, neither power can expect to cope with the increasing disorder of international relations at political and military levels. As nuclear weapons spread, some joint "crisis control" measures may have to be taken. Common positions on peaceful nuclear explosions and their implications for arms control and development will have to be worked out. There will have to be a substitute for the now defunct Soviet-American trade agreement. In the Middle East there must be a greater concert both to prevent war and to agree on the outlines of future

233

peace. Perhaps there should be informal bureaucratic links across the range of ministries and functions. The issue becomes all the more important as the prospect of change in either Soviet or American leadership beckons. Short of such major ties, the fruitful but still insubstantial rapprochement of the last few years could dissolve as its authors leave the political scene.

IS DETENTE WORTH SAVING? *

George F. Kennan

Presenting a historical view of the relationship between the United States and the Soviet Union, George F. Kennan contends that these societies basically have much in common, but certain differences between them prevent completely harmonious relationships. Kennan argues that this situation would have been able to work itself out with little long-term impact except for the advent of two radical changes after World War II: the direct confrontation between the two nations, and their acquisition of nuclear arms. He concludes that the new and awesome danger implicit in these weapons makes imperative American efforts to expand cooperation with the Soviet Union.

Some years ago, for reasons I have never entirely understood, an impression got about that there was beginning, in our relationship with the Soviet Union, a new period of normalization and relaxation of tensions, to be sharply distinguished from all that had gone before and to be known by the term *détente*.

This image of détente, in which, for all I know, there may have been at one time some slender basis of reality, came to be rather seriously oversold. It was oversold—for different reasons in each case—by our government, by the Soviet government, and by the American press; and as a result of this overselling, many people came to address to the behavior of both countries expectations that were unreal and could not be met fully.

Today an almost predictable reaction has set in—a reaction against what people understand to be "détente." It has set in partly as a consequence of the earlier overselling of this idea; partly because real mistakes have been made here and there, on both sides; partly

---

* Source: *Saturday Review* (6 March 1976), pp. 12-17.

because an improvement in political relations appeared to threaten the formidable interests vested in a continuing state of high military tension. In addition, there seem to be a number of people in our political and journalistic world for whom a certain cold war rhetoric has long been the staff of life, who have been alarmed by an apparent favorable trend in our relationship to Russia that has threatened to undermine the basis for this rhetoric, and who now welcome the chance to attack that trend. The result has been the emergence of a school of thought which appears to believe that something useful could now be achieved in our relations with Russia by a policy of strident hostility on our part, by reversion to the cold war slogans of the fifties, by calling names and making faces, by piling up still greater quantities of superfluous armaments, and by putting public pressure on Moscow to change its internal practices, and indeed the very nature of Soviet power.

Granted this tangle of motivations and outlooks, just where should the United States stand regarding détente? Is it a mere governmental public-relations ploy, without grounding in the realities? Or is it a major fact of international life, which will lead on to ever-widening vistas of mutual Soviet-American support?

The best way of getting at these questions is, it seems to me, to step back from them so that the riddle of détente can be brought into historical perspective.

There is no need to dwell at any great length on the curious sort of symmetry—sometimes one of similarity, sometimes of diametrical opposition—that has marked the development of the Russian and American peoples, particularly in the modern age—by which term I am thinking of the past 200 to 250 years. Many thoughtful observers —including even Tocqueville, who had never been to Russia—have noted it and commented on it. At the start of that period, the two peoples were marked by their respective inhabitation of vast, under-populated, and relatively underdeveloped but potentially enormously fruitful territories in the north temperate zone of the planet. In the eighteenth century both were just emerging out of a former obscurity onto the great stage of the international life of the civilized world. The Russians were emerging into this limelight after several centuries of relative isolation—which one might call a historically compelled isolation—from the main cultural and religious and political centers of Western civilization. They were emerging in the manner with which we are all familiar. By that time a limited westward territorial expansion had brought them to Poland and to the Baltic Sea. The construction of a new and partially Europeanized capital on the banks of the Neva was creating a governmental center reasonably open to contact with Western Europe, in contrast to the former remote and self-immolating Grand Duchy of Moscow, with its religious intolerance, its dark suspicion of the heretical outside world, its pious abhorrence of contact with the individual Western foreigner.

In that same century, we Americans were emerging onto the world scene for the first time as a discrete entity, but emerging in quite a different way: not as an old people, isolated from Europe by the workings of a long and unhappy history, but as a young people newly born, so to speak, out of the wombs of old England and Scotland and certain parts of the Continent. We bore with us, to be sure, the traditions, the customs, the inherited outlooks of the European societies that had mothered us. But we were now in the process of being changed to some degree by the very discipline of our physical encounter with the great American wilderness and were, in any case, appearing now for the first time as something in our own right, something visible and active on the landscape of world politics, preparing to take an independent part in the affairs of the world.

To this concept we must add, now, the reflection that around the same time both of these two peoples, starting from a position of what we might call proximity to the main centers of Western European power and culture, began in earnest their respective processes of developmental expansion away from those centers: the Russians eastward across the Volga and the Urals into the immense expanses of central Asia and Siberia; the Americans westward across their own empty, magnificent, and underdeveloped continent. Both were destined, in the late nineteenth and early twentieth centuries, to close the circle and to meet, in a sense, on the shores of the Pacific—to meet as peoples by this time of immense demographic, physical, and potential military power, each towering already in these respects over any of the individual entities, if not the totality, of the old Europe from which they had taken, in so high degree, their origins and their inspirations.

So far I have dealt mostly with similarities. But these similarities in physical and geographic experience were accompanied by profound almost antithetically related differences in political and social outlook. With these differences, too, most of us are familiar. The Russians inherited the outlook of a great continental land power, almost totally cut off from the world oceans, surrounded over great periods of their history by fierce and dangerous land neighbors; and they became accustomed to that intense concentration of political authority that marks all societies and communities that find themselves virtually in

a state of siege. The Russians learned to regard as natural the subordination of the individual to this concentration of authority. They
were grateful, no doubt, for whatever liberties and immunities might
be conceded to the individual at any given moment, but they tended
to accept these as the product of an act of grace on the part of constituted authority rather than as absolute rights, inherent in the condition of individual man. We Americans, on the other hand, were heirs
to the mercantile and commercial traditions of latter-day England and
Scotland. Shielded in effect on the oceanic side—whether we recognize the fact or not—by English sea power, and facing on our mainland only insignificant military challenges, we were able to proceed
in relative peace to the development of our continent, enjoying, indeed
taking increasingly for granted, these rights and procedures of self-
government that were actually in high degree the achievements of
the European civilizations out of which we had emerged.

The differences between these two outlooks were, as you see,
profound. But the two peoples had one thing in common: a tendency
to attribute to their own political ideology a potential universal
validity—to perceive in it virtues that ought, as one thought, to command not only imitation on the part of other peoples everywhere but
also recognition of the moral authority and ascendancy of the respective national center from which these virtues were proceeding. The
Russians had inherited this messianic view of their own place in the
world from old Byzantium, with its strong sense of religious orthodoxy and its universalistic political pretensions. We Americans had it
because, failing to recognize the relationship between our freedoms
and achievements on the one hand, and the uniquely favorable conditions in which it was given to us to lead our national life on the other,
we mistook those achievements and freedoms as the products of some
peculiar wisdom and virtue on our own part and came to see in the
system of government we were now enjoying the ultimate salvation
of most of the rest of the world. So each of these great peoples went
along into the twentieth century nurturing vague dreams, if not of
world power, at least of a species of exemplary and moral world
leadership, which entitled it to some special form of admiration, defer-
ence, imitation, or authority—call it what you will—at the hands of
other less favorably endowed peoples.

It was, then, against this background that the relations between
the two peoples and their governments developed up to the end of
the nineteenth century. In the geopolitical sense there were no serious
conflicts between them; on the contrary, there was much, particularly
in their respective relationships to England, that gave to each of them

a certain limited positive value in the other's eyes. But ideologically the two official establishments remained poles apart. They viewed each other with uneasiness and distaste. The image of tsarist autocracy remained no less repulsive in American eyes than did American republicanism in the eyes of the court and bureaucracy of Petersburg. And over the whole period of tsarist power these differences continued to constitute a complicating factor in Russian-American relations, not wholly inhibiting the development of those relations but limiting in some degree the dimensions and intensity they could assume.

Toward the end of the nineteenth century, another complication began to make itself felt in the form of the growing restlessness of the non-Russian nationalities within the framework of the Russian Empire and the growing power of their appeals to congressional and, to some extent, popular sympathies within this country. This was a factor that has to be distinguished from the general incompatibility of the two political systems to which I have just referred, because this restlessness arose not mainly from discontent with the general political system prevailing in Russia (although there was this, too), but rather from the treatment by the tsarist regime of the particular non-Russian nationality in question, which was a different thing. The phenomenon became a complicating factor in Russian-American relations only when individuals from among these minority nationalities began to appear in significant numbers among the immigrants to this country. Particularly was this true, of course, of the Jews—Russian, Polish, and Lithuanian—whose migration to this country in considerable numbers began in earnest in the 1880s, and whose powerful resentment of the treatment of their coreligionists in Russia soon began to become a factor of importance in American political life. The legislative branch of the American government has always had, it would seem, a peculiar sensitivity to the feeling of compact blocks of recent immigrants residing in our great urban communities. So, at any rate, it was in this case, with the result that the tales of the sufferings of these non-Russian nationalities soon came to exercise upon political and congressional opinion in this country an influence stronger than anything ever evoked by the tales of the sufferings of the Russian people themselves at the hands of their autocratic government. It is curious, in a certain melancholy way, to recall that in December 1911 the House of Representatives adopted almost unanimously a resolution calling on the President to terminate the old trade treaty with Russia that had been in force ever since 1832; and the purpose of this resolution was to compel the Russian government to liberalize its treatment of the Jews within Russia. The one vote cast against the resolution in the

House of Representatives was cast by a man who complained that this sort of pressure by a foreign government would not help the Jews in Russia but would appreciably damage American business; President Taft, pursuant to this resolution, did so terminate the treaty, with the result that Russian-American relations, down to the Revolution of 1917, remained very cool and unhappy indeed.

This, then, was the general shape of Russian-American relations as they existed in the final years of the tsarist empire, and it was against this background that the whole question was overtaken by the Russian Revolution, in 1917.

The initial impact of this revolution on the relationship consisted primarily of sheer confusion. The reaction of the American public was confused by the fact that it was not one revolution but two: a moderate-democratic one in February 1917, with which all Americans tended to sympathize; and an extreme, left-wing-Marxist one, dictatorially oriented, in November, the seriousness and durability of which was at first widely questioned. This reaction was even more confused by the fact that there was at that time a war in progress—a great European war which the United States was then just in the process of entering. The emotional reaction to the experience of being at war soon came to dominate American opinion and to distort all other issues. Thus the Russian Provisional Government, resulting from the first revolution, was idealized because it attempted to carry on in the war against Germany, whereas the Bolshevik regime, taking over in November 1917, was scorned, resented, and opposed in large measure because its first official act was to take Russia out of the war entirely.

Similar confusions prevailed, of course, on the Bolshevik side. Lenin and his associates attached enormous significance to their own seizure of power. They saw it as the first step in a political transformation of the world far more important than any of the issues over which the world war was being fought. And for this reason they insisted on seeing America's reluctant and trivial participation in the allied military intervention in Russia, in 1918–1920, as the expression of an ideological hostility to themselves, rather than as an event in the prosecution of the war against Germany, which it really was.

These early confusions and misunderstandings yielded only slowly and partially to the passage of time, and they helped to engender a deep mutual antagonism between the two parties concerned. But they were not the most important cause of the antagonism. The most important cause was another situation produced by the revolution—a situation that was not at all a misunderstanding: the fact, namely, that the Bolshevik leaders looked upon the political and social

239

system of this country as a misconceived, regressive, iniquitous one, disreputable in its origins and purposes and deserving of violent overthrow; and they conceived it as their duty, however poor the prospects for success, to encourage such an overthrow and to contribute to its realization wherever they could. This, too, of course, bred a reciprocal reaction here. It was a reaction flowing in part from resentment of the Soviet attitude—resentment, that is, of the hostility addressed by the Bolshevik leaders to cherished American ideals and institutions. But it also flowed from a very genuine distaste on the part of most Americans for what they could learn of the ideology of the new Communist leaders and of the manner in which their dictatorial authority was being exercised.

So the Russian-American relationship came to be burdened in the twenties and thirties not only by the great differences in historical experience and political tradition of which I have spoken but also by those special elements of ideological and political antagonism introduced by the establishment of Communist power in Russia.

All of this was sufficient to render relations in the period between the two wars—not just in the early years of nonrecognition but even after diplomatic relations were established in 1933—distant, meager, and unpleasant. Now these sources of contention were in their entirety a serious burden on an international relationship (and no one could have been more aware of their seriousness, I think, than those of us who served in the American Embassy in Moscow at the time). But they were not, I would point out, the source of any particular military tension between the two countries; and there was no great urgency about the resolution of the conflicts they produced. They represented serious long-term problems, but these were not problems wholly immune to those immutable laws of change that eventually affect all societies, transform all customs, and erode all militant ideologies; and for this reason there was no need to despair of their ultimate peaceful resolution. Above all, the preservation of world peace, not to mention the inviolability of civilized life on the planet, did not depend on their early solution.

It was in this last respect, above all, that the outcome of World War II worked its most significant and most fateful changes. There were two of these changes that stand out in my mind. Both were of a quasi-military nature.

The first was the elimination of Germany and Japan as major military powers standing between the United States and the Soviet Union, the attendant creation of great political and military vacuums, and the advance of Soviet military power, by way of filling one of these vacuums, into the heart of Europe. This produced a direct confrontation between American and Soviet military power that had never existed before.

As far as conventional forces were concerned, even this was not necessarily a fatal complication. The presence of both Soviet and American forces in the heart of Europe is an anomaly of history, awkward in some ways to both parties and to the peoples whose territory is affected. For this very reason, given continuing restraint and patience on both sides, it may be expected to yield eventually to a more normal and less dangerous state of affairs.

The same, unfortunately, cannot be said of the second of the two great military-political consequences of World War II, for this was the acquisition and cultivation by both American and Soviet governments of the nuclear capability—of the capability, that is, of putting an end to civilized life not only on the territory of the other party but on great portions of the remainder of the surface of the planet as well.

The fears and other reactions engendered by this nuclear rivalry have now become a factor in our relations with Russia of far greater actual importance than the underlying ideological and political differences. The real conflicts of interest and outlook, for all their seriousness, are limited ones. There is nothing in them that could not yield to patience, change, and a readiness for accommodation. There is nothing in them, above all, that could really be solved by—and, therefore, nothing that could justify—a major war, let alone the sort of global cataclysm that seems to preempt so many of our plans and discussions. Yet this fact is constantly being crowded out of our consciousness by the prominence, and the misleading implications, of the military competition. An image arises, if only initially for purposes of military planning, of an utterly inhuman adversary, committed to our total destruction and committed to it not for any coherent political reason but only because he has the capacity to inflict it. This unreal image presents itself to both parties; and in the name of a response to it whole great economies are distorted, whole populations are to some extent impoverished, vast amounts of productive capacity needed for constructive purposes in a troubled world are devoted to sterile and destructive ones; a proliferation of nuclear weaponry is encouraged and pursued that only increases with every day the dimensions and dangers of the problem to which it is supposed to be responsive; and the true nature of our relations with the Soviet Union and its peoples becomes obscured and distorted by the cloud of anxieties and panicky assumptions that falls across its face. The

241

nuclear rivalry, in other words, begins to ride along of its own momentum, like an object in space, divorced from any cause or rationale other than the fears it engenders, corrupting and distorting a relationship that, while not devoid of serious problems, never needed to be one of mortal antagonism.

Our first task, then, is to master, and to bring under rational control, this fearful capacity for suicidal destruction that has been let loose among us; and of this I would say only that so terrible are the dangers of a continued failure to master it that we would be fully warranted in accepting very considerable risks to avoid this failure. The risks, for example, of a total ban on the testing of nuclear weapons seem to me to be trivial in comparison with the risks involved in the continued proliferation of these weapons on a world scale. Yet we shrink from it. Is this timidity really justified? Is the tail of military fear not wagging the dog of constructive and hopeful political opportunity at this point?

I find myself disturbed by these reactions not only because of their obvious negativeness and sterility, and not only because they stimulate exaggerations and distortions of the real situation in world affairs, but also because they tend to obscure both the real limitations and the real possibilities to which our relations with the Soviet Union are subject. Let us remember that for the reasons I have just outlined there has always been an area where collaboration with Russia, as we would like to see it, has not been possible. This was true before the revolution. It is true today. It will continue to be true long into the future. But there is another area in which collaboration—and mutually profitable collaboration—*is* possible. The relative size and nature of these two areas is not immutable; it has not failed to change with the years; and only someone unfamiliar with the history of Soviet-American relations could fail to recognize that since Stalin's death the direction of this change has been in general a favorable one —the one we would like to see.

This has been, if you will, a small gain, but it has been a real one and the only kind we can hope to make. And it should be recognized that none of the complicating factors—neither the asperities of our military rivalry, nor the apparent conflict of our aims with those of the Soviet Union in specific geographic areas and countries, nor the somewhat dated but now traditional Communist rhetoric to which the Soviet leadership is committed—none of these things constitutes any adequate reason, nor do all of them together, why we should not exploit to the full those areas in which our relations with Russia are or might be capable of constructive development and where exchanges might be pursued, cultural as well as commercial, which would be mutually profitable and would give greater depth and stability to the relationship as a whole.

We have burdens enough in Soviet-American relations without adding to them by the neglect of those areas where possibilities for improvement do actually exist. In a world so troubled as ours of today, the favorable opportunities have to be cherished and nurtured, not sacrificed to prejudice, vanity, or political ambition.

AMERICA: YOU MUST THINK ABOUT THE WORLD *

Alexander Solzhenitsyn

In this address, the Nobel Prizewinning author and Soviet expatriate, Alexander Solzhenitsyn enumerates abuses against human rights perpetrated by the Soviet Union, and takes the West to task for its implicit support of the U.S.S.R. He finds the Soviet government guilty of domestic repression and international aggression; it does not merit the trust necessary for a relationship like détente. In Solzhenitsyn's view, the West has made numerous compromises with totalitarian regimes, often on grounds of expediency, but in the process has betrayed higher moral standards that should govern interstate relationships. This address, delivered in Washington, D.C., on 30 June 1975, under the sponsorship of the AFL-CIO, was his first major public address after his expulsion from the Soviet Union in 1974.

Through the decades of the 1920s, the 1930s, the 1940s, the 1950s, the whole Soviet press wrote: Western capitalism, your end is near.

But it was as if the capitalists had not heard, could not understand, could not believe this.

Nikita Khrushchev came here and said, "We will bury you!" They did not believe that, either. They took it as a joke.

Now, of course, they have become more clever in our country. Now they do not say "we are going to bury you" anymore, now they say "détente."

Nothing has changed in Communist ideology. The goals are the same as they were, but instead of the artless Khrushchev, who could not hold his tongue, now they say "détente."

---

* Source: American Federation of Labor and Congress of Industrial Organizations, *Publication No. 152* (Washington, D.C.: AFL-CIO, 1975).

In order to understand this, I will take the liberty of making a short historic survey—the history of such relations, which in different periods have been called "trade," "stabilization of the situation," "recognition of realities," and now "détente." These relations now are at least forty years old.

Let me remind you with what sort of system they started.

The system was installed by armed uprising.

It dispersed the Constituent Assembly.

It capitulated to Germany—the common enemy.

It introduced execution without trial.

It crushed workers' strikes.

It plundered the villagers to such an unbelievable extent that the peasants revolted, and when this happened it crushed the peasants in the bloodiest possible way.

It shattered the church.

It reduced twenty provinces of our country to a condition of famine. This was in 1921, the famous Volga famine. . . .

I repeat, it was a system that introduced concentration camps for the first time in the history of the world. A system that, in the twentieth century, was the first to introduce the use of hostages, that is to say, to seize not the person whom they were seeking, but rather a member of his family or someone at random, and shoot that person.

This system of hostages and persecution of the family exists to this day. It is still the most powerful weapon of persecution, because the bravest person, who is not afraid for himself, still shivers at the threat to his family.

It is a system which was the first—long before Hitler—to employ false registration, that is, to say: "Such and such people have to come in to register." People would comply and then they were taken away to be annihilated.

We did not have gas chambers in those days. We used barges. A hundred or a thousand persons were put into a barge and then it was sunk.

It was a system which deceived the workers in all of its decrees—the decree on land, the decree on peace, the decree on factories, the decree on freedom of the press.

It was a system which exterminated all additional parties, and let me make it clear to you that it not only disbanded the party itself, but also destroyed its members. All members of every other party were exterminated. It was a system which carried out genocide of the peasantry; 15 million peasants were sent off to extermination.

It was a system which introduced serfdom, the so-called passport system.

It was a system which, in time of peace, artificially created a famine, causing 6 million persons to die in the Ukraine in 1932 and 1933. They died on the very edge of Europe. And Europe did not even notice it. The world did not even notice it—6 million persons!

I could keep on enumerating these endlessly, but I have to stop because I have come to the year 1933 when, with all I have enumerated behind us, your President Roosevelt and your Congress recognized this system as one worthy of diplomatic recognition, of friendship and of assistance. . . .

The scope and the direction of my speech today do not permit me to say more about prerevolutionary Russia. I will just say that information about prerevolutionary Russia was obtained by the West from persons who were either not sufficiently competent or not sufficiently conscientious. I will just cite for the sake of comparison a number of figures which you can read for yourself in *Gulag Archipelago*, volume one, which has been published in the United States, and perhaps many of you may have read it. These are figures:

- According to calculations by specialists, based on the most precise objective statistics, in prerevolutionary Russia, during the eighty years before the revolution—years of the revolutionary movement when there were attempts on the Tsar's life, assassination of a Tsar, revolution—during these years about seventeen persons a year were executed. The famous Spanish Inquisition, during the decades when it was at the height of its persecution, destroyed perhaps ten persons a month. In the *Archipelago*—I cite a book which was published by the Cheka in 1920, proudly reporting on its revolutionary work in 1918 and 1919 and apologizing that its data were not quite complete—in 1918 and 1919 the Cheka executed, without trial, more than a thousand persons a month! This was written by the Cheka itself, before it understood how this would look to history.

- At the height of Stalin's terror in 1937-38, if we divide the number of persons executed by the number of months, we get more than forty thousand persons shot per month! Here are the figures: seventeen a year, ten a month, more than a thousand a month, more than forty thousand a month!

Thus, that which had made it difficult for the democratic West to form an alliance with prerevolutionary Russia had, by 1941, grown to such an extent and still did not prevent the entire united democracy of the world—England, France, the United States, Canada, Australia, and small countries—from entering into a military alliance with the Soviet Union. How is this to be explained? How can we understand it? Here we can offer a few explanations. The first, I think, is that the entire united democracy of the world was too weak to fight against Hitler's Germany alone. If this is the case, then it is a terrible sign. It is a terrible portent for the present day. If all these countries together could not defeat Hitler's little Germany, what are they going to do today, when more than half the globe is flooded with totalitarianism? I do not want to accept this explanation.

The second explanation is perhaps that there was simply an attack of panic—of fear—among the statesmen of the day. They simply did not have sufficient confidence in themselves, they simply had no strength of spirit, and in this confused state decided to enter into an alliance with Soviet totalitarianism. This is also not flattering to the West.

Finally, the third explanation is that it was a deliberate device. Democracy did not want to defend itself. For defense it wanted to use another totalitarian system, the Soviet totalitarian system.

I am not talking now about the moral evaluation of this, I am going to talk about that later. But in terms of simple calculation, how shortsighted, what profound self-deception!

We have a Russian proverb: "Do not call a wolf to help you against the dogs." If dogs are attacking and tearing at you, fight against the dogs, but do not call a wolf for help. Because when the wolves come, they will destroy the dogs, but they will also tear you apart.

World democracy could have defeated one totalitarian regime after another, the German, then the Soviet. Instead, it strengthened Soviet totalitarianism, helped bring into existence a third totalitarianism, that of China, and all this finally precipitated the present world situation. . . .

There is another Russian proverb: "The yes-man is your enemy, but your friend will argue with you." It is precisely because I am the friend of the United States, precisely because my speech is prompted by friendship, that I have come to tell you: "My friends, I am not going to tell you sweet words. The situation in the world is not just dangerous, it is not just threatening, it is catastrophic."

Something that is incomprehensible to the ordinary human mind has taken place. We over there, the powerless, average Soviet people, could not understand, year after year and decade after decade, what was happening. How were we to explain this? England, France, the United States were victorious in World War II. Victorious states always dictate peace; they receive firm conditions; they create the sort of situation which accords with their philosophy, their concept of liberty, their concept of national interest.

Instead of this, beginning in Yalta, your statesmen of the West, for some inexplicable reason, have signed one capitulation after another. Never did the West or your President Roosevelt impose any conditions on the Soviet Union for obtaining aid. He gave unlimited aid, and then unlimited concessions. Already in Yalta, without any necessity, the occupation of Mongolia, Moldavia, Estonia, Latvia, Lithuania was silently recognized. Immediately after that, almost nothing was done to protect eastern Europe, and seven or eight more countries were surrendered.

Stalin demanded that the Soviet citizens who did not want to return home be handed over to him, and the Western countries handed over 1.5 million human beings. How was this done? They took them by force. English soldiers killed Russians who did not want to become prisoners of Stalin, and drove them by force to Stalin to be exterminated. This has recently come to light—just a few years ago—a million and a half human beings. How could the Western democracies have done this?

And after that, for another thirty years, the constant retreat, the surrender of one country after another, to such a point that there are Soviet satellites even in Africa; almost all of Asia is taken over by them; Portugal is rolling down the precipice.

During those thirty years, more was surrendered to totalitarianism than any defeated country has ever surrendered after any war in history. There was no war, but there might as well have been.

For a long time we in the East could not understand this. We could not understand the flabbiness of the truce concluded in Vietnam. Any average Soviet citizen understood that this was a sly device which made it possible for North Vietnam to take over South Vietnam when it so chose. And suddenly, this was rewarded by the Nobel Prize for Peace—a tragic and ironic prize.

A very dangerous state of mind can arise as a result of this thirty years of retreat: give in as quickly as possible, give up as quickly as possible, peace and quiet at any cost.

This is what many Western papers wrote: "Let's hurry up and end the bloodshed in Vietnam and have national unity there." But at the Berlin Wall no one talked of national unity. One of your leading newspapers, after the end of Vietnam, had a full headline: "The

247

Blessed Silence." I would not wish that kind of "blessed silence" on my worst enemy. I would not wish that kind of national unity on my worst enemy.

I spent eleven years in the Archipelago, and for half of my lifetime I have studied this question. Looking at this terrible tragedy in Vietnam from a distance, I can tell you, a million persons will be simply exterminated, while 4 to 5 million (in accordance with the scale of Vietnam) will find themselves in concentration camps and will be rebuilding Vietnam. And what is happening in Cambodia you already know. It is genocide. It is full and complete destruction but in a new form. Once again their technology is not up to building gas chambers. So, in a few hours, the entire capital city—the guilty capital city—is emptied out: old people, women, children are driven out without belongings, without food. "Go and die!"

This is very dangerous for one's view of the world when this feeling comes on: "Go ahead, give it up." We already hear voices in your country and in the West—"Give up Korea and we will live quietly. Give up Portugal, of course; give up Japan, give up Israel, give up Taiwan, the Philippines, Malaysia, Thailand, give up ten more African countries. Just let us live in peace and quiet. Just let us drive our big cars on our splendid highways; just let us play tennis and golf, in peace and quiet; just let us mix our cocktails in peace and quiet as we are accustomed to doing; just let us see the beautiful toothy smile with a glass in hand on every advertisement page of our magazines."

But look how things have turned out: Now in the West this has all turned into an accusation against the United States. Now, in the West, we hear very many voices saying, "It is your fault, America." And, here, I must decisively defend the United States against these accusations.

I have to say that the United States, of all the countries of the West, is the least guilty in all this and has done the most in order to prevent it. The United States has helped Europe to win the First and the Second World Wars. It twice raised Europe from postwar destruction—twice—for ten, twenty, thirty years it has stood as a shield protecting Europe while European countries were counting their nickels, to avoid paying for their armies (better yet to have none at all), to avoid paying for armaments, thinking about how to leave NATO, knowing that in any case America will protect them anyway. These countries started it all, despite their thousands of years of civilization and culture, even though they are closer and should have known better.

I came to your continent—for two months I have been travelling in its wide open spaces and I agree: here you do not feel the nearness of it all, the immediacy of it all. And here it is possible to miscalculate. Here you must make a spiritual effort to understand the acuteness of the world situation. The United States of America has long shown itself to be the most magnanimous, the most generous country in the world. Wherever there is a flood, an earthquake, a fire, a natural disaster, disease, who is the first to help? The United States. Who helps the most and unselfishly? The United States.

And what do we hear in reply? Reproaches, curses, "Yankee Go Home." American cultural centers are burned, and the representatives of the Third World jump on tables to vote against the United States.

But this does not take the load off America's shoulders. The course of history—whether you like it or not—has made you the leaders of the world. Your country can no longer think provincially. Your political leaders can no longer think only of their own states, of their parties, of petty arrangements which may or may not lead to promotion. You must think about the whole world, and when the new political crisis in the world will arise (I think we have just come to the end of a very acute crisis and the next one will come any moment) the main decisions will fall anyway on the shoulders of the United States of America.

And while already here, I have heard some explanations of the situation. Let me quote some of them: "It is impossible to protect those who do not have the will to defend themselves." I agree with that, but this was said about South Vietnam. In one-half of today's Europe and in three-quarters of today's world the will to defend oneself is even less than it was in South Vietnam.

We are told: "We cannot defend those who are unable to defend themselves with their own human resources." But against the overwhelming powers of totalitarianism, when all of this power is thrown against a country—no country can defend itself with its own resources. For instance, Japan does not have a standing army.

We are told, "We should not protect those who do not have full democracy." This is the most remarkable argument of the lot. This is the leitmotif I hear in your newspapers and in the speeches of some of your political leaders. Who in the world, ever, on the front line of defense against totalitarianism has been able to sustain full democracy? You, the united democracies of the world, were not able to sustain it. America, England, France, Canada, Australia together did not sustain it. At the first threat of Hitlerism, you stretched out your hands to Stalin. You call that sustaining democracy?

And there is more of the same (there were many of these speeches in a row): "If the Soviet Union is going to use détente for its own ends, then we. . . ." But what will happen then? The Soviet Union has used détente in its own interests, is using it now and will continue to use it in its own interests! For example, China and the Soviet Union, both actively participating in détente, have quietly grabbed three countries of Indochina. True, perhaps as a consolation, China will send you a ping-pong team. And just as the Soviet Union once sent you the pilots who once crossed the North Pole, in a few days you are flying into space together.

* * *

To understand properly what détente has meant all these forty years—friendships, stabilization of the situation, trade, et cetera—I would have to tell you something, which you have never seen or heard, of how it looked from the other side. Let me tell you how it looked. Mere acquaintance with an American, and God forbid that you should sit with him in a cafe or restaurant, meant a ten-year term for suspicion of espionage.

In the first volume of *Archipelago* I tell of an event which was not told me by some arrested person, but by all of the members of the Supreme Court of the U.S.S.R. during those short days when I was in the limelight under Khrushchev. One Soviet citizen was in the United States and on his return said that in the United States they have wonderful automobile roads. The KGB arrested him and demanded a term of ten years. But the judge said: "I do not object, but there is not enough evidence. Couldn't you find something else against him?" So the judge was exiled to Sakhalin because he dared to argue and they gave the other man ten years. Can you imagine what a lie he told? And what sort of praise this was of American imperialism—in America there are good roads? Ten years.

In 1945–46 through our prison cells passed a lot of persons—and these were not ones who were cooperating with Hitler, although there were some of those, too. These were not guilty of anything, but rather persons who had just been in the West and had been liberated from German prison camps by the Americans. This was considered a criminal act: liberated by the Americans. That means he has seen the good life. If he comes back he will talk about it. The most terrible thing is not what he did but what he would talk about. And all such persons got ten-year terms.

* * *

Everything poisonous which could be said about the United States was said in Stalin's days. And all of this is a heavy sediment which can be stirred up anytime. Any day the newspapers can come out with the headlines: "Bloodthirsty American imperialism wants to seize control of the world," and this poison will rise up from the sediment and many people in our country will believe this, and will be poisoned by it, and will consider you as aggressors. This is how détente has been managed on our side.

The Soviet system is so closed that it is almost impossible for you to understand from here. Your theoreticians and scholars write works trying to understand and explain how things occur there. Here are some naive explanations which are simply funny to Soviet citizens. Some say that the Soviet leaders have now given up their inhumane ideology. Not at all. They have not given it up one bit.

Some say that in the Kremlin there are some on the left, some on the right. And they are fighting with each other, and we have to behave in such a way as not to interfere with those on the left side. This is all fantasy: left . . . right. There is some sort of a struggle for power, but they all agree on the essentials.

There also exists the following theory, that now, thanks to the growth of technology, there is a technocracy in the Soviet Union, a growing number of engineers, and the engineers are now running the economy and will soon determine the fate of the country, rather than the party. I will tell you, though, that the engineers determine the fate of the economy just as much as our generals determine the fate of the army. That means zero. Everything is done the way the party demands. That is our system. Judge it for yourself.

It is a system where for forty years there have not been genuine elections but simply a comedy, a farce. Thus a system which has no legislative organs. It is a system without an independent press; a system without an independent judiciary; where the people have no influence on either external or internal policy; where any thought which is different from what the state thinks is crushed.

And let me tell you that electronic bugging in our country is such a simple thing that it is a matter of everyday life. You had an instance in the United States where a bugging caused an uproar which lasted for a year and a half. For us it is an everyday matter. Almost every apartment, every institution has got its bug and it does not surprise us in the least—we are used to it.

It is a system where unmasked butchers of millions like Molotov and others smaller than him have never been tried in the courts but retire on tremendous pensions in the greatest comfort. It is a system where the show still goes on today and to which every foreigner is introduced surrounded by a couple of planted agents working according to a set scenario. It is a system where the very constitution has never been carried out for one single day; where all the decisions mature in secrecy, high up in a small irresponsible group and then are released on us and on you like a bolt of lightning.

And what are the signatures of such persons worth? How could one rely on their signatures to documents of détente? You yourselves might ask your specialists now and they'll tell you that precisely in recent years the Soviet Union has succeeded in creating wonderful chemical weapons, missiles, which are even better than those used by the United States.

So what are we to conclude from that? Is détente needed or not? Not only is it needed, it is as necessary as air. It is the only way of saving the earth—instead of a world war to have détente, but a true détente, and if it has already been ruined by the bad word which we use for it—*détente*—then we should find another word for it.

I would say that there are very few, only three, main characteristics of such a true détente.

In the first place, there would be disarmament—not only disarmament from the use of war but also from the use of violence. We must stop using not only the sort of arms which are used to destroy one's neighbors but the sort of arms which are used to oppress one's fellow countrymen. It is not détente if we here with you today can spend our time agreeably while over there people are groaning and dying and are in psychiatric hospitals. Doctors are making their evening rounds, for the third time injecting people with drugs which destroy their brain cells.

The second sign of détente, I would say, is the following: that it be not one based on smiles, not on verbal concessions, but it has to be based on a firm foundation. You know the words from the Bible: "Build not on sand but on rock." There has to be a guarantee that this will not be broken overnight and for this the other side—the other party to the agreement—must have its acts subject to public opinion, to the press, and to a freely elected parliament. And until such control exists there is absolutely no guarantee.

The third simple condition—what sort of détente is it when they employ the sort of inhumane propaganda which is proudly called in the Soviet Union "ideological warfare." Let us not have that. If we are going to be friends, let us be friends, if we are going to have détente, then let us have détente, and an end to ideological warfare.

The Soviet Union and the Communist countries can conduct negotiations. They know how to do this. For a long time they do not make any concessions and then they give in a little bit. Then everyone says triumphantly, "Look, they have made a concession; it is time to sign." The European negotiators of the thirty-five countries for two years now have painfully been negotiating and their nerves were stretched to the breaking point and they finally gave in. A few women from the Communist countries can now marry foreigners. And a few newspapermen are now going to be permitted to travel a little more than before. They give a thousandth of what natural law should provide. Matters which people should be able to do even before such negotiations are undertaken. And already there is joy. And here in the West we hear many voices, saying: "Look, they are making concessions; it is time to sign."

During these two years of negotiations, in all the countries of eastern Europe, the pressure has increased, the oppression intensified, even in Yugoslavia and Romania, leaving aside the other countries. And it is precisely now that the Austrian chancellor says, "We have to sign this agreement as rapidly as possible."

What sort of an agreement would this be? The proposed agreement is the funeral of eastern Europe. It means that western Europe would finally, once and for all, sign away eastern Europe, stating that it is perfectly willing to see eastern Europe be crushed and overwhelmed once and for all, but please do not bother us. And the Austrian chancellor thinks that if all these countries are pushed into a mass grave, Austria at the very edge of this grave will survive and not fall into it also.

And we, from our lives there, have concluded that violence can only be withstood by firmness.

You have to understand the nature of communism. The very ideology of communism, all of Lenin's teachings, are that anyone is considered to be a fool who does not take what is lying in front of him. If you can take it, take it. If you can attack, attack. But if there is a wall, then go back. And the Communist leaders respect only firmness and have contempt and laugh at persons who continually give in to them. Your people are now saying—and this is the last quotation I am going to give you from the statements of your leaders—"Power, without any attempt at conciliation, will lead to a world conflict." But I would say that power with continual subservience is no power at all.

But from our experience I can tell you that only firmness will make it possible to withstand the assaults of Communist totalitarian-

253

ism. We see many historic examples, and let me give you some of them. Look at little Finland in 1939, which by its own forces withstood the attack. You, in 1948, defended Berlin only by your firmness of spirit, and there was no world conflict. In Korea in 1950 you stood up against the Communists, only by your firmness, and there was no world conflict. In 1962 you compelled the rockets to be removed from Cuba. Again it was only firmness, and there was no world conflict. And the late Konrad Adenauer conducted firm negotiations with Khrushchev and thus started a genuine détente with Khrushchev. . . .

We, we the dissidents of the U.S.S.R., do not have any tanks, we do not have any weapons, we have no organization. We do not have anything. Our hands are empty. We have only a heart and what we have lived through in the half century of this system. And when we have found the firmness within ourselves to stand up for our rights, we have done so. It is only by firmness of spirit that we have withstood. And if I am standing here before you, it is not because of the kindness or the good will of communism, not thanks to détente, but thanks to my own firmness and your firm support. They knew that I would not yield one inch, not one hair. And when they could not do more they themselves fell back.

This is not easy. In our conditions this was taught to me by the difficulties of my own life. . . . Now, I do not want to mention a lot of names because however many I might mention there are more still. And when we resolve the question with two or three names it is as if we forget and betray the others. We should rather remember figures. There are tens of thousands of political prisoners in our country and—by the calculation of English specialists—7,000 persons are now under compulsory psychiatric treatment. Let us take Vladimir Bukovsky as an example. It was proposed to him, "All right, we will free you. Go to the West and shut up." And this young man, a youth today on the verge of death, said: "No, I will not go this way. I have written about the persons whom you have put in insane asylums. You release them and then I will go West." This is what I mean by that firmness of spirit to stand up against granite and tanks.

Finally, to evaluate everything that I have said to you, I would say we need not have had our conversation on the level of business calculations. Why did such and such a country act in such and such a way? What were they counting on? We should rather rise above this to the moral level and say: "In 1933 and in 1941 your leaders and the whole western world, in an unprincipled way, made a deal with totalitarianism." We will have to pay for this, some day this deal will come back to haunt us. For thirty years we have been paying for it and we are still paying for it. And we are going to pay for it in a worse way.

One cannot think only in the low level of political calculations. It is necessary to think also of what is noble, and what is honorable —not only what is profitable. Resourceful Western legal scholars have now introduced the term "legal realism." By legal realism, they want to push aside any moral evaluation of affairs. They say, "Recognize realities; if such and such laws have been established in such and such countries by violence, these laws still must be recognized and respected."

At the present time, it is widely accepted among lawyers that law is higher than morality—law is something which is worked out and developed, whereas morality is something inchoate and amorphous. That is not the case. The opposite is rather true! Morality is higher than law! While law is our human attempt to embody in rules a part of that moral sphere which is above us, we try to understand this morality, bring it down to earth and present it in a form of laws. Sometimes we are more successful, sometimes less. Sometimes you actually have a caricature of morality, but morality is always higher than law. This view must never be abandoned. We must accept it with heart and soul.

It is almost a joke now in the Western world, in the twentieth century, to use words like *good* and *evil*. They have become almost old-fashioned concepts, but they are very real and genuine concepts. These are concepts from a sphere which is higher than us. And, instead of getting involved in base, petty, shortsighted political calculations and games, we have to recognize that the concentration of World Evil and the tremendous force of hatred is there, and it is flowing from there throughout the world. And we have to stand up against it and not hasten to give to it, give to it, give to it everything that it wants to swallow.

Today there are two major processes occurring in the world. One is the one which I have just described to you which has been in progress more than thirty years. It is a process of shortsighted concessions; a process of giving up, and giving up and giving up and hoping that perhaps at some point the wolf will have eaten enough.

The second process is one which I consider the key to everything and which, I will say now, will bring all of us our future; under the cast-iron shell of communism—for twenty years in the Soviet Union and a shorter time in other Communist countries—there is occurring a liberation of the human spirit. New generations are growing up

255

which are steadfast in their struggle with evil; which are not willing to accept unprincipled compromises; which prefer to lose everything —salary, conditions of existence, and life itself—but are not willing to sacrifice conscience; not willing to make deals with evil.

This process has now gone so far that in the Soviet Union today, Marxism has fallen so low that it has become an anecdote, it is simply an object of contempt. No serious person in our country today, not even university and high school students, can talk about Marxism without smiling, without laughing. But this whole process of our liberation, which obviously will entail social transformations, is slower than the first one—the process of concessions. Over there, when we see these concessions, we are frightened. Why so quickly? Why so precipitously? Why yield several countries a year?

I started by saying that you are the allies of our liberation movement in the Communist countries. And I call upon you: let us think together and try to see how we can adjust the relationship between these two processes. Whenever you help the persons persecuted in the Soviet Union, you not only display magnanimity and nobility, you are defending not only them but yourselves as well. You are defending your own future.

So let us try and see how far we can go to stop this senseless and immoral process of endless concessions to the aggressor—these clever legal arguments for why we should give up one country after another. Why must we hand over to Communist totalitarianism more and more technology—complex, delicate, developed technology, which it needs for armaments and for crushing its own citizens? If we can at least slow down that process of concessions, if not stop it altogether —and make it possible for the process of liberation to continue in the Communist countries—ultimately these two processes will yield us our future.

On our crowded planet there are no longer any internal affairs. The Communist leaders say, "Do not interfere in our internal affairs. Let us strangle our citizens in peace and quiet." But I tell you: Interfere more and more. Interfere as much as you can. We beg you to come and interfere. . . .

KISSINGER'S GRAND DESIGN *

G. Warren Nutter

G. Warren Nutter finds fault with the American policy of détente with the Soviet Union on conceptual and operational levels. He contends that détente as articulated by Henry Kissinger is focused on peace as a goal in itself, a position that is inherently self-defeating, and that détente contains no ethical concept capable of providing a substantive base for U.S. foreign policy. Nutter sees the implementation of détente, especially in the economic and military realms, as shifting power toward the U.S.S.R. through the misguided adoption of incentives as a gradual means of ameliorating aggressive behavior. Nutter advocates a revitalized diplomacy, based on a realistic assessment of the dangers confronting the West and emphasizing straightforward bargaining.

Secretary of State Henry A. Kissinger has implicitly renounced his earlier conviction that only the exercise of power can check Soviet strife with the Western world and that, unless Soviet weakness is exploited, détente will merely hasten Soviet hegemony by demoralizing the West. "Détente is an imperative," he now says. "In a world shadowed by the danger of nuclear holocaust, there is no rational alternative to the pursuit of relaxation of tensions." [1] That is, avoidance of the *risk* of war must be the supreme and overriding goal of U.S. policy, almost regardless of cost in other respects.

This attitude stands in stark contrast to the sober warning on the opening page of Kissinger's first book:

> Those ages which in retrospect seem most peaceful were least in search of peace. Those whose quest for it seems unending appear least able to achieve tranquillity. Wherever peace—conceived as the avoidance of war—has been the primary objective of a power or a group of powers, the international system has been at the mercy of the most ruthless member of the international community. Whenever the international order has acknowledged that certain principles could not be compromised even for the sake of peace,

---

* Source: G. Warren Nutter, *Kissinger's Grand Design* (Washington, D.C.: American Enterprise Institute, 1975), pp. 10-25.
[1] Speech to the Pilgrims of Great Britain, *Department of State Bulletin*, December 31, 1973, p. 779.

stability based on an equilibrium of forces was at least conceivable.[2]

He made the same point in those early years when he noted that "the dilemma of the nuclear period can, therefore, be defined as follows: the enormity of modern weapons makes the thought of war repugnant, but the refusal to run any risks would amount to giving the Soviet rulers a blank check."[3] And, in his basic treatise on foreign policy, he added:

> Much as we deplore it, most historical changes have been brought about to a greater or lesser degree by the threat or use of force. Our age faces the paradoxical problem that because the violence of war has grown out of all proportion to the objectives to be achieved, no issue has been resolved. We cannot have war. But we have had to learn painfully that peace is something more than the absence of war.[4]

The change in attitude between then and now may seem subtle, but it is fundamental. Kissinger's détente is conceived as a no-risk policy: it aims not merely at avoiding war or the risk of war, but at eliminating all risk of confrontation that could eventually generate a risk of war. Kissinger the public official could find no more severe a critic of his policy of détente than Kissinger the scholar, who would say that the search for a no-risk policy is self-defeating, that a so-called no-risk policy incurs the greatest risk of all.

Risk aversion has gained ascendancy all the same, and along with it reactive diplomacy.[5] Hence Kissinger's previous exhortations to the West to take the initiative in diplomacy, to stand fast on principle, to place the onus of failure on the Soviet Union, to insist on unification of Germany and full preservation of Allied rights in Berlin, to isolate East Germany, to deny legitimacy to Soviet hegemony in Eastern Europe—all have become inconsistent with détente. The emphasis on institutional as opposed to personal diplomacy has been reversed, and summitry has become the standard operating procedure.

---

[2] *A World Restored*, p. 1.

[3] *Nuclear Weapons and Foreign Policy* (New York: Harper and Brothers, for the Council on Foreign Relations, 1957), p. 4.

[4] *Necessity for Choice*, p. 170.

[5] The opening to China is a notable exception. Mediation in the Middle East may also seem to be, but our diplomatic efforts there, while obviously intensive and innovative, have clearly been reactive since they were brought into motion only by eruption of the October War and imposition of the Arab oil embargo.

Secretary Kissinger hails agreements that Professor Kissinger would have strenuously opposed. Some are acclaimed as landmarks in détente: ratification of the status quo in Berlin, recognition of East Germany, and legitimization of the existing political order in Eastern Europe. SALT I is called an unqualified success in limiting nuclear arms even though it permits a sizable expansion of the Soviet arsenal and contains serious terminological loopholes, both the product of Soviet intransigence. The Soviet Union, once portrayed as a revolutionary power beyond reassurance and incapable of compromise, is now viewed as a conciliatory member of the family of nations practicing restraint in its economic, political, and military relations with others.

One can only speculate on what caused such a profound change in outlook. A case can be made that Kissinger simply saw no other way to turn as he watched the tide of history sweep away, one by one, the elements he had identified as essential for establishing an international order. No progress had been made in resolving the German question, so that Atlantic unity may have seemed beyond reach. Frustration may have become complete when West Germany launched the Ostpolitik, as he had feared it would, and thereby effectively abandoned the cause of reunification, coming to terms instead with the existing order of things in Eastern Europe. A collapse of will and a scramble for accommodation on the part of other Western nations may well have seemed in the offing. Finally, for one reason or another, the strategy of limited warfare proved a dismal failure, tearing American society apart in the process. Little remained out of which to build the edifice of peace envisaged by Kissinger the scholar.

It should be noted that, despite all the other changes in his thinking, Kissinger has not wavered in his insistence on strong conventional forces to defend Europe. He has steadfastly opposed any reduction in U.S. forces and pressed for a buildup in European military strength. We must, he seems to be saying, keep a military anchor to windward while groping for a steady political course.

But all that is speculation. Kissinger has publicized quite a different rationale for détente, one that makes no reference to the evolution of his own thinking, let alone what may have stimulated it. If détente is an imperative, the official statements say, it is also an opportunity for building an international order conducive to peace, for "the United States and the Soviet Union, after decades of profound suspicion, have perceived a common interest in avoiding nuclear holocaust and in establishing a web of constructive relationships." [6] Diplomacy need only take advantage of the relaxation of tensions to create, within the spreading environment of global interdependence, a web of mutual involvement and vested interest. The forecast progression is to be from détente to mutual involvement, then to world community, and finally to world society. The evolving order will acquire legitimacy because the great powers will recognize that they stand to lose more in the way of critical vested interests than they would gain if they defied the rules of international conduct and broke the bonds of interdependence. How fortunate, then, that détente is necessary, for it is also good.

Whereas Kissinger stressed in his scholarly days that diplomacy plays only a symbolic role in a revolutionary age, he now argues that negotiation with the Soviet Union will result in great substantive achievements. The diplomacy of détente is based on the principle of linkage, which means something quite different from what one might think. Normally, linkage is used to describe a quid-pro-quo relationship: an action by one country is linked to a reciprocal action by another. But to Kissinger linkage means the interrelationship between issues, which he explains as follows:

> Our approach proceeds from the conviction that, in moving forward across a wide spectrum of negotiations, progress in one area adds momentum to progress in other areas. If we succeed, then no agreement stands alone as an isolated accomplishment vulnerable to the next crisis. We did not invent the interrelationship between issues expressed in the so-called linkage concept; it was a validity because of the range of problems and areas in which the interests of the United States and the Soviet Union impinge on each other. We have looked for progress in a series of agreements settling specific political issues, and we have sought to relate these to a new standard of international conduct appropriate to the dangers of the nuclear age. By acquiring a stake in this network of relationships with the West, the Soviet Union may become more conscious of what it would lose by a return to confrontation. Indeed, it is our hope that it will develop a self-interest in fostering the entire process of relaxation of tensions. [7]

---

[6] Speech to the American Legion, *Department of State Bulletin*, September 16, 1974, p. 375. See also his speech to the U.N. General Assembly, *Department of State Press Release*, no. 496 (September 22, 1975), p. 4.

[7] Statement to the Senate Foreign Relations Committee, *Department of State Bulletin*, October 14, 1974, p. 508.

In other words, one thing leads to another, and, once the network of relations is established, the Soviet Union risks losing it all if it renounces any part.

This approach is one of moving diplomatically "along a broad front" rather than step by step, settling one issue at a time. There is no reckoning of quid pro quo, either for each agreement or for the outcome as a whole. The only criterion to be met is that each arrangement should derive from mutual interest and dispense mutual benefit. There is no need for concern if the Soviet Union gains more than the West along the way since the fundamental balance of power will not be altered by such incidental marginal adjustments. What is important is that the Soviet Union, the unruly power being tamed, perceive sufficient gain from the ultimate network of relations to be induced, for fear of losing the gain, to behave in accord with agreed rules of international conduct. Part of the unfolding diplomatic process is the joint declaration from time to time of principles to guide relations among nations (witness the Moscow Statement of Principles, the Agreement on the Prevention of Nuclear War, and the Helsinki Declaration), the purpose being to accustom nations to the notion of paying attention to agreed rules and gradually to establish a sense of obligation to conform to them. The diplomacy of détente should not, he therefore says, be judged piece by piece but as an indivisible process, and the judgment to be rendered is whether a stable international order will emerge from the web of mutual involvement being spun.

Though Kissinger has not put it quite so bluntly, agreements aimed at creating Soviet vested interests in peace will naturally focus on economic and technological issues, since these are the areas of greatest Soviet weakness and hence greatest potential gain. "As political relations have improved on a broad front," he says, "economic issues have been dealt with on a comparably broad front." So far we have concluded "primarily regulatory agreements conferring no immediate benefits on the Soviet Union but serving as blueprints for an expanded economic relationship if the political improvement continued." The prospect is that "over time, trade and investment may leaven the autarkic tendencies of the Soviet system, invite gradual association of the Soviet economy with the world economy, and foster a degree of interdependence that adds an element of stability to the political equation." [8]

---

[8] Ibid., pp. 511-512.

Kissinger has never altered his position that transformation of Soviet society, insofar as it takes place, will be a slow evolutionary process essentially beyond the influence of outside pressure. Believing détente to be imperative, he therefore considers it counterproductive, as well as futile, to demand (for example) that Soviet emigration be liberalized as a precondition for improved economic relations. He is not so explicit about why a quid-pro-quo approach should not be used when intervention in domestic affairs is not involved, as would be the case if an economic concession by the United States were offered only in exchange for a political concession by the Soviet Union not directly affecting its internal affairs. Presumably he views such an approach as inconsistent with the commanding objective of constructing a network of mutual interests.

While it would be difficult to exaggerate the significance Kissinger claims for the diplomacy of détente, one should not leave the impression that he considers the envisaged network of interdependency adequate, once built, to preserve the peace by itself. On the contrary, he continues to emphasize that deterrence of aggression, so obviously important today, must remain an essential component of Western policy, new order or not, and that the foundation of deterrence must be built out of strong conventional forces. As in the past, he views SALT as the cornerstone of negotiations with the Soviet Union, having the purpose of stabilizing nuclear parity while preventing an arms race. The question—to which we next turn—is whether deterrence, arms control, and ultimately peace can long coexist with détente.

A Critique

Fault can be found with the very conceptual foundation of Kissinger's grand design: his paradigm of a stable world order. Is legitimacy of the international order, conceived as consensus on rules of conduct, synonymous with stability and ultimately with peace? Suppose we reduce the notion to absurdity and let the major powers agree that might makes right—that violence is to be the means for settling disputes. Is this a legitimate and stable order? Or let one power force all others to accept its way of resolving conflict. Is acquiescence the same as consensus?

Clearly, something is missing from Kissinger's paradigm, and the missing element is the ethic of a peaceful order, which involves more than the principle of agreement on rules, for the question immediately arises of how agreement is to be reached and at what cost in terms of other values. If the only goal is an agreed set of rules, why resist the revolutionary power? Why not simply accede to its intransigent demand for a new order? The way out would seem to be simple: if you can't beat 'em, join 'em. But of course that is not the way out, because principles and ideology are at stake.

Kissinger certainly knows this, but he does not face the issue. Perhaps he fears being cast as an ideologue if he reveals his vision of the good society, spelling out the ethical substance he attributes to it. But failure to do so empties his system of moral content and hence deprives it of relevance to the great issues of our time.

This is merely to say that the West has been resisting Soviet expansion, not just to preserve the legitimacy of international relations, but to save Western civilization. The Soviet system menaces a cherished way of life, and the problem has been to find a course of resistance that works—that preserves Western civilization—while avoiding catastrophic war. Kissinger's grand design, by ignoring this moral dilemma, cannot provide a relevant solution to the problem.

Part of the trouble comes from Kissinger's obsession with purity of concept. In his view, a statesman is, for example, either creative or ideological, one or the other. He cannot be both. But why not? The one does not contradict the other: being ideological does not prevent one from being creative or vice versa, even as a matter of degree. Rather, extreme cases aside, the one complements the other, and whether a particular creative process is likely to produce good results or bad can hardly be judged without reference to an underlying ideology. What is the sense of value-free creativity?

This tendency to put concepts into pigeonholes and to pose choices in terms of mutually exclusive alternatives pervades Kissinger's thought. There is either political unity or disintegration, either negotiation or confrontation, either détente or disaster. Nations are either status-quo powers or revolutionary ones; an institution belongs either to an international system or to a domestic structure; a statesman either uses history or is used by it.

Perhaps limited exposure to the subject of economics helps explain this cast of mind. The economist thinks in terms of scarce means, competing uses (values), substitutability and complementarity of goods, comparative advantage, optimal mixes of goods—all quantitative concepts involving more or less of things, not all or nothing. He also reasons stochastically and defines concepts through frequency distributions. Above all, he attributes the unfolding state of affairs more to the operation of impersonal forces than to the activities of specific individuals.

Institutions do not attract Kissinger's attention, for history looms personified before him. There is no evidence of strong interest on his part in comprehending American institutions, their evolution, the forces they exert, or the governmental processes consistent with them. His writings are essentially bare of reference to such issues: he does not ponder the institutional foundations of various political systems or speculate on the significance of particular institutions. When he contrasts personal and institutional diplomacy, he does not have in mind the nature of the process but the relations being developed, whether they are between individuals or structures. To institutionalized diplomacy he gives the name bureaucratic statesmanship, which he then deplores. Diplomacy simply assumes a personalized shape in Kissinger's eyes.

And so we have the familiar style: personalistic, secretive, mysterious. The public is asked to trust the creative statesman implicitly while he sculpts a new order visible to his mind's eye alone. How can he impart to the masses a comprehension of why and how it will work when it has never existed before?

Perhaps he cannot, but then too bad for creative statesmanship, so called: it is something our political system cannot afford, for nothing is more at odds with the tenets of democracy than the principle of truth by authority. It is not in the American style to bet everything on a horse before knowing its track record and what course it is going to run. American foreign policy must rest on consensus, and it can do so only if its grand design is fully revealed and openly discussed. Similarly, American diplomacy must rest on an institutional foundation, even at the risk of being contaminated by bureaucracy.

Whatever verdict is rendered on the issue of personalized diplomacy, there remains the question, at least equally important, of whether the substance of détente constitutes the best foreign policy for the United States. For brevity, we shall use "détente" to mean the already described configuration of policies and procedures specifically associated with Kissinger's stewardship of foreign affairs, not the relaxation of international tensions in the abstract. The issue is whether détente, so defined, is the best way to preserve the security of the West.

Détente involves a mixed strategy: interdependency is the carrot, deterrence the stick, and arms control the rein. Let us examine the relative importance of these elements, their mutual consistency, and the compatibility of this strategy with the attainment of peace and tranquillity.

Deterrence is obviously the key element, for without it security of the West would depend solely on Soviet good will and self-restraint, scarcely a strong reed to lean upon in the light of Soviet history and ideology. By definition, effective arms control would reduce the level of Western military strength required for deterrence, but the relation between deterrence and interdependency is far more complex. Greater gains from so-called interdependency might, by enhancing the Soviet stake in the existing international order, provide an incentive to the Soviet Union to restrain its expansionist instinct. But the unilateral concessions yielding those gains will cause us to appear all the more weak-willed in the eyes of Soviet leaders, while the gains themselves increase Soviet power commensurately. Soviet leaders will consequently be tempted to seek even greater gains through power politics and to treat the United States as a weakling deserving contempt. Meanwhile, the atmosphere of détente is certain, as we now witness, to sway Western psychology toward downgrading the Soviet threat, cutting defense budgets, and disrupting alliances, the effect being a further tipping of the power balance in the Soviet Union's favor. The dynamics of this process can, as Kissinger once constantly warned, lead to demoralization of the West and Soviet victory by default.

Kissinger's grand design rests on the thesis that the dominating effect of greater interdependency will be to restrain Soviet behavior, but he has little backing from history. Economic interdependence is scarcely new: on the eve of World War I, Norman Angell argued in *The Great Illusion* that the intricate network of world commerce had destroyed all possibility of gain from war. Yet the warring nations of Europe in the twentieth century, as in the nineteenth, normally were close trading partners. As Professor Gregory Grossman reminds us, "history provides little reassurance that trade ensures peace, and Russia's own history least of all. Germany was her largest trading partner just before each of the two World Wars, while China was her largest trading partner (and Russia China's) before the break between Moscow and Peking around 1960." [9]

It is doubtful in any case that the interdependency seemingly envisaged by Kissinger can grow out of normal trading relations, since there is no reason to believe that the Soviet Union is about to abandon

---

[9] Gregory Grossman, Statement before the Joint Economic Committee, in *Hearings on the Soviet Economic Outlook*, 93rd Congress, 1st session, July 17-19, 1973, p. 143. In each case, Germany accounted for 40 percent of Russia's foreign trade. On the general issue of trade and peace, see also Albert Wohlstetter, "Threats and Promises of Peace: Europe and America in the New Era," *Orbis*, Winter 1974, p. 1112 ff.

its traditional policy of autarky. Soviet planners are, however, eager for a generous infusion of Western technology if the price is right—which is to say, if available on cheap long-term credit or otherwise concessionary terms. The response called for is economic aid, which might seem to weld a stronger bond of dependency than a network of trade. But, historically, tribute has been no more successful than trade in preventing conquest or domination by a foreign power.

Perhaps the weakest link in Kissinger's argument is the insistence that any gains accruing to Soviet power from détente are irrelevant "because when both sides possess such enormous power, small additional increments cannot be translated into tangible advantage or even usable political strength." [10] This does not make sense, as Professor Albert Wohlstetter succinctly demonstrates:

> The reasoning supporting this view of the present equilibrium proceeds from the notion that adding an increment of military power to the "overwhelming arsenals of the nuclear age" does not effectively change anything. But is it true that because both the Soviet Union and the United States have many thousands of nuclear warheads, it makes no difference at all if one of the superpowers adds to its arsenal wire-guided anti-tank weapons or surface-to-air missiles or laser-guided bombs or the like for use in limited contingencies? And, can neither gain some political end by transferring such weapons (or even some day a few nuclear weapons) to an ally? On the evidence of October 1973 the Soviet Union feels that one-sided gains are feasible. Statements about the sufficiency or stability of military balances cannot be derived from the mere size of the superpowers' nuclear stockpiles. "Power" is much more complex and varied than that. Neither military nor political nor economic power can be measured by one simple scalar number.[11]

In other words, the power balance is still subject to infinite variation through "marginal adjustments."

Consider what has been happening to Soviet and American defense efforts in real terms. Ours has fallen by almost a sixth since 1964 while theirs (according to our official estimate) has risen by more than a third, coming to surpass ours by 1970. When the incremental cost of the Vietnam War is eliminated, our defense effort

---

[10] *U.S. Foreign Policy for the 1970's: Shaping a Durable Peace*, A Report to the Congress by Richard Nixon, President of the United States (Washington, D. C.: Government Printing Office, 1973), p. 232.

[11] Wohlstetter, "Threats and Promises of Peace," pp. 1116-1117.

shows virtually a steady decline, year by year, since 1963. Theirs shows a steady rise.[12] Are we to believe that this "marginal adjustment" has had no effect on the global power balance?

The most immediate impact has been on relative forces in being. In the strategic nuclear sphere, the Soviet Union has moved from a position of substantial inferiority to rough parity, a development that has made the balance of conventional forces, whose importance Kissinger has always stressed, all the more significant. The Soviet Union now has almost twice as many men under arms as we do; a decade ago it had only a sixth more than we did. Our surface combat fleet has shrunk in numbers to become smaller than the Soviet fleet; a decade ago it was a third larger. And so on and on.[13] These divergent trends in military strength surely have implications for diplomacy as well as deterrence, as Kissinger, an avid practitioner of show of force, well knows. And, however unthinkable nuclear war has become, use of conventional force remains habitual: witness the instances of the last quarter century in Korea, Hungary, the Middle East, Africa, South Asia, Cuba, Southeast Asia, Czechoslovakia, and Cyprus.

Over the longer run, diverging defense efforts are likely to disturb the power balance more fundamentally, because the technology of weaponry, offensive and defensive, is in constant flux along with the military arts. There is no way to regulate this dynamic process through arms control without rigorous on-site inspection, and whichever power gains the upper hand in innovation achieves the potential for commanding the future heights of power. The nature of the military balance a decade hence is therefore being determined in the laboratories and on the proving grounds of today. Who knows what new miracles of horror science has in store for us? Perhaps they will metamorphose the balance of terror in the same way that nuclear explosives once did. Whether radical or not, change is certain in military art and science, and relative strength in research and development now is likely to be translated directly into future relative strength in being.

---

[12] *Annual Defense Report: FY1976 and FY197T* (Washington, D. C.: Government Printing Office, 1975), charts facing I-6 and D-1.

[13] For relevant data, see ibid., and statement by the chairman, Joint Chiefs of Staff, before the Senate Armed Services Committee on United States Military Posture for FY1975, in *Hearings on S. 300*, 93rd Congress, 2d session, February 5, 1974, part 1.

Much more could be said against détente, but it would repeat what can be found in a voluminous literature already in print.[14] Enough has been said here to enable us to turn to the questions put by Secretary Kissinger to his critics:

> What is the alternative they propose? What precise policies do they want us to change? Are they prepared for a prolonged situation of dramatically increased international danger? Do they wish to return to the constant crises and high arms budgets of the cold war? Does détente encourage repression—or is it détente that has generated the ferment and the demands for openness that we are now witnessing? Can we ask our people to support confrontation unless they know that every reasonable alternative has been explored? [15]

The questions are quite loaded, of course, because they imply that the critics must choose either white hat or black, either détente or cold war. If that is the only choice open, one wonders what has happened to the "new stable structure of peace" under construction these last six years. As Professor Wohlstetter points out, "what is odd about this metaphor is its desire to have it both ways. The Structure of Peace in the nuclear era is solid and unshakable. Yet we must tiptoe carefully to make sure that we do not bring the whole apparently ramshackle affair crashing down about our ears in the final apocalypse of shattered glass and toppling masonry." [16]

The metaphor is wrong on both counts: the structure is in fact shaky, but there is no need to tiptoe around our relations with the Soviet Union. Not yet. An alternative stance is still achievable for American foreign policy that avoids the perils of Kissinger's détente at the one extreme and stark cold war at the other. It involves restoring Western confidence and resolve, reconstituting deterrence, basing negotiation firmly on the principles of reciprocal concession and unimpaired security, and bargaining accordingly.

As already stressed, Kissinger's diplomacy has created too much one-sided détente, an overrelaxation of tension in the United States and throughout the West. Tension is after all the natural defensive

---

[14] The following are some of the more effective and authoritative critiques of détente: Robert Conquest et al., "Detente: An Evaluation," *Survey*, Spring-Summer 1974, pp. 1-27; Theodore Draper, "Detente," *Commentary*, June 1974, pp. 25-47; Gregory Grossman, Statement before the Joint Economic Committee; and Albert Wohlstetter, "Threats and Promises of Peace."

[15] Speech in Minneapolis, *Department of State Bulletin*, August 4, 1975, p. 166.

[16] Wohlstetter, "Threats and Promises of Peace," p. 1116.

reaction to a perceived threat, and it alerts and stimulates the will to resist. Tension had become excessive in the West, Kissinger concluded, because the cold war associated with it contained a more perilous risk—nuclear annihilation—than the threat being resisted. Tension was relaxed by a diplomatic blitz that had the effect of accenting the nuclear risk while belittling the Soviet threat. The consequence has been a dangerous weakening of the will to resist, as a confused public tries to understand whether resistance is unnecessary or whether it is futile.

What needs to be done first is to restore a healthy state of alert based on appreciation of the external dangers threatening the Western way of life and a sense of confidence that they can be overcome. This can be done gradually by nudging diplomacy away from a quest for ways of getting the Soviet Union involved and toward the practice of quid-pro-quo bargaining. The differing nature of Eastern and Western problems provides a basis for reciprocal concessions benefitting both sides while improving Western security, or at least leaving it unimpaired.

The Soviet Union suffers chronically from a defective economy, which constantly thwarts the ambition of Soviet leaders to maximize power in the future as well as now. The economy simply cannot meet the heavy demands placed on it for both maintaining strength in being and providing growth, including a rising living standard. The problems stem from the inefficient organization and deficient incentives of a huge command economy hampered by, among other things, a policy of basic autarky. Hence the economy experiences periodic agricultural crises in the short run and inability to generate a broad front of technological innovation over the long run.

One way out would be fundamental reform of the economic system, but the totalitarian rulers have carefully avoided such a venture for fear of undermining their monolithic power. Curing the patient might eliminate need for the doctor. And so they have turned predictably to the West for help.

Whatever economic help we give is bound to enhance Soviet power—to make it stronger than it otherwise would be. Gains to the West, if any, will be trivial economically and even more so strategically, because Western military and political strength is not constrained significantly by economic factors. Hence we should not help the Soviet Union economically and technologically unless we receive political concessions in return that leave our security at least unimpaired. In general we should insist on improvement of security since what the Soviet Union gains from economic aid and expanded trade strengthens the leadership internally as well as externally. It should be required to reduce the Soviet threat to the West in exchange for the gain in domestic power. It is on this basis that we should parley for Soviet movement on SALT, MBFR, arms control in the Middle East, neutralization of Southeast Asia, and so on.

We must not delude ourselves that our foreign policy has no effect on conditions inside the Soviet Union and Eastern Europe. On this score, Solzhenitsyn is right[17] and Kissinger wrong. If Soviet rulers know the West will bail them out of every economic difficulty, they will be under no pressure to liberalize the regime. Similarly, the relaxing of external tension has always been accompanied in the East by a tightening internally. Kissinger asks whether détente encourages repression or ferment, and the answer is repression. Dissent reached its high mark in the Soviet Union before détente, and the movement has been virtually stamped out since. The various parts of Eastern Europe have experienced a like reactionary policy. Kissinger attacks a straw man when he stubbornly insists that Western foreign policy cannot transform the Soviet domestic structure, for no one seriously believes that outside pressure can cause democracy or anything like it to spring forth overnight in Soviet society. That is not the issue at all, but rather how best to endorse and strengthen the liberal cause in the East.

Businesslike bargaining based on the principle of unimpaired security is hardly confrontation or cold war. If Soviet leaders blindly reject opportunities to make arrangements yielding mutual gains but not undermining our strategic position, we have all the less reason to believe that they will behave responsibly merely to continue enjoying the goodies of involvement.

A revitalized diplomacy will help raise Western morale and confidence and lay the way for repairing our crumbling ramparts and alliances. The downward trend of defense must be reversed or all else is in vain. NATO must be put back together again and its strategic dilemmas resolved. It is a sad fact that Western military strategy has lagged far behind technology, particularly in not appreciating the revolutionary significance of smart weapons, non-nuclear as well as nuclear.[18] Selective strategic targeting, the product of

---

[17] See his Washington speech as reported in *U.S. News and World Report*, July 14, 1975, especially p. 49 ff.

[18] See Wohlstetter, "Threats and Promises of Peace," p. 1122 ff., and Earl Voss, "Defending Europe with Blunderbusses," Reprint 24 (Washington, D. C.: American Enterprise Institute, April 1974).

intensive deliberation in the Pentagon in recent years, is an early sign of overdue revision of strategic doctrine.

The issue, then, is how to make best use of our assets in the continuing struggle to defend Western civilization against the threat from the East. Stripped of rhetoric, Kissinger's détente amounts to giving the assets away without requiring any strategic benefits in return, this being done on the premise that the Soviet rulers will so treasure what they are receiving that they will carefully avoid upsetting the strategic equilibrium. But, as we have argued, they will hardly need to do anything since the power balance will steadily move in their favor anyhow. The alternative proposed here would exchange our assets only for compensatory strategic benefits. Such a diplomacy of reciprocal concession holds far more promise for meaningful peace than the drift of détente.

PART THREE
DEFENSE

5

DEFENSE: SELECTED DOCUMENTS

U.S.-SOVIET MILITARY BALANCE:
A FRAME OF REFERENCE FOR CONGRESS *

Congressional Research Service

This study by John M. Collins and John Steven Chwat of the Library of Congress discusses and details the comparative military strengths of the United States and the Soviet Union. Imbalances between these forces exist, but they are often ascribable to the different military requirements and approaches of the two nations, which complicate examinations and comparisons of capabilities. In several key areas, however, where meaningful analyses are possible, American forces either are significantly inferior to those possessed by the U.S.S.R. or are incapable of performing tasks deemed important for U.S. defensive needs.

Causes of Asymmetries

Quantitative and qualitative analyses of United States–Soviet armed forces simply identify salient asymmetries. To assess the importance of imbalances, it is necessary first to know *why* they exist. Critical U.S. deficiencies then can be isolated from those of slight concern.

Inequities for and against the United States can be traced in part to geographic circumstance, technological peculiarities, and U.S.

---

* Source: U.S. Congress, Senate, *United States/Soviet Military Balance: A Frame of Reference for Congress*, prepared for the Committee on Armed Services by the Congressional Research Service, 94th Congress, 2d session, January 1976, pp. 13–45.

threat appraisals, but the preponderance ensued because of deliberate policy decisions by *both* superpowers, beginning three decades ago.

Geographic Influences. Soviet armed forces safeguard the world's largest state, which stretches 3,000 miles north-to-south and 7,000 east-to-west, the latter distance being equal to the expanse between Washington, D.C., and Burma. NATO's forward defense forces abut Warsaw Pact buffer states, whose loyalty depends in part on a strong Soviet presence. A hostile China shares Siberia's lengthy southern frontier. Huge Soviet standing armies, air defenses, and tactical air establishments thus are understandable.[1] Carrier-based fighters are unnecessary. IRBMs–MRBMs [intermediate range ballistic missiles–medium range ballistic missiles] and medium bombers provide the requisite reach across Eurasia's land mass. The United States, still isolated by oceans despite technological developments, currently has different homeland defense problems.

The U.S. economy, including aspects associated with national security, relies extensively on imports. Intercontinental commerce is important. Most of our defense commitments are overseas. We therefore enjoin the U.S. Navy to keep critical sea lanes open in exigency and project offensive power onto foreign shores in support of American and allied interests. Strategic airlift plays imperative roles.

The Soviet situation of course is quite different. That country is relatively self-sufficient in raw materials. Most allies under its aegis are directly accessible by land avenues. The Kremlin has been reluctant to commit its own combat forces in far distant states since Khrushchev got his comeuppance in Cuba.[2] The Soviet Navy consequently is still structured primarily to protect the mother country by checking U.S. carrier air power and SSBNs [nuclear-powered ballistic missile submarines], to shortstop U.S. reinforcements for NATO, cut U.S. supply lines whenever required, and challenge the Sixth Fleet's control of the Mediterranean. Attack submarines, antiship missiles, and fast patrol boats serve those purposes best. An embryonic core of aircraft carriers and amphibious ships is the first indication that Moscow *may* intend to extend its offensive reach and improve its ability to project political power.

---

[1] Many U.S. military men contend that Soviet forces far exceed those required for deterrence and defense, but Soviet standards for "how much is enough?" may be significantly different from ours.

[2] Soviet training teams, service troops, SAM [surface-to-air-missile] crews, and interceptor pilots, all noncombatant or defensive in nature, once flooded the Nile Delta to help protect the Kremlin's massive investment in military aid but offensive forces in Egypt were always exclusively Arab. Cuban, not Soviet, forces now fight in Angola.

Technological Influences. Soviet quantitative advantages in fighter-attack aircraft count several models whose capabilities are grossly inferior to F-4 Phantoms, which have set the U.S. standard since 1962.[3] Even modern MIG-25s lack multipurpose adaptability, being mainly for reconnaissance and air defense. None equal our F-4's unrefueled combat radius, and none can be refueled in flight. Their ability to accomplish ground support missions falls far short of F-4s, which have a 16,000 lb. payload capacity in comparison with an estimated 2,000 lb. for MIG-21s and 2,800 lb. for MIG-23s.[4] Some Soviet fighters could outperform F-4s in air-to-air combat, being fast, more maneuverable, and able to operate at higher altitudes, although U.S. avionic packages, electronic countermeasures (ECM), and missile armaments reduce the margin. F-15 and F-16 aircraft hopefully will preserve our qualitative edge in the 1980s.[5] As a result, U.S. decision makers currently accept unspecified degrees of Soviet numerical superiority without undue compunction.

The Soviet Army, with 1,710,000 more men than its U.S. counterpart, requires much more tactical airlift, as the balance sheet shows. The disparity in numbers, however, is disproportionate, because nothing in the Soviet inventory matches performance characteristics of the U.S. C-130 fleet, which is easily the world's best.

Threat Characteristics. Giant Soviet ground forces would imperil the continental United States only if accompanied by adequate amphibious assault, strategic airlift, and logistic support apparatus, which is not the case. Part of those forces, together with tactical air elements, are pinned down semipermanently along the Chinese border, where they pose no immediate threat to U.S. associates or allies. A substantial percentage of Soviet troops serve internal security purposes in satellite states. Such factors all limit U.S. general purpose force requirements.

Pervasive Policy Decisions. Deliberate U.S. policy decisions account for the quantitative and qualitative ascendancy of Soviet armed forces in several areas. The seven summarized below overarch all others.

---

[3] About half of all Soviet counter air and a quarter of all close air support aircraft have been deployed since 1970, according to U.S. Air Force sources.

[4] SU-19A Fencer ground attack aircraft have a payload of about 7,500 pounds. No unclassified payload figures are available for SU-17/20 Fitter Cs, which are designed for deep interdiction. Both were deployed in 1974.

[5] U.S. Joint Chiefs of Staff, *Statement by George S. Brown before the Senate Armed Services Committee on United States Military Posture for FY 1976,* 5 February 1975, pp. 106-107.

Quantum instead of incremental improvements. The prevailing U.S. approach to research and development, predicated on technological initiative, features "pioneering and aggressive innovation." [6] Quantum improvements are the aim. That policy stimulates creativity in one sense, but paradoxically cultivates conservatism. Many modest advancements are accused of approaching obsolescence before they can be deployed. Successors for aging systems thus are often delayed indefinitely while U.S. scientists strain for breakthroughs.

The Soviets since World War II have espoused incremental improvements of the existing establishment.[7] Moderately modernized arms and equipment are procured as they become available. That procedure ensures continually improved capabilities which narrow or close qualitative gaps while U.S. forces "make do" with products in hand.[8]

Quality instead of quantity. The United States honors a principle of war called economy of force. Conversely, the Soviets implicitly prefer the principle of mass. This country therefore chooses quality instead of quantity, and generally retires outdated items when new ones enter the inventory.[9] The opposition, which opts for *both*, adds recent arrivals to existing stocks, winnowing out predecessors only when they cease to serve useful purposes. The effects of those diametrically different policies accentuate quantitative imbalances between U.S. and Soviet armed forces.

Firepower instead of manpower. The United States places a high premium on human life. This country therefore replaces manpower with firepower wherever possible. High dollar costs for pay and allowances reinforce that policy, which keeps personnel strengths down and support requirements up in U.S. armed forces, but not in the Soviet Union.

---

[6] U.S. Congress, House, Committee on Appropriations, *Hearings on Department of Defense Appropriations for 1976: Part 4, Research and Development, Test and Evaluation*, 94th Congress, 1st session, 1975, pp. 366-369, 531-532, 553-554.

[7] Ibid.

[8] In practice, neither the United States nor the Soviet Union subscribes exclusively to quantum jump or incremental improvement policies. U.S. tanks, guns, aircraft, and other items often undergo repeated modifications that add to or alter original capabilities without replacing basic systems. The Soviets began emphasizing *both* approaches about four years ago. (Ibid., pp. 553-554.) Nevertheless, the differentiations described are essentially correct.

[9] There are exceptions, as with any rule of thumb. The U.S. Army, for example, no longer uses M-48 tanks, but M-48A5s are being equipped with new diesel engines and 105mm guns for our marines. Many items retired by U.S. armed forces still serve some allies.

Sustained combat concepts. Title 10 of the United States Code, which prescribes an army, navy, and air force that could, if required, conduct "sustained" combat operations, has a profound influence on U.S. force structure.[10] All three services must maintain solid logistic and administrative establishments to fulfill that function wherever U.S. interests are involved.

The Soviet Union seems to have a different philosophy. Its air and ground forces are best adapted for a short, decisive conflict if NATO and the Warsaw Pact clash.[11] Admiral Sergei Gorshkov also has shaped a first-strike, "one-shot" navy, without much staying power.[12] "Tooth-to-tail" ratios therefore reflect poorly on U.S. general purpose forces, which are long on logistic support and sometimes short on combat power in comparison with Soviet counterparts.

Total force concepts. When the United States began to retrench during final stages of the conflict in Vietnam, the Defense Department placed increasing emphasis on so-called total force concepts, which count on collective security and reserve components to offset reductions in our active duty establishment.[13] Soviet leaders rely more on active forces and less on allies to support national interests. Those conflicting policies contribute substantially to comparative force postures. . . .

Cyclical cutbacks. Cutbacks in U.S. armed forces have followed every American war since we won our independence. The current cycle began about 1970. Since then, drawdowns have been drastic. No service escaped the knife, as the air force did after the Korean conflict. The army has been sliced in half since personnel strengths reached high points in 1968 (1,570,000 then, 790,000 now). Soviet personnel, which exceeded our own by 857,000 in 1965, currently

---

[10] Title 10, United States Code, Chapter 307, Section 3062; Chapter 503, Section 5012; and Chapter 807, Section 8061. . . .

[11] See, for example, Steven L. Canby, "NATO Muscle: More Shadow Than Substance," *Foreign Policy* (Fall 1972), pp. 44-46; also Richard D. Lawrence and Jeffrey Record, *U.S. Force Structure in NATO: An Alternative* (Washington, D.C.: The Brookings Institution, 1974), pp. 6-26. Some authorities suggest that both studies underestimate Soviet staying power, but, if so, differences in U.S.-Soviet concepts still are clearly evident.

[12] Office of the Chief of Naval Operations, *Understanding Soviet Naval Developments*, April 1975, p. 19, and Russell Spurr, "Moscow: Drawing the Asian Battlelines," *Far Eastern Economic Review* (31 October 1975), pp. 26-34.

[13] U.S. Department of Defense, *Statement by Melvin R. Laird before the House Armed Services Committee on the FY 1972-1976 Defense Program and the 1972 Defense Budget*, 9 March 1971, p. 21.

surpass us by about 2.7 million.[14] Their weapons inventory dilates similarly, while ours declines.

U.S. decision makers intended to constitute a smaller force which modernization measures would endow with greater capabilities than its predecessors. However, rates of retraction exceeded those of refurbishment. Size, therefore, was reduced without concomitant increases in strength. Moreover, the higher performance of new systems does not always compensate for the sharp reduction of flexibility caused by fewer numbers.

All-volunteer force. Three decades of U.S. conscription ended in January 1973, when draft calls registered zero, although the Selective Service System still functions on a standby basis.[15]

America's withdrawal from Indochina, implementation of the Nixon Doctrine (which demanded fewer general purpose forces than previous containment policies), budgetary difficulties, public opinion, and reevaluations of pressing threats led U.S. leaders to establish manpower requirements at 2.2 million in 1973.[16] That ceiling has remained almost constant.[17]

The United States probably could slightly exceed stated recruiting limits in these times of tight economy, but if society were more affluent, we would face serious problems filling quotas. In either event, this country is *compelled* to stress reserve components. Influences on the balance of U.S. and Soviet active forces thus are adverse.

Money for manpower. The cost of U.S. defense manpower has doubled during the past decade, owing to the initiation of annual comparability pay raises and a one-time increase to make our all-volunteer force feasible. Pay and allowances now absorb about 53 percent of the defense budget. Associated outlays for troop housing, recruiting,

---

[14] See the following table:

	1965	1975
Soviet personnel	3,510,000	4,812,000
U.S. personnel	2,653,000	2,134,000
Difference	857,000	2,678,000

Figures include strategic offensive and defensive personnel, army, navy, air force, marines, and Soviet border guards.

[15] U.S. Department of Defense, *Military Manpower Requirements Report for FY 1974*, February 1973, pp. 1-2.

[16] Ibid., p. 5.

[17] The FY 1976 manpower authorization is slightly less than 2.1 million. Public Law 94-106, 8 October 1975.

human relations, and various other activities presently push the total close to sixty-five cents out of every dollar.[18] Relative shares for manpower have been stabilized, but absolute outlays will continue to climb as programmed cost-of-living increases periodically take effect.[19]

The impact on force modernization is immense. Manpower costs added to inescapable expenditures for operations and maintenance sharply reduce funds for research, development, and procurement programs in an inflationary environment that causes prices to escalate.[20] The Soviet Union, with far lower pay scales and a controlled economy less afflicted by inflation, could afford a larger force and modernize at a more rapid rate if its total defense budget were exactly the same as that of the United States.[21]

Particular Policy Decisions. A spate of subordinate policies, most of them derived at least indirectly from the seven above, affect United States–Soviet asymmetries in specific functional areas. The following list is depictive, rather than definitive.

Strategic nuclear policies. U.S. defense decision makers settled on a strategic nuclear triad of bombers, ICBMs [intercontinental ballistic missiles], and SLBMs [submarine sea-launched ballistic missiles] in the late 1950s, and have clung to it ever since, whereas the Soviets stress land-based ballistic missiles and downplay manned aircraft.[22] America's mixed force matrix was focused primarily on city targeting early in the 1960s to accommodate our second-strike strategy of

---

[18] U.S. Department of Defense, *Annual Defense Department Report to the Congress on the FY 1976 and Transition Budgets, FY 1977 Authorization Request and FY 1976-1980 Defense Programs,* 1975, pp. 123-126.

[19] Public Law 90-207, 90th Congress (81 Stat. 649), Section 8.

[20] Department of Defense, *Annual Report to the Congress on the FY 1976 and Transition Budgets,* p. D1.

[21] Soviet pay and allowances were an estimated 18-25 percent of the total defense budget in 1969, the latest date for which unclassified data are available. U.S. Congress, Joint Economic Committee, "Economic Burden of Defense Expenditures," by Stanley H. Cohn, in *Soviet Economic Prospects for the Seventies,* 93d Congress, 1st session, 1973, p. 150.

Such comparisons are always suspect. The Soviet defense budget is secret. Segments are concealed under civil headings. Expenditures are enumerated differently than in the United States. Rubles are difficult to convert accurately into dollars. Most Western calculations therefore are based on one of two methodologies. The first, which manipulates published Soviet data to correspond with U.S. categories and exchanges rubles for U.S. currency, risks underestimating the Kremlin's expenditures. The second, which judges how much it would cost to duplicate visible Soviet defense efforts in U.S. dollars, risks overestimations.

[22] About 30 percent of all U.S. warheads are on ICBMs, as opposed to 80 percent for the Soviet Union. MIRVing [multiple independently targetable reentry vehicle] Soviet ICBMs may push that proportion to well over 90 percent unless Moscow elects to install multiple warheads on SLBMs.

assured destruction, which preserved deterrence by means of a "balance of terror." Capabilities were required to eradicate "say, one-fifth to one-fourth of the [Soviet] population and one half of [Soviet] industrial capacity." [23]

Beyond those finite demands, U.S. decision makers believed that relative strengths were irrelevant. The Defense Department placed less credence in the number of delivery vehicles than in the stock of separately targetable nuclear warheads.[24] That conclusion strongly influenced this country to install MIRVs instead of augmenting its inventory of bombers and ballistic missiles. Our ICBM–SLBM holdings have stayed static at 1,054 and 656, respectively, since 1967, while Soviet launchers increased.

None of the U.S. weapons systems was expressly engineered with the requisite combinations of accuracy, payload, yield, and responsiveness to neutralize time-sensitive hard targets like missiles in silos, because city targets are soft, sprawling areas. The Soviets, by way of contrast, specialize in heavy ICBMs and high megatonnage.

Arms control accords have also shaped the balance since 1972. Phase I of the Strategic Arms Limitation Talks (SALT I) produced an ABM [antiballistic missile] Treaty that, with the amending protocol two years later, restricts each side to a single ABM site containing no more than 100 missiles.[25] The SALT I interim agreement on strategic offensive systems "froze" selected force levels for the period May 1972–October 1977 (Table 1) pending more lasting arrangements now addressed by SALT II negotiators. U.S. officials seek essential equivalence.[26]

---

[23] U.S. Department of Defense, *Statement by Robert S. McNamara before the Senate Armed Services Committee on the FY 1969-73 Defense Program and 1969 Defense Budget*, 22 January 1968, p. 50.

[24] Ibid., p. 52. Decisions, for example, were taken in 1961 to reduce the planned number of Titan squadrons. Atlas ICBMs were retired in 1964. The Minuteman program was compressed from 1,200 to 1,000 missiles that same year. Data received telephonically from Air Force Systems Command Historical Office, 9 January 1976.

[25] The SALT ABM Treaty permitted each side two ABM sites, one to defend the capital city, a second to cover ICBMs. The protocol reduces authorization to one site each. U.S. Congress, House, Committee on Foreign Affairs, and Senate, Committee on Foreign Relations (joint committee print), *Legislation on Foreign Relations, with Explanatory Notes*, 93d Congress, 2d session, March 1974, pp. 1175-1179; U.S. Congress, Senate, Committee on Foreign Relations, "Protocol on the Treaty with the U.S.S.R. on the Limitation of ABM Systems, Executive I, 93-2, 19 September 1974," in *Legislative Calendar*, 93d Congress, 1st session, 2 January 1975, p. 14.

[26] SALT I and II interrelationships, together with current stumbling blocks, are summarized in John M. Collins, *SALT II Issues* (Issue Brief Number IB 75074), Congressional Research Service, updated as of 13 November 1975.

Table 1
SALT I FORCE LEVELS

Delivery System	United States	U.S.S.R.
ICBMs:		
"Freeze" level, May 1972[1]	1,054	1,608[2]
Max conversion[3]	1,000	1,399
Already converted	0	32
Current status	1,054	1,603
"Heavy" ICBMs:[4]		
Pre-1964 models:		
"Freeze" level, May 1972[1]	54	209
Exchanged for SLBMs	0	32[5]
Current status	54	177
Post-1964 models: "Freeze" level, May 1972[1]	0	413
Current total	54	590
SLBMs:		
"Freeze" level, May 1972[1]	656	740
Maximum conversion[3,6]	710	950
Current status	656	725
"Modern" ballistic missile submarines:[7]		
"Freeze" level, May 1972[8]	41	43
Maximum conversion	44	62
Current status[9]	41	45
Heavy bombers	(10)	(10)
Total ICBM, SLBM launchers:		
"Freeze" level, May 1972[1]	1,710	2,328
Current status	1,710	2,328

[1] The "freeze" level of 26 May 1972, reflects Soviet delivery systems in operation and under construction at that time. All Soviet figures are U.S. intelligence estimates, since Moscow refused to furnish statistics.

[2] Open sources originally charged the U.S.S.R. with 1,618 ICBM silos, but U.S. officials since have accepted about 10 of those as command and control centers or training sites, rather than launchers for operational missiles.

[3] Pre-1964 ICBMs could be exchanged for SLBMs on a 1-for-1 basis, according to SALT I rules. Figures shown indicate ceilings if that course were chosen. The U.S. ceiling of 710 SLBMs was mathematically unattainable. We could trade 48 of our 54 Titan ICBMs for 3 Poseidon boats with 16 launchers each or for 2 Trident boats with 24 launchers each. Either alternative would increase the number of SLBMs to 704, unless we switch to SSBNs with more than 16 tubes.

[4] Pre-1964 "heavy" ICBMs, by U.S. definition, included U.S. Titan IIs (1962), Soviet SS-7s (1961), and SS-8s (1963). Post-1964 models, by U.S. definition, included

all land-based ballistic missiles significantly larger than Soviet SS-11s. When the SALT I Interim Agreement was signed, only SS-9s qualified. This study counts 100 SS-19s (as of January 1976) although SALT II accords may eventually consider them in the "light" ICBM category.

[5] Some Soviet SS-7s and SS-8s have been dismantled and exchanged for 2 nuclear-powered SLBM submarines.

[6] Soviet pre-1964 SLBMs on diesel submarines did not count, but those on H-class nuclear-powered boats did. Figures shown indicate the ceiling if the maximum allowable number of ICBMs were converted to SLBMs.

[7] SALT I limitations did not include 10 Soviet H-class nuclear-powered submarines or 22 G-class diesel-powered boats. The former are armed with 3 SS-N-5 SLBMs each (range about 750 nautical miles). The latter carry 3 SS-N-5s or 3 SS-N-4s (range 350 nautical miles).

[8] Only 25 Y-class Soviet ballistic missile submarines were in service in May 1972. All 41 U.S. SSBNs were operational.

[9] Soviet submarines 44 and 45 replace an estimated 32 SS-7s and SS-8s. See footnote 5 above.

[10] Not covered by SALT I.

Tactical nuclear policies. A smorgasbord of tactical nuclear weapons was technologically feasible in the late 1950s. The United States experimented with all or most before deciding to stress adaptable aircraft and artillery that hopefully have sufficient accuracy and small enough yields to fight a limited nuclear war in crowded NATO Europe without causing unconscionable civilian casualties and collateral damage, yet still function effectively in conventional combat.[27]

The Soviets in contrast elected to emphasize unipurpose intermediate- and medium-range ballistic missiles, along with free rockets. None of their systems is capable of discriminating nuclear combat—the yields are too large and they are too erratic. Airfields, ports, logistical bases, command–control installations, and other area targets (many of which are collocated with German cities) could be engaged most effectively.[28]

General purpose force policies. Records are replete with general purpose force policies that account for asymmetries in the United States–Soviet military balance. This section silhouettes four (one for each service) as illustrations.

---

[27] For general background, see U.S. Department of Defense, *The Theater Nuclear Posture in Europe: A Report to the United States Congress in Compliance with Public Law 93-365*, 1975.

Honest John rockets, the least accurate of U.S. tactical nuclear weapons, have largely been replaced by Lance missiles.

U.S. R & D programs for mobile MRBMs were cancelled in 1964. Thor and Jupiter missiles were removed from Western Europe and Turkey that same year. Data received telephonically from Air Force Historical Office, 9 January 1976.

[28] Thomas W. Wolfe, *Soviet Power and Europe, 1945-1970* (Baltimore: The Johns Hopkins Press, 1970), pp. 197-199, 203, 209, 211, 456-458.

Soviet assembly lines turned out about 9,000 heavy tanks before they ceased production about 1962. An estimated 2,500 still are combat-effective. This country, however, never put much store in heavy tanks, and discontinued development a decade earlier than the Soviets. None remains in service. Instead, U.S. armored elements are equipped with more versatile mediums that trade steel plate protection for speed, maneuverability, air mobility, and ability to operate in areas where bridge capacities are low and terrain is somewhat restrictive.[29]

The Soviet Navy specializes in ship-killing cruise missiles. An estimated 108 major combatants (including sixty-eight submarines) and 135 fast patrol boats are so equipped. The U.S. Navy, which has nothing comparable, assigns such roles to fourteen aircraft carriers [30] and traditional submarines armed with torpedoes, as an outgrowth of policy decisions taken two decades ago.[31] The consequent imbalance will persist until the United States begins to deploy Harpoon missiles in quantity (beginning late in 1976).

America's fighter-attack aircraft (navy and marine, as well as air force) all perform deep interdiction missions and provide close air support for ground combat units as a matter of policy. The Soviet Union would depend heavily on MRBMs and IRBMs for the former task in a nuclear war, and emphasizes massed tube artillery, mortars, and multiple rocket launchers along lines of contact between Soviet and enemy forces.

Differences between tactical fighter inventories of U.S. and Soviet Air Forces thus are greater than statistics in Table 8 indicate. Our aircraft generally have greater range, payload capacities, choices of ordnance, and loiter abilities. Soviet counterparts are comparatively simple, light, maneuverable, and less vulnerable on the ground, since they can fly from primitive strips that permit far greater dispersal than that enjoyed by U.S. forward-based fighters.[32]

The United States Marine Corps, organized, trained, equipped, and psychologically conditioned as an elite air-ground team, exists primarily to seize and defend lodgments on foreign shores in support

---

[29] U.S. Congress, House, Committee on Government Operations, *Military Tank Procurement*, Tenth Report, 85th Congress, 1st session, 1957, p. 16.

[30] One U.S. attack carrier was decommissioned in January 1976. Another will leave active service before the close of FY 1976.

[31] U.S. Congress, House, Subcommittee No. 3 (Seapower) of the Committee on Armed Services, *Hearings on Military Posture and H.R. 12564*, Part 2, 93d Congress, 2d session, 1974, p. 1003.

[32] U.S. Air Force Systems Command, *Military Forces Handbook: Military Forces of the U.S.S.R. and People's Republic of China*, 1975, pp. 13-14.

of U.S. foreign policy predicated on collective security principles.[33] The Soviet Union, which conducts its few overseas operations through proxies, as yet has no analogous policy, although an emerging amphibious assault force suggests that the Kremlin soon may have more than token intervention capabilities in Africa and South Asia.

Strategic mobility policies. U.S. policies have supported strategic air transport since the early 1960s, when Congress and the executive branch collaborated in efforts to correct shortcomings. Succeeding crises, such as those in Berlin, Cuba, Vietnam, and Israel, underscored the importance of adequate intercontinental airlift to project U.S. power and supply allies. Assets afforded by C-5As and C-141s thus are unparalleled anywhere in the world.[34]

Deploying U.S. forces without being able to sustain them could sow the seeds of disaster. Corollary sealift forces consequently are required,[35] but our merchant marine has been allowed to languish. Only 118 ships remain in the Military Sealift Command Controlled Fleet, including 14 in ready reserve—reduced operating status.[36] In accord with national policy, we therefore place extraordinary dependence (95 percent) on U.S.-owned, but privately operated, commercial carriers that fly foreign flags and are manned by alien crews who owe this country no allegiance.[37] Many of the ships are poorly suited for military purposes. Total force policies also pass heavy responsibility to selected allies, who are expected to provide ships and related services in times of common emergency, including offloading assistance and operations to clear supplies from terminal areas.

The Soviet Merchant Marine, by contrast, consists mainly of modern, highly automated ships that currently carry more than half of all the Kremlin's transoceanic cargo. Coordination with the Soviet Navy is complete.[38]

Assessing Asymmetries

U.S. Quantitative Superiority. Areas of U.S. quantitative superiority over the Soviet Union are indicated in Table 2. Some are negative or

---

[33] See "Operational Functions of Armed Forces," Annex B [not included in this selection].

[34] Department of Defense, *Statement on the FY 1969-73 Defense Budget*, pp. 139-140.

[35] More than 95 percent of all U.S. military bulk cargo bound for Vietnam moved by sea, including aviation fuel.

[36] Statistics furnished by Military Sealift Command, as of 3 October 1975.

[37] *Understanding Soviet Naval Developments*, p. 39.

[38] Ibid., pp. 39-40.

Table 2
U.S. QUANTITATIVE SUPERIORITY
(active forces only)

	United States	Soviet Union	U.S. Margin
Strategic offensive:			
MIRVed ICBM	550	110	440
MIRVed SLBM	416	0	416
ALCM	1,140	185	955
Heavy bombers [1]	463	135	328
Tankers	615	50	565
ICBM–SLBM warheads	6,794	3,442	3,352
Strategic defense: none	NA	NA	NA
Ground forces:			
Airmobile divisions	1	0	1
Infantry divisions	6	0	6
Marine divisions	3	0	3
Nuclear artillery pieces	700	0	700
Helicopters [2]	9,492	2,580	6,912
Naval forces:			
Personnel [3]	515,400	386,000	129,400
Attack carriers	14	0	14
Helicopter carriers	7	2	0
Cruisers [4]	27	13	14
Destroyers [4]	70	65	5
Nuclear-powered attack subs [4]	62	35	27
Carrier aircraft	1,508	53	1,455
Marine fighter–attack aircraft [5]	468	0	468
Mobility forces: Strategic airlift	300	60	240

[1] Excludes United States FB-111s and Soviet Backfire bombers.
[2] Helicopters include 487 in the U.S. Marine Corps.
[3] Excludes ballistic missile submarine forces.
[4] Cruisers and destroyers exclude SSM types.
[5] U.S. Air Force and Marine shore-based fighter–attack aircraft combined fail to equal Soviet counterparts (2,768 to 3,590).
Note: See Table 8 for sources and explanatory notes.

neutral in value. Some facilitate strong leverage in other contexts but have almost no significance in terms of the United States–Soviet balance. Some perhaps affect perceptions but provide few credible capabilities. Only a few confer conclusive advantage on the United States.

Superiority disadvantageous. The United States has 129,000 more general purpose navy personnel than the Soviet Union. Differences are due principally to U.S. logistic support and administrative elements that afford unparalleled staying power. Nonetheless, this country uses many more people than the opposition to operate fewer ships. That phenomenon deprives other defense sectors of much-needed funds in this era marked by high manpower costs.

Superiority deceptive. Token U.S. superiority in infantry, airmobile, and marine divisions is smothered by the Soviet total (19 to 168). Even if one U.S. division equalled two of the Kremlin's, which sometimes is true for personnel strengths but surely not combat power,[39] forty Soviet Category 1 divisions in north-central Europe outnumber our five by four to one. Using that same criterion, Warsaw Pact divisions still outnumber NATO counting all ready reinforcements.

America's numerical advantage in conventional cruisers and destroyers disappears when Soviet SSM [surface-to-surface missile] ships are included in the tally (twenty-seven U.S. cruisers, thirty-three Soviet; seventy U.S. destroyers, eighty-five Soviet). Moscow's overall edge in escort-type vessels is 223 to 195, if one counts ships in our naval reserve, but excludes coast guard vessels.[40]

Similarly, the two-to-one U.S. numerical predominance in nuclear attack submarines is almost nullified if Soviet nuclear-powered cruise missile submarines (which carry torpedoes as well as SSMs) are considered: sixty-two U.S.; seventy-five Soviet.

Superiority an ambiguous asset. Manned bombers, the original component of the U.S. strategic nuclear triad, must penetrate increasingly effective enemy defenses-in-depth to reach targets. They have little ability to engage time-sensitive targets (such as ICBMs), since flights are measured in many hours, not minutes. Consequently, some skeptics assert that U.S. superiority in strategic aircraft and short-

---

[39] Soviet tank divisions have half as many men as ours. Their motorized rifle divisions are two-thirds the size of U.S. mechanized divisions. Tank strengths in each case are about equal.

[40] Total escort figures include cruisers, destroyers, frigates, corvettes, and other escorts of all types.

range attack missiles (SRAM) is a dubious asset.[41] As they see it, U.S. deterrent powers depend much more on ballistic missiles, which could strike swiftly and would be "home free" in the absence of a sound Soviet ABM shield.[42]

Immense U.S. superiority in MIRV launchers and ballistic missile warheads is often lauded. American preeminence clearly affects peacetime perceptions to our benefit, at home and abroad. Fixed-site ICBMs could survive a sneak attack with greater retaliatory capabilities than would be preserved if each silo contained a single warhead.

Beyond that, however, the practical utility of many MIRVs is problematic, in the opinion of many observers. Most Soviet counterforce targets would be immune to a U.S. second strike, since Soviet reserves could be launched on warning. Huge stocks of U.S. MIRVs will be inessential for assured destruction missions until Moscow deploys a comprehensive and credible ABM system (presently proscribed by SALT), because a handful of survivable MIRVed missiles could cover sufficient targets. MIRVs would be equally superfluous for fighting a "tit-for-tat" war. Some critics therefore believe that maintaining U.S. superiority in MIRVs would divert dollars that could be used better to correct known deficiencies elsewhere in our defense establishment.

Helicopters are another ambiguous asset. They provided unsurpassed battlefield mobility in Vietnam, but whether similar employment would be possible in NATO Europe's high-risk air defense environment is subject to conjecture. If not, our numerical superiority would lose significance.

---

[41] SRAMs can be used to improve the penetration powers of manned bombers by suppressing enemy defenses. They can also engage static targets of other kinds. To do so, however, the bombers they accompany must first breech enemy defenses-in-depth, since SRAM's effective range is only about 100 miles.

[42] Many military men discourage attempts to analyze components of the U.S. strategic nuclear triad in isolation, since the synergistic effects of mixed forces far exceed the capabilities of any given system. Ballistic missiles and manned aircraft (or other airbreathers, like cruise missiles) create wholly dissimilar difficulties for defenders. The Soviets, not knowing where U.S. bombers might strike, must cover all critical points, whether we have many aircraft or few. Further, the current mix of U.S. forces confronts the Kremlin with insoluble first-strike scheduling problems. SLBMs, with flight times of six to ten minutes from firing positions along our continental shelf, might catch B-52s on strip alert, but still lack the accuracy and yields to crush missile silos. Soviet ICBMs, enroute about half an hour, are best-suited for such targets, but would allow SAC ample time to "scramble" its bombers. U.S. SSBNs at sea are almost invulnerable in any case, given Moscow's present antisubmarine-warfare capabilities.

This section, which acknowledges the need for mixed forces, simply suggests that future effectiveness *might* be improved by amending the mix to counter Soviet countermeasures.

Superiority an assured asset. America's amphibious landing forces (but not amphibious lift) are much more numerous than three marine divisions indicate, because several army divisions are also qualified. The consequent flexibility opens up U.S. options not otherwise available.

U.S. carrier air power is also greater than statistics show. Marine, as well as navy, fighter–attack squadrons are trained to operate afloat when required. Soviet and proxy forces in underdeveloped areas still rely almost exclusively on land-based air support, and entirely lack high-performance carrier aircraft. The U.S. edge thus is absolute.

United States–Soviet Quantitative Equality. Between U.S. quantitative superiority on one hand and Soviet quantitative superiority on the other is a zone of approximate equality, where asymmetries are minor (Table 3).

The balance between light ICBMs is important, because that category contains most of the land-based ballistic missiles on both sides.

Neither country enjoys credible ABM capabilities. The U.S. site at Grand Forks, North Dakota, which functioned briefly as an active R & D facility, is being shut down, except for perimeter acquisition

Table 3
UNITED STATES / SOVIET QUANTITATIVE EQUALITY
(active forces only)

	United States	Soviet Union	Difference
Strategic offensive: light ICBMs [1]	1,000	1,013	13
Strategic defensive: ABM missiles	100	64	36
Ground forces: none	NA	NA	NA
Naval forces:			
Escorts [2]	98	105	7
Patrol–ASW aircraft ashore	450	360	90
ASW helicopters afloat	80	53	27
Air forces: total tactical aircraft	5,000	5,350	350
Mobility forces: none	NA	NA	NA

[1] This study counts all Soviet SS-19 ICBMs as "heavies," although SALT II accords may eventually consider them in the "light" category.

[2] Escorts in this table exclude cruisers, destroyers, and U.S. Coast Guard vessels. They include 34 U.S. Naval Reserve ships.

Note: See Table 8 for sources and explanatory notes.

radar and related facilities. The Congress expects "that the interceptor missiles and warheads will be expeditiously evacuated." [43] Even so, parity will continue to pertain for all practical purposes. The sixty-four Soviet ABM missiles around Moscow could be easily saturated.

The quantitative standoff in fixed- and rotary-wing ASW [anti-submarine warfare] aircraft is meaningful only when measured against missions. Neither side has sufficiency, given current submarine strengths.[44]

Equal totals of tactical aircraft are far less important than superiority in particular types, such as fighter–attack.

Soviet Quantitative Superiority. *United States–Soviet correlations militarily immaterial.* Soviet quantitative superiority in any given category is of little concern when offensive forces or weapons systems compete against dissimilar defenses. If the Kremlin increased its cruise missile holdings by many multiples, there would be no call for this country to reciprocate in kind. Stronger SAM defenses would serve our purposes better. Inequities are irrelevant where noncombat forces are concerned. Each side sizes according to missions, not enemy counterparts. Table 4 indicates cases where correlations consequently are immaterial, except perhaps for perceptions.

United States–Soviet correlations militarily important. The balance in any given category affects military capabilities directly when like offensive forces or weapons systems compete against each other: U.S. divisions versus Soviet divisions; U.S. fighter aircraft versus similar Soviet aircraft; and so on. Examples are indicated in Table 5. Regional balances frequently are more important than total inventories, as already noted.

U.S. quality compensates for quantities in different degrees. U.S. overages in some categories *could* counteract shortages elsewhere (more SAMs, fewer interceptors, for example, but we are strong in neither). However, certain imbalances create distinct disadvantages.

Soviet quantitative superiority in ICBMs may soon imperil the U.S. second-strike force of ballistic missiles in silos. At the very least, America's ICBM *launchers* should outnumber Moscow's anticipated stock of *warheads* with single-shot kill probabilities. Otherwise, the

---

[43] U.S. Congress, House, *Department of Defense Appropriations, Fiscal Year 1976, Conference Report to accompany H.R. 9861*, Report No. 94-710, 94th Congress, 1st session, 10 December 1975, p. 28.

[44] Soviet ASW concentrates essentially on U.S. ballistic missile submarines. Our ASW efforts are directed primarily against Soviet attack submarines, which challenge U.S. abilities to control sea lanes and protect shipping in emergency.

Table 4

SOVIET QUANTITATIVE SUPERIORITY, CORRELATION
BETWEEN LIKE FORCES MILITARILY IMMATERIAL
(active forces only)

	United States	Soviet Union	Soviet Margin
Strategic offensive:			
SLBMs	656	725	69
SLCMs	0	348	348
Ballistic missile submarines	41	73	32
Medium bombers	66	500	434
Strategic defensive:			
SAM launchers	330	9,500	9,170
Interceptors	396	2,700	2,304
Ground forces: SSM	180	1,853	1,673
Naval forces:			
Amphibious ships [1]	57	85	28
Patrol boats	7	230	223
Shore-based bombers	0	480	480
Air forces: reconnaissance aircraft	340	750	410
Mobility forces:			
Strategic sealift	1,009	2,358	1,349
Tactical airlift [2]	500	800	300

[1] Amphibious ships exclude helicopter carriers.
[2] U.S. tactical airlift includes reserve C-130s.
Note: See Table 8 for sources and explanatory notes.

U.S.S.R. at some time in the future might compromise one leg of the U.S. triad.

Numerical imbalances between U.S.–Soviet and NATO–Warsaw Pact ground forces are considerable.[45] Disparities in both deployed strengths and ready reserves are especially evident in central Europe, where our troops are spread very thinly. Five division equivalents in the U.S. zone, including two armored cavalry regiments, cover a 250-kilometer (155-mile) front, approximately twice the desired distance. Those forces are insufficient to conduct a mobile defense, featuring selected strong points well forward. We have *no* locally available reserves above division level.

---

[45] Refer back to Figure 2 [not included in this selection].

Table 5

SOVIET QUANTITATIVE SUPERIORITY, CORRELATION BETWEEN LIKE FORCES MILITARILY IMPORTANT
(active forces only)

	United States	Soviet Union	Soviet Margin
Strategic offense:			
ICBMs:			
Heavy [1]	54	613	559
Total	1,054	1,603	549
Strategic defense: none	NA	NA	NA
Ground forces:			
Army personnel	789,100	2,500,000	1,710,900
Divisions [2]	19	168	149
Main battle tanks [2]	8,975	34,650	25,675
Armored carriers	19,000	40,000	21,000
Tube artillery [3]	3,510	17,150	13,640
Naval forces:			
SSM cruisers	0	20	20
SSM destroyers	0	20	20
Attack submarines	73	253	180
Air forces: fighter/attack [4]	2,300	3,590	1,290
Mobility forces: none	NA	NA	NA

[1] This study counts all Soviet SS-19 ICBMs as "heavies," although SALT II accords may eventually consider them in the "light" category.

[2] Includes army and marines.

[3] Artillery includes army and marine conventional and nuclear capable pieces.

[4] Fighter–attack aircraft exclude those based on carriers.

The "small" U.S. contingent presently in place is to be reinforced rapidly in emergency by elements now in the United States. Expeditious arrival would depend on strategic warning, readily available airlift–sealift assets in adequate amounts, rapid action by NATO's politico–military leaders, and the preservation of vulnerable reception facilities in Europe, none of which is assured.[46]

Asymmetries between U.S. and Soviet cruisers, destroyers, and attack submarine strengths also are important, because all such ships can engage each other in combat. There is no direct relationship

---

[46] For fuller discussion, see John M. Collins, *U.S. Military Support for NATO*, prepared for the Senate Armed Services Committee (19 January 1973), pp. 21-28.

between like systems, as there is for ICBMs, because submarines sink surface ships, and vice versa, but numerical superiority nonetheless would assist the so-called one shot Soviet Navy if a war of attrition occurred.

Appraising U.S. Ends and Means

There is no consensus concerning the implications of many asymmetries identified in foregoing sections. Those who believe in bald U.S. superiority across the board discern impending disaster for the United States. They recommend that America's military establishment be reinforced immediately. Even those who prefer quantitative parity as the U.S. force posture standard feel some queasiness when confronted with statistics like those in Table 8.

Superiority and parity, however, are oriented exclusively on *Soviet holdings*, without regard for real *U.S. requirements*. Sufficiency, a better standard, concentrates on what this country can *do* despite Soviet opposition, not on what each side *has*.[47]

The following exposition therefore focuses on possible conflicts between available U.S.–Soviet assets (Tables 2–5) and announced U.S. aims (Table 6). Findings are summarized in Table 7.[48]

Present Balance. *Strategic nuclear problems.* The present balance between U.S. and Soviet strategic offensive forces would be degraded dramatically by pre- and post-launch attrition at the onset of a general nuclear war. Our ICBMs and bombers both are vulnerable in different degrees. This country, having absorbed a Soviet first strike, would have to retaliate with truncated elements whose coordination and control could be disrupted. Our forces would have to function in a chaotic atmosphere, where nuclear effects (blast, heat, radiation) might drastically decrease expected capabilities.

U.S. strategic defensive problems are perhaps even greater. If deterrence should fail for any reason, and massive Soviet attacks hit

---

[47] Superiority is a force planning concept which demands markedly greater capabilities of certain kinds than those possessed by opponents. Parity-essential equivalence is predicated on particular capabilities that are approximately equal in overall effectiveness. Friendly and enemy numbers need not jibe in either case, but statistical strengths tend to be overemphasized, because friendly force levels depend on the extent of enemy deployments. By way of contrast, sufficiency as a force-sizing criterion calls for adequate abilities to attain desired ends without undue waste. Superiority thus is essential in some circumstances; parity suffices under less demanding conditions; and inferiority (qualitative as well as quantitative) sometimes is acceptable.

[48] See Annex B for force sufficiency factors [not included in this selection].

Table 6
U.S. AIMS TO BE ACCOMPLISHED

National Security Interests
Survival
Physical security
Stability
Credibility
Peace
World power
Self-determination
Freedom of action

National Security Objectives
Deter aggression
Defend United States if deterrence fails
Safeguard other states whose security is linked with our own

Military Roles and Missions
Title 10, United States Code
Overcome aggressors that imperil U.S. peace and security
Conduct prompt and sustained operations on order
Protect U.S. shipping
DOD Amplification
Gain general air superiority
Gain general naval supremacy
Deal with one major and one minor contingency concurrently

U.S. Objectives in NATO Europe
Deter Warsaw Pact aggression
Defend without major loss of territory if deterrence fails
Maintain a high tactical nuclear threshold

Strategic Mobility Aims
Reinforce and resupply NATO Europe in emergency
Facilitate U.S. operations elsewhere as required
Supply selected allies

U.S. Defense Commitments
Treaties
Congressional resolutions
Executive agreements
Policy declarations, communiques

Table 7
KEY U.S. SHORTCOMINGS[1]

Strategic Nuclear Problems
    Prelaunch survivability of ICBMs
    Postlaunch survivability of bombers
    Defense for U.S. population, production base

NATO–Related Problems
    Active army small compared with global commitments
    Key assets extremely concentrated
    Absence of ABM defense in Europe
    Cracks in the NATO alliance
    Readiness–responsiveness of U.S. reserve components

Naval Combat Problems
    Protect U.S. shipping–reinforce NATO
        Navy small compared with global commitments
        Surface combatants exposed to short-range missiles
        ASW unable to cope with large-scale submarine threat
    Amphibious lift insufficient for landing forces

Strategic Mobility Problems
    Airlift insufficient to move ready reserves rapidly
    Sealift depends on foreign-flag carriers

---

[1] The Soviet Union is plagued with its own set of problems. Some are precise counterparts of those shown above. Others are different. This study concentrates on *U.S.* problems that call for *U.S.* solutions.

the United States, we would be exposed to the full effects, unable to protect our population or production base. The Soviet Union, like the United States, lacks sizable ABM capabilities but, unlike this country, still stresses strong air and civil defenses.[49] Some studies in fact claim that city evacuation plans shortly will enable the Soviets to engage in nuclear combat with far fewer casualties than this coun-

---

[49] M. N. Titov, P. T. Yegorov, B. A. Gayko, and others, *Civil Defense,* ed. G. A. Cristy (Oak Ridge [Tenn.] National Laboratory, 1975); Leon Gouré, *Soviet Civil Defense in the Seventies* (Coral Gables, Fla.: Center for Advanced International Studies, University of Miami, 1975); Harriet Fast Scott, "Civil Defense in the U.S.S.R.," *Air Force Magazine* (October 1975), pp. 29-33; U.S. Department of Defense, Defense Civil Preparedness Agency, *Fact Sheet: Soviet Civil Defense* (1973), p. 4.

try.[50] That contention is unconfirmed, but even partial defenses could buttress the Kremlin's bargaining power in times of intense international crisis, by undercutting our second-strike assured destruction threat.

NATO-related problems. The vulnerability of U.S. and allied ground combat, tactical air, support, and command-control forces in central Europe increased sharply when France withdrew from military participation in NATO. At West Germany's waist, the theater now is barely 130 miles wide, less than one-third the distance from Los Angeles to San Francisco. Maneuver room for armies is at a premium. Congestion at air bases approaches supersaturation. Some U.S. aircraft and logistical installations were repositioned in the United Kingdom, but most U.S. supplies, including ammunition, are stored within a thirty-mile radius of Kaiserslautern. The first sharp Soviet surge could sever friendly supply lines, which radiate from Bremerhaven, Rotterdam, and Antwerp, then run closely behind and parallel to the prospective front. Airfields also could be overrun. Every lucrative military target, including command–control centers, air bases, ports, and supply depots is within easy reach of Soviet IRBMs and MRBMs.[51] The absence of ABM defenses thus is critical. The Soviets, who have less need for a tactical ABM system and possess strong anti-aircraft capabilities, are not so disadvantaged.[52]

Total force concepts applied to NATO Europe also exhibit flaws. The entire south flank, for example, is shaky from the Atlantic seaboard to Asia Minor. Portugal has been politically unstable and

---

[50] U.S. Congress, Senate, "Reassessing and Refining Our Foreign Policy: Remarks by Howard H. Baker, Jr.," *Congressional Record* (24 June 1975), p. S11410; Eugene P. Wigner, "The Myth of Assured Destruction," *Survive* (July-August 1970), pp. 2-4; U.S. Department of Defense, Defense Civil Preparedness Agency, *Briefing of Post Nuclear Attack Study (PONAST) II,* prepared by the Joint Chiefs of Staff Studies Analysis and Gaming Agency, 23 May 1973.

[51] John W. Bowen, then chief of staff for the U.S. European Command, in personal correspondence to the author, 27 November 1967. The situation he perceived at that time remains essentially unchanged.

France has not undertaken any agreement to realign herself militarily with NATO. The use of French forces and territory in time of crises would be subject to a political decision. NATO therefore does not plan on French participation. U.S. Congress, Senate, Armed Services Committee, *Hearings on Fiscal Year 1973 Authorization for Military Procurement,* 93d Congress, 1st session (1972), Part 2, p. 523. For implications of de Gaulle's decision to evict NATO forces from France, see Gordon A. Moon, II, "Uncertain Future," *Army* (March 1967) and "Invasion in Reverse," *Army* (February 1967).

[52] French and British ballistic missiles can reach targets on Soviet soil, but those in fixed sites are vulnerable to surprise attacks by IRBMs, MRBMs, and SLBMs with short flight times. They might not be destroyed, but their reliability would be in doubt.

militarily unreliable since Spinola was ousted in autumn 1974. Italy, with continual government crises, a sick economy, and a strong Communist Party, faces serious problems. Greece and Turkey are more concerned with threats from each other than from the Warsaw Pact. French forces would assist in NATO's forward defense only if *French* leaders concluded that *French* interests were endangered.

U.S. reserve components display spotty degrees of responsiveness. Some tactical fighter, reconnaissance, and airlift units reputedly could be enroute to Europe almost immediately, others in less than ten days.[53] Army National Guard divisions, despite recent improvements in readiness, still would require weeks to receive personnel and equipment fillers, complete team training, and deploy. (Soviet Category 2 divisions allegedly could be on site in days.) [54] If war with the Warsaw Pact were short and decisive, as some students of the subject suggest, only those elements mobilized and positioned early would count. The remainder would be ineffective, no matter how impressive they might look on paper.[55]

Naval combat problems. The scarcity of U.S. surface combatants compared with global commitments and contingency requirements strains capabilities. The U.S.S.R. can concentrate power where and when it wants *before* hostilities break out, while the U.S. Navy must cover extended sea lanes.

Carrier aircraft and shipboard SAM defenses would afford a fair shield for U.S. fleets if the Soviets fired antiship cruise missiles from long range, but the U.S. Navy has almost no protection against surprise attacks launched from close quarters. Soviet ships so armed could stand close in during crises, perhaps interspersed with U.S. elements, then strike suddenly with a high probability of success.

The Soviet inventory of ballistic missile and attack submarines is a bit smaller than it was ten years ago (376 then, 326 now), but capabilities have expanded significantly, while U.S. cruiser, destroyer, and escort strength declined by 131 ships.[56] We discarded nine aged ASW carriers during the same decade. That shift in the quantitative balance, coupled with continued ASW detection difficulties, seriously

---

[53] U.S. Congress, Senate, Armed Services Committee, *Hearings on FY 1973 Authorization for Military Procurement*, p. 1123.

[54] Data received from Office of the Joint Chiefs of Staff (J-5) on 16 January 1976.

[55] Greater reliance on brigade and battalion-sized Army National Guard forces, and less on full divisions, recently was announced by former Defense Secretary Schlesinger. He contended that "we should stop pretending that we can use [National Guard and Reserve divisions] as full substitutes for active duty ground forces," in "Guard Divisions Played Down," *Army Times* (12 March 1975), p. 31.

[56] Includes ships in U.S. Naval Reserve, but excludes Coast Guard.

impairs America's ability to protect sea lanes required for important U.S. commerce and NATO resupply–reinforcement purposes. Steps to bottle up Soviet boats before war began might well provoke combat, not prevent it. Outnumbered U.S. forces therefore would initially be compelled to find, fix, fight, and finish Soviet submarines beneath open seas. Enemy boats returning to base for refills would have to transit attrition barriers at choke points, but before then they could deal great damage.[57]

Assault sealift problems are also imposing. One marine amphibious force (MAF)—a marine division with its associated air wing—normally embarks on forty-eight amphibious ships.[58] U.S. Navy holdings today total just sixty-four, including seven helicopter carriers. Ten on the average are undergoing overhaul at any one time. The forty-eight-ship requisition thus constitutes 88 percent of all operational assets. Only half of our amphibious lift is available in the Atlantic area. The remainder is located along the U.S. West Coast and elsewhere in the Pacific. Lead times to assemble, load, move, and conduct a division-sized amphibious assault would approximate two months from time of alert.[59] Whether such operations could succeed under general war conditions is contentious.

Strategic mobility problems. Increased dependence on strategic reserves in the United States instead of forward deployment places increased demands on mobility forces.

America's airlift assets, the world's best, still exhibit shortcomings. Table 2 shows 300 aircraft (seventy C-5As and 230 C-141s) in operational squadrons, but a substantial slice is grounded for maintenance at any given moment.[60] Moving our only airborne division to the Middle East (where Brezhnev threatened to commit ground combat troops during the 1973 Arab-Israeli crisis) would take a week if

---

[57] Sea control problems related to potential Middle East oil crises are covered in U.S. Congress, House, *Oil Fields as Military Objectives: A Feasibility Study*, prepared for the Special Subcommittee on Investigations of the Committee on International Relations by the Congressional Research Service, 94th Congress, 1st session, 1975, pp. 19-20, 66-67.

[58] Statistics were drawn from a marine corps command and staff manual. They would be modified to meet specific contingencies, but requirements would be similar.

[59] Department of Defense, *Annual Report to the Congress on the FY 1976 and Transition Budgets*, p. II-93. Supplemented by telephone conversation with Operations and Amphibious Matters Branch, Headquarters, U.S. Marine Corps, 27 June 1975.

[60] Airlift availability rates were reviewed in Comptroller General of the United States, *Report to the Congress: Airlift Operations of the Military Airlift Command during the 1973 Middle East War* (1975), pp. 10-15, 57-58.

alert times permitted prior preparation, longer if not.[61] Flights to NATO Europe are shorter, but lift requirements are much larger. A lengthy period thus would elapse before all airlifted elements closed.

U.S. sealift dependence on foreign flags has already been discussed (see strategic mobility policies).

Projected Balance. Nothing in United States–Soviet R & D, deployment, or budgetary trends is likely to eliminate the problems just enumerated. A few will be eased. Others will be exacerbated.

Research and development. Air- and land-mobile missiles now in design stages would reduce pre-launch attrition threats to U.S. ICBMs, if a sizable percentage of our present force were converted. Better low-level performance and penetration aids should improve post-launch survival prospects for future U.S. bombers, although evolving Soviet countermeasures ensure continued sharp competition.[62] Other strategic offensive R & D programs, like bigger ballistic missiles and maneuverable reentry vehicles (MaRV), do little to circumvent key shortcomings. Perfecting cruise missiles might strengthen short-term U.S. deterrence, but might also prove to be a long-term liability if the Soviets deploy equivalent systems: they have stout air defenses, whereas we do not.

U.S. and Soviet scientists both seek to solve ABM problems, but no breakthroughs appear imminent. The Department of Defense has no programs that specifically concern air defense for the United States. R & D related to U.S. civil defense receives very low priority.

Laser-guided antitank weapons, "smart" bombs, new artillery ammunition, and SAM-D are among the R & D innovations U.S. forces count on to compensate for superior Soviet numbers in NATO Europe, but science offers no other relief for U.S. shortcomings. One crucial problem, the absence of ABM defenses, is susceptible to R & D solutions, but if a suitable system surfaced tomorrow, the SALT I Treaty would preclude deployment. Additional complications actually are anticipated, since the Soviets already are testing mobile IRBMs in a MIRVed mode.

R & D programs seem unlikely to ease basic naval combat problems in the predictable future. On the contrary, quieter, faster Soviet submarines, long-range Soviet SLBMs that allow larger operational

---

[61] Includes roughly 11,000 men, a basic load of ammunition, and five-day supplies of rations and fuel. Statistics furnished telephonically by staff members of the 82d Airborne Division, 8 April 1975.

[62] U.S. bombers on final approaches to many Soviet targets would have to overfly open water or flat terrain that facilitate low-level radar coverage for air defenders.

areas, and improved ECM for Soviet antiship missiles will increase U.S. ASW detection and fleet air defense difficulties.

Neither the United States nor the Soviet Union is experimenting with any equipment expected to alter strategic mobility means essentially.

Procurement–deployment programs. Replacing B-52s with B-1s is the only strategic nuclear procurement–deployment plan directly related to current *U.S.* shortcomings. Introducing Trident simply will complicate *Soviet* ASW problems. SALT accords prohibit increasing the number of American ICBMs to equal or exceed those of the Soviet Union. Multiplying MIRVs to include all U.S. missiles would maintain a lead in warheads, but be of limited value in light of our key shortcomings.

Soviet modernization efforts, in contrast, are of unsurpassed magnitude. They feature four new ICBM families, all with greater payload capacities than their predecessors, and all being tested with MIRVs. Two systems incorporate "cold launch" techniques that allow refire capabilities using larger missiles in existing silos. Backfire bombers, vastly superior to aged Bear and Bison aircraft, are entering the inventory.[63] Eight new Delta-class submarines with twelve long-range missiles each have already been launched. "Stretched" versions with sixteen launch tubes are now under construction.[64]

America's strategic defensive plans include no procurement and extensive cutbacks. All antiballistic missiles will be removed this year.[65] All six air national guard F-101 interceptor squadrons will phase out by the end of FY 1977, partly because of budgetary priorities, partly because of beliefs that "without effective ABM defenses, air defenses are of limited value against aggressors armed primarily with strategic missiles."[66]

Soviet strength is growing rapidly in central Europe, according to recent statements by the chairman of NATO's Military Committee.[67] This country, which annually considers sharp force cutbacks,

---

[63] Backfire bombers, a SALT II issue, could strike targets in the United States without in-flight refueling, then recover in Cuba or some neutral country in Latin America. The Soviets have only a few tankers, and only a few of those could serve Backfires.

[64] Department of Defense, *Annual Report to the Congress on the FY 1976 and Transition Budgets*, pp. II12–II16. Updated informally.

[65] U.S. Congress, House, *Department of Defense Appropriations: Fiscal Year 1976*, Conference Report, p. 28.

[66] Department of Defense, *Annual Report to the Congress on the FY 1976 and Transition Budgets*, p. II41.

[67] "NATO Warned of Soviet Offensive Power," *Aviation Week* (15 December 1975), p. 19.

has no plans to significantly alter the present balance by adding forces.[68] Exchanging F-4 squadrons for F-15s and F-16s will *curtail* tactical nuclear capabilities, since neither new aircraft can carry nuclear weapons.[69] No solution to congestion problems or exposed supply lines is seen to be soon forthcoming.

One U.S. attack carrier was retired in January 1976. Another will be decommissioned before the end of this fiscal year. At that time, the navy will be able to maintain no more than two on station in the Pacific and two in the Atlantic–Mediterranean at any one time. Only twelve ships will be available for active duty. The thirteenth is designated for training.[70] Carrier aircraft, a prime means of projecting naval power and protecting U.S. fleets, will be reduced commensurately.

Meanwhile, the Soviets are equipping gun destroyers with anti-ship cruise missiles as an extra capability. The U.S. Harpoon, when deployed, should strengthen deterrence by promising counterbattery fire in kind, but Soviet first strikes could still be destructive. The Soviets' forward deployment posture is improving in Cuba and along the littorals of Africa and South Asia, where several countries already service Soviets ships.[71] The United States is experiencing difficulties, especially in Turkey and Greece.[72]

The United States is doing nothing to reduce dependence on merchant ships flying foreign flags. Few ships suitable for military purposes are being built. Soviet programs, which emphasize small ships for use in small ports, ensure responsive forces under firm control that support operations in underdeveloped areas and assist in projecting political power.

---

[68] Adding two or three U.S. Army brigades and associated elements to USAREUR will have little effect on the overall U.S.-Soviet military balance in Europe.

[69] "New U.S. Fighters a Worry in Europe," *New York Times* (22 December 1975), p. 17. F-15s are not wired to handle nuclear weapons. Modifications could be incorporated only at great cost. F-16s are designated as "nuclear capable," but could carry nuclear weapons only if retrofitted. F-111 squadrons could be dedicated to NATO in emergency, at the expense of other missions. Clarification received from air force staff members on 13 January 1976.

[70] "Sea Power Cut in the Pacific," *Washington Star-News* (24 December 1975), p. D-10. Updated by Office of the Chief of Naval Operations, 19 January 1976.

[71] See, for example, U.S. Congress, House, *Means of Measuring Naval Power, with Special Reference to U.S. and Soviet Activities in the Indian Ocean*, prepared for the Subcommittee on the Near East and South Asia of the Committee on Foreign Affairs by the Congressional Research Service, 93d Congress, 2nd session (1974), pp. 4, 10-12.

[72] See especially U.S. Congress, House, *Greece and Turkey: Some Military Implications Related to NATO and the Middle East*, prepared for the Special Subcommittee on Investigations of the Committee on Foreign Affairs by the Congressional Research Service, 1975.

Budgetary emphasis. U.S. budgetary projections paint a bleak picture when related to pressing U.S. problems, even though absolute outlays are very large.

DOD's baseline budget has been cut by 20 percent since 1964. Expenditures continue to decline in terms of purchasing power, percent of the total federal budget, and U.S. gross national product.[73] High disbursements for pay, allowances, and other manpower costs will persist, given prevailing policies. Comparatively little will be left over for expansion and modernization after unavoidable operations-maintenance outlays are deducted.

Such trends sap quality as well as quantity, since consequences include fewer flying hours and less ship steaming time, fewer maneuvers and other exercises, maintenance slowdowns, and program stretchouts. (The latter actually increase costs in the long run.)

The Soviet Union, according to some authorities, is outspending this country at a rapid rate.[74] Those conclusions are almost impossible to substantiate, for reasons already enumerated. It seems clear, however, that the Kremlin is willing to commit sizable resources for national defense. Even if pessimistic U.S. estimates were radically erroneous, and rival budgets were equal, the Soviets would have more money for modernization, being less bothered by inflation and immense manpower costs.

Still, the U.S. situation is not all bad. Budgetary crimps, real or imagined, stimulate the search for innovative, less expensive solutions to our national defense problems. Necessity *really is* the mother of invention.

Predicting Soviet Intentions. No appraisal of the United States–Soviet military balance would be complete without some note of Soviet intentions, which reflect changeable states of mind among men in the Kremlin. Otherwise, there would be no way to predict the imminence or intensity of prospective perils.

Two opposing schools of thought (with kaleidoscopic shades in between) currently collide. A quick summary of associated philosophies points up the differences.[75]

---

[73] Department of Defense, *Annual Report to the Congress on the FY 1976 and Transition Budgets*, pp. 123-126. The baseline budget excludes incremental war costs, foreign military assistance, and retired pay.

[74] See, for example, "CIA Finds Soviet Arms Budget Now Is Ahead of U.S.," *New York Times* (22 July 1974), p. 2 and James R. Schlesinger, letter to Senator John L. McClelland, chairman, Subcommittee on Defense of the Committee on Appropriations, 23 October 1975, p. 2.

[75] For discussion, see Barry M. Blechman, "Handicapping the Arms Race: Are the Soviets Ahead?" *New Republic* (3 and 10 January 1976), pp. 19-21.

School "A" discounts the significance of Soviet strides since the mid-1960s. America's assured destruction capabilities afford a sound nuclear deterrent, so the argument goes. Accommodations in Europe, including those at Helsinki in 1974, stabilize that area, reducing risks of armed conflict. Soviet influence elsewhere allegedly depends more on diplomacy than military power. Equally important, Moscow's adventures in uncommitted countries, such as Somalia and Angola, are little related to compelling U.S. interests.

School "B" is less sanguine. As its members see it, the sapping of U.S. relative strength has far-reaching implications for a foreign policy predicated on partnership and negotiation. Inability to provide a strategic nuclear shield for the free world, coupled with failure to defeat a ninth-rate country like North Vietnam, erodes America's alliance system. Consequently, reciprocal arms control accords, which once were strategic adjuncts, assume crucial proportions. U.S. national security, School "B" contends, quite literally depends to a high degree on cooperation by a canny competitor, whose incentives to collaborate are slight.

Ascertaining which school is correct exceeds the scope of this unclassified study. Suffice it to say here that the extent to which *suspected* Soviet intentions should shape *actual* U.S. capabilities is a subject that calls for caution. Intentions can change overnight, but improving military capabilities is a time-consuming process.

* * *

Wrap-Up

Quantitative and, in some instances, qualitative deficiencies, disadvantageous deployments, and attributes ill-designed to accomplish essential aims all contribute to imbalances between U.S. and Soviet armed forces. That condition is by no means static. Table 8 clearly shows a thrust that likely will continue unless U.S. decision makers take dynamic steps to ratify, reinforce, retard, or repeal current trends.

As it stands, the quantitative balance continues to shift toward the Soviet Union. U.S. qualitative superiority never compensated completely and, in certain respects, is slowly slipping away. America's global responsibilities, coupled with U.S. reliance on reserve components, permit the Soviet Union to concentrate power while we remain dispersed, depending heavily on allies and arms control accords to safeguard our national interests. Force structure standards that stress essential equivalence instead of sufficiency encourage overemphasis on arms and equipment that bear scant relationship to pressing requirements.

Quantitative asymmetries that favor the Soviet Union attract the most attention, but the absence of comparable capabilities is only occasionally cause for concern, as Tables 4 and 5 indicate. Mismatched U.S. ends and means are much more important (see Tables 6 and 7). Very few positive U.S. programs, contemplated or in progress, will alleviate associated problems.

Some of the cogent U.S. shortcomings identified in earlier sections would lose significance if this country scaled down its overseas interests, accepting uncertain costs related to reduced world power status, the possible loss of free-world leadership, and long-range U.S. security. Others could be corrected (entirely or in part) by policy changes, such as amending military pay scales to allow more money for modernization without a bigger budget. A third course of action could contribute by scrapping inessential and inappropriate capabilities, present or proposed—the contemplated expansion of our strategic nuclear triad from three to seven systems typifies programs that are ripe for review.[76] Some steps, like reshaping the U.S. Navy to meet emerging Soviet threats, might demand expending additional funds. Risks courted by allowing any or all shortcomings to remain uncorrected should be carefully calculated.

Which combination would be most suitable (indeed, whether *any* action is essential) might best be ascertained by a national debate to sharpen issues and identify optimum options. This study lays the groundwork for congressional participation.

Sound conclusions would allow Congress and the executive branch in concert to chart a course that matches ends and means in ways that assure America's ability to deter and, if need be, defend successfully against any sort of Soviet armed aggression for the rest of the twentieth century.

Trends in the Quantitative Balance

Statistics contained in Table 8 are calculated to show changes in the U.S.–Soviet quantitative balance over the last ten years. Columns for 1965 and 1975 first indicate comparative force levels, then identify how far ahead or behind the United States was at those selected

---

[76] Manned bombers, hard-site ICBMs, and submarine-launched ballistic missiles comprise our current triad. Air-launched and land-mobile ballistic missiles, along with air- and sea-launched cruise missiles, are in various stages of R & D. All are considered as add-ons, rather than replacements for present systems.

Table 8
U.S.–SOVIET QUANTITATIVE BALANCE

	1965			1975			Net U.S. Change
	United States	Soviet	U.S. (difference)	United States	Soviet	U.S. (difference)	
STRATEGIC OFFENSIVE							
Personnel[1]	220,800	308,000	−87,200	76,700	414,000	−337,300	−250,100
Navy	16,550	8,000	+8,550	18,400	14,000	+4,000	−4,150
Air Force	204,250	300,000	−95,750	58,300	400,000	−341,700	−245,950
Ballistic/cruise missiles:							
ICBM	854	224	+630	1,054	1,603	−549	−1,179
Heavy[2]	54	224	−170	54	590	−536	−366
Light[3]	800	0	+800	1,000	1,013	−13	−813
MIRVed	0	0	(40)	550	110	+440	+440
SLBM	496	120	+376	656	725	−69	−445
MIRVed	0	0	(40)	416	0	+416	+416
ALCM[4]	1,260	190	+1,070	1,140	185	+955	−115
SLCM[5]	0	140	−140	0	348	−348	−208
Submarine	0	92	−92	0	300	−300	−208
Surface	0	48	−48	0	48	−48	−0
Bombers	935	1,420	−485	529	635	−106	+379
Heavy[6]	630	210	+420	463	135	+328	−92
Medium[7]	305	1,210	−905	66	500	−434	+471
Tankers[8]	1,000	0	+1,000	615	50	+565	−435
Ballistic missile submarines	31	40	−9	41	73	−32	−23
Nuclear	31	15	+16	41	54	−13	−29
Diesel	0	25	−25	0	19	−19	+6

ICBM/SLBM warheads	1,702	344	+1,358	6,794	3,886	+2,908	+1,550
MRV	528	0	+528	480	1,542	−1,062	−1,590
MIRV	0	0	(40)	5,810	640	+5,170	+5,170
STRATEGIC DEFENSIVE							
Personnel 9	120,750	500,000	−379,250	25,100	600,000	−574,900	−196,850
Army	23,050	400,000	−376,950	900	500,000	−499,100	−122,150
Navy	3,750	0	+3,950	1,200	0	+1,200	+2,750
Air Force	93,750	100,000	−6,250	23,000	100,000	−77,000	−70,750
ABM missiles 10	0	0	(40)	100	64	+36	+36
SAM launchers 11	2,694	8,900	−6,206	330	9,500	−9,170	−2,964
Interceptors 12	1,113	3,800	−2,687	396	2,700	−2,304	+383

1 U.S. reductions reflect the inactivation of strategic bomber squadrons.

2 Definition of "heavy" ICBMs conforms to U.S. SALT I unilateral statements. Includes U.S. Titans; Soviet SS-7, SS-8, SS-9, SS-18, SS-19, although SALT II accords may eventually consider SS-19s in the "light" category. An estimated 100 of them were deployed in January 1976.

3 Definition of "light" ICBMs conforms to U.S. SALT I unilateral statements. Includes U.S. Minuteman II, III; Soviet SS-11, SS-13, SS-17.

4 ALCMs with nuclear warheads include U.S. Hound Dog, SRAM; Soviet AS-3 (Kangaroo), AS-4 (Kitchen), AS-6. Where statistics are lacking, but mass production confirmed, figures shown reflect standard force loadings—for example, 2 Hound Dogs per B-52, 1 AS-3 per Bear bomber, 2 AS IIIs per Backfire.

5 Strategic sea-launched cruise missiles currently are limited to Soviet Shaddock, which has a maximum range of about 250 nautical miles (NM). Its estimated effective range is closer to 150 NM. Figures shown are tubes only, not missiles. Their primary mission probably is antiship.

6 "Heavy" bombers include U.S. B-52; Soviet Bear, Bison.

7 "Medium" bombers include U.S. B-47, B-58, FB-111, Soviet Badger, Blinder, and Backfire.

8 U.S. 1965 tanker figure includes 50 squadrons (average 20 aircraft each).

9 U.S. reductions reflect the inactivation of interceptor squadrons, SAM batteries, and radar sites.

10 Soviet 1965 ABM figure excludes abortive deployment of possible first-generation missiles around Leningrad.

11 SAM air defense launchers include U.S. Bomarc, Hawk, Nike-Hercules, both active and national guard. Soviet forces include SA-1 through SA-6. Soviets have 12,000 missiles for 9,500 launchers.

12 Interceptors include U.S. Air National Guard squadrons as well as those in the regular air force.

Table 8 (continued)

	1965			1975			
	United States	Soviet	U.S. (difference)	United States	Soviet	U.S. (difference)	Net U.S. Change
GROUND FORCES							
Army: Personnel[13]	939,950	1,800,000	−860,050	789,100	2,500,000	−1,710,900	−850,850
Divisions[14]	16	147	−131	16	168	−152	−21
Infantry	8	0	+8	6	0	+6	−2
Mechanized	1	90	−89	4	113	−109	−20
Armor	4	50	−46	4	47	−43	+3
Airborne	2	7	−5	1	8	−7	−2
Airmobile	1	0	+1	1	0	+1	0
Tanks[15]	10,200	30,500	−20,300	10,100	40,000	−29,900	−9,600
Heavy	0	2,500	−2,500	0	2,500	−2,500	0
Medium	8,200	25,000	−16,800	8,500	34,500	−26,000	−9,200
Light	2,000	3,000	−1,000	1,600	3,000	−1,400	−400
Armored carriers[16]	20,700	35,000	−14,300	19,000	40,000	−21,000	−6,700
SSM[17]	—	—	—	180	1,853	−1,673	+14
IRBM	0	101	−101	0	87	−87	+112
MRBM	0	608	−608	0	496	−496	—
SRBM	—	—	—	180	1,170	−990	—
LRCM	—	—	—	0	100	−100	—
Nuke artillery[18]	1,750	0	—	+700	0	+450	−1,050
Other artillery[19]	1,750	—	—	2,100	17,000	−14,900	—
At missiles[20]	16,500	—	—	2,400	6,000	−3,600	—
Helicopters	4,000	—	—	9,000	2,580	+6,420	—

	190,000	10,000	+180,000	197,000	12,000	+185,000	+5,000
Marines: Personnel							
Divisions	3	0	+3	3	0	+3	0
Separate regiments 21	0	0	(40)	0	5	-5	-5
Tanks	545	75	+470	475	150	+325	-145
Artillery	840	75	+765	710	150	+560	-205
Aircraft	478	0	+478	468	0	+468	-10
Fighter	229	0	+229	204	0	+204	-25
Attack	249	0	+249	264	0	+264	+15
Helicopters	419	0	+419	487	0	+487	+68
Border Guards	0	200,000	-200,000	0	400,000	-400,000	-200,000

13 Army strengths exclude strategic nuclear elements. U.S. figure for 1965 parallels that prior to the Vietnam war buildup. The peak in fiscal year 1968 was 1,570,000.

14 U.S. figures exclude separate brigades and regiments which sometimes are used to calculate "division equivalent" strengths. Soviet tank divisions are shown as armor. Soviet motorized infantry divisions are shown as mechanized.

15 U.S. medium tanks include M-48 and M-60; all others are light tanks. Soviet heavy tanks include JS-2/3, T-10; T-54/55, T-62 are mediums; PT-76 is light.

16 U.S. figures are limited to armored personnel carriers. Soviet statistics include scout cars.

17 U.S. SRBMs include Pershing, Lance, and Honest John (Lance has entirely replaced H.J. in Europe). Soviet SRBMs include Scud A/B, Scaleboard, Frog. The Soviet LRCM is Shaddock, a land-based version of their strategic nuclear SLCM.

18 U.S. nuclear artillery includes 155 mm and 8-in howitzers. The Soviets may have nuclear rounds for 203 mm gun-howitzers and 240 mm mortars, but perhaps only for training purposes.

19 Conventional artillery excludes mortars, antitank guns, rocket launchers, recoilless weapons, and anti-aircraft artillery.

20 U.S. antitank missiles include Dragon and Tow. Soviet models include Snapper, Swatter, and Sagger. No Soviet missiles are helicopter mounted.

21 Soviet marines (naval infantry) in 1965 comprised small units with the 4 fleets (Northern, Baltic, Black Sea, and Pacific). They now are organized into regiments.

309

Table 8 (continued)

NAVAL FORCES	1965			1975			Net U.S. Change
	United States	Soviet	U.S. (difference)	United States	Soviet	U.S. (difference)	
Personnel[22]	650,500	292,000	+358,500	515,400	386,000	+129,400	−229,100
Aircraft carriers	32	0	+32	21	3	+18	−14
Attack[23]	16	0	+16	14	0	+14	−2
ASW	9	0	+9	0	1	−1	−10
Other[24]	7	0	+7	7	2	+5	−2
Cruiser[25]	33	22	+11	27	33	−6	−17
SSM[26]	0	14	−14	0	20	−20	−6
Other	33	8	+25	27	13	+14	−11
Destroyer[25]	217	150	+67	70	85	−15	−82
SSM[26]	0	24	−24	0	20	−20	+4
Other	217	126	+91	70	65	+5	−86
Other escorts[25,27]	(38) 38	103	(−27) −65	(34) 64	105	(−7) −41	(+20) +24
Attack submarines[28]	169	336	−167	73	253	−180	−13
Conventional	169	322	−153	73	185	−112	+41
Nuclear	29	12	+17	62	35	+27	+10
Diesel	140	310	−170	11	150	−139	+31
SSM[26]	0	14	−14	0	68	−68	−54
Nuclear	0	0	(40)	0	40	−40	−40
Diesel	0	14	−14	0	28	−28	−14
Boats	0	460	−460	7	230	−223	+237
SSM[26]	0	110	−110	4	135	−131	−21
Motor torpedo	0	350	−350	3	95	−92	+258
Amphibious ships[29]	118	14	+104	57	85	−28	−132

Tactical aircraft [30]	4,729	800	+3,929	3,543	768	+2,775	−1,152
Ashore/amphibious	352	800	−448	450	715	−265	+183
Bombers [31]	0	400	−400	0	480	−480	−80
Patrol/ASW [32]	352	400	−48	450	360	+90	+138
Afloat [33]	2,132	0	+2,132	1,508	53	+1,455	−677
Fighter	712	0	+712	473	0	+473	−239
Attack	961	0	+961	836	0	+836	−125
ASW [34]	459	0	+459	199	53	+146	−313
Fixed wing	222	0	+222	119	0	+119	−103
Helicopter	237	0	+237	80	53	+27	−210
Sealift [35]	2,778	1,345	+1,433	1,009	2,358	−1,349	−2,782

22 Naval personnel strengths include naval air elements, but exclude ballistic missile submarine forces.

23 The Soviet VSTOL carrier Kiev is sometimes called a cruiser.

24 Soviet helicopter carriers of the Moskva class are sometimes called helicopter cruisers. U.S. counterparts are commonly categorized as amphibious ships.

25 U.S. Navy reclassified many cruisers, destroyers, and other escorts in the spring of 1975 to conform more closely to international terminology. The 1965 column reflects 1975 classifications to facilitate comparisons.

26 SSM refers to anti-surface-ship cruise missiles in this table. Soviet SS-N-2, 3, 9, 10, and 11 are included. SS-N-3s (Shaddocks) are shown as strategic missiles, but have antiship missions.

27 Escorts include frigates, destroyer escorts, and other comparable oceangoing craft of 1,000 tons or more. U.S. Naval Reserve ships, shown in parentheses, are immediately available to augment active forces in emergency. U.S. Coast Guard vessels are omitted.

28 Soviet coastal submarines are excluded.

29 Amphibious ships exclude helicopter carriers and landing craft (such as LCU, LCM, LCVP).

30 Total aircraft for navy and air force include all types. Subordinate entries, which include selected types only, do not equal the total.

31 Soviet naval bombers include Badger, Blinder, Beagle, Backfire.

32 Soviet naval patrol-ASW aircraft include Bear, May, and Mail. The latter is an amphibian.

33 U.S. naval aircraft afloat exclude those assigned to marine squadrons.

34 The sharp drop in U.S. Navy ASW aircraft between 1965 and 1975 reflects the decommissioning of 9 ASW aircraft carriers.

35 U.S. sealift included 329 vessels in the Military Sealift Command (MSC)-controlled fleet in 1965 and 118 in 1975. (MSC was called Military Sea Transport Service in 1965). The remainder are merchant marine. No such breakout is possible for Soviet ships.

Table 8 (continued)

	1965			1975			Net U.S. Change
	United States	Soviet	U.S. (difference)	United States	Soviet	U.S. (difference)	
AIR FORCES:							
Personnel[36]	531,000	400,000	+131,000	530,700	500,000	+30,700	−100,300
Tactical aircraft[30]	5,800	3,250	+2,550	5,000	5,350	−350	−2,900
Fighter/attack[37]	3,800	2,800	+1,000	2,300	3,590	−1,290	−2,290
Recon/ECM	820	450	+370	340	750	−410	−780
Airlift:							
Strategic[38]	26	8	+18	300	60	+240	+214
Tactical[39]	620	750	−130	500	800	−300	−170

36 Air Force personnel strengths exclude strategic nuclear and naval air elements.

37 Current Soviet fighter-attack figures include 2,000 aircraft intended primarily for counterair missions and 1,500 earmarked primarily for close air support of ground forces.

38 Strategic airlift forces include U.S. C-5 and C-141 aircraft, Soviet Cock and Candid.

39 Tactical airlift forces include U.S. C-130s, active and reserve. Soviet figures indicate Cub only.

40 Par.

times. The right hand column reflects cumulative shifts in U.S. status. In 1965, for example, we had 630 more ICBMs than the Soviet Union. Today, they have 549 more than we do. The net change in balance thus is 1,179 in favor of the U.S.S.R. Some entries in the net change column are positive, although this country currently is behind. Those circumstances occur when Soviet reductions exceed those of the United States, but Soviet inventories remain numerically superior. Other entries are negative, although the United States currently is ahead. Those conditions are caused by Soviet expansion that narrows, but does not close, specific gaps.

Comparisons include active inventories only, except as noted. Reserve components and allied forces are addressed in the text.

Multiple open sources were used to compile basic data. Various staff sections in the Pentagon amended and supplied many statistics.

THE PERMANENT CHALLENGE OF PEACE:
U.S. POLICY TOWARD THE SOVIET UNION *

Henry A. Kissinger

In this address, Secretary of State Henry Kissinger argues that America's world situation has changed dramatically since World War II: the United States now is permanently involved in international affairs and faces a formidable rival in the Soviet Union. With the increased dangers caused by the development of nuclear weapons, a shift of the relationship between these powers into constructive channels has become imperative. Kissinger contends that such a shift hinges upon offering the U.S.S.R. incentives for cooperation and penalties for intransigence, and he presents two important cases illustrating this point. Both nations can profit from strategic arms controls, Kissinger explains, and America's national interest has already benefited from the accords that have been reached. In Angola, however, the United States should have checked the Soviet military intervention, but failed to do so.

America enters its third century and its forty-eighth presidential election with unmatched physical strength, a sound foreign policy

---

* Source: An address made at San Francisco, California, on 3 February 1976 before a luncheon sponsored by the Commonwealth Club of San Francisco and the World Affairs Council of Northern California (text from press release 44). *Department of State Bulletin* (23 February 1976), pp. 201-211.

design—yet scarred by self-doubt. In the past decade and a half, we have seen one President assassinated, another driven from office, and a third resign. We have lived through the agony of Vietnam and Watergate. We are still struggling to overcome the bitterness and division that have followed in their wake. We face no more urgent task than to restore our national unity and our national resolve.

For we, the strongest free nation, cannot afford the luxury of withdrawing into ourselves to heal our wounds. Too much depends upon us—peace or war, prosperity or depression, freedom or tyranny. Too much is at stake for America to paralyze itself tearing up the past, seeking sensational headlines in the present, or offering panaceas for the future. For our own well-being—American lives and American jobs—will be affected if we permit our domestic disunity and turmoil to cause us to falter in meeting our international responsibilities.

And so it is imperative that the national debate in this election year—the greatest demonstration of how free people govern themselves—strengthen, not undermine, our confidence and our capacity to carry out an effective national policy. It is essential that we quickly rebuild our national unity, the sense that we are all part of a shared enterprise.

It is in this spirit that I intend today to discuss America's relations with the world's other superpower, the Soviet Union. In recent months that relationship has become, as it should be, an important part of our national debate. I want to explain the Administration's view of the conditions that gave rise to the policy known as détente, the goals we seek, and the relationship of our Soviet policy to the overall design of American diplomacy.

The United States is today confronted by one challenge unprecedented in its own history and another challenge without precedent in the history of the world. America finds itself for the first time permanently and irrevocably involved in international affairs. At the same time, the catastrophic nature of nuclear war imposes upon us a necessity that transcends traditional concepts of diplomacy and balance of power: to shape a world order that finds stability in self-restraint and, ultimately, cooperation.

For the first century and a half of our history, our peace and security were provided for us by two oceans, the shield of the British navy, and equilibrium among the European powers. The success of our democracy at home, and the absence of direct threat from abroad, nourished our sense of uniqueness and fostered the illusion that it was up to America to choose whether and when we would participate in the world.

*　　*　　*

Today, while we still have massive strength, we no longer enjoy meaningful nuclear supremacy. We remain the world's most productive and innovative economy—but we must now share leadership with Western Europe, Canada, and Japan; we must deal with the newly wealthy and developing nations; and we must make new choices regarding our economic relations with the Communist countries. Our democratic principles are still far more valued by the world's millions than we realize, but we must also compete with new ideologies which assert progressive goals but pursue them by oppressive methods.

Today, for the first time in our history, we face the stark reality that the challenge is unending, that there is no easy and surely no final answer, that there are no automatic solutions. We must learn to conduct foreign policy as other nations have had to conduct it for so many centuries—without escape and without respite, knowing that what is attainable falls short of the ideal, mindful of the necessities of self-preservation, conscious that the reach of our national purpose has its limits. This is a new experience for Americans. It prompts nostalgia for a simpler past. As before in our history, it generates the search for scapegoats, holding specific policies responsible for objective conditions.

It is precisely because we no longer predominate but must pursue a long-term course that there is a premium today on our constancy and purposefulness. We cannot afford to swing recklessly between confrontation and abdication. We must not equate tough rhetoric with strong action, nor can we wish away tough realities with nostalgic hopes. We can no longer act as if we engage ourselves in foreign affairs only when we choose, or only to overcome specific problems, so that we can then shift our priorities back to our natural concern with ourselves. The reality is that there can be no security without our vigilance and no progress without our dedication.

It is in this context that U.S.–Soviet relations must be seen.

The Contemporary Challenge of Relations

The issue of how to deal with the Soviet Union has been a central feature of American policy for three decades. What is new today is the culmination of thirty years of postwar growth of Soviet industrial, technological, and military power. No American policy caused this; no American policy could have prevented it. But American policy can keep this power from being used to expand Soviet influence to our detriment; we have the capacity to enable allies and friends to live

315

with a sense of security; we possess the assets to advance the process of building an international order of cooperation and progress.

We must do so, however, in unprecedented conditions. In previous periods, rivalry between major powers has almost invariably led to war. In our time, when thermonuclear weapons threaten casualties in the hundreds of millions, such an outcome is unthinkable. We must manage a fundamental clash of ideologies and harness the rivalry of the nuclear superpowers, first into coexistence, and then mold coexistence into a more positive and cooperative future. For as President Kennedy once said: "In the final analysis our most basic common link is that we all inhabit this small planet. We all breathe the same air. We all cherish our children's future. And we are all mortal." [1]

In the period after World War II, our nightmare was that the Soviet Union, after consolidating its occupation of Eastern Europe, might seek to spread its control to other contiguous areas in Europe and Asia. Our policies therefore sought to build alliances and positions of military strength from which we could contain and isolate the Soviet Union. In this manner the Soviet Union might be forced to settle for peace; transformations might occur within Soviet society that would curb expansionist tendencies and make the U.S.S.R. over time into a more cooperative participant in the international system.

These policies served us and our allies well. Soviet expansion was checked. Behind our shield of security and with our assistance, our friends and allies in Western Europe restored their economies and rebuilt their democratic institutions.

*   *   *

Gradually, with the acquisition of nuclear technology and the transformation of the international system through decolonization, the Soviet Union began to emerge as a first-class military power.

In strategic military terms, the U.S.S.R. has achieved a broad equality with the United States, as was inevitable for a large nation whose rulers were prepared to impose great sacrifices on their people and to give military strength the absolute top priority in resources. With only half of our gross national product, Soviet military expenditures exceed those of the United States.

For the first time in history, the Soviet Union can threaten distant places beyond the Eurasian landmass—including the United States. With no part of the world outside the range of its military forces, the U.S.S.R. has begun to define its interests and objectives in global terms. Soviet diplomacy has thrust into the Middle East, Africa, and

[1] For President Kennedy's address at American University, Washington, D.C., on 10 June 1963, see *Department of State Bulletin* of 1 July 1963, p. 2.

Asia. This evolution is now rooted in real power, rather than a rhetorical manifestation of a universalist doctrine which in fact has very little validity or appeal.

Coping with the implications of this emerging superpower has been our central security problem for the last several years. This condition will not go away. And it will perhaps never be conclusively "solved." It will have to be faced by every Administration for the foreseeable future.

Our policy must deal with the consequences. The emergence of ambitious new powers into an existing international structure is a recurrent phenomenon. Historically, the adjustment of an existing order to the arrival of one or more new actors almost invariably was accompanied by war—to impede the upstart, to remove or diminish some of the previously established actors, to test the balance of forces in a revised system. But in the nuclear era, when casualties in a general nuclear war will involve hundreds of millions in a matter of days, the use of force threatens utter catastrophe. It is our responsibility to contain Soviet power without global war, to avoid abdication as well as unnecessary confrontation.

This can be done, but it requires a delicate and complex policy. We must strive for an equilibrium of power, but we must move beyond it to promote the habits of mutual restraint, coexistence, and ultimately cooperation. We must stabilize a new international order in a vastly dangerous environment, but our ultimate goal must be to transform ideological conflict into constructive participation in building a better world.

This is what is meant by the process called détente—not the hunger for relaxation of tension, not the striving for agreements at any price, not the mindless search for friendly atmosphere which some critics use as naïve and dangerous caricatures.

The policies pursued by this Administration have been designed to prevent Soviet expansion but also to build a pattern of relations in which the Soviet Union will always confront penalties for aggression and also acquire growing incentives for restraint. These goals are well within our capacities. Soviet power is evolving with considerable unevenness. Soviet society is no longer totally cut off from contact with or the influences of the world around it, nor is it without its own needs for outside relationships. It is the great industrial democracies, not the Soviet Union, that are the engine of the world economy and the most promising partners for the poorer nations.

The industrial democracies, if they face their challenges with confidence, if they do not mesmerize themselves with the illusion of

317

simple solutions, possess vast strengths to contain Soviet power and to channel that power in constructive directions.

Our essential task is to recognize the need for a dual policy that simultaneously and with equal vigor resists expansionist drives and seeks to shape a more constructive relationship. We must prevent the Soviet Union from translating its growing strength into global or regional preponderance. But we must do so without escalating every crisis into a massive confrontation. In recent years, the United States has firmly resisted attempts by the Soviet Union to establish a naval base in Cuba, to impede the access routes to Berlin, to exploit the explosive situation in the Middle East. Recently we have sought to halt blatant intervention in Angola—until prevented from doing so by congressional action.

At the same time, we have a historic obligation to mankind to engage the Soviet Union in settlements of concrete problems and to push back the shadow of nuclear catastrophe. At the very least, we owe it to our people to demonstrate that their government has missed no opportunity to achieve constructive solutions and that crises which have occurred were unavoidable. For whatever the rhetoric, Americans will not support confrontations they consider contrived.

This is why the United States has set forth principles of responsible relations in the nuclear age: Respect for the interests of all, restraint in the uses of power, and abstention from efforts to exploit instability or local conflicts for unilateral advantage. The United States has sought to give life to these principles in major negotiations on arms control, the prevention of accidental war, and in the settlement of political issues such as Berlin. And we have begun to construct a network of cooperative agreements in a variety of functional areas—economic, scientific, medical, environmental, and others— which promise concrete benefits if political conditions permit their full implementation and further development.

It has been our belief that, with patience, a pattern of restraints and a network of vested interests can develop which will give coexistence a more hopeful dimension and make both sides conscious of what they would stand to lose by reverting to the politics of pressure, confrontation, and crisis.

This policy reflects the deepest aspirations of the American people.

*　　*　　*

In the Administration's view the country needs a balanced policy, combining firmness and conciliation, strong defense and arms control, political principles and economic incentives. And it must be a policy for the long term that the American people can sustain, offering promise of a constructive future.

* * *

So let us understand the scope and limits of a realistic policy:

- We cannot prevent the growth of Soviet power, but we can prevent its use for unilateral advantage and political expansion.
- We cannot prevent a buildup of Soviet forces, but we have the capacity, together with our allies, to maintain an equilibrium. We cannot neglect this task and then blame the Soviet Union if the military balance shifts against us.
- We have the diplomatic, economic, and military capacity to resist expansionism, but we cannot engage in a rhetoric of confrontation while depriving ourselves of the means to confront.
- We must accept that sovereign states, especially of roughly equal power, cannot impose unacceptable conditions on each other and must proceed by compromise.
- We must live with the reality of the nuclear threat, but we have it in our power to build a new relationship that transcends the nuclear peril.

So let us end the defeatist rhetoric that implies that Soviet policy is masterful, purposeful, and overwhelming while American policy is bumbling, uncertain, and weak. Let us stop pretending that somehow tough rhetoric and contrived confrontations show confidence in America. The opposite is true. Those who are prepared to base their policy on reality, those who assert that the American people will support a complex policy of firmness and conciliation and that this policy will succeed, show a real faith in our capacities and our future. We have a design and the material assets to deal with the Soviet Union. We will succeed if we move forward as a united people.

Against this background let me discuss two current issues that illustrate the two strands of policy that we are concurrently pursuing:

- The Strategic Arms Limitation Talks, in which we are seeking to shape a more positive future.
- The Angolan situation, where we are attempting to curb Soviet expansionism.

Strategic Arms Limitation

There is one central fact that distinguishes our era from all previous historical periods: the existence of enormously destructive weapons

319

that can span unlimited distances almost instantaneously. No part of the globe is beyond reach. No part of the globe would be spared the effects of a general nuclear exchange.

For centuries it was axiomatic that increases in military power could be translated into almost immediate political advantage. It is now clear that new increments of strategic weaponry do not automatically lead to either political or military gains. Yet, in the nature of things, if one side expands its strategic arsenal, the other side will inevitably match it. The race is maintained partly because a perceived inequality is considered by each side as politically unacceptable even though it has become difficult to define precisely what purely military purpose is served.

We thus face a paradox: At current and foreseeable levels of nuclear arms, it becomes increasingly dangerous to invoke them. In no crisis since 1962 have the strategic weapons of the two sides determined the outcome. Today these arsenals increasingly find their purpose primarily in matching and deterring the forces of the opponent. For under virtually no foreseeable circumstance could the United States—or the Soviet Union—avoid 100 million dead in a nuclear exchange. Yet the race goes on because of the difficulty of finding a way to get off the treadmill.[2]

This condition imposes a unique and heavy responsibility on the leaders of the two nuclear superpowers. Sustaining the nuclear competition requires endless invocations of theoretical scenarios of imminent or eventual nuclear attack. The attempt to hedge against all conceivable contingencies, no matter how fanciful, fuels political tensions and could well lead to a self-fulfilling prophecy. The fixation on potential strategic arms imbalances that is inherent in an unrestrained arms race diverts resources into strategically unproductive areas—particularly away from forces for local defense, where shortfalls and imbalances could indeed be turned rapidly to our disadvantage. If no restraint is developed, the competition in strategic arms can have profound consequences for the future of international relations and indeed of civilization.

The United States therefore has sought and achieved since 1963 a series of arms control agreements which build some restraint into

---

[2] To be sure, there exist scenarios in planning papers which seek to demonstrate how one side could use its strategic forces and how in some presumed circumstance it would prevail. But these confuse what a technician can calculate with what a responsible statesman can decide. They are invariably based on assumptions such as that one side would permit its missile silos to be destroyed without launching its missiles before they are actually hit–on which no aggressor would rely where forces such as those possessed by either the United States or the U.S.S.R. now and in the years ahead are involved.

nuclear rivalry. There was a significant breakthrough to limit strategic weapons in 1972. If the 1974 Vladivostok accord leads to a new agreement, an even more important advance will have been made.

Yet, at this critical juncture, the American people are subjected to an avalanche of charges that SALT is a surrender of American interests. There are assertions that the United States is falling behind in the strategic competition and that SALT has contributed to it. There are unsupportable charges that the Soviets have systematically violated the SALT agreements.

None of this is accurate. What are the facts?

First of all, American policy decisions in the 1960s set the level of our strategic forces for the 1970s. We then had the choice between continuing the deployment of large, heavy-throw-weight missiles like the Titan or Atlas or undertaking development and deployment of large numbers of smaller, more flexible ICBMs [intercontinental ballistic missiles] or combinations of both types. The Administration then in office chose to rely on an arsenal of 1,000 small, sophisticated, and highly accurate ICBMs and 656 submarine-launched missiles on forty-one boats, along with heavy bombers; we deployed them rapidly and then stopped our build-up of launchers unilaterally in the 1960s when the programs were complete. Only fifty-four of the heavy Titans were retained and still remain in the force.

The Soviets made the opposite decision; they chose larger, heavier missiles; they continued to build up their forces through the 1960s and 1970s; they passed our numerical levels by 1969–70 and continued to add an average of 200 missiles a year until stopped by the first SALT agreement.

Thus, as a consequence of decisions made a decade ago by both sides, Soviet missiles are superior in throw weight while ours are superior in reliability, accuracy, diversity, and sophistication and we possess larger numbers of warheads. In 1972 when the SALT agreement was signed, the Soviet Union was still building at the rate of ninety land-based and 120 sea-based launchers a year—while we were building none, as a result of our own repeatedly reaffirmed unilateral decisions of a decade previously. Since new American programs to redress the balance had only recently been ordered, there was no way to reduce the numerical gap before the late seventies when more modern sea-based missiles and bombers were scheduled to become operational.

The interim SALT agreement of 1972 froze overall numbers of launchers on both sides for five years, thereby limiting the momentum of Soviet programs without affecting any of ours. It stopped the

Soviet build-up of heavy missile launchers. It forced the Soviets to agree to dismantle 210 older land-based missiles to reach permitted ceilings on missile-carrying submarines. The agreed-upon silo limitations permitted us to increase the throw weight of our own missiles, if we decided on this avenue of improving our strategic forces. We have so far chosen not to do so, although, through research and development, we retain the option. By any measure, the SALT agreements prevented the then-evolving gap in numbers from widening while enabling us to retain our advantage in other categories and easing the problem of redressing the balance when new programs became operational. What no negotiation could do is reverse by diplomacy the results of our own long-standing decisions with respect to weapons design and deployment.

Moreover, the SALT agreements ended for an indefinite period the prospect of a dangerous and uncertain competition in antiballistic missile defense—a competition that promised no strategic advantage, but potentially serious instabilities and the expenditure of vast sums of money.

The first SALT agreements were therefore without question in the American national interest. In the five-year respite gained by the 1972 interim agreement, it was our intention to negotiate a long-term pact on offensive weapons that would firmly fix both sides at an equal level once our new programs became operational. This is precisely what President Ford achieved at Vladivostok in November 1974.

In this accord in principle, both sides agreed on a ceiling of 2,400 strategic weapons covering strategic systems and heavy bombers—but not counting any of our forward-based aircraft in Europe, or our allies' strategic weapons, many of which can reach Soviet soil. The ceiling of 2,400 is lower than the level the Soviet Union already has reached; it would require the dismantling of many Soviet weapons, while the planned levels and composition of our forces would not need to be reduced or changed. An equal ceiling of 1,320 was placed on numbers of strategic weapons with multiple warheads. Soviet heavy missile launchers will remain frozen. These limits would cap the strategic competition in numbers for a ten-year period, yet preserve all the programs we need to assure deterrence and strategic sufficiency.

Obviously no single agreement can solve every problem. This is not a question of loopholes, but of evolving technology, with respect to which we intend to remain vigilant. We will negotiate carefully to make certain that the national interest and national security are protected. But if we succeed in turning the Vladivostok accord into a ten-year agreement, we will have crossed the threshold between total unrestrained competition and the difficult but promising beginning of long-term strategic equilibrium at lower levels of forces. The United States and the Soviet Union have already agreed to turn to reductions in strategic forces in the next phase of the negotiations, starting in 1977.

One would have thought that these accomplishments would speak for themselves. Instead, they have triggered a flood of charges which mislead the American people and our friends, give a wrong impression of irresoluteness to our adversaries, and complicate the prospects for a new agreement that is in the overriding national interest.

No charge is more irresponsible and potentially more dangerous than the allegation that the United States has knowingly tolerated violations of the first SALT agreements.

What are the facts? A Standing Consultative Commission was created by the agreements of 1972 precisely to consider disputes or ambiguities in implementation. Such incidents were almost certain to arise in a first, quite limited agreement between longstanding adversaries possessing weapons systems of great complexity whose growth is verified not by some neutral policing mechanism but by each side's own intelligence systems. Every questionable activity that has arisen has been systematically analyzed by this government and considered by the President and his advisers. Whenever any question remained, it was then promptly raised with the Soviets. All instructions to the American representative on the Consultative Commission reflected the unanimous views of all U.S. agencies concerned and the data and assessment produced jointly by them. No one had a bias in favor of absolving the Soviets—an inherently malicious charge. No one prevented all questionable or suspicious activities from being raised with the Soviets. And not all the questioned activities were on the Soviet side.

All of these issues have been and will continue to be seriously handled and dealt with through a process that has proved effective. Yet irresponsible charges continue to lump together incidents that have been explained or are still being considered with wild allegations that have no foundation. They sometimes put forward inaccurate figures and data which often can be refuted only by divulging sensitive intelligence information. Yet with all the recent flurry of allegations, no recommendations are made of what countermeasures we should take or how to assess the significance of any given alleged violation.

323

In what way do the alleged violations affect the strategic equation? In what manner, if any, have we been foreclosed from protecting ourselves? Would those who inaccurately allege violations simply throw over all the agreements regardless of the benefits they provide the United States? Would they halt the negotiation of further agreements? What purpose is served by leading our public and the Soviet Union to believe—totally incorrectly—that the United States is blind to violations or that its government deliberately deceives its people? Can anyone seriously believe that this Administration which has strenuously resisted Communist advances in every part of the world—and is often strongly criticized for it—would ignore Soviet violations of a formal agreement?

I can assure you that this Administration will not tolerate violations. It will continue to monitor Soviet compliance meticulously. It will pursue energetically all ambiguities or signs of noncompliance. But it will not be driven by demagoguery to make false or hasty judgments. No department or agency charged with responsibility for this problem holds the view that any violations have occurred.

As we assess SALT we must face squarely one question: What is the alternative to the agreement we have and seek? If the SALT process falters, we must consider what new or additional strategic programs we would undertake, their likely cost, and above all, their strategic purpose.

An accelerated strategic build-up over the next five years could cost as much as an additional $20 billion. Failing a satisfactory agreement, this will surely be the path we must travel. It would be a tragically missed opportunity. For in the process of such a build-up, and the atmosphere it would engender, it would be difficult to return to serious negotiations for some time. Tensions are likely to increase; a new, higher baseline will emerge from which future negotiations would eventually have to begin. And in the end, neither side will have gained a strategic advantage. At the least, they will have wasted resources. At worst, they will have increased the risks of nuclear war.

Of course the Soviet Union must ponder these alternatives as well. Their sense of responsibility must equal ours if there is to be an equitable and durable agreement based on strict reciprocity. We consider a SALT agreement important, but we will take no chances with our national security.

Let me sum up:

- We will never stand for the violation of a solemn treaty or agreement, and we will remain alert.

- We will never tolerate a shift in the strategic balance against us—by violations of agreements, by unsatisfactory agreements, or by neglect of our own programs. We will spend what is necessary to maintain strategic sufficiency.
- The President is determined to pursue the effort to negotiate a saner strategic balance on equitable terms—because it is in our interest and because we have an obligation to our own people and to world peace.

The Soviet Union and Angola

As the United States strives to shape a more hopeful world, it can never forget that global stability and security rest upon an equilibrium between the great powers. If the Soviet Union is permitted to exploit opportunities arising out of local conflicts by military means, the hopes we have for progress toward a more peaceful international order will ultimately be undermined.

This is why the Soviet Union's massive and unprecedented intervention in the internal affairs of Africa with nearly $200 million worth of military equipment, its advisers, and its transport of the large expeditionary force of 11,000 Cuban combat troops must be a matter of urgent concern.

Angola represents the first time that the Soviets have moved militarily at long distance to impose a regime of their choice. It is the first time that the United States has failed to respond to Soviet military moves outside the immediate Soviet orbit. And it is the first time that Congress has halted national action in the middle of a crisis.

When one great power tips the balance of forces decisively in a local conflict through its military intervention—and meets no resistance—an ominous precedent is set, of grave consequence even if the intervention occurs in a seemingly remote area. Such a precedent cannot be tolerated if a lasting easing of tensions is to be achieved. And if the pattern is not broken now, we will face harder choices and higher costs in the future.

The United States seeks no unilateral goals in Angola. We have proposed a ceasefire; withdrawal of all outside forces, Soviet, Cuban, and South African; cessation of foreign military involvement, including the supply of equipment; and negotiations among all three Angolan factions. This approach has the support of half the nations of Africa.

Last summer and fall, to halt a dangerously escalating situation, the United States provided financial support through African friends to those in Angola—the large majority—who sought to resist Soviet and Cuban domination. Using this as leverage, we undertook an active diplomacy to promote an African solution to an African problem. We acted quietly, to avoid provoking a major crisis and raising issues of prestige.

At first it was feared that the Soviet-backed faction, because of massive Soviet aid and Cuban mercenaries, would dominate totally by Independence Day, 11 November. Our assistance prevented that. African determination to oppose Soviet and Cuban intervention became more and more evident. On 9 December the President warned Moscow of the consequences of continued meddling and offered to cooperate in encouraging a peaceful outcome that removed foreign influence. The Soviet Union appeared to have second thoughts. It halted its airlift from 9 December until 24 December.

At that point, the impact of our domestic debate overwhelmed the possibilities of diplomacy. It was demanded that we explain publicly why our effort was important—and then our effort was cut off. After the Senate vote to block further aid to Angola, Cuba more than doubled its forces and Soviet military aid was resumed on a large scale. The cooperativeness of Soviet diplomacy declined. Since then the situation has continued to deteriorate.

As our public discussion continues, certain facts must be understood. The analogy with Vietnam is totally false; this nation must have the maturity to make elementary distinctions. The President has pledged that no American troops or advisers would be sent to Angola, and we were prepared to accept legislative restrictions to that effect, in addition to the War Powers Act which already exists. What was involved was modest assistance to stabilize the local balance of forces and make possible a rapid political settlement in cooperation with African countries.

*　　*　　*

It is said that the Russians will inevitably be eased out by the Africans themselves over a period of time. This may or may not prove true. But such an argument, when carried to its logical conclusion, implies that we can abandon the world to interventionist forces and hope for the best. And reliance on history is of little solace to those under attack, whose future is being decided now. The degree of Soviet and Cuban intervention is unprecedented; they will have effectively determined the outcome. There is no evidence to support the claim that they will be quickly removed or that other nations may not draw damaging conclusions dangerous to our long-term interests.

It is maintained that we should meet the Soviet threat in Angola through escalated methods of pressure such as altering our position on SALT or grain sales. But these arrangements benefit us as well as the Soviet Union and are part of the long-term strategy for dealing with the Soviet Union. History has proved time and again that expansion can be checked only when there is a local balance of forces; indirect means can succeed only if rapid local victories are foreclosed. As the President has pointed out, the Soviet Union has survived for nearly sixty years without American grain; it could do so now. Cutting off grain would still lose Angola. We would duplicate the experience of the Trade Act, which interrupted the trade relationship with the U.S.S.R. to insure emigration—and ended up with neither.

Let us not bemuse ourselves with facile slogans about not becoming the world's policeman. We have no desire to play such a role. But it can never be in our interest to let the Soviet Union act as the world's policeman. There are many crises in the world where the United States cannot and should not intervene. But here we face a blatant Soviet and Cuban challenge, which could have been overcome if we had been allowed to act prudently with limited means at the early stage. By forcing this out onto center stage, our divisions simultaneously escalated the significance of the crisis and guaranteed our impotence.

To claim that Angola is not an important country, or that the United States has no important interests there, begs the principal question. If the United States is seen to waver in the face of massive Soviet and Cuban intervention, what will be the perception of leaders around the world as they make decisions concerning their future security? And what conclusions will an unopposed superpower draw when the next opportunity for intervention beckons?

Where are we now? The government has a duty to make clear to the Soviet Union and Cuba that Angola sets no precedent, that this type of action will not be tolerated again. It must reassure adjacent countries they will not be left exposed to attack or pressure from the new Soviet-Cuban foothold. Congress and the executive must come together on this proposition—in the national interest and in the interest of world peace.

The Administration will continue to make its case, however unpopular it may be temporarily. Let no nation believe that Americans will long remain indifferent to the dispatch of expeditionary forces and vast supplies of arms to impose minority governments—especially when that expeditionary force comes from a nation in the Western Hemisphere.

National Strength and the Debate at Home

We live in a world without simple answers. We hold our values too dear to relinquish defending them; we hold human life too dear to cease the quest for a secure peace. The first requirement of stability is to maintain our defenses and the balance of power. But the highest aim of policy in the nuclear age must be to create out of the sterile equilibrium of force a more positive relationship of peace.

America has the material assets to do the job. Our military might is unmatched. Our economic and technological strength dwarfs any other. Our democratic heritage is envied by hundreds of millions around the world.

Our problems therefore are of our own making—self-doubt, division, irresolution. We must once again become a confident, united and determined people.

ANNUAL DEFENSE DEPARTMENT REPORT
FY 1977 *

In his fiscal year 1977 report, Secretary of Defense Donald Rumsfeld discusses the status of United States defense efforts. The objectives assigned to the military forces derive from broad foreign policy and national security considerations and require sufficient flexibility to respond to a range of challenges. The capabilities of other nations determine the make-up of our strategic nuclear forces, which must provide effective deterrence and strategic stability. Our general purpose forces are organized to protect vital American interests, especially in Central Europe and Northeast Asia and must maintain the ability to fight—with the aid of allies—one major and one minor conflict simultaneously.

U.S. Defense Programs

A strong U.S. military posture is a vital ingredient in deterring adventurism by others in areas important to our interests and in providing the necessary incentive for the Soviets and others to pursue policies of political cooperation and arms limitation negotiations with us.

---

* Report of Secretary of Defense Donald H. Rumsfeld to the Congress on the FY 1977 Budget and its Implications for the FY 1978 Authorization Request and the FY 1977-1981 Defense Programs, 27 January 1976, pp. 14-26.

Specifically, our major defense programs seek to ensure the military capability of the United States, in concert with its allies, to:

- maintain a strategic balance with the Soviet Union;
- maintain conventional combat forces which enable us credibly to deter, and if necessary, to defend against a conventional attack in Europe and which are sufficient to meet the most likely threats to our security and that of our allies elsewhere;
- maintain naval forces adequate to deter attacks on sea lines of communication, project forces ashore, and keep essential sea lanes open;
- achieve a more stable military environment through negotiation of equitable arms control measures.

In its defense planning, the United States is following two parallel tracks: we design and deploy the forces necessary to maintain military equilibrium with the Soviet Union and its allies, while at the same time we explore the possibility of achieving, through mutual arms control agreements, a more stable balance at reduced levels of forces.

In military planning, the United States seeks to develop forces that can respond to a wide range of challenges and which are applicable with precision, control, and restraint. This flexibility is crucial if U.S. forces are to be perceived by ourselves, our allies, our adversaries, and the rest of the world, as providing us with the capability to respond appropriately to a wide range of threats. Without such flexibility, the deterrent would be degraded.

The difficult and classical force planning problem lies in deciding just how much defense is enough. The details of the department's solution to this problem are reviewed in the body of this *Annual Report*. It should be noted that we have proposed only the most fundamental defense needs. For example, we do not program forces to deal with every conceivable contingency. Nor, with the exception of the strategic nuclear forces, do we attempt to counterbalance potential enemies with U.S. resources alone. One factor of importance in shaping our planning should be mentioned here. During the past thirty years, not only have we seen a rise in U.S. external interests, and an expansion of Soviet military power, we have also witnessed an explosion in the technology of warfare.

The Impact of Technology. Prior to World War II, we could spend less than 2 percent of our GNP on defense not simply because of the illusion of isolation but also because military requirements appeared to be reasonably well understood and straightforward. Ground forces and navies were the product of long experience and gradual evolution. The increasing mobility of the tank and the long-range firepower of the aircraft were beginning to reshape the face of war, but even they were evolutionary platforms and had undergone trials in World War I and subsequent conflicts. Force planning could be, and was, largely traditional and incremental, although occasional and annoying innovators such as airpower and tank enthusiasts threatened to disturb the customary patterns of warfare by suggesting novel uses for newer military instruments.

Now, however, conditions are dramatically different. Because of technology, we find ourselves in the position of having to maintain three basic types of forces—strategic nuclear, theater nuclear, and nonnuclear—and while the first two are more specialized in their functions than the third (and less costly), they add appreciably to the burden of defense. Technology also obliges us to examine closely proposals for totally new weapons, and frequently to replace old ones before the end of their previously anticipated life cycles. We know the phenomenon of "trading up" in the automobile industry, but the pressures here are different. With so much of current military competition focused on qualitative improvements in weapons systems, the need grows stronger to stay abreast of the competitor, to avoid block obsolescence in major capabilities, and to modernize systematically.

We have passed well beyond the era of improving the horse. Not only must we contend with the awesome novelty of nuclear weapons, space platforms, and exotic sensors, we must also try to visualize, mostly without combat experience, the types of campaigns that an enemy might attempt to conduct, and the weapons he might decide to use. Only then can we seriously design our deterrent forces.

Strategic Nuclear Forces. Strategic nuclear forces occupy a unique position in the planning process. Owing to the power of nuclear weapons, the high technology involved in modern delivery systems, and the need to preclude the possibility of devastating surprise attack at intercontinental distances, strategic nuclear forces must be shaped much more by the specific capabilities of other nations and our deterrent goals than by the shifting currents of international politics and the tactics of U.S. foreign policy.

The facts about the evolution of the Soviet strategic forces should be well known. Their growing technical sophistication—with high-yield MIRVs and rapidly improving accuracies—suggests a considerable interest in continuing force improvements and in flexibility. It is likely, moreover, that even within the limits foreshadowed by the

Vladivostok understanding, they will continue their rapid rate of strategic force modernization which will improve the capabilities of their forces against a wide range of targets.

Our basic objectives continue to be credible deterrence and continued strategic stability. The conditions under which our main offensive forces satisfy these objectives are when they:

- contain a highly survivable second-strike capability that can, if necessary, retaliate with devastating force against an enemy's basic economic and political assets;
- have the combination of warheads, accuracy, command-control, and retargeting capability so that, whatever the contingency, they can execute a variety of second-strike attacks on military and other targets of value to an enemy, and at the same time minimize collateral damage to civilian populations;
- are known to be equivalent to the enemy's offensive forces in the important dimensions of military power;
- remain well-hedged, through active research and development programs, against future vulnerabilities that an enemy might attempt to exploit.

The effectiveness of our strategic nuclear forces in providing credible deterrence and strategic stability continues to be of fundamental concern to the United States and its allies. Without the foundation of our strategic forces, the security and cohesion of our alliances could be jeopardized. The United States, as the strongest nation among the Western allies, bears a particularly heavy responsibility to ensure that its nuclear forces protect our allies as well as ourselves, and that they avoid present and future vulnerabilities. Deterrence needs to be comprehensive and credible. Too much is at stake to tolerate or tempt the serious consideration by opponents of even very high risk attacks.

Under present circumstances, and by these standards, we believe that we have an adequate strategic offensive force. Even after a well-coordinated surprise attack, the United States could (if necessary) retaliate with enough power to destroy its enemy as a modern, functioning society. Furthermore, because this retaliatory capability is diversified among a triad of offensive forces, the potential for unprecedented damage is well assured.

At the same time, selected portions of our offensive forces are acquiring the flexibility to respond to more discriminating attacks. Not only is our inventory of preplanned options increasing; we are acquiring the retargeting and command-control capabilities to respond rapidly to unforeseen events. No hostile and reckless power can assume that our hands will be tied because our only choices in response to a limited nuclear attack are inactivity and the holocaust. More appropriate options now exist. We propose to go on refining them—and making systems improvements such as increased accuracy—so as to ensure that any attack can be met by a deliberate and credible response.

This degree of flexibility, which is strengthening and broadening deterrence, necessarily includes the option and the capability to strike accurately at military targets, including some hardened sites. But it does not permit, and our programs do not aim to acquire, a disarming first-strike capability against the U.S.S.R. Such an objective is not even attainable at present because the Soviets themselves maintain a triad of offensive forces—along with massive active strategic defenses—that preclude a successful simultaneous attack on all three forces.

We can pursue such a policy not only because of our nonaggressive stance in the world, but also because our primary capabilities for second-strike, counter-economic, and other types of targeting are currently well assured. In fact, precisely for these reasons, our strategic nuclear forces are roughly equivalent to those of the U.S.S.R. Despite the differences between the two offensive forces, the overall capabilities of our forces—however measured—compare favorably with those of the Soviets.

Whether or not this basic equivalence will continue through the next decade is the most serious issue that we face in our decisions about our strategic nuclear programs. We must now move forward with force modernization programs which ensure the maintenance of a strategic equilibrium for the future and thereby support our SALT objectives. Two difficulties we anticipate in this connection are of special significance. The first is that our heavy bomber force and SSBNs are aging. However, the B-1 and Trident programs give us a sound basis for modernizing these two essential parts of the strategic triad.

The second difficulty is more profound. The modernization of the Soviet ICBM force that is now under way will increase the vulnerability of the Minuteman ICBMs. We would prefer to forestall any danger to both ICBM forces by mutual agreement. But if we are unsuccessful on that score, we must decide what to do about Minuteman. One superficially tempting option is unilaterally to phase out fixed, hard ICBMs without any replacement. However, that would heighten the vulnerability of our other forces and deprive us of the tight control, retargeting, and accuracy that are such important characteristics of the Minuteman. We would have diminished the means to respond to the more limited nuclear attacks with which we must be concerned, and our deterrent coverage would be less complete.

The consequences of a mistake or a failure of deterrence are so appalling that we cannot afford to ignore any significant vulnerabilities or prospective loss of capability. Accordingly, we must ensure that we have enough warheads for a second-strike to cover targets we deem important, and that we maintain the flexibility and control to deliver them as directed by the President. In a world containing totalitarian and antagonistic powers, vulnerable allies, and possible increases in nuclear proliferation, the capability for controlled and deliberate responses is essential.

Although we seek greater flexibility for the strategic nuclear forces, we recognize that they cannot credibly deter all of the threats that could develop in the future. To cover the full range of contingencies, we must maintain and strengthen our other capabilities.

The General Purpose Forces. Our general purpose forces do not need to be coupled as closely to their counterparts in the U.S.S.R. as our strategic nuclear forces. In part, this is because of the major nonnuclear contributions made by our allies. But it is also the case because the Soviets currently orient a significant fraction of their general purpose forces toward the People's Republic of China. We therefore focus on maintaining two principal strong deployments outside the Western Hemisphere—in Central Europe and Northeast Asia—and on being able, in conjunction with allies, to hold a forward defense line against a major attack in either theater.

Of the capabilities currently deployed in the European theater, our NATO allies provide a vast preponderance of the ground forces, most of the ships, and 75 percent of the aircraft. A similar situation prevails in the other bastion of free world strength—Northeast Asia. Without the contributions of our allies, either we would have to offset the military power of our adversaries entirely by ourselves—with much larger defense expenditures than we are currently making—or we would have to redefine our interests in much more restrictive terms and risk the erosion of our own security.

The day has passed when, because of overwhelming U.S. strength, we could look upon our mutual security treaties as guaranteeing the security of others by the pledge and the presence of the United States alone. We now depend on the defense contributions of our allies to provide the main barrier to hostile expansion in both Western

Europe and Northeast Asia. Our general purpose forces are largely designed to complement theirs.

We believe that a conventional attack should be met by a conventional response, but that we should also maintain a back-up theater nuclear capability—not as a substitute for nonnuclear forces, but as a deterrent to the use of nuclear weapons and as a hedge against failure of our conventional defenses. This is particularly important in view of the extensive improvements in Soviet theater-level, nuclear-capable forces in the European region, such as the development of the SS-X-20 IRBM and the introduction of modern, dual capable aircraft to replace older tactical systems.

These objectives, which also support deterrence, stability, and a higher nuclear threshold, require that we maintain some forces deployed forward in those theaters where opposing strength already is or can readily be concentrated. We also maintain a central strategic reserve in the Continental United States (CONUS), long-range mobility forces, and the capability to protect our sea lines of communication.

It is essential that we maintain positions of strength both in Europe and in Northeast Asia. Because both great theaters are of fundamental importance to the security of the United States, we must size general purpose forces to assist in meeting a major contingency in at least one of these theaters while we help to garrison a forward defense in the other. But since we cannot preclude the use of the general purpose forces in other theaters and for other purposes, the basic objective of our planning must be to provide the forces to deter a major nonnuclear conflict, and in the process, gain the flexibility to deal with lesser contingencies. With this approach, we place a reasonable constraint on our force requirements while providing a capability that is sufficient, we believe, to deal with the most dangerous challenges of a volatile and uncertain international environment.

In recent years, some countries where U.S. forces are stationed have reexamined the terms of arrangements now in effect for the use of U.S. bases and facilities. As a result, we are now engaged in renegotiating agreements with several host nations, such as Spain, Greece, and Turkey. Although we believe that the outcome of these negotiations will prove mutually acceptable, the terms of the new agreements are likely to be shorter than in the past, and our freedom of use adjusted. The force structure we have developed and the programs we propose take these changing considerations into account.

Although general purpose forces are not tied to any single commitment or contingency, and can be used as directed, the most severe test of their adequacy arises in Central Europe. NATO faces a standing force of twenty-seven Soviet and thirty-one East European divisions, comprising close to a million men, a tactical air force of some three thousand aircraft, and what must be the largest concentration of tanks in the world. With little advance preparation, this force could launch a substantial attack into Germany. After a short period of mobilization and deployment, it could be substantially reinforced by divisions and tactical aircraft from the Western Military Districts of the U.S.S.R. Thus we face two demanding but conceivable contingencies: first, an attack launched with little or no warning by the deployed forces of the Warsaw Pact; and second, an assault undertaken with the main immediately deployable strength of the pact after perhaps only a few weeks of warning to NATO.

The United States would not have to face either of these contingencies alone. Allied forces in the Central Region (excluding forces located in France, Denmark, and the United Kingdom) consist of about six hundred thousand men in the ground forces and about thirteen hundred tactical aircraft—not counting Seventh U.S. Army and the United States Air Forces, Europe (USAFE). By most of the measures of effectiveness and force adequacy, these allied divisions would not be able by themselves to halt an attack by the in-place force of the Warsaw Pact. The four U.S. divisions and three additional maneuver brigades deployed in Germany, along with eight wings from USAFE, would make the critical difference in ensuring that force and firepower ratios do not favor the Warsaw Pact to an excessive degree.

This is not to say that the current mobilization day (M-day) situation is entirely satisfactory. In the event it were subjected to a surprise attack, if the West had larger ready forces with greater firepower and mobility, it would obviously lessen the risk of a major breakthrough. We are adding two brigades to Seventh Army for that reason. But the bulk of any additional in-place capability will have to come from our allies. Unless such a contribution is forthcoming, our best judgment must be that while we cannot have high confidence of stopping a surprise pact attack, the pact cannot have high confidence of succeeding in one. Deterrence is served, but not as conclusively as it might be.

To deal with the contingency of a pact mobilization and deployment, NATO has a reinforcing capability which, if brought to the front in a timely fashion, should be adequate to conduct an effective forward defense. Although the pact could deploy three times as many tanks and a few more aircraft, NATO could actually have more men in the theater and an edge in fighter-attack aircraft. Whether this would actually be the line-up of forces depends critically on several factors: the time it would take the pact to deploy and organize such a large attacking force; the amount of warning NATO would have of this effort and the speed of its reaction; and the ability of the United States, in particular, to deploy its active divisions and air wings to Europe.

In light of what our allies are capable of doing, the United States needs to deploy a substantial number of additional divisions and fighter-attack wings to the Center Region in a relatively short time. If we could provide this force on-line in a timely manner, NATO would have the manpower, the force and firepower ratios, the division frontages, and the operational resources necessary to conduct a strong, sustained defense.

The department is providing the necessary number of active army divisions for this purpose and improving their deployability. The air force plans to fill its twenty-six-wing fighter-attack structure with additional aircraft to improve U.S. firepower still further. In order for us to have high confidence in our ability to deploy all the required ground forces in time to meet a full pact attack, we need to improve our airlift capability to move outsize cargo.

We also face the problem that the length of a conventional war in Europe is quite uncertain. Despite confident forecasts of a short, intense conflict, it is within the realm of probability that we would have to sustain and support our forces in the Center Region over a period of many months, as well as provide reinforcements to the northern and southern flanks. How effective we would be in these functions depends critically on the availability of amphibious forces, supporting airpower, and logistic resources and our ability to protect vital sea lines of communication.

In Northeast Asia we are concerned primarily about the military balance on the Korean Peninsula. North Korea has built up an impressive military capability and devotes almost 15 percent of its GNP to military purposes. Its military forces are armed with modern Soviet air and ground equipment. The North enjoys an advantage over the South in numbers of tanks, artillery, and modern aircraft.

The Republic of Korea (ROK) has also improved and strengthened its military forces in the past decade. Its half million army is among the best trained forces in Asia and is numerically superior to the North Korean army. Moreover, in the event of attack from the North, the ROK would be defending from prepared defensive positions. On balance we believe the ROK is in a strong position to defend itself against the North if timely U.S. support is provided. While South Korea now finances almost all its defense effort, it continues to need significant foreign military sales credits to continue its force modernization program.

Under the Mutual Defense Treaty with the Republic of Korea, the United States maintains the Second Infantry Division as well as an air force tactical wing to supplement ROK air capabilities. The U.S. forces support our overall security objectives in Northeast Asia and are a stabilizing element in the area generally. As such they are important to Japan's sense of security (which is also bolstered by the presence of U.S. forces in Japan) and the continuation of moderate Soviet and Chinese policies toward the Korean peninsula.

Although our naval and amphibious forces provide us with enormous reach and flexibility, it is primarily in the context of a European contingency that we measure their adequacy. It should be emphasized also that a war in Europe could spread to other areas and that, even if the actual combat were more closely confined, we would still be concerned with protecting the sea lanes to Northeast Asia, standing guard against the Soviet Pacific fleet, and maintaining access to the Persian Gulf.

These tasks are demanding, but we believe that the combined U.S. and allied naval forces could perform them at the present time. Our assessment indicates that our forces remain at least equal to their counterparts in the Soviet Union and the Warsaw Pact as a whole. The Soviet Navy, with surface ships, submarines, and long-range aircraft, continues to maintain a powerful defense of Russian territory and nearby waters against U.S. sea-based tactical air and amphibious forces. It also continues to develop the potential to interdict U.S. and allied shipping. However, while NATO would probably incur major losses in an antishipping campaign, these losses would not be prohibitive—as far as we can tell—and the effect on our combat capability would be severe but not crippling. Existing U.S. and allied sea control forces should be able to take a heavy toll of the enemy's submarines and surface combatants and, within an acceptable time, reestablish full control of sea lanes in the Atlantic and Pacific.

These conclusions are essentially the same as last year, and must be qualified in the same fashion. The Soviets could do grave damage to our surface combatants if they were to attack by surprise, and they might well be able to deny us, at least temporarily, the use of certain seas. Moreover, our ability to continue at even the current level of effectiveness and protect the main sea lanes is directly related to a modernization and expansion of the U.S. Navy. Without such a program, U.S. control of the essential seas will inevitably decline.

Security Assistance. Security assistance (which includes grant materiel assistance under the Military Assistance Program, credits and sales under the Foreign Military Sales Act, and Security Supporting Assistance) continues to be an important instrument of U.S. policy. In its early years, grant aid was used to strengthen collective security arrangements against Communist expansion by improving the conventional forces of European and Asian allies. Since then, security assistance also has been used to maintain regional security arrangements, help promote recipients' internal security, contribute to base rights and facilities for U.S. forces and, to a degree, increase U.S. influence in recipient countries.

Grant aid has declined as more recipients have reached the point of economic development where they can shift to foreign military sales, either credit or cash, and to commercial sales. In the past few years, cash sales have grown rapidly, with the bulk of the increase occurring in the Middle East.

The change in character and in primary recipients of security assistance has raised some serious questions regarding the need to continue grant military aid as a policy tool and the wisdom of accepting the role of a major seller and exporter of defense articles and services. Additionally, because the total of recent arms transfers is large and because the materiel sought is often first-line equipment in demand both by U.S. forces and by friends and allies, military exports should come generally from production, or excess or overage equipment in order to avoid adverse impact on overall Defense Department programs and resources.

An evaluation of security assistance suggests that it has on the whole supported U.S. foreign policy. Security assistance has helped maintain a military balance between NATO and Warsaw Pact in Western Europe and contributes to a stabilized balance in Northeast Asia by helping to deter North Korea. In the Middle East, military assistance to Saudi Arabia and Iran has supported the development of regional security in the Persian Gulf area and assistance to Israel has been vital to her security.

Military assistance does not result in the unquestioning support of foreign governments for U.S. policies. Security assistance credits and sales are expected to help further our security interests by providing recipient states with sufficient confidence in their own military security to engage in regional political negotiations, and thus decrease opportunities for the Soviet Union or any other power to intimidate them or gain dominant influence over them.

The demand for articles and services (primarily through foreign military cash sales) is likely to continue as nations acquire the means. The United States is dealing with sovereign nations determined to establish their own defense requirements and who do not wish to be told how to allocate resources. The United States supports multilateral efforts including regional arrangements to limit arms transfers, but this is a sensitive issue involving strongly held feelings of national sovereignty, and progress will be slow and difficult. At the same time, we are decreasingly able, unilaterally, to influence the arms acquisition policies of other nations because military materiel is available from many Communist countries and Western nations.

The Foreign Policy–Military Posture Relationship Reviewed

The U.S. military force structure is derived from U.S. national security and foreign policy objectives, our appreciation of the most likely threats to the achievement of those objectives, and an assessment of the military force that would be most effective in preventing those threats from materializing, in overcoming them if they should arise, or in generally sustaining U.S. diplomatic efforts to maintain a credible deterrent.

In strategic force planning, the pace and character of U.S. improvements are based on the degree of success we experience in restraining a strategic arms race through arms limitation negotiations and on our estimates of what steps are necessary to prevent Soviet strategic forces from upsetting the current strategic balance.

General purpose force planning is based primarily on our policies of deterring war in Europe and Northeast Asia, and on the necessity to maintain the flexibility to protect major interests elsewhere in the world should they be threatened. The security assistance program remains an important means of helping friends meet their own security needs and undergirding our other foreign policies.

The defense posture has been developed to meet the military requirements of U.S. policy as efficiently as possible, recognizing the range of demands on total national resources.

Budgetary Needs

Meeting the military requirements of U.S. foreign policy is a dynamic process created in part by changes in technology, military capabilities, and the international situation. There are no grounds for slackening current defense programs. On the contrary, our assessments strongly support the case for a properly focused real increase in the resources devoted to our military posture.

A rough balance now exists at the level of the strategic nuclear forces, and, whatever the ambitions of the U.S.S.R., essential equivalence is the foundation we must maintain. If challenged, we and our allies have the resources to defend the two bastions of Western Europe and Northeast Asia, and hold open the main sea lanes to our shipping—although not without serious initial losses. To the extent that we could meet these two basic challenges, we should have in hand the capability to meet other and less demanding contingencies. But our posture, unless strengthened, has potential vulnerabilities, such as aging of forces and readiness which is lower than it should be.

Debates no doubt will continue on how to compare Soviet defense expenditures with ours; differences will arise as to whether and when their outlays have exceeded U.S. expenditures. Much or little can be made of the Sino-Soviet dispute and the hard fact that the U.S.S.R. has tripled its forces in the Far East during the past decade. What cannot be in question, however, are these trends:

- Soviet defense expenditures have been increasing more or less steadily for more than ten years;
- Soviet military power—nuclear and nonnuclear, strategic and tactical, quantitative and qualitative—has been expanding, not contracting;
- Much of the expansion has taken place in the forces that constitute a direct threat to the United States and its allies.

We have responded to these developments by extracting greater combat power out of existing defense assets. If we are to maintain the necessary conditions of deterrence and stability in the years ahead, we must provide real increases to the defense budget. The need now is not so much for expanded force structure as it is for the replacement of aging systems and improved capability, readiness, and mobility in the structure that is now planned.

6

IS AMERICA'S DEFENSE ADEQUATE?

HOW TO LOOK AT THE
SOVIET-AMERICAN BALANCE *

Les Aspin

Representative Les Aspin (Democrat, Wisconsin) contends that the threat to the United States resulting from the growth in the Soviet defense budget is overstated. He reasons that the aggregate difference in the spending levels of the two nations is not as great as frequently portrayed. Increased Soviet expenditures do not automatically signify hostile intentions, and a significant portion of the Soviet military expansion has been channeled in directions that do not threaten the United States. American defense capabilities, he concludes, are sufficient in areas that often are criticized as inadequate.

The Soviet Union, we hear these days from the Pentagon, is now outspending the United States on defense. Yesterday's missile gap is today's dollar gap.

It is legitimate to ask two questions about the figures being bandied about. First, do the statistics fairly reflect reality? As Disraeli remarked, "There are three kinds of lies: lies, damned lies, and statistics." Second, if there has been an increase in the Soviet defense budget, is it really something we have to worry about? After all, the U.S. military could add a billion dollars to its subsidies for commissaries or its budget for uniforms without generating any worries in the Soviet equivalent of the Pentagon.

---

* Source: *Foreign Policy*, no. 22 (Spring 1976), pp. 96-106.

When James Schlesinger was defense secretary, he said, "If one strips away pensions and other such considerations, the Soviets may at this point, in terms of the American dollar, be outspending us by 50 percent. They are outspending us, even including pensions, by approximately 30 percent." This has been echoed by others, inside and outside Defense.

The key phrase is "in terms of the American dollar." The Soviets, of course, do not spend dollars. But somehow, Soviet expenditures must be translated into figures comparable to American expenditures. The Pentagon does this by putting both defense budgets into dollars. Starting from observed Soviet defense activity (manpower, equipment, construction, and operations), analysts calculate the cost of procuring a similar force in this country. They ask, "What would it cost to buy the Soviet defense establishment in the United States at U.S. prices?" Based on preliminary figures, this calculation shows that last year the Soviets spent $107 billion on defense while the United States spent $79 billion, both in 1974 dollars.

A Trap Door

This method of calculation seems fair on the surface. But there's a trap door. Soviet wages are generally much lower than American wages. But by computing Soviet manpower costs at U.S. rates, one discovers a huge Soviet defense manpower "budget" of over $50 billion that exists only in American documents.

Using this methodology, the largest single reason that Soviet defense spending exceeds our own has been the American decision to switch to an all-volunteer army and to pay its servicemen civilian-level wages. The absurdity of this calculation then becomes clear: If the United States were to shave its military pay scales, Soviet defense "spending" would fall.

To be sure, calculating the cost of Soviet defenses in American dollars is one way of getting a perspective on the size of their effort. But it is not the only way. An alternative is to compute U.S. and Soviet defense expenditures in rubles.

This method is admittedly much more difficult. For example, we have no good way to estimate what it would cost the Soviets to produce the whole range of American equipment. We cannot turn a new tank over to a Soviet manufacturer and ask him what it would cost to produce it.

Nevertheless, a meaningful ruble comparison can still be made. The result is the reverse of the dollar comparison. Whereas the dollar comparison is weighted by the fact that it prices the manpower-intensive Soviet forces in terms of high U.S. personnel costs, the ruble comparison is weighted by the fact that it prices the technology-intensive U.S. forces in terms of the high costs of Soviet technology. When the calculations are done with rubles, the United States is the bigger spender.[1]

Actually, the ruble comparison understates the American lead in spending. Many of the more sophisticated items in the U.S. arsenal are beyond Soviet production capabilities: computers and other advanced electronics are prime examples. The standard estimate counts the cost in rubles of the closest item the Soviets can actually make. Since we alone have a TV homing, steerable bomb, for example, in rubles it would be priced as an ordinary bomb.

So the answer to the question, "who is spending more on defense," depends on the price system used.

A Question of Trends

Beyond the absolute levels of defense spending, there is the question of trends. It is impossible to ascertain with any relevant measure if the Soviets are out-spending the United States in any given year, but the trends in spending over several years are not so ambiguous.[2]

According to the best estimates available, real Soviet defense spending has increased an average of 2.7 percent a year over the decade 1964 to 1974.[3] U.S. defense spending, on the other hand, increased from 1964 to 1968, because of Vietnam, but has declined in real (not inflated dollar) terms since. The curve results in an annual net decline of 1 percent per year.

---

[1] The results differ because the relative costs of manpower and equipment in the countries differ. Where relative costs vary, using a single monetary unit from either one of the two countries to make the comparison produces a bias—what economists call the "index number" problem.

[2] Trend calculations were worked from the dollar costs of Soviet spending. Although dollar figures give a misleading view of the absolute level of Soviet outlays, if applied consistently, they are valid in describing changes and trends.

[3] Former Secretary Schlesinger has put the long-term Soviet growth at between 3 and 5 percent per year. Deputy Defense Secretary William Clements has claimed that the Soviet military budget "in real terms is increasing about 5 percent a year . . ." (*Defense Space Business Daily*, 31 May 1975). Actually, the rate of growth has fluctuated between 1 and 5 percent annually. And, in the 1964–74 period, the annual rate of growth averaged 2.7 percent, which corresponds to a 3 percent slope in the long-term trend line.

Former Defense Secretary Melvin R. Laird believes the Soviet increase is evidence that "the Soviet Union has engaged in a relentless effort to attain military supremacy."[4] For him and others, détente is a smoke screen behind which the Soviets are hiding while still trying to surpass the United States in all dimensions of military power.

But there are two other possible explanations for Soviet behavior—explanations that are not so cataclysmic. The first is the timing of budget decisions. Right now the driving force behind rising Soviet expenditures is the new generation of intercontinental ballistic missiles (ICBMs). These systems have a long gestation period, and were being developed before the 1972 SALT agreements ushered in the era of détente.

This means that we cannot automatically assume that recent budget growth is a reflection of the current attitudes of the Soviet leaders. If the attitudes have changed, we may see a change in defense expenditures in late 1976 or 1977 when the current ICBM deployment nears completion.

The second possibility is that the growth in Soviet defense expenditures is a function of internal, bureaucratic–political factors in the Kremlin. Brezhnev, trying to keep a majority for détente in the Politburo, cannot afford to alienate the armed forces. Using increased defense expenditures to keep the military on board for political purposes is not unknown in this country and may also be an accepted ploy in the Soviet Union.

But whatever the reason, the trends are there. To quote Schlesinger again: "By most of the available measures, American power is declining and Soviet power is rising. No one can say precisely where the peril points lie as this process unfolds. But if real expenditures by the United States remain constant or continue to fall, while real Soviet outlays continue to rise, the peril points will occur in the relatively near future."[5]

However, the crucial issue is what the Soviets are spending their extra rubles on. If the increases are in forces that threaten the United States and its NATO allies, that is one thing. If the increases are for more troops on the Chinese border, that is something else. The accompanying table, based on previously unavailable data, shows what proportions of the total growth in Soviet defense spending have been devoted to each military mission.

---

[4] Melvin R. Laird, "Is This Detente?" *Reader's Digest* (July 1975), p. 57.
[5] Letter to Senator John L. McClellan, chairman of the Senate Appropriations Defense Subcommittee, 23 October 1975, p. 5.

Identifying the Increases

Not all increases directly threaten U.S. interests. These include higher spending on four missions that comprise 36 percent of the increase in Soviet spending in the 1964–74 decade:

1. Since the Sino-Soviet split, the Soviet Union has boosted the number of troops and amount of equipment stationed along the Chinese border. (This accounts for 16 percent of the budget increase.)

2. In response to the 1968 uprising in Czechoslovakia, the Soviets stationed five divisions there in order to restore control. They remain there. (This accounts for 5 percent of the increase.)

Table 1

DISTRIBUTION OF CHANGES IN SOVIET DEFENSE SPENDING, 1964–1974
(as a percentage of the total increase)

Mission	% Change
Research and development	+18
Intercontinental range offense	+26
Intermediate range offense	−8
Strategic defense	+7
Navy, general purpose forces	+3
Tactical air forces	+2
Chinese border	+16
Eastern Europe (minus Czechoslovakia)	+10
Czechoslovakia	+5
Internal security	+8
Other changes (unidentifiable by mission)	+13
	+100

Note: All changes in the missions listed in the table are cumulative (cumulative change equals the sum of the differences between spending in 1964 and in each of the succeeding years) and are expressed as percentages of the cumulative increase in total spending for the 1964-74 period. Outlays for command and general support were allocated to various mission categories based primarily on those categories' proportions of the total budget in any given year. Research and development costs are not included in any mission categories apart from that entitled "research and development."

Source: Estimates provided in the table were derived from the following sources: *The Military Balance,* various years, published by the International Institute for Strategic Studies; U.S. Congress, Joint Economic Committee, Subcommittee on Priorities and Economy in Government, *Allocation of Resources in the Soviet Union and China*, 1974 and 1975; and the best available intelligence community estimates as of January 1976.

3. In the 1964–74 period, the Soviet Union significantly augmented the border troops of the KGB (Committee of State Security) and the security troops of the MVD (Ministry of Internal Affairs). These forces are "essentially paramilitary formations whose principal functions are to police Soviet borders [and] cannot credibly be included in the Soviet land order of battle."[6] (This accounts for 8 percent of the increase.)

4. The Soviet Union has traditionally been extremely sensitive about its vulnerability to attack and has made enormous investments in surface-to-air missiles and fighter-interceptor aircraft, even as the limited effectiveness of air defense led the Pentagon to trim outlays in that area drastically. (This accounts for 7 percent of the increase.)

Other increases in Soviet defense spending directly threaten U.S. interests, at least in part.

Intercontinental-range offensive forces, composed of ICBMs, submarine-launched ballistic missiles (SLBMs), and long-range bombers, are generally considered the most threatening and account for 26 percent of the increase. However, this increase was offset somewhat by a decline in spending for shorter-range strategic forces, such as medium- and intermediate-range missiles, which can threaten NATO.

Many of the Soviet allocations for research and development (R & D) can pose a potential threat to the United States and its allies. Spending for military R & D accounted for 18 percent of the total growth in Moscow's defense budgets, although the proportion that went for programs affecting U.S. interests is uncertain. Furthermore, Soviet R & D efforts are less efficient. One estimate suggests that Soviet R & D outlays are only 40 percent as productive as U.S. R & D outlays.

An estimated 100,000 additional Soviet troops were moved into the Eastern European satellites, excluding Czechoslovakia, during the decade. (This accounts for 10 percent of the increase.) It should be noted, however, that the Soviets were not the only ones to expand their force in the area; West Germany increased its army by 80,000 men in the 1964–74 period and, as Schlesinger told Congress, ". . . the capacity of our [NATO] allies has improved substantially in the last decade."[7]

---

[6] Jeffrey Record, *Sizing Up the Soviet Army* (Washington, D. C.: The Brookings Institution, 1975).

[7] U.S. Congress, House, Subcommittee on the Department of Defense of the Committee on Appropriations, *Hearings on the Department of Defense Appropriations for Fiscal Year 1976*, 94th Congress, 1st session, 1975, Part 1, p. 27.

A moderate amount of the increase, 5 percent, has gone into the navy (excluding ballistic missile submarines) and the tactical air forces—a portion of which went for squadrons assigned to the Far East for possible use against China.

In sum, about 36 percent of the expansion in Soviet defense spending falls into categories that are not directly threatening and 51 percent into areas that might threaten us. The 51 percent, however, should be reduced somewhat because, as we have seen, it contains some built-in exaggerations of the threat to the United States.

There is a danger here of drawing this argument too finely and getting too absorbed in the statistics. It is impossible to neatly categorize every defense dollar (or ruble) as nonthreatening or threatening. Forces can be shifted from a nonthreatening front to a threatening one. Still, in the event of a European war, it is unlikely that the Soviets would uncover their Chinese flank by removing forces from the Far East. With regard to Czechoslovakia, the Soviet occupation forces there would have to contend with the possibility of an uprising in the event of general war in Europe. With these qualifications in mind, we can say that only about half of the Soviet growth in military spending of 2.7 percent per year is threatening to America.

A Look at Throw-Weight

Three specific areas of Soviet spending are often pointed to with alarm—the Soviet strategic forces, navy, and ground forces.

In the strategic weapons area, the Soviets have indeed expanded rapidly, especially considering the fact that much of the R & D increase is for strategic weapons. About a third of the additional spending has gone here. As a result, the Soviets have moved from inferiority to rough parity in the missile area—a shift the Nixon Administration publicly accepted on taking office. But still, some people fear that the Soviets have spent themselves into superiority. For them, "throw-weight" is now in vogue.[8]

Paul Nitze, for example, recently tried to show a Soviet advantage in throw-weight.[9] But the simple fact is that the United States has a commanding lead of 27 million pounds to 12 million pounds when total missile throw-weight and maximum bomber payload are combined.

---

[8] Throw-weight is the maximum useful weight that can be carried to a target by a missile.

[9] Paul H. Nitze, "Assuring Strategic Stability in an Era of Détente," *Foreign Affairs* (January 1976), pp. 207-232. [This article appears later in this volume.]

Nitze appears to worry most that if the Soviets strike first and hit U.S. missile silos, they could, by his calculations, improve their throw-weight advantage, hold American cities hostage, and therefore "win" a nuclear war. He neglects one point: The superpower with the postattack advantage is the superpower that strikes first. If Washington were to launch a first strike against Soviet missile fields, we would end up with an absolutely enormous throw-weight advantage because much more Soviet throw-weight is carried on their vulnerable land-based missiles.

So it looks as if both superpowers face a throw-weight gap. But does it matter? Even if the Soviets successfully carried out a devastating attack on our forces,[10] the United States would still have about 3,100 surviving warheads—and that is 10 percent more than the Soviet arsenal has now, before an attack. Even if the Soviets attacked first, the United States would still have enough surviving warheads to drop thirteen on every Soviet city of more than one hundred thousand people. Is the Politburo really going to sniff at the possibility of warheads raining down on the Kremlin by arguing, "We have more throw-weight than the Americans"? If they are really that irrational, then they are not smart enough to understand the concept of throw-weight advantage in the first place. In the last analysis, both countries enjoy a surfeit of missilery. In light of that, the significance of any throw-weight advantage is nil.

In the other two areas—the navy and ground forces—the spending growth, as shown in Table 1, was modest for those missions and locales that threaten the United States and its NATO allies.

Only 3 percent of the growth in Soviet defense spending went to navy conventional forces (excluding strategic missile submarines that are covered in the strategic forces category). The Soviet Navy has grown, but it has been able to do this within relatively level budgets because few ships were retired during the decade and it enjoyed a large budget growth prior to the base year 1964, used in the table. The Soviets have built more ships than the United States, but every year we produce more tons of ships; U.S. Navy warships are larger and more capable and have greater firepower. The Soviet Navy has grown, but according to many specialists, it is still largely designed for defensive purposes.[11]

---

[10] One that eliminated 50 percent of our SLBMs, 90 percent of our ICBMs, and 80 percent of our B-52s.

[11] See Michael T. Klare, "Superpower Rivalry at Sea," *Foreign Policy*, no. 21 (Winter 1975-76), pp. 86-96, 161-167.

The latest rage among those who view the Soviet military budget with alarm is the spending on ground forces. The numbers being published about Soviet production of tanks, trucks, cannon, and other equipment as well as figures on Soviet military manpower are impressive.

But is the equipment and manpower being sent where it is threatening to U.S. interests? And what kind of quality are they buying with their rubles?

Roughly one-third of Soviet ground forces and equipment are deployed to the Far East, another third faces NATO, while the remaining third is elsewhere. Thus, a sizable fraction does not endanger U.S. security interests. Moreover, as the table indicates, most of the increased spending on Soviet ground forces has gone for men and arms along the Chinese border and in Czechoslovakia, not Eastern Europe.

Tanks, artillery, and other equipment are ground out in quantity but do not measure up to the quality of American weaponry. For example, Soviet tanks have a lower rate of fire, are less accurate at long range, and do not have as much armor protection. The crew space is also cramped, making it difficult for Soviet tankers to work as effectively as their American counterparts.

The issue of quality also applies to manpower. The Soviets have added 1 million men in the last decade and now have twice as many in uniform as the United States. But Soviet troops are employed in agricultural and construction projects, and large numbers of Soviet officers are really party functionaries. Furthermore, the Soviet enlisted man is not as experienced as the American volunteer who serves longer tours in the U.S. Army. As Lieutenant General Daniel Graham, then director of the Defense Intelligence Agency, testified, "Every six months they replace a quarter of their draftees, and the Soviet army's enlisted strength is almost all draftee." [12] Because of this turnover, many of the men assigned to combat units are still undergoing training.

This is not to say that superior numbers are irrelevant. But part of the reason the United States trails in quantities of equipment is that the U.S. armed forces have decided they want their armories filled with high-quality and sophisticated items. If the services feel that quantity should now be the primary concern, then they can tell their designers to take that into account.

---

[12] In testimony before the U.S. Congress, Joint Economic Committee, Subcommittee on Priorities and Economy in Government, *Allocation of Resources in the Soviet Union and China—1975*, p. 125.

Numerical comparisons are important in any assessment of the military balance. But this does not mean that any simple statistic showing the Soviets ahead of the United States is cause for hand wringing.

I do not mean to suggest that Soviet defense spending should be ignored. Some of the increase in spending is certainly threatening. Additional spending in threatening areas can mount up over the years and this warrants our close attention. But a lot of statistics are abused when we talk of the Soviet military. We must put those numbers in perspective and not jump to the conclusion that the Soviet bear is ten feet tall.

SOVIET STRENGTH AND PURPOSE *

Amos A. Jordan, R. W. Komer, Les Aspin

In this exchange, Amos A. Jordan and R. W. Komer dispute the analysis of increased Soviet military expenditures presented by Les Aspin in the previous article. Both writers accuse Aspin of statistical trickery; by any measure, they say, the U.S.S.R. outspends the United States and possesses numerically superior forces. They also argue that Aspin underestimates the direct threat posed to the United States by these developments. Aspin rebuts these charges within the framework of his initial analysis: an accurate comparison of the levels of military expenditures is difficult, and a large portion of the recent Soviet build-up either is not aimed against American interests or is more menacing quantitatively than qualitatively. He concludes that Soviet actions do not justify a large increase in the U.S. defense budget.

Amos A. Jordan

The article by Les Aspin is an important contribution to the on-again, off-again Great Debate about the significance of the American military strength in the world. . . . The overall thrust of the Aspin piece is clear: the statistics which the U.S. Administration has been using about

* Source: *Foreign Policy*, no. 23 (Summer 1976), pp. 32-48.

the relative size of the U.S. and Soviet defense efforts are being distorted to serve the Pentagon's purposes; moreover, even if Soviet defense budgets have been increasing, we need not worry particularly, for only half of the purported increases can be viewed as "threatening" to the United States.

Although the facts force Aspin to admit that U.S. and Soviet defense program trends are adverse to the United States—the central point of the article—he spends the bulk of his essay deprecating the significance of this. The remainder of the article is devoted largely to the red herring of conceptual problems in the CIA's method of comparing the absolute size of the Soviet and U.S. defense program. Thus, he mostly ignores the data showing that, for the better part of a decade, in manpower, force levels, equipment, and various other measures, Soviet military strength has been increasing while ours has been declining. Instead he focuses on what should have been a methodological footnote. Although estimating what the Soviet program would cost if it were procured in the United States, with the same manpower and the same quantities and quality of equipment, overstates Soviet resource inputs, it is the best comparative method available. In any case, it is clear that any distortion inherent in the method could not vitiate the conclusion that the Soviet Union's overall defense program is very much the larger of the two.

Further, despite Aspin's statement to the contrary, basing the comparative costing on rubles produces the same conclusions. Since the data for ruble-based comparisons are not as reliable as those for dollar-based analyses (the intelligence community now has under way a major effort to improve them), a meaningful ruble comparison is difficult; nevertheless, as former CIA Director William E. Colby publicly stated a year ago, "a very rough" ruble-based comparison indicates that the Soviet program is indeed significantly larger than ours.

In short, Aspin's thesis that "the answer to the question, 'who is spending more on defense,' depends on the price system used" is contrary to the facts, as best non-Soviet analysts can ascertain them. Examination of the quantity and quality of Soviet forces procured tends to confirm this judgment.

On the key question of relative trends, Aspin attempts to minimize the significance of the adverse changes he admits. He advances—in the first instance—two weak explanations for Soviet increases which strike him as less cataclysmic than the Pentagon's explanation that the Soviet Union is striving for military supremacy: first, that recent budget growth may be merely a reflection of pre-Strategic Arms Limitation Talks (SALT) attitudes by Soviet leaders and second, that it is a function of "internal, bureaucratic-political factors in the Kremlin." In his first case, if the Soviets were budgeting for four new intercontinental ballistic missiles (ICBMs), one new intermediate range ballistic missile (IRBM), one new submarine-launched ballistic missile (SLBM), and one new bomber, while—at the same time—negotiating for arms controls with the United States, I can question whether it was a search for stability which impelled the Soviets to complete all these expensive systems—and to promptly begin the next generation of several new ICBMs and SLBMs which are now under development (the latter systems undoubtedly conceived after the signing of the 1972 SALT agreement).

Turning to Aspin's second, "bureaucratic-political" explanation for rising Soviet defense budgets, it is difficult to take comfort from the proposition that major Soviet program and force increases mean little because they have occurred as a consequence of Brezhnev's "trying to keep a majority for détente in the Politburo" and still maintain his support in the armed forces. If the Soviet armed forces with their preoccupation with military might are so influential, concern about the military balance would seem doubly warranted.

In a third, and, to Aspin, crucial, prong to his argument for deflating the significance of rising Soviet military budgets, he identifies "threatening" and "nonthreatening" mission categories in those budgets with surprising precision. In the absence of adequate ruble data, apparently he has used the dollar costing figures he scorns to manipulate the information with far more precision and rigidity than warranted. Throughout, his figures are so obviously out of line with what we clearly know that his information base can be called into question. Thus, in his discussion of throw-weight advantage, he observes that the United States has the lead—27 million pounds to 12 million pounds. The Soviet figure is roughly correct but, including both missile throw-weight and bomber payload, U.S. figures are overstated by a factor of roughly three. In fact, in terms of strategic systems, the Soviet Union not only now has a throw-weight advantage but will likely increase its lead over the next few years. Its advantage is focused in the most dangerous aspect of the equation, namely, *missile* throw-weight, which holds the potential for counterforce or first-strike use which bomber payload does not.

Aspin's statement that roughly one-third of Soviet ground forces are deployed in the Far East and another one-third against NATO is also erroneous. An analyst could only arrive at these figures by torturing the data so that Soviet divisions opposite Turkey (which are really anti-NATO) and Iran and in central Russia become "Far

Eastern" divisions. In fact, only about one-fourth of the Soviet ground forces are in the Far East, and one-half are facing NATO—a very important difference for defense planners. (Of overall Soviet forces, far less than 25 percent are committed against China.) His related observation that Soviet Far Eastern deployments do not threaten U.S. interests (or, indeed, Japan's), presumably because they are anti-Chinese, not only ignores the security interests and troop deployments of the United States in Northeast Asia but also pre-supposes an unwarranted Soviet force inflexibility.

Indeed, apart from data inadequacies, the flexibility of Soviet forces and the variability of Soviet marginal resource allocations over time are crucial weak points in his case. In the past several years, for instance, the Soviets have not put increased military resources into a build-up against China or in other areas Aspin delineates as "non-threatening," but overwhelmingly into "threatening" strategic offensive systems and associated research and development (R & D). An objective observer can only echo the congressman's sentiment that the overall Soviet build-up should be placed in appropriate perspective.

R. W. Komer

Les Aspin often makes good sense in criticizing our defense posture. But his attack on comparisons of Soviet and U.S. defense spending in the last issue of *Foreign Policy* is not one of his better efforts. While accusing the Defense Department of making meaningless comparisons, he in turn rebuts them by using largely meaningless comparisons of his own. In effect he plays the same numbers game that he charges the Defense Department with playing.

I agree that gross estimates of annual Soviet versus U.S. military spending can be misleading by themselves. Not only are they neces-sarily based on esoteric ruble–dollar conversion ratios, but they hardly tell the whole story. However, Aspin's attack on what they do tell us is also quite misleading. He says that costing both force postures in dollar terms tends to overstate Soviet manpower costs, which are much lower than ours. But the CIA was not quite so dumb as to overlook this obvious point. Contrary to what Aspin claims, it did make a special correction for lower Soviet manpower costs.

Nor is Aspin right in stating that when the two budgets are compared in terms of rubles instead of dollars," the United States is the bigger spender." The only detailed U.S. estimate done on this basis, again by the CIA, makes clear that, on the contrary, Soviet spending still greatly exceeds that of the United States.

Of course, Aspin is quite right that in any case "the crucial issue is what the Soviets are spending their extra rubles on," and not just the total size of their budget. It is a pity that he then undermines his own argument by such dubious allocations of Soviet military budget changes in 1964–74 to various mission categories. This is unsupported by any known analysis I am familiar with—classified or unclassified. He must have done it on the back of an envelope.

I doubt that any qualified expert would agree with him that "only about half of the Soviet growth in military spending of 2.7 percent a year is threatening to America" or NATO. Since his artful chart [Table 1] shows only the distribution of *changes* in Soviet defense spending, it also nicely conceals the total allocations involved. And by using the entire decade 1964–74 as a base, he highlights the build-up on the Chinese border while obscuring the more recent sharp growth of Soviet strength opposite Europe. True, the Soviet Union budgets for some forces that do *not* directly threaten the United States. But the United States also buys forces that do not threaten the Soviet Union. Moreover, we spent a cool $150 billion on the incremental cost of the Vietnam war, which, by Aspin's definition, surely did not directly threaten Moscow. While this was going down the drain, comparable Soviet outlays were contributing directly to the growth in Soviet strength. Where does this leave Aspin's argument?

Perhaps Aspin's best point, made in a later press release, is that NATO vesus Warsaw Pact (WP) budget comparisons are more meaningful than those between the United States and Soviet Union alone. I agree that total NATO spending exceeds that of the WP. But for reasons I gave in an earlier *Foreign Policy* article,[1] this too is grossly misleading. Here Aspin disregards his own admonition to look not only at totals but at where the money goes.

In strong contrast to the Soviet-dominated WP forces, equipped and organized on the Soviet model, NATO is only a loose coalition of fourteen disparate national military establishments. The resulting waste, overlap, and duplication in NATO-country spending vitiates any comparison. For example, T. A. Callaghan conservatively estimates that NATO wastes over $11 billion a year by failing to consolidate research and development, procurement, and support alone.[2] And the adverse impact on military capability through lack of common training or doctrine, lack of standardization or even interopera-

---

[1] R. W. Komer, "Treating NATO's Self-Inflicted Wound," *Foreign Policy*, no. 13 (Winter 1973-74), pp. 34-48.

[2] T. A. Callaghan, *U.S./European Economic Cooperation in Military and Civil Technology* (Arlington, Va.: EX-IM Tech, August 1974), pp. 22-36.

bility of equipment and procedures, is even more worrisome. In short, NATO's whole is actually less than the sum of its parts, which makes gross NATO-WP budget comparisons no more valid an index than those between the United States and the Soviet Union alone.

Finally, we need hardly rely on gross budget comparisons to document the growth in Soviet military power. A simple bean count will suffice. In most categories, the Soviet Union not only greatly outproduces us, but has far more active divisions, ships, aircraft, missiles, artillery, and the like than would seem consistent with a defensive stance. True, quality as well as quantity must be taken into account. We do still have a technological edge in many key respects. But Aspin acknowledges that superior numbers are not irrelevant either. And he also agrees that the trend is what is most disturbing. So while sharing his view that we need sober appraisal, not just numbers games, I regret that he invented one of his own to counter that of the Pentagon.

Les Aspin

Let me address the criticisms of Amos A. Jordan and R. W. Komer in the context of my original article.

The article's first point was that the key to determining which superpower spends more on defense is the currency used in the comparison. Putting both budgets in dollar terms shows the Soviets spending more—and we all agree on that. But this calculation contains a bias against the United States.[1] Jordan dismisses the severe limitation of the dollar comparison as a mere "methodological footnote." I wish we could. But since the Pentagon relies heavily on the dollar comparison in its appeal for more money,[2] it is necessary to elevate this humble footnote to underscore the fallacies of the Pentagon argument.

If we put both defense budgets in ruble terms, the United States would clearly be outspending Russia. Komer contests this, saying

---

[1] Komer says the CIA made "a special correction for lower Soviet manpower costs." Not according to the CIA. It does calculate Soviet levels for pensions and a few other personnel costs like training, but then CIA Director William E. Colby has testified, "Our dollar cost estimates for personnel are derived by applying U.S. compensation rates to our estimates of Soviet manpower. Compensation rates are based on U.S. pay and allowances, rations, and clothing allowances for 1973."—U.S. Congress, Joint Economic Committee, Subcommittee on Priorities and Economy in Government, *Allocation of Resources in the Soviet Union and China—1975*, 1975, Part 1, p. 21.

[2] Defense Secretary Rumsfeld, for example, used his dollar comparison chart four times during his budget presentation to the House Armed Services Committee. No other chart rated such frequent attention.

the only detailed ruble comparison shows Soviet spending "still greatly exceeds that of the United States." There is indeed such a study. It shows the Soviets outspending the United States by 10 percent. But the methodological footnote in this study reveals that the margin of error is so large that a 10 percent lead is meaningless. Although Komer doesn't mention it, the ruble figures in this study are derived from a partial list of 1955 Soviet machine tool prices. In other words, the cost of a T-62 tank is extrapolated from the twenty-year-old cost figures for a lathe. The CIA itself now puts no faith in the study, noting it has "significant technical and theoretical problems [which] tend to understate the ruble cost of U.S. programs." [3]

Komer and Jordan ignore the statement in my article that many sophisticated American defense items simply cannot be made by the Soviets and that the ruble price of such items is therefore theoretically infinite. If realistic ruble price tags were attached to these weapons, there is no doubt that a ruble comparison would show the United States as the bigger spender.[4]

The second point made in my article was that Soviet defense spending has been growing by 2.7 percent a year over the past decade —not by the tremendous amounts claimed by some Pentagon spokesmen—and about half the growth is destined for the Chinese border, internal security, and other areas that are not directly threatening to the United States. Komer and Jordan do not dispute the first point, I am happy to see, but they do dispute the second.

Komer says he has not seen any analysis to support my conclusions concerning the nonthreatening spending which he thinks must have been done "on the back of an envelope." [5] Actually the basic information comes from the CIA.[6]

---

[3] Edward W. Proctor, deputy CIA director for intelligence, in Joint Economic Committee, *Allocation of Resources in the Soviet Union and China—1975*, p. 90.

[4] A natural question is why the CIA does these studies. It should be noted that the agency does not necessarily pick its own topics. It is often told to make a certain study by another agency which feels the study and the CIA cachet will help sell a point.

[5] Komer also cites the cost of Vietnam as a U.S. expenditure which is not threatening to the Soviet Union. I had already deducted those funds before noting in my article that real spending on baseline U.S. forces had declined about 1 percent per annum in the past decade.

[6] Komer also says I bias the results by using the 1964-74 period and by citing spending "increases" rather than totals. Komer ought to take his argument to the Pentagon, for I was responding to their official plaint that we are being overwhelmed because the Soviets "increased" their defense spending during those years. The Pentagon picked the years. The Pentagon framed the argument in terms of increases.

Jordan suggests that the figures have been manipulated and says that only by "torturing the data" could anyone suggest that roughly one-third of the Soviet ground forces face China. May I then nominate as chief torturer Lieutenant General Daniel O. Graham, then director of the Defense Intelligence Agency, who testified, "You have a third of [Soviet ground forces] facing west against NATO, a third of them in the middle . . . and a third of them opposite China." [7]

But the issue here is not precise numbers. Whether the CIA or Komer is right, whether Graham or Jordan is right, is not crucial. The point is that of the 2.7 percent increase in the Soviet defense budget, a significant part has gone to nonthreatening areas.

The third point in the original article noted that the Soviets are indeed producing a lot of tanks, ships, and artillery—what Komer appropriately calls a "bean count." But the point is that many of their beans have been sent to the Chinese border and that our beans are generally of a higher quality than theirs. [8]

Take ships as one example. They have more. They grind out dozens of small ships. But the United States has built more tons of ships than the Soviets every year since World War II. The United States concentrates ship tonnage in a few ships like the huge carriers, each with more firepower than the combined might of every Soviet ship of greater than 1,000 tons. If the low numbers of ships in the U.S. fleet is a problem, the fault lies not with the size of the defense budget but with the way the navy designs its ships.

Komer notes that it is production trends rather than whole numbers that are "most disturbing." Trends are important, but the Pentagon's figures on Soviet production rates neatly chose a period, 1972–74, that takes in a hump in Soviet production and a trough in American production. In several weapons areas, Soviet output dropped last year while ours rose. [9] As Komer said, it is the trends that matter.

Defense planning, of course, is based on something more sophisticated than bean counts. In recent years we have ceased planning to fight two-and-a-half wars simultaneously and have shifted our

---

[7] Joint Economic Committee, *Allocation of Resources in the Soviet Union and China—1975*, p. 134.

[8] Jordan and I have another bean count problem with throw-weight and bomber payload, which he says comes to 9 million pounds or one-third what I stated. This is a good example of what can be done with numbers. His numbers are right— if you assume that each Soviet missile carries its *maximum* payload but each of our B-52s carries only 15,000 pounds. But B-52s can carry 60,000 pounds on some models and 75,000 pounds on others. I said in the article that my calculation was based on the "maximum" payload.

[9] Les Aspin, "Budget Time at the Pentagon," *The Nation*, 3 April 1976, pp. 399-402.

forces to a one-and-a-half war strategy. At the same time, the Russians have confronted China and are presumably shifting from a one-war to a two-war strategy. The slow but steady increase in Soviet defense spending is driven in part by China's military expansion which has averaged 8 percent a year recently.[10]

The purpose of this long exercise, of course, is not really to discover how much the Soviets are spending on defense, but to determine how much the United States should spend on defense.

The Russians are increasing their defense budget by 2.7 percent per year, minus some percentage which is not threatening to the United States. What should be the U.S. response? To approve the President's proposed budget, which contains a real increase of 7 percent in overall defense spending and 22 percent in the weapons accounts, would be an overreaction.

I shall close on Komer's opening salvo. He suggests I am playing a numbers game. But let us look at some history when we talk of numbers games.

Back in 1959, Allen Dulles, then director of the CIA, argued that the Soviets had recently caught up to the United States in defense spending and he expected "the massive build-up to continue." [11]

Today the Pentagon argues that the Russians have only recently exceeded the United States in defense spending and Secretary Rumsfeld warns that "the momentum of the build-up shows no sign of slackening." [12]

I expect that in another fifteen years some administration figure will step forward to announce solemnly to the nation that the Russians have just overtaken us in defense spending and the momentum of their recent build-up will continue without slackening.

Where's the numbers game?

---

[10] Jordan also questions the Russians' motives and cites as evidence the new missiles and bomber they had in the works during the SALT negotiations. As I said in my article, the Russians clearly are not filled with love for the Western democracies, but in the missile field the Russians have long been playing a game of catch up with the United States. For example, all through the SALT talks they were trying to perfect the MIRV technology which we were already deploying. Furthermore, we were budgeting for at least one new intercontinental ballistic missile, three new submarine-launched ballistic missiles, and a new bomber during the SALT talks. By Jordan's logic our motives must also be questioned.

[11] Allen Dulles, address before Edison Electric Institute, text reprinted in the *New York Times*, 7 April 1959, p. 8.

[12] U.S. Defense Department, *Annual Defense Department Report, Fiscal Year 1977*, 27 January 1976, p. 4.

THE BUREAUCRATIC SALTSCREEN *

Robert L. Bartley

Robert L. Bartley, editor of the Wall Street Journal's *editorial page, questions the propriety of procedures used by the foreign policy bureaucracy and Henry Kissinger to negotiate the SALT I agreement and to handle possible violations of it. He accuses Kissinger of using secrecy and manipulation to acquire support for the accords. Bartley argues that recent Soviet deployments have violated the intent of the SALT agreements, but these have been ignored by the national security bureaucracy for reasons of its own. He questions whether future treaties negotiated in this bureaucratic environment would place any effective restrictions on the Soviet Union.*

Secretary of State Kissinger will be flying off to Moscow, perhaps as soon as this coming weekend, in an effort to firm up a second strategic arms pact with the Soviet Union. In doing so, he is brushing off both Soviet activities in Angola and charges by former U.S. defense officials that the Soviets are cheating on the first arms pact.

Some of these charges were detailed in an article in this space [the editorial page of the *Wall Street Journal*] on 19 December [1975]. Its theme was that the Soviets have been exhibiting shysterlike behavior on SALT I, which concerns easily monitored things like huge missile silos, and that thus it would be foolish to rely on SALT II to limit their deployment of small and elusive cruise missiles.

To the charges of Soviet misbehavior, Secretary Kissinger offers a fundamentally bureaucratic answer—government officialdom agrees there are no "violations," so forget it. Even at this late date in Mr. Kissinger's career such arguments apparently impress some people, at least to judge by a column in the *Washington Post* by Stephen S. Rosenfeld. So a few words are needed on Dr. Kissinger and the bureaucracy.

Specifically, Secretary Kissinger assures us that in the Verification Panel, a high-level inter-agency group on SALT, all decisions have been unanimous. In fact, the Verification Panel is a discussion and bargaining forum; whether there is any meaningful sense in which it makes decisions is a moot question. Certainly it does not operate by voting, as Mr. Kissinger's phraseology suggests. What actually

---

* Source: *The Wall Street Journal* (13 January 1976), p. 18.

happens there might be understood by studying the way SALT I was negotiated, as described by John Newhouse in *Cold Dawn*, a book written on information probably supplied with Mr. Kissinger's authorization.

One issue stalling the SALT I negotiations was submarine-launched ballistic missiles; the U.S. had a numerical lead but the Soviets were building rapidly. In April 1972, Mr. Kissinger—then President Nixon's security advisor—flew off to Moscow, so secretly that even the head of the U.S. SALT delegation did not know he was there. In those meetings Soviet Party Chairman Brezhnev said submarines could be included in the agreement if the Soviets were allowed sixty-two submarines with 950 missiles, compared with the then-existing U.S. total of forty-one submarines and 656 missiles.

A Verification Panel meeting had been scheduled for 28 April. One conceivable way to proceed would have been to put the Soviet offer on the table for discussion and decision, unanimous or otherwise. Instead, Mr. Kissinger pondered the problem of how to move what Mr. Newhouse describes as a "deal worked out" from the "back channel" into the "front channel." Mr. Kissinger ordered a briefing paper on what submarine numbers the Russians *"might propose"* (italics from the original). The mid-range number turned out to be sixty-two. As the meeting was convened, Mr. Newhouse reports, "some, though probably not all of the principals knew that Brezhnev had put forward an SLBM proposal with specific numbers."

In the meeting Mr. Kissinger bargained with Admiral Thomas H. Moorer, chairman of the joint chiefs of staff. The Pentagon wanted a speed-up of development of new Trident submarines, and Mr. Kissinger asked how many boats the Russians would have without an agreement by 1978, when the first Tridents could be ready. The answer was eighty, and Mr. Kissinger said the agreement should hold them to a lower number. Mr. Newhouse reports, "The meaning of the exchange between Kissinger and Moorer was clear to those who heard it. The Navy would have Trident, assuming congressional approval, and the President would have the support of the Chairman of the Joint Chiefs of Staff for an SLBM deal that gave the Soviets nearly half again as many missile-carrying submarines as the United States."

Arguably the Verification Panel was indeed the site of a budget decision on the Trident program. But the SALT deal had already been "worked out" between Mr. Kissinger and Secretary Brezhnev. Mr. Kissinger concealed this information from the Verification Panel as he bargained with and manipulated its members to win their acquiescence to the Soviet proposals. Now comes Secretary Kissinger to point to "unanimous" Verification Panel decisions as a reason for confidence in the judgments of government officialdom.

That the issue of Soviet compliance with SALT I has been treated in a similar fashion can scarcely be doubted by anyone who reads the documents recently released by Congressman Pike's Select Committee on Intelligence. A 1973 memo to the acting director of the CIA from Edward W. Proctor, deputy director for intelligence, complains that twenty-four days after detection of a possible violation, the information was still being withheld from, among others, Secretary of State Rogers, the head of our SALT delegation, and our representative to the Standing Consultative Commission, the Soviet-American body that deals with possible violations.

"A principal reason for establishment of the 'hold' on this information was to insure that there be no leakage while the Soviets were being queried on the matter," the memo reads. In short, Mr. Kissinger was again keeping U.S. officials ignorant while he tried to strike a bargain with the Russians. The CIA concern over Mr. Kissinger's habit of withholding information is summed up in the rather urgent advice to "get concrete assurance from Dr. Kissinger that the President is aware of the decision to withhold this information from key officials."

Another Pike Committee document is a memo of a phone conversation between a member of the NSC staff and the CIA director of strategic research. It reads in part, "in the reports of the intelligence community concerning SALT monitoring, Dr. Kissinger wanted to avoid any written judgments to the effect that the Soviets have violated any of the SALT agreements. If the Director believes that the Soviets may be in violation, this should be the subject of a memorandum from him to Dr. Kissinger. The judgment that a violation is considered to have occurred is one that will be made at the NSC level."

Having ordered the bureaucracy not to find violations, Secretary Kissinger now asks us to take comfort in the fact that the bureaucracy has found no violations.

To be fair, the words "NSC level" could in practice mean Mr. Kissinger's personal NSC staff, or they could mean the official members of the National Security Council. Dr. Kissinger has said that there is "no memorandum" by department heads or chiefs of staff raising "any of the issues" recently discussed. This is spectacularly untrue in at least one instance, since in his closing days as chief of naval operations, Admiral E. R. Zumwalt sent a personal letter to

President Nixon raising, among other things, Soviet compliance with SALT. Before the assembled NSC, the former President dismissed the letter as a "cheap shot."

Members of the NSC scarcely need to be told that the President had staked his political future, and later much of his political survival, on détente and SALT. His treatment of Admiral Zumwalt's letter served to bring home the point: Do not press the compliance issue unless you are prepared to resign.

With the accumulating evidence of withheld information, some senators have started to worry about whether anything was withheld from them when they ratified the 1972 accords. In particular, some of them are intrigued by Secretary Kissinger's 9 December statement that the Soviet Union has "specifically disavowed" American unilateral statements, particularly the one defining the "heavy" missile limited but left undefined in the formal pact. The senators would like to know the date of this "specific disavowal," since when ratification was pending Mr. Kissinger mentioned no such thing, though he did point to the terms of the unilateral statement as a "safeguard."

The Soviets have in fact deployed missiles that clearly breach the U.S. definition, in the process increasing their missile throw weight, or lifting power, to an extent other parts of the treaty were intended to preclude. Today, U.S. officialdom does not consider this a violation. The impression U.S. officialdom succeeded in leaving in 1972 is recorded by Mr. Newhouse:

> Language worked out in Helsinki probably assures adequate protection against any increase in the number of missiles in the SS-9 class; but it is nonetheless a bit vague and incomplete, lacking, for example, a definition of what constitutes a "heavy" missile. The Soviets were determined to keep it that way. And they did. Still, any violation of this language, let alone the letter, would probably oblige the United States to withdraw from the agreements. Moscow understands that.

An outsider has no chance, of course, to keep up with the bureaucratic politics being played this week in preparation for Mr. Kissinger's Moscow trip. But there are glimmers on what is happening with the cruise missile, a drone aircraft with super-accurate guidance. The weapon sharply raises the issue of "verification," or the American ability to detect Soviet violations.

The cruise missile is totally mobile, and small enough to fit in a submarine tube. It flies at the same altitudes and speeds as an ordinary aircraft. Based on familiar aviation technology, it need not be tested at full range. The vehicle is recoverable, and thus could record much data usually broadcast and subject to detection. The crucial guidance technology could conceivably be tested on an ordinary aircraft. For that matter, the Soviets already have a number of cruise missiles without the modern guidance; the verification problem is to tell when such guidance is developed and installed.

Forget it, Mr. Kissinger and his allies are arguing within the government. Officialdom has decreed that verification can be handled. A good part of the reasoning behind this assurance is that while the U.S. could not be sure of detecting any such tests, the Russians could not be sure the U.S. would fail to detect them. So Russians would not take the chance of blowing up the whole pact.

Sure, just as they would not take the chance of deploying missiles that breached the U.S. definition of "heavy."

When Secretary Kissinger goes to Moscow this weekend, he will be dealing with people who refused to define "heavy" and then ignored the stated U.S. definition, who built new ABM radars with no respect to the procedures the treaty requires under anything but a shyster's interpretation of their own statements, who justify missile silos as "command and control" centers though they have blow-away lids. In dealing with such people on something as elusive as the cruise missile, whatever an officialdom under pressure to reach an agreement might decree, the only safe assumption is this: A limit on the cruise missile will be a limit on the United States but not on the Soviet Union.

SALT ACCORDS DEBATE *

Henry M. Jackson, J. William Fulbright, Alan Cranston

The Senate's resolution approving the SALT I agreements included an amendment introduced by Senator Henry M. Jackson (Democrat, Washington) calling for equality in intercontinental strategic forces in future arms accords with the aim of maintaining the strategic balance between the U.S. and the U.S.S.R. Jackson contends that America's technological and geographical advantages will not permanently com-

---

* Source: *Congressional Record*, 92d Congress, 2d session, vol. 118, no. 130 (14 August 1972), pp. S13467-S13469, and vol. 118, no. 138 (7 September 1972), pp. S14280-S14283.

*pensate for fewer and smaller ICBMs and bombers. During the floor
debate on this amendment, Senators J. William Fulbright (Democrat,
Arkansas) and Alan Cranston (Democrat, California) countered that
the existence of American and allied nuclear forces based outside of
the United States (so-called forward-based systems) complicates
simple notions of nuclear parity.*

Mr. JACKSON. Mr. President, senators who share my view
that the Senate ought to go on record in support of the policy of the
United States to seek a follow-on agreement that limits the threat to
the survivability of our deterrent forces will welcome my amendment.
The first part does precisely that. It urges restraint on the part of the
Soviet Union by indicating that a failure to achieve a threat-limiting
agreement could jeopardize the supreme national interests of the
United States. In so doing, the amendment takes account of the fact
that while the interim agreement may have some slight effect on the
rate of growth of the Soviet threat to the survivability of our deterrent, it does not halt it. Therefore, should the threat overtake the
negotiation of a follow-on agreement at any time within the next
five years, our supreme national interests could be jeopardized. I will
be surprised, Mr. President, to learn that there is any substantial
opposition to this view within the Senate.

Mr. President, I have elsewhere described the present agreement
as providing the United States with "interim subparity." The agreement confers on the Soviets a 50 percent advantage in numbers of
land- and sea-based launchers and a 400 percent advantage in throw-
weight. Now, the argument is made that this enormous disparity in
numbers of launchers and throw-weight is offset by superior technology and numbers of warheads on our side. There is a certain
limited truth to this claim. It is not an enduring truth: for while
numbers are limited under the agreement, technology is not. It stands
to reason, therefore, that in the long run "superior" technology cannot be relied upon to offset inferior numbers.

The inability of technology to compensate for numbers is not
only true in general but is, in the present case, true for specific
reasons as well. The greatest part of our presumed technological
advantage lies in our lead over the Soviets in the development and
deployment of MIRV warheads on our missile forces.

This lead is not one that can be maintained at anything approaching our current margin. On the contrary, when the Soviets develop a
MIRV capability—and they are expected to do so at "any moment"—
the combination of that capability and their vastly superior throw

weight will give them, given time and effort on their part, superiority in numbers of warheads.

There is an enormous volume of misinformation on the subject of alleged U.S. advantages arising from technology and geography. There is no doubt that in the long run technology will tend toward equalization. How well I remember those who argued that the Soviets would require a decade or more to catch up with the United States in developing hydrogen weapons. The same sort of scientists who today argue that we can rest comfortably with inferior numbers of launchers because of an unbridgeable advantage in technology miscalculated by about 9½ out of 10 years back in 1947. The Russians, of course, were only months behind us, and our scientists were behind the eight ball.

As to geography, I have heard it argued—the chairman of the Foreign Relations Committee made the case himself last week—that owing to our possession of forward bases for our submarine fleet we need fewer submarines than the Soviets in order to maintain on-station times equal to theirs. Now, sea-based strategic forces are assuming increasing importance; so it is essential that we be correct on this point. Despite some statements to the contrary, the geographical asymmetries favor the Soviet submarine fleet and not our own. With the increased range such as that of the Soviet SSNX-8 submarine launched missile, the importance of forward bases is greatly diminished. Russian submarines will be on-station with respect to a large number of U.S. targets within one day's travel time from Murmansk or Petropavlovsk. This is not substantially different from the situation of our submarines operating out of their forward bases. What is more important, however, is that the Russians have a very large land mass between our submarines and their vulnerable points while we do not. Most of the U.S. points that are targets for Soviet submarine-launched missiles are coastal or near-coastal.

So there is little substance to the claim that we are in a favorable geographical situation.

The point I wish to make, Mr. President, is that, over the long run, there is no substitute for equal numbers of launchers taking account of throw-weight differentials. I believe that the Senate should join with our negotiators and administration spokesmen in rejecting, for the future, the sort of disparities that we have agreed to, on an interim basis, in the present agreement. And in so doing I believe that we ought to insist that the principle that was applied in the case of the ABM treaty—the principle of equality on which the Russians insisted—ought to be applied to a treaty on offensive weapons.

I was concerned, Mr. President, that our consent to the interim agreement, containing, as it does, the wide disparities to which I have referred, might be misunderstood as reflecting on the acceptability of such disparities in a follow-on treaty. In order to make the record clear I asked a number of witnesses before the Armed Services Committee to comment on this issue.

On 18 July, I asked Ambassador Gerard Smith, the director of the Arms Control and Disarmament Agency and head of our SALT delegation: "Would the present Interim Agreement be acceptable as a permanent agreement?"

Ambassador Smith replied: "Not to me."

I then directed the same question to other members of the SALT delegation. The former deputy secretary of defense and now assistant to the secretary of defense for SALT, Mr. Paul Nitze, said: "No." General Royal Allison, a member of the delegation and assistant to the chairman of the joint chiefs of staff for strategic arms negotiations, also said "No."

On 24 July, I directed a similar question to Secretary Laird, with respect to whether a SALT II agreement should continue the numerical relationships established in the interim agreement. Secretary Laird, speaking for the Administration, said:

> I would hope that in these negotiations we could move in the direction of equality as far as numbers and also as far as some of the other important areas dealing with offensive strategic weapon systems. I feel that this should be a very important thrust of our negotiations because this is very basic to the continued support of the obligations that we have undertaken with our friends and allies throughout the world in order to prevent the possibility of a nuclear exchange in the future.

The chief of naval operations, Admiral Zumwalt, testified:

> It is my view that in SALT II, we must achieve an equality of numbers. Just as the Soviets insisted on symmetry with regard to the ABM treaty, if we are going to go into a permanent treaty on the strategic side, I think we absolutely must insist on symmetry.

I know of no one in a responsible position in the Administration who is in disagreement with this widely expressed view.

My amendment provides the Senate with an opportunity to declare itself in favor of equality in a follow-on agreement; and I am certain that in view of the basic good sense of that position and the overwhelming testimony before us, we will act to affirm it.

Mr. President, the question of what is to be included in the computation of equal forces in a follow-on agreement is related to the difficult issue of our forward deployments in Europe which are dedicated to the defense of our European allies and which are at sea.

The intent of my amendment as it bears on this matter is, I believe, perfectly clear and straightforward. In stating that "the Congress recognizes the principle of United States-Soviet Union equality reflected in the antiballistic missile treaty" and that accordingly "the Congress requests the President to seek a future treaty that, *inter alia*, would not limit the United States to levels of intercontinental strategic forces inferior to the limits provided for the Soviet Union" it is unmistakably clear that so-called forward based systems, which are not intercontinental, should not be included in that calculation of equality. It is my view, and the intent of the pending amendment, that any eventual treaty must recognize the necessity that the intercontinental strategic forces of the U.S. and the U.S.S.R., by which I mean to include ICBMs, submarine-launched nuclear missiles, and intercontinental range bombers of the two powers, should bear an equal relationship to one another. This says nothing about the eventual role of or disposition of the issue of forward based systems.

With regard to the question of forward based systems it has been my understanding, as clearly set forth by representatives of the Administration in testimony before the Senate, that the United States has refused to negotiate the issue of forward based systems in a bilateral U.S.-U.S.S.R. negotiation. I understand that this position was based on the entirely justifiable view that such systems are part and parcel of our alliance defense commitment and could not appropriately be considered without satisfactory alliance participation. I fully support the Administration's view on this matter and there is nothing in my amendment which in any way contradicts that position.

My amendment, in its final sentences, simply points to the need for a vigorous program of research, development, and modernization leading to a prudent strategic posture. I wish to emphasize that adoption of this language is not intended to bear upon the wisdom of any particular procurement item. Decisions on procurement ought to be taken on a case-by-case basis. So while it is useful for the Senate to go on record to the effect that we must continue our efforts in the research, development, and modernization area, senators can rest assured that this does not constitute an endorsement of any particular weapons system or any particular research and development effort. I emphasize this, Mr. President, because I would not wish senators

367

to gain the impression that in voting for my amendment they are committing themselves to any future action on procurement items.

Mr. President, I began my remarks by observing that international agreements always involve unwritten hopes and expectations and reservations. Sometimes it helps to set them down. In the present case I hope, and I am sure my colleagues share this hope, that a follow-on agreement will limit the threat to the survivability of our strategic deterrent forces. It is, in my view, well to underline this hope by language that lets the Soviets know that a failure to achieve this result would jeopardize our supreme national interests. My amendment does that.

I fully expect that our negotiators at SALT II will insist upon equality just as the Soviets insisted upon equality in the ABM treaty. The issue of whether the present agreement adds up to equality is beside the point; and there will be differences of opinion on that. But what I am certain we can agree on is the necessity that we not accept in SALT II levels of intercontinental strategic weapons that are inferior to the levels of intercontinental forces permitted for the Soviet Union. My amendment does that.

Finally, I am confident that the Senate would wish to reaffirm its confidence in the importance of our research and development efforts.

Mr. President, the overriding hope and expectation of all of us is that the SALT deliberations will eventually produce a treaty that will assure the survivability, and therefore the credibility, of our deterrent posture. Such a treaty would be an enormous step toward world peace.

Mr. President, I want to see the Senate of the United States play a full and equal role in the effort to bring about such a treaty. The place to start is by giving our advice as well as our consent to the present agreement. We have an obligation to give direction to the future efforts of the government on SALT policy. I believe that direction must be toward survivable forces and toward equality. I am confident the Senate shares this view and that it will act to support my amendment.

* * *

Mr. FULBRIGHT. The senator from Washington stated a moment ago that he had over forty cosponsors. I think he raises a question that is very important. It is my belief that some of those cosponsors do not understand the way the senator from Washington uses the word "equality." In his statement here a moment ago to the Senate, and as he made it before, he used the word "equality" without qualification. He said all his amendment seeks to do in the future is to lay down guidelines that our negotiators should seek equality.

I think I would understand and I think many members in the public would understand that to mean overall equality, and that is overall equality of nuclear weapons, equality of capacity to develop new ones, either offensive or defensive weapons. That is what I take the statement to mean.

I do not believe it is understood that what the senator from Washington is really saying is that—regardless of the degree of superiority we may have in the field of airplanes and the capacity to deliver nuclear weapons by airplanes or from forward bases, or our superiority in other areas—these are excluded from his concept of equality and that all that the senator is contemplating when he uses the word "equality" is in numbers of intercontinental missiles.

I believe in view of that circumstance, and aside from others, that a thorough discussion of the significance of the senator from Washington's amendment is necessary if the Senate is to vote intelligently and with understanding on what is involved in this agreement.

Within the last few days there have been indications that this is the way at least the Russians understand the agreement. The article I referred to earlier in *Izvestia* makes clear the Russians believe this amendment is an effort to undermine the interim agreement, it is an indication of lack of desire on our part to proceed with significant restrictions on nuclear arsenals.

* * *

I emphasize that this interim agreement is not a routine matter in my opinion. It could be the most significant move by this Congress in many years, if it is properly implemented and if we accept it in the spirit in which it was intended at the time of the summit meeting. It, along with the ABM agreement, could be a landmark action by Congress and the country if it is carried through properly, and by that I mean if we accept genuine parity or sufficiency, to use the word of the President, in this area rather than trying to manipulate this whole matter to the point that we have superiority and continuing superiority.

We had superiority for a long time. But the clear fact is that if we insist upon superiority, there will be no further progress in the control of armaments. On the contrary, it would result in a vast increase, in the acceleration of the arms race, in my opinion, because the reaction against the failure of Phase II in the SALT agreements would be an increase in the arms race because of the disappointment, as well as because of suspicion that would arise then, on the part of both sides, that the other side was going for that myth of first strike capability. I do not believe first strike capability is a possibility under present conditions, or the foreseeable conditions, but it is a concept which has been sold and much talked about and could be easily distorted into a justification for an unlimited arms race.

*   *   *

Mr. JACKSON. May I say I think it is amazing for the chairman of the Foreign Relations Committee to tell over forty members of the Senate that they do not know what the Jackson amendment is about, that they do not know what equality in intercontinental strategic forces is about . . . My amendment does not say intercontinental strategic missiles; it says intercontinental strategic forces. Read the amendment. That includes bombers. That includes missiles fired from land bases. It includes missiles fired from submarines.

Mr. FULBRIGHT. If that is true, why does the senator object to the words *overall strategic?*

Mr. JACKSON. For the obvious reason.

Mr. FULBRIGHT. What is the reason?

Mr. JACKSON. For the obvious reason that the addition of the term *overall* would of necessity mean more than my amendment intends. I have said repeatedly that the intercontinental strategic forces to be balanced on the basis of equality are ICBMs, SLBMs and intercontinental range bomber forces. I am not including, for example, tactical weapons. Addition of the word *overall* could prejudice the position of our NATO partners and other allies who are not participating directly in the SALT negotiations.

Mr. FULBRIGHT. Of course, we are getting into the type of debate which is appropriate to the senator's amendment. I think that is quite proper. The only thing is, I think it would be more appropriate to make these arguments—and we shall make them—when and if the senator's amendment is offered. They are legitimate questions of our differences of view. But I do not think it is clear at all from the senator's amendment and what has been said in the press that he is talking about overall nuclear equality in strategic weapons. It is not only weapons in Europe that we have, but we have weapons all around the periphery of the Soviet Union. We have them in Turkey. We have control of when they are used. We have them in the Far East. We have them on aircraft carriers. We have fourteen of them commissioned now, and we soon will have sixteen, and the Russians have none. Are these intercontinental or not? If they fly off an aircraft carrier in the North Sea, I admit they are not from our continent, but they are the same kind of destructive weapon.

. . . I reiterate that when the senator presents his proposal that all he asks is equality—equality of intercontinental strategic forces—I say that the average person would be impressed. Certainly I would be included in the definition of an average person. If he came to me, I would say, 'Sure, I am for equality." Everybody is for equality. The interim agreement is for equality. The President says it gives equality—at least equality.

The argument can be made that the Russians have inferiority at the moment, and that is why the permission was given in the interim agreement to increase their numbers of submarines.

. . . I suspect a number of senators think the senator means over-all equality, that he takes all the weapons systems, offensive, defensive, puts them up against the Russians, and that there is approximate equality. That is what the interim agreement actually provides for, but the senator is offering an amendment which does not say that at all, and it is clear that is not proposed. His amendment calls for numerical equality in intercontinental ballistic missile forces, and he ignores all the other areas of nuclear weaponry where we have advantages or superiority, including the weapons that we already have in place around the periphery of the Soviet Union, on our aircraft carriers, and in Europe.

The other members of the Armed Services Committee—he does not have to take my word about it; the senator from Missouri [Stuart Symington] has had considerable experience, and is a former secretary of the air force; he has said and will say that these weapons in Europe can be put on a fighter-bomber and, with one refueling, delivered to Moscow. The weapon does not come from the United States, but a two- or three-kiloton weapon delivered on Moscow, coming from Germany, is just as destructive as one coming out of a submarine.

All of these factors were taken into consideration by the President. Dr. Kissinger, at the White House, described this, and answered all of the questions as to whether there was parity as well as sufficiency, and he said there was. He said in no uncertain terms that this was not an imprudent agreement which leaves the United States in an inferior position.

Inferiority is clearly the implication in the senator's amendment. It is very cleverly written. He says, "Strategic forces inferior to the limit provided for the Soviet Union." The implication is clear that we are inferior in our strategic forces.

Well, what does he mean by our strategic forces? Again he comes back; the only thing he can mean is ICBMs.

Nobody denies that there is a numerical inferiority. However, our country, years ago, deliberately rejected the idea of weapons such as the SS-9s and the Titans, big multimegaton weapons. We deliberately chose the smaller, one-megaton Minuteman, because it is a more efficient way to use our capacity for destruction. . . .

Mr. JACKSON. Would the senator say that an SS-9 might be designed for a first-strike capability, in order to knock out a hardened site? Otherwise, why would they want to have a twenty-five-megaton warhead capability? . . . The forces we sought were totally different. We never sought a first-strike capability to knock out hardened sites. That is the difference, and that is what is disturbing about the huge Soviet missiles and the still larger missiles they are now developing.

Mr. FULBRIGHT. The senator assumes all of this. I do not think he has any basis for that at all. He is trying to read the minds of the Russians.

The first effort we made was to develop a big one, bigger than we now have. We were far ahead in technology, and so on, and our own military people, looking at it, decided that it was less efficient to put ten or twenty or twenty-five megatons in one missile, less efficient than to put the same or less megatonnage in four or five missiles, for various reasons. First, there is flexibility; you can fire at more targets more easily. It is more accurate; and four megatons, in the calculations I have, which come from expert sources, four megatons properly delivered in a Minuteman will cause the equivalency, they call it, in destruction, of sixteen megatons, or about four to one. If you concentrate it all in one, it is not efficient.

We started out that way, and simply as a matter of sophistication and knowledge, we decided it was more efficient to go to the Minuteman.

I think that is true. Everything we have been doing is to that effect, that that is correct. We are not about to go back to the big one.

When you MIRV a weapon, you have fewer megatons, but they divided it up. Why did they divide it up? Because it is more efficient to put MIRVed missiles in submarines. They are still so destructive no one can withstand it. . . .

Mr. JACKSON. Did the senator want to leave the record as I understood he left it, that we had the choice of several warheads for Minuteman, and could deliver up to a total of four megatons? Is that what the senator said?

Mr. FULBRIGHT. No; four separate megatons, I mean four missiles, one megaton per missile, is a more efficient way to use it than one big missile. We decided that years ago, more efficient than one missile with ten or fifteen megatons in it. We made the decision that it was more efficient and more effective.

Mr. JACKSON. It is not a matter, I would say, of efficiency. I think it is a matter of strategic policy.

Mr. FULBRIGHT. I mean efficiency in destructive power, the deliverability of destructive power. . . .

Mr. CRANSTON. The senator from Washington, in colloquy with the senator from Arkansas, stated that the trouble with the word *overall* was that nuclear tactical weapons would then be included.

Would the senator accept the word *overall* if it was followed by the words *exclusive of nuclear tactical weapons?*

Mr. JACKSON. What would it mean then? Can the senator explain what it would mean?

Mr. CRANSTON. It would mean that all relevant factors in measuring sufficiency of force would be considered but nuclear tactical weapons would not be considered.

Mr. JACKSON. What relevant factors?

Mr. CRANSTON. There are many factors that we have gone over in this debate. The great ring of forward position forces that are used on sea, in the air, and from the ground. You would consider more than simply the number of missiles and throw-weight.

Mr. JACKSON. Well, I would just point out that obviously you have to consider the relative posture, as we are talking about it, first in intercontinental strategic terms, to determine whether or not you are going to have any basis of equality or parity.

When the Soviets get 1,618 land-based missiles, and we have our thousand, when the Soviets get 950 launching tubes for sixty-two Y-class submarines, and we have forty-four ballistic missile submarines with a total of 710 tubes, I think it is apparent to the people of this country and to members of the Senate that this is not equality; and when you add on top of that that they have a four-to-one advantage in throw-weight, that is, in the capacity of these items that we are talking about, it is clear that we have not achieved parity.

I remember in the arguments over the ABM that the contention against the ABM was that when the Soviet Union got around our number of land-based missiles, they would stop development of ICBMs at around a thousand. Here they are at 1,618 already.

You know, you have to ask, Why was not some determination made by those who constantly worry about U.S. forces to get the Russians to cut back and reduce theirs? There is a golden opportunity for the Russians to agree to a thousand land-based missiles and to the forty-two Y-class submarines they now have, or to forty-four.

There is a golden opportunity, Madam President, to have a real arms limitation agreement that will save money and resources on both sides.

Mr. FULBRIGHT. Madam President, this comes back, I submit to the senator from Washington, to the same argument as before. One reason the Russians thought they should have more ICBMs was that they had no capacity to put weapons around our borders, as we have around theirs in such places as Turkey, Korea, and elsewhere as well as in aircraft carriers. They do not have a single aircraft carrier.

This is a matter of each country's decision as to how it looks after its defense. Not having the capacity to do what we have done, to have in being 7,000 warheads in Europe and other large numbers on aircraft carriers, and so on, scattered around the world, how do they offset that to reach even a degree of equality? They cannot do that under the situation in which they operate.

The senator is taking one area—ICBMs. He talks about the submarines. We believe, and we have been told, that we have superior submarines. We already have superior submarines. They are beginning to develop a missile that can travel a couple of hundred miles more than ours, but we have underway the Trident submarine, and so forth. There is the ever-increasing sophistication.

I think that the way the senator presents his case is very deceptive. I would have thought the same thing. If I had no background on it and the senator approached me cold and said, "Aren't you for equality with the Russians on strategic missiles?" I would say, "Sure, I am."

He would say, "Would you cosponsor my bill?"

I would say, "Sure. I'm for equality."

But it never would have occurred to me that the kind of equality he is talking about is superiority—equality in one area, and we are clearly superior in the others.

It can mean nothing, in truth, but superiority if we accept the senator's idea that we must have 1,618 ICBMs and 740 submarine tubes, just what the Russians could have, and they all, of course, would have to be exactly of the same explosive power and length. The whole idea that this one category should be balanced off nicely so that each side has the same amount is absolutely irrelevant and is a wrong way to look at it.

When you consider the power of destruction of one-fourth of all these weapons on the other country, in view of the fact that we have already agreed to the ABM treaty, in which each country has said it is not going to proceed to develop a defense against these weapons, then we do not need 1,600.

374

Then comes into play what the President has called sufficiency. I submit that 400 on each side is sufficient, because the other side has said, "We do not propose to develop and we do not have a defense against intercontinental ballistic missiles or against submarine missiles." The only kind of defense either would have at the present time, I suppose, is some kind of defense against those missiles delivered by airplanes, because we both have antiaircraft defenses of some kind, but we have nothing that could deal with a submarine launched missile or an intercontinental ballistic missile. So when you get above 400, which often has been used as a figure adequate to destroy three-fourths of each other's industrial capacity and kill 300 million people—that is enough to completely demoralize and destroy the other country's society.

So in talking about this, the senator is confusing the issue by equating nuclear weapons with conventional weapons. It is true that there is considerable merit in saying, with respect to conventional weapons, that we ought to have so many .45s against their .45s, so many different guns. There is some relevance in that argument. But with nuclear weapons, if there is no defense against it, I submit that the senator is playing around with the numbers game of a thousand or sixteen hundred or two thousand, and it is utterly meaningless. It has no significance. The concept of equality under those circumstances is meaningless.

The idea of first-strike capability seems to me also to be meaningless, because there is literally no possibility of a straight first-strike capability on either side with weapons of this kind and deployed as they are, including submarine weapons. Assume, for example—and I do not think they could—that the Russians could destroy 1,000 Minutemen, which is a fantastic and ridiculous assumption, what are they going to do about the submarines?

A first-strike capability means that the country attacked could not effectively retaliate. With 700 or 500 or even 400, they could render unacceptable damage to the other.

So I think the whole idea of equality, as submitted by the senator, is simply not a meaningful term under the circumstances, because it is not understood that way, and I would not have understood it that way. . . .

Mr. JACKSON. The senator has dwelt at great length on the subject of the 7,000 warheads in Europe. Would the senator give the Senate the benefit of his views as to the number of bombs or warheads we could put on Soviet soil in connection with a move on our part and, second, how many we could put on Soviet soil in the event of a Soviet first strike against our forces in Europe?

Mr. FULBRIGHT. This has been discussed, as I have said, at considerable length. The senator from Missouri discussed it the other day. He stated time and again that with one refueling, the fighter bombers, of which we have several hundred, could take a nuclear weapon of about 200 kilotons, I think he said ——

Mr. JACKSON. How many weapons?

Mr. FULBRIGHT. To Moscow.

If the senator is asking how many they could shoot down, nobody knows how efficient they are, but if you send enough of them over, you can. . . . We have plenty of weapons.

ASSURING STRATEGIC STABILITY *

Paul H. Nitze

In this article Paul H. Nitze contends that the Soviet Union is attempting to acquire a theoretical nuclear war-winning capability through the expansion of its nuclear arsenal and civil defense programs. Russia possesses expansionist aims and is able to pursue them in the current détente environment. The SALT process has failed to increase stability because it has focused on overall delivery system quantities, allowing the development of a large throw-weight imbalance. In order to restore the effectiveness of the United States nuclear deterrent, steps should be taken to decrease missile vulnerability through adoption of a mobile ICBM system and to increase missile quality.

Even though the translation of the Vladivostok Accord on strategic arms into a SALT II treaty has not yet been resolved, I believe it is now timely to take stock of the strategic arms balance toward which the United States and the Soviet Union would be headed under the terms of such a treaty. To that end it is necessary to raise certain basic questions about the maintenance of strategic stability—in terms of minimizing both the possibility of nuclear war and the possibility that nuclear arms may be used by either side as a means of decisive pressure in key areas of the world.

---

* Source: *Foreign Affairs* (January 1976), pp. 207-232.

It appears to be the general belief that while such strategic stability may not be assured by the SALT agreements, it is not and will not be substantially endangered—that on the contrary it has been furthered by the SALT negotiations and agreements since 1969— and that in any event the best hope of stability lies in further pursuit of negotiations with the aim of reducing the level of strategic weapons and delivery systems on both sides. Unfortunately—and to the profound regret of one who has participated both in the SALT negotiations and in a series of earlier U.S. decisions designed to stabilize the nuclear balance—I believe that each of these conclusions is today without adequate foundation.

On the contrary, there is every prospect that under the terms of the SALT agreements the Soviet Union will continue to pursue a nuclear superiority that is not merely quantitative but designed to produce a theoretical war-winning capability. Further, there is a major risk that, if such a condition were achieved, the Soviet Union would adjust its policies and actions in ways that would undermine the present détente situation, with results that could only resurrect the danger of nuclear confrontation or, alternatively, increase the prospect of Soviet expansion through other means of pressure.

While this highly disturbing prospect does not mean that strategic arms limitation should for a moment be abandoned as a U.S. (and world) goal, the practical fact we now face is that a SALT II treaty based on the Vladivostok Accord would *not* provide a sound foundation for follow-on negotiations under present trends. If, and only if, the United States now takes action to redress the impending strategic imbalance, can the Soviet Union be persuaded to abandon its quest for superiority and to resume the path of meaningful limitations and reductions through negotiation.

Finally, I believe that such corrective action *can* be taken: (a) within the framework of the Vladivostok Accord; (b) with costs that would increase the strategic arms budget marginally above present levels (themselves less than half the strategic arms budget we supported from 1956 through 1962, if the dollar values are made comparable); (c) with results that would encourage the diversion of the Soviet effort from its present thrust and in directions compatible with long-range strategic stability. At the close of this article I shall outline the key elements in such a corrective program.

II

Let us start with a brief review of the overall state of Soviet-American relations. The use of the word *détente*, in its current sense, began in 1971. U.S. efforts to improve its relations with the Soviet Union go back to 1933. They dominated the war and the immediate postwar period, and the early years of the Eisenhower Administration. They formed an important strand of U.S. foreign policy in both the Kennedy and Johnson Administrations. The word *détente* as currently used implies something different from these efforts; it implies that their goal has now been achieved and that all that remains to be done is to make détente "irreversible."

The chain of events leading to the present situation goes back to the Sino-Soviet split and the great buildup of Soviet forces facing China. There were about fifteen Soviet divisions facing China in the mid-1960s; between 1968 and 1972 the number grew to at least forty-five divisions. This caused the Chinese Communists to be deeply concerned about the danger of an attack by the Soviet Union on China. The Chinese turned to the one power that could help deter such an attack; they opened the Ping-Pong diplomacy that resulted in the so-called normalization of U.S. relations with China.

Mr. Nixon was, I think, correct in taking the position that he wished good relations with both China and the U.S.S.R. and did not want an alliance with either. Moscow, however, wanted to be sure that the new relationship between China and ourselves did not deepen into something closer to an alliance and thus impede Soviet policy toward China. For this and other reasons the Russians began to go out of their way to be friendly to Mr. Nixon and Mr. Kissinger. They opened up a vista of relaxation of tensions and of a growing collaboration between the United States and the Soviet Union. In 1972 not only were the SALT I agreements—the Anti-Ballistic Missile (ABM) Treaty and the Interim Agreement—entered into, but also there was signed at Moscow a document called Basic Principles of Relations between the United States and the Soviet Union. Together with a subsequent agreement signed in Washington in 1973, this laid out what appeared to be a good basis for continuing relations between the U.S.S.R. and ourselves. Among other things, these agreements called for collaboration to see to it that crisis situations in other parts of the world did not build up into confrontations which could increase the risk of war between the two countries. It was understood that this collaboration was to have special reference to Southeast Asia and to the Middle East. These bilateral agreements were accompanied by the Paris agreements with respect to Vietnam, and the Soviet Union was among those guaranteeing that the Paris agreements would be implemented and abided by.

These understandings, however, produced no positive Soviet actions. With respect to the final North Vietnamese takeover in Southeast Asia, the Soviets actually took actions to help the North Vietnamese violate the agreements. With respect to the Middle East, it is hard to sustain the argument that is often made that the Soviets exercised restraint in the October 1973 crisis. There appears to have been little that they refrained from doing to encourage and make possible the attack by Egypt and Syria on Israel and the OPEC action on oil prices and the embargo. The Soviets not only trained and equipped the Egyptians and the Syrians for their surprise attack, but also failed to warn us when they knew that an attack was imminent. When the battle turned against the attackers, they threatened to intervene with their forces.

These two experiences in Southeast Asia and in the Middle East are bound to make us skeptical that the Soviet leaders are in fact moving toward any lasting reduction in tensions, or any abandonment of expansionist aims. A further ground for skepticism comes from what Soviet leaders are saying to their own people, and especially what they are saying in authoritative pronouncements aimed at leadership circles. Here readings of the past year are all too clear. To take but one example, there were published in January 1975 companion articles, one by Boris Ponomarev, a deputy member of the Politburo, the other by Aleksandr Sobolev, a leading theoretician, each arguing that the evolution of the correlation of forces—in which they include not only military but economic and social forces—has moved very favorably from the standpoint of the Soviet Union over recent years.[1] Hence, they say, it is now possible to shift the target of Communist action from the formerly colonial world to the developed world— particularly Europe. This shift in target is made possible by two things: one of them is "détente" and the other is "nuclear parity" (as they interpret the term, in a way we shall examine shortly).

In the sum total there are strong grounds for concluding that in Soviet eyes "détente" is not that different from what we used to call the "cold war." When we talked about the "cold war" we were in part emphasizing the fact that despite the deep hostility of the U.S.S.R. to the West in general and to the United States in particular, it would be a terrible thing if there were to be a "hot war" with the

---

[1] B. N. Ponomarev, "The Role of Socialism in Modern World Development," *Problemy Mira i Sotsializma* [Problems of peace and socialism] (January 1975), pp. 4-13; A. I. Sobolev, "Questions of the Strategy and Tactics of the Class Struggle at the Present Stage of the General Crisis of Capitalism," *Rabochiy Klass in Sovremennyy Mir* [The working class and the contemporary world] (January 1975), pp. 3-20.

Soviet Union. When the Soviets use the word *détente* in their internal writings, they make it clear that they intend *détente* to mean the same thing as *peaceful coexistence*. Peaceful coexistence, they make it clear, implies no change in their basic objectives, while they expect that current tactics will weaken the West and strengthen the socialist states.[2]

III

However one reads these broader signs of present Soviet behavior, a prime touchstone of the reality of détente—not only now but for the future—must lie in the area of strategic arms. If the Soviets are acting (and negotiating) in a way that gives promise of a stable nuclear balance (with meaningful reduction in due course), then the future of détente is clearly much brighter. If they are not, however, then the disturbing signs must be taken more seriously, and the long-term dangers are great indeed.

Let us begin by discussing the similarities and contrasts between Soviet and American views on certain strategic questions.

"Is the avoidance of war—particularly a nuclear war—between the two countries desirable?" On this question I think both sides are in agreement. However, there is a certain difference of approach. Clausewitz once said that the aggressor never wants war; he would prefer to achieve his objectives without having to fight for them. The Soviets take seriously their doctrine that the eventual worldwide triumph of socialism is inevitable; that they are duty bound to assist this process; and that, as the process progresses, the potential losers may stand at some point and feel impelled to fight back. On the U.S. side some say that there is no alternative to peace and therefore to détente. This attitude misses two points. The first is that capitulation is too high a price for free men. The second is that high-quality deterrence, not unilateral restraint to the point of eroding deterrence, is the surest way of avoiding a nuclear war.

This thus leads to a second pair of questions: "Is nuclear war unthinkable? Would it mean the end of civilization as we know it?" We in the United States tend to think that it is, and this view prevailed (except for a small group of believers in preventive war, who never had strong policy influence) even in the periods when the United States enjoyed a nuclear monopoly and, at a later time, a clear theoretical war-winning capability.[3] When the effort was made in the late

---

[2] See comments by Aleksey Rumiantsev, at a conference sponsored by *Problemy Mira i Sotsializma* (summer 1975).

[3] To see how top officials viewed American nuclear power even in the period of American monopoly, one can now consult the recently declassified text of the

1950s and early 1960s to create a significant civil defense capability, public resistance soon aborted the effort, so that today the United States has only the most minute preparations in this area. Rather, Americans have thought throughout the last thirty years in terms of deterring nuclear war, with the debate centering on how much effort is necessary to maintain deterrence, to keep nuclear war unthinkable.

In the Soviet Union, the view has been quite different. Perhaps initially because of the U.S. monopoly, Soviet leaders from the outset discounted the impact of nuclear weapons to their people. But as the Soviet nuclear capability grew, the Soviet leaders still declined to depict nuclear war as unthinkable or the end of civilization. On the contrary, they directed, and still direct, a massive and meticulously planned civil defense effort, with expenditures that run at approximately a billion dollars a year (compared to U.S. civil defense expenditures of approximately $80 million a year).[4] The average Soviet citizen is necessarily drawn into this effort, and the thinking it represents appears to permeate the Soviet leadership. In the Soviet civil defense manual issued in large numbers beginning in 1969 and 1970, the estimate is made that implementation of the prescribed evacuation and civil defense procedures would limit the civilian casualties to 5 to 8 percent of urban population or 3 to 4 percent of the total population—even after a direct U.S. attack on Soviet cities. The Soviets may well overestimate the effectiveness of their civil defense program, but what is plain is that they have made, for twenty years or more, an approach to the problem of nuclear war that does assume, to a degree incomprehensible to Americans (or other Westerners), that nuclear war could happen, and that the Soviet Union could survive.

These differences in approach and attitude appear to be basic and deeply rooted. In essence, Americans think in terms of deterring nuclear war almost exclusively. The Soviet leaders think much more of what might happen in such a war. To the extent that humanitarian and moral objections to the use of nuclear weapons exist in the Soviet Union—as of course they do—such objections are subordinated for

---

NSC 68 policy paper dated in the spring of 1950. Even though Soviet nuclear capacity (after the first Soviet test of August 1949) was assessed as small for some years to come, that paper rejected any idea of reliance on American nuclear power for the defense of key areas. To be sure, in the 1950s under John Foster Dulles, the United States had a declaratory policy of "massive retaliation." But in the actual confrontations of that period, this declaratory policy was not in fact followed; instead, conventional force was used, for example in the Lebanon crisis of 1958 and, less directly, in the Offshore Islands crisis of the same year. After 1961, massive retaliation was abandoned.

[4] Eugene Wigner, "The Atom and the Bomb," *Christian Science Monitor* (13 November 1974), p. 4.

practical planning purposes to what Soviet leaders believe to be a realistic view.

It may be argued that these differences are more apparent than real, and that with the passage of time and the emergence of near-equality in the respective nuclear capabilities the differences are today less significant. Unfortunately, as the civil defense picture suggests, the trend in comparative nuclear weapons capabilities has if anything accentuated them.

That this is so can be seen in the more concrete realm of nuclear strategic concepts, and the postures that result from them. Often overrefined or expressed in terms hard for the layman to grasp, the range of strategic nuclear concepts available to any nuclear-weapons nation in fact boils down roughly to five:

1. Minimum Deterrence. This means a capacity to destroy a few key cities with little if any counterforce capacity to attack a hostile nation's military forces. In essence, it relies on the threat alone to deter. As between the Soviet Union and the United States, in the event deterrence failed, this level of American capacity would concede to the Soviet Union the potential for a military and political victory. The Soviets would risk U.S. retaliation against a portion of their industry and population, if our action policy in the event deterrence failed turned out to be the same as our declaratory policy before deterrence failed. To reduce this risk of retaliation, the Soviets could limit their attack to U.S. forces and continue to hold the U.S. population as hostage. In sum, the effect of this level of deterrence would be to provide limited deterrence of a full-scale attack on the U.S. population. It would have less strength in deterring a Soviet attack on U.S. forces or on allies whose security is essential to our own.

2. Massive Urban-Industrial Retaliation. As the name implies, this posture is designed to destroy many cities, many millions of people and much productive capacity, and to do so on an assured second-strike basis. This level of deterrence, sometimes called assured destruction, would concede to the Soviet Union the potential for a military victory if deterrence failed, but (it would be anticipated) would make any such victory worthless in political terms. This form of deterrence differs from minimum deterrence largely in the degree of damage to Soviet industry and population it would threaten.

3. Flexible Response. In this form of deterrence the United States would have the capability to react to a Soviet counterforce attack without going immediately to a counter-city attack. It would thus increase the credibility of deterrence. The question of military or political victory if deterrence fails would depend upon the net surviving destructive capacity of the two sides after the initial counterforce exchanges. If the net surviving capacity after such a flexible response were grossly to favor the Soviet Union, or if each limited exchange placed the United States in a progressively weaker relative position, we are back to the minimum deterrence or massive urban-industrial retaliation situation, depending on the amount of surviving effective nuclear capability on the U.S. side.

4. Denial of a Nuclear-War-Winning Capability to the Other Side. This means a nuclear posture such that, even if the other side attacked first and sought to destroy one's own strategic striking power, the result of such a counterforce exchange would be sufficiently even and inconslusive that the duel would be extremely unattractive to the other side. This level of deterrence, in addition to deterring an attack on U.S. population centers, should also deter a Soviet attack on U.S. forces or those of its allies. In practice, against any major nuclear nation, the posture would also include a capacity for effective massive urban-industrial retaliation if such a strategy were called for.

5. A Nuclear-War-Winning Capability. This would be a position so superior that, whatever the initial forms of nuclear exchange, one's own surviving capacity would be enough to destroy the war-making ability of the other nation without comparable return damage. Such a U.S. posture would deter any Soviet attack on the United States and could also limit other serious Soviet military initiatives contrary to U.S. and allied interests. However, Soviet weapons technology and program momentum are such that the United States probably could not obtain this capability.

A review of the choices made by the United States and the Soviet Union among these five concepts goes, I believe, further than any other form of analysis in explaining and clarifying the changes in the strategic balance since 1945. Until roughly 1954, the United States retained nuclear superiority without extraordinary effort. By the late 1950s, the vulnerability of American bomber bases (bombers then being the only effective delivery method) emerged as a serious weakness in the American posture.[5] This weakness, and the rapid advances in missile technology of the period, led the United States between 1956

---

[5] See Albert Wohlstetter, "The Delicate Balance of Terror," *Foreign Affairs* (January 1959), pp. 211-234.

and 1962 to place great emphasis on ensuring the survivability of its nuclear striking power; average strategic obligational authority during these years was about $18 billion a year in 1974 dollars.[6] As a result the feared intercontinental ballistic missile (ICBM) "gap" of the 1960 presidential campaign never in fact became reality, but on the contrary the United States reestablished a clearly superior nuclear capability by 1961–62. This was the situation at the time of the only true nuclear confrontation of the postwar period, the Cuban missile crisis of the fall of 1962.

Up to that point something approaching a war-winning capability seemed to most Americans the best possible form of deterrence, and thus desirable. However, as it became clear that the Soviet Union, too, was developing massive and survivable missile delivery capabilities, this view changed to the belief that even though a nuclear war might be won in a purely military sense, it could not be won in a political sense. That led to the further view that mutual deterrence through mutually assured destruction was the best feasible objective.

I have explained elsewhere at greater length the decisions of the early 1960s, in which I was one of those who participated with Robert McNamara, then secretary of defense.[7] In essence, the United States opted at that point to stress technological improvement rather than expanded force levels. While numerical comparisons were not ignored, the basic aim was an underlying condition of what may be called "crisis stability," a situation where neither side could gain from a first strike, and of "mutual assured destruction," where each side would have a fully adequate second-strike capability to deter the other. In such a condition it was believed that neither could realistically threaten the other in the area of strategic weapons, and that the result would be much greater stability and higher chances of the peaceful resolution of crises if they did occur. While nuclear weapons would always be a major deterrent, the conventional arms balance at any point of confrontation would remain important (as it had been in the Berlin crisis of 1958–62 and also in the Cuban missile crisis itself). In short, the aim was to downgrade nuclear weapons as an element in U.S.–Soviet competition and to prepare the way for systematic reduc-

---

[6] It should be noted that this figure refers to the amounts obligated annually for equipment, materiel, and personnel that can be directly attributed to the program mission, including all support costs that follow directly from the number of combat units. It does not include allocable costs of such related activities as communications, general support, and intelligence.

[7] See Paul H. Nitze, "The Vladivostok Accord and SALT II," *The Review of Politics* (University of Notre Dame) (April 1975), pp. 147-160, especially pp. 149-150.

tions in nuclear arms. If both sides were to adopt such a concept, it should be possible, over time, to move from what might be called a "high deterrent" posture to a "low deterrent" posture, with the deterrent remaining essentially equivalent on both sides but at successively lower levels.

As the United States thus adjusted its posture, the invitation for the Soviet Union likewise to seek a similar posture—and stop there—was patent both from statements of American policy and from the always-visible American actions. Unfortunately, however, the Soviet Union chose to pursue a course that was ambiguous: it could be interpreted as being aimed at overtaking the United States but then stopping at parity; it could, however, be interpreted as being aimed at establishing superiority in numbers of launchers and in throw-weight[8] and, perhaps ultimately, a nuclear-war-winning capability on the Soviet side.

It is important to consider the reasons that may have entered into this choice. In part, the Soviet leaders may have been motivated by technological factors—that they had already moved to heavy rockets but were behind in other areas, such as solid propellant technology, accuracy and MIRVing (the development of multiple, independently targetable reentry vehicles). In part, there may have been an element of traditional Soviet emphasis on mass and size. But it is hard to avoid the conclusion that an important factor was the reading the Soviet leaders gave to the Cuban missile crisis and, to a lesser extent, the Berlin crisis. In the latter case, Khrushchev had briefly sought to exploit the first Soviet rocket firings of 1957—by a series of threats to Berlin beginning in late 1958—but then found that the West stood firm and that the United States quickly moved to reestablish its strategic superiority beyond doubt. And in the Cuban missile case, the very introduction of the missiles into Cuba in the fall of 1962 must have reflected a desire to redress the balance by quick and drastic action, while the actual outcome of the crisis seemed to the Soviet leaders to spell out that nuclear superiority in a crunch would be an important factor in determining who prevailed.

Harking back to the Soviet penchant for actually visualizing what would happen in the event of nuclear war, it seems highly likely that

---

[8] "Throw-weight" is a measure of the weight of effective payload that can be delivered to an intended distance. In the case of intercontinental ballistic missiles (ICBMs) and submarine-launched ballistic missiles (SLBMs), the throw-weight is a direct measure of such a payload in terms of the potential power of the missiles' boosters. In view of the more variable loads carried by heavy bombers, a formula for equivalence is needed to take account of all factors including explosive power. This point is addressed in footnote 14.

the Soviet leaders, in those hectic October days of 1962, did something that U.S. leaders, as I know from my participation, did only in more general terms—that is, ask their military just how a nuclear exchange would come out. They must have been told that the United States would be able to achieve what they construed as victory, that the U.S. nuclear posture was such as to be able to destroy a major portion of Soviet striking power and still itself survive in a greatly superior condition for further strikes if needed. And they must have concluded that such a superior capability provided a unique and vital tool for pressure in a confrontation situation. It was a reading markedly different from the American internal one, which laid much less stress on American nuclear superiority and much more on the fact that the United States controlled the sea lanes to Cuba and could also have expected to prevail in any conflict over Cuba waged with conventional arms.[9]

One cannot prove that this was the Soviet reasoning. But the programs they set under way about 1962—above all the new family of weapons systems, embodying not only numbers and size but also greatly advanced technology, the development and deployment of which began to be evident beginning in 1971 but which must have been decided upon some years earlier—seem to reflect a fundamental state of mind on the Soviet side that contains no doubt as to the desirability of a war-winning capability, *if feasible*. Believing that evacuation, civil defense and recuperation measures can minimize the amount of damage sustained in a war, they conclude that they should be prepared if necessary to accept the unavoidable casualties. On the other hand, the loss of a war would be irretrievable. Therefore, the best deterrent is a war-winning capability, if that is attainable.

There have been, and I believe still are, divisions of opinion on the Soviet side as to whether such a capability *is* feasible. There are those who have argued that the United States is a tough opponent with great technical expertise and that the United States can be expected to do whatever is necessary to deny such a war-winning capability to the Soviet side. Others have taken the view that the developing correlation of forces—social, economic, and political as well as military and what they call the deepening crisis of capitalism—may prevent the United States and its allies from taking the necessary countermeasures and that the target of a war-winning capability, therefore, is both desirable and feasible. Again, this is not to say that Soviet leaders would desire to initiate a nuclear war even if they

---

[9] See Maxwell D. Taylor, "The Legitimate Claims of National Security," *Foreign Affairs* (April 1974), p. 582.

had a war-winning capability. They would, however, consider themselves duty bound by Soviet doctrine to exploit fully that strategic
advantage through political or limited military means.

IV

The SALT negotiations got under way in late 1969. As a participant in those talks from then until mid-1974, I have described
elsewhere some of the difficulties that attended the U.S. side.[10] What
was most fundamental was that the U.S. delegation sought at every
level and through every form of contact to bring home to the Soviet
delegation, and the leaders behind it, the desirability of limitations
which would assure "crisis stability" and "essential equivalence"—
and that the Soviet side stoutly resisted these efforts. . . .

The Vladivostok Accord, in essence, limits the total number
of strategic launchers—ICBMs, submarine-launched ballistic missiles
(SLBMs) and heavy strategic bombers, to 2,400 on both sides, and
the number of MIRVed missile launchers to 1,320 on both sides.
It limits the Soviet Union to the number of modern large ballistic
launchers (MLBMs) that they now have, while prohibiting the United
States from deploying any modern launchers in this category.[11] The
accord calls for air-to-surface missiles with a range greater than
600 kilometers, carried by heavy bombers, to be counted against
the 2,400 ceiling. The treaty would allow freedom to mix between the
various systems subject to these limitations. . . .

A notable feature of the Vladivostok Accord is that it does not
deal with throw-weight. The agreement would not effectively check
the deployment of the new Soviet family of large, technically improved
and MIRVed offensive missiles. While both sides are permitted equal
numbers of MIRVed missiles, the new Soviet SS-19s have three times
the throw-weight of the U.S. Minuteman III, and the new SS-18s,
seven times. What this comes down to is that under the accord the
Soviets can be expected to have a total of about 15 million pounds of
missile throw-weight and bomber throw-weight equivalent. If the
Congress goes forward with the B-1 and the Trident system but the

---

[10] Paul H. Nitze, "The Strategic Balance between Hope and Skepticism," *Foreign Policy* (Winter 1974-75), pp. 136-156.

[11] There has been no agreed definition of a heavy ballistic missile. However, both sides acknowledge that the SS-9 and the SS-18 are MLBMs and that the U.S. Titan missile, while it is considered heavy, does not fall within the definition of "modern." The U.S. has no launchers for MLBMs and is prohibited from converting any of its silos to such launchers. The Soviets are estimated to have had 308 launchers for MLBMs and are permitted to convert the SS-9 launchers into launchers for the even larger and much more capable SS-18s.

United States does not add further strategic programs, the Soviets can be expected to end up with an advantage of at least three-to-one in missile throw-weight and of at least two-to-one in overall throw-weight, including a generous allowance for the throw-weight equivalent of heavy bombers, and two-to-one or three-to-one in MIRVed missile throw-weight. This disparity leaves out of consideration the Backfire, the FB-111, and the highly asymmetrical advantage in air defenses that the Soviet Union enjoys.[12]

Thus, the Vladivostok Accord, while a considerable improvement upon the prior negotiating positions presented by the Soviet Union, continues to codify a potentially unstable situation caused by the large disparity in throw-weight, now being exploited by Soviet technological improvements.

V

The prospects for SALT III center on reductions in the strategic forces on both sides, an aim of the SALT talks since their inception. My personal view is that meaningful reductions are highly desirable, and that the aim of reductions should be to increase strategic stability. But this aim is not served by reducing numbers of launchers, unless throw-weight is also reduced and made more equal.[13]

The agreed reduction of the throw-weight of large, land-based MIRVed missiles, however, would increase stability. I see no reason why the Soviet Union needs to replace its SS-9s with SS-18s, nor why it needs to replace a large number of its SS-11s with SS-19s. Although it is perfectly feasible and permissible under the Vladivostok Accord for us to develop missiles of equally large or even greater throw-weight than the SS-19s and fit them in Minuteman III silos, would it not be far better for both sides if there were sub-limits of, say, fifty on the number of SS-18s the Soviets were permitted to deploy and five hundred or less on the number of SS-19 and SS-17 class ICBMs that either side was permitted to deploy? Even in a context of no other changes in the postures of the two countries, the reduction

---

[12] In mid-1973 the United States had 602 fighter interceptors and 481 surface-to-air missiles, compared to the Soviet Union's 3,000 fighter interceptors and 10,000 surface-to-air missiles. Edward Luttwak, *The U.S.-U.S.S.R. Nuclear Weapons Balance*, The Washington Papers (Beverly Hills: Sage Publications, 1974).

[13] Indeed, if total throw-weight is not reduced while the number of launchers is, the fewer launchers become more vulnerable and critical to each side and crisis stability is actually lessened. See Lt. Gen. (then Col.) Glenn A. Kent, "On the Interaction of Opposing Forces under Possible Arms Agreements," Occasional Papers in International Affairs, No. 5, Center for International Affairs, Harvard University (March 1963).

in missiles to these numbers would change the missile throw-weight asymmetry to one-and-a-half to one.

It might then be more feasible to work out subsequent reductions in numbers of vehicles which would include the Soviet older un-MIRVed missiles, such as the SS-9, along with our Minuteman II and Titan. But in the absence of throw-weight limitations of some sort, reduction per se will not improve stability.

However, the Russians are opposed to considering throw-weight limitations and have also taken the position that a future negotiation for reductions has to take into account all forward-based systems—all the systems we have in Europe and in East Asia, and on aircraft carriers. Thus, it is hard to see how we can have high hopes of getting anything in SALT III that will provide relief for the anticipated strain on the U.S. strategic posture as the Soviet deployments proceed and as their accuracy improves.

VI

The country as a whole has looked at strategic nuclear problems during the last six years in the context of SALT, hoping to make the maintenance of our national security easier through negotiations. It now appears, however, for the reasons outlined above, that we are not likely to get relief from our nuclear strategic problems through this route. Therefore, we have to look at our strategic nuclear posture in much the way we used to look at it before the SALT negotiations began and determine what is needed in the way of a nuclear strategy for the United States and what kind of posture is needed to support it. A fundamental aim of nuclear strategy and the military posture to back it up must be deterrence: the failure to deter would be of enormous cost to the United States and to the world.

Once again, two important distinctions should be borne in mind: the distinction between the concept of deterrence and the concept of military strategy, and the accompanying distinction between declaratory policy and action policy. Deterrence is a political concept; it deals with attempts by indications of capability and will to dissuade the potential enemy from taking certain actions. Military strategy deals with the military actions one would, in fact, take if deterrence fails. A responsible objective of military strategy in this event would be to bring the war to an end in circumstances least damaging to the future of our society.

From the U.S. standpoint, just to level a number of Soviet cities with the anticipation that most of our cities would then be destroyed would not necessarily be the implementation of a rational military strategy. Deterrence through the threat of such destruction thus rests on the belief that in that kind of crisis the United States would act irrationally and in revenge. Yet serious dangers can arise if there is such a disparity between declaratory deterrence policy and the actual military strategy a nation's leaders would adopt if deterrence fails— or if there is a belief by the other side that such a disparity would be likely. I think former Secretary James Schlesinger's flexible response program was, in effect, an attempt to get our declaratory policy closer to a credible action policy and thus improve deterrence.

Ultimately, the quality of that deterrence depends importantly on the character and strength of the U.S. nuclear posture versus that of the Soviet Union. In assessing its adequacy, one may start by considering our ability to hold Soviet population and industry as hostages, in the face of Soviet measures to deter or hedge against U.S. retaliation directed at such targets.

In 1970 and 1971—when the focus was almost exclusively on mutual assured destruction—the congressional debates on whether or not to deploy a U.S. antiballistic missile system recognized clearly the importance to deterrence of hostage populations. Critics of the ABM argued—and with decisive impact on the outcome of the debate—that an effective ABM defense of urban-industrial centers could be destabilizing to the nuclear balance: if side A (whether the United States or the U.S.S.R.) deployed an ABM defense of its cities, side B could no longer hold side A's population as a hostage to deter an attack by A on B. And in 1972 the same argument carried weight in the negotiation and ratification of the ABM limits in the SALT I agreements.

Yet today the Soviet Union has adopted programs that have much the same effect on the situation as an ABM program would have. And as the Soviet civil defense program becomes more effective it tends to destabilize the deterrent relationship for the same reason: the United States can then no longer hold as significant a proportion of the Soviet population as a hostage to deter a Soviet attack. Concurrently, Soviet industrial vulnerability has been reduced by deliberate policies, apparently adopted largely for military reasons, of locating three-quarters of new Soviet industry in small and medium-sized towns. The civil defense program also provides for evacuation of some industry and materials in time of crisis.

In sum, the ability of U.S. nuclear power to destroy without question the bulk of Soviet industry and a large proportion of the Soviet population is by no means as clear as it once was, even if one assumes most of U.S. striking power to be available and directed to this end.

A more crucial test, however, is to consider the possible results of a large-scale nuclear exchange in which one side sought to destroy as much of the other side's striking power as possible, in order to leave itself in the strongest possible position after the exchange. As already noted, such a counterforce strategy appears to fit with Soviet ways of thinking and planning; it is a strategy we must take into account.

Figures 1 and 2 apply this test over a period of years running from 1960 to (as it happens) 1984. For past periods, fairly assured estimates are available for both sides. For future years, a median estimate of U.S. programs, based on published data, has been used, while on the Soviet side there are two alternative projections—an "A-threat" based on a representative estimate of Soviet force deployments and accuracy capabilities, and a "B-threat" reflecting the possibility of increased Soviet emphasis on accuracy and other strategic force factors. Both forces are assessed in terms of total available throw-weight, measuring this directly for assumed missile inventories and making full allowance for the bomber equivalent of missile throw-weight for both sides.[14]

The figures assume an exchange in which the Soviet Union has attacked U.S. forces, and the United States has retaliated by trying to reduce Soviet strategic throw-weight to the greatest extent possible. To assess the opposing forces *before* attack in terms of their relative throw-weight is of course only a partial measure of their comparative original capability. In working out what would actually happen in the assumed exchange, full account has been taken of all relevant factors—in particular the number, yield, accuracy, and reliability of the reentry vehicles associated with that throw-weight, and the hardness of the targets against which they are assumed to have been targeted.

It is the situation *after* attack, of course, that is most important. And here, since the targets remaining after the exchange would almost all be soft ones, missile accuracy and other refinements in the original postures no longer have the same significance. Surviving throw-

---

[14] A B-52 has been assigned an equivalent throw-weight of 10,000 lbs. and a B-1 about 19,000 lbs. The SRAM air-to-surface missile has a yield about equal to that of a Minuteman III warhead; hence, for every three SRAMs carried by a bomber, that bomber is given a throw-weight equivalent equal to the throw-weight of one Minuteman III. Laydown bombs are assumed to have roughly the yield of Minuteman II; hence, for each laydown bomb carried by a bomber it is given a throw-weight equivalent equal to the throw-weight of a Minuteman II. The alert bomber force is assumed to be 40 percent of the B-52 inventory and 60 percent of the B-1 inventory, degraded to incorporate penetration factors.

Figure 1
SOVIET–U.S. THROW-WEIGHT RATIOS

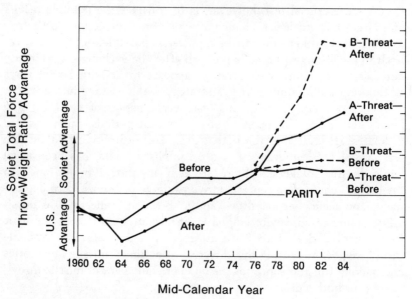

Figure 2
SOVIET–U.S. THROW-WEIGHT DIFFERENTIALS

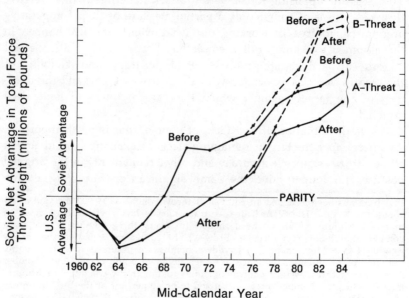

weight thus becomes an appropriate *total* measure of the residual capability on both sides.

As worked out by Mr. T. K. Jones, who served as my senior technical advisor when I was a member of the U.S. SALT delegation, the results of such an assessment are shown in Figure 1, expressed in terms of the ratios, and Figure 2, expressed in terms of the absolute units of weight—by which one side exceeds the other before and after attack in the various periods and alternative cases examined.[15]

Based on this method of assessment, the United States in 1960 held a slight but increasing advantage over the Soviet Union, and this advantage became greatest in about mid-1964. Thereafter, however, Soviet programs—greatly accelerated, as earlier noted, after the Cuban missile crisis—started to reverse the trend, so that by mid-1968 the total deployed throw-weights on both sides, before a hypothetical nuclear exchange, were roughly equal. However, as the "after" curve shows, the U.S. operational military advantage persisted for some time thereafter, offsetting the Soviet superiority in deployed throw-weight. For example, if in 1970 the Soviets had attacked U.S. forces, their entire prewar advantage would have been eliminated, leaving the United States with substantial superiority at the end of the exchange. However, this situation began to be reversed in 1973, with the Soviets gaining the military capability to end an exchange with an advantage in their favor. Moreover, in 1976 the "before" and "after" curves of Figure 1 cross, signifying that the Soviets could, by initiating such an exchange, increase the ratio of advantage they held at the start of the exchange. By 1977, after a Soviet-initiated counterforce strike against the United States to which the United States responded with a counterforce strike, the Soviet Union would have remaining forces sufficient to destroy Chinese and European NATO nuclear capability, attack U.S. population and conventional military targets, and still have a remaining force throw-weight in excess of that of the United States. And after 1977 the Soviet advantage after the assumed attack mounts rapidly.

In addition to the ratios and absolute differences that apply to the remaining throw-weights of the two sides, there is a third factor which

---

[15] I regret that, even if space permitted, the full assumptions used in Mr. Jones's study cannot be spelled out here. Security considerations necessarily enter in for some of the underlying data. I have myself gone over Mr. Jones's data and assumptions with care and believe that they represent a careful and objective analysis of the relevant factors. Above all, since his methods are self-consistent from one period to the next, they show a valid trend-line and pace of change—which I believe the more expert readers of this article will find conform to their more general judgments.

should be borne in mind. That factor is the absolute level of the forces remaining to the weaker side. If that absolute level is high, continues under effective command and control, and is comprised of a number of reentry vehicles (RVs) adequate to threaten a major portion of the other side's military and urban-industrial targets, this will be conducive to continued effective deterrence even if the ratios are unfavorable. These considerations reinforce the desirability of survivable systems and methods of deployment.

VII

In sum, the trends in relative military strength are such that, unless we move promptly to reverse them, the United States is moving toward a posture of minimum deterrence in which we would be conceding to the Soviet Union the potential for a military and political victory if deterrence failed. While it is probably not possible and may not be politically desirable for the United States to strive for a nuclear-war-winning capability, there are courses of action available to the United States whereby we could deny to the Soviets such a capability and remove the one-sided instability caused by their throw-weight advantage and by their civil defense program.

To restore stability and the effectiveness of the U.S. deterrent: (1) the survivability and capability of the U.S. strategic forces must be such that the Soviet Union could not foresee a military advantage in attacking our forces, and (2) we must eliminate or compensate for the one-sided instability caused by the Soviet civil defense program. Specifically, we must remove the possibility that the Soviet Union could profitably attack U.S. forces with a fraction of their forces and still maintain reserves adequate for other contingencies.

As to the civil-defense aspect, the absence of a U.S. capability to protect its own population gives the Soviet Union an asymmetrical possibility of holding the U.S. population as a hostage to deter retaliation following a Soviet attack on U.S. forces. Although the most economical and rapidly implementable approach to removing this one-sided instability would be for the United States to pursue a more active civil defense program of its own, such a program does not appear to be politically possible at this time. Its future political acceptability will be a function of the emerging threat and its appreciation by U.S. leadership and by the public.

Two more practicable avenues of action suggest themselves. First, all of the options which would be effective in diminishing the one-sided Soviet advantage involve some improvement in the *accuracy* of U.S. missiles. Differential accuracy improvements can, at least temporarily, compensate for throw-weight inequality.

This is a controversial issue which has been studied extensively. The results of one such study by a member of Congress are shown in the *Congressional Record* of 20 May 1975. According to that study the United States presently holds a four-to-one superiority in the hard-target kill capability of missile forces. The congressman notes in his opposition to a U.S. high-accuracy maneuvering reentry vehicle (MaRV) program that MaRV would by the late 1980s improve U.S. accuracy to .02 n.m. (120 feet), incorrectly estimating that this would increase the U.S. advantage to seven-to-one over the U.S.S.R.— assuming the latter was unable to develop MaRV by that time. How- ever, the congressman's data also predict that the hard-target kill capability of the Soviet missile force will by the 1980s have increased a hundredfold, so that if the United States took no action to improve the accuracy of its missiles, the Soviet Union would have an advantage of twenty-five-to-one. While it is unnecessary to equip more than a portion of U.S. missiles with high-accuracy RVs, it is clear that sub- stantial accuracy improvements are essential to avoid major Soviet superiority in a critical respect.

Others argue that improvements in U.S. missile accuracy would be "destabilizing." More specifically, such programs "could spur Soviet countermeasures such as new programs to increase their second-strike capabilities by going to (1) more sea-launched strategic missiles, (2) air- and sea-launched cruise missiles, (3) expanded stra- tegic bomber forces, and (4) mobile ICBMs." [16] These arguments ignore the central fact that deterrence is already being seriously under- mined by unilateral actions of the Soviet Union. Hence, further self- restraint by the United States cannot but worsen this condition.

Moreover, the Soviet programs cited as consequences of U.S. accuracy improvement are in fact stabilizing rather than destabilizing. Under the SALT agreements on force ceilings, such reactions would compel offsetting reductions in the Soviet silo-based ICBM force, thereby reducing their total force throw-weight. Moreover, the replacement ICBM systems are not likely to achieve accuracy equal to that of the silo-based ICBMs, while throw-weight moved to bombers and cruise missiles, because of the long flight time to targets, cannot be effectively used in a first-strike counterforce role.

---

[16] Additional views of Representative Schroeder, "Alternative Defense Posture Statement," Report 94-199 of House Armed Services Committee (May 10, 1975), p. 130.

PAUL H. NITZE

In sum, even on the information furnished by those generally opposing improved accuracy of U.S. missiles, improvement *is* necessary to avoid a major Soviet advantage, and the logical Soviet counter to such improvements would move the Soviets in a direction which would stabilize the strategic relationship and reduce the Soviet throw-weight advantage.

Second, the prospective Soviet advantage could be offset by measures to decrease the *vulnerability* of U.S. strategic nuclear forces. Here there are several ongoing programs already under way, notably the development of the Trident submarine and the B-1 bomber; both these delivery systems will be inherently less vulnerable to a counter-force attack than fixed ICBM installations, the submarine by reason of its mobility at sea and the B-1 by virtue of its mobility and escape speed as well as the potential capacity to maintain a portion of the B-1 force airborne in time of crisis. In addition, programs to increase the prelaunch survivability of U.S. bomber forces generally, as well as programs to increase air defense capability through the so-called AWACS [airborne warning and control system] system, operate to reduce vulnerability of the total U.S. force. To a considerable extent, however, these programs are already taken into account in the calculations shown on Figures 1 and 2—if they were to be delayed, the effect would be negative, and the contrary if they were to be stepped up and accelerated.

I believe, however, that these measures do not go far enough. The most vulnerable U.S. delivery system today is that of our fixed and hardened ICBM installations, including Minuteman silos. Under present trends, it is only a question of time until a combination of the large throw-weight available to the Soviets and improved accuracy will threaten the destruction of a high percentage of these installations—so that today there is considerable talk in some quarters of actually phasing out U.S. ICBM installations.

I believe such action would be unwise, and that it is entirely feasible, at not excessive cost, to adopt a new system of deployment that would not only permit the retention of our ICBMs—which contribute heavily to the total U.S. throw-weight—but would actually make these a more critical and effective component of the U.S. striking force. The system that would accomplish these ends would be a proliferation of low-cost shelters for what is called a multiple launch-point system. The essence of such a system would be to construct a large number of shelter installations, so that the smaller number of actual missile launchers could be readily moved and deployed among these installations on a random pattern deliberately varied at adequate intervals of time.

The ingredients for such a system are, I believe, already in existence, notably through the availability of sufficiently large areas of western desert land now owned by the Department of Defense. On this land there could be created a large number of hardened shelters, or alternatively the missiles themselves could be encased in hardened capsules redeployable among a large number of "soft" shelters. Preliminary study indicates that the research, development and procurement costs of a system along these lines would average approximately $1.5 billion a year in 1975 dollars over the next eight to ten years. Inasmuch as the current level of obligational authority for strategic weapons systems is on the order of $7 billion per year—much less, as already noted, than the comparable amounts obligated annually in 1956–62—I believe this is a cost we should be prepared to accept.

The objective of creating such a new system of deployment would be to greatly increase the throw-weight costs to the Soviets of destroying a substantial portion of our deterrent forces. This is achieved with a multiple launch-point system, since in order to destroy the system virtually all of the relevant shelter installations would need to be destroyed. There would be many more hardened shelters or encapsulated missiles than the present number of fixed installations, so that the Soviets would be required to commit a larger portion of their throw-weight to this task than they would to the task of attacking fixed installations—the trade-off of U.S. throw-weight destroyed to Soviet throw-weight used would greatly favor the United States. Thus the Soviet advantage in a counterforce exchange would be drastically reduced or eliminated.

Furthermore, I believe that such a U.S. move would be likely to lead to Soviet countermoves that would have a constructive impact on the overall balance. The logical answer to such a U.S. move would be for the Soviet side to substitute either multiple launch-point missiles or SLBMs for a portion of their large fixed ICBMs. They would thereby increase the survivability of their systems, but at the cost of substantially reducing their throw-weight advantage. Such moves by both sides would greatly improve crisis stability and thus significantly reduce the risk of a nuclear war.

In essence, the multiple launch-point idea is a method of preserving and increasing the effectiveness of land-based systems by making them partially mobile. It is, however, necessary to take account of the usual argument advanced for banning land-based mobile missile systems. This argument is that it is more difficult to verify with confidence the number of mobile and thus redeployable launchers deployed by either side than it is to verify the number of fixed silos. The merit of this argument fades in a situation where up to 10 or 12 million pounds of MIRVed throw-weight can be expected to be available to the Soviet side under the limits contemplated by the Vladivostok Accord. With improved accuracy, less than 4 million pounds of MIRVed throw-weight could threaten the destruction of a high percentage of the fixed silos on the U.S. side. No practicable addition through unverified mobile launchers to the 10 to 12 million pounds of throw-weight permitted the Soviet side would compensate strategically for the additional throw-weight requirement that a U.S. multiple launch-point system would impose. A significant portion of a U.S. multiple launch-point system should survive even if the Soviet Union were to devote to the task of attacking it double the 4 million pounds of MIRVed throw-weight it would have to allocate to the destruction of our Minuteman silos.[17]

---

[17] Under the Vladivostok Accord, both sides are permitted 1,320 MIRVed missile launchers. The maximum MIRVed throw-weight the Soviets could obtain within this limit with the missiles they are currently testing and beginning to deploy is:

    4,500,000 pounds on 308 SS-18s (about 15,000 pounds each)

    7,100,000 pounds on 1,012 SS-19s (about 7,000 pounds each)

for a total MIRVed throw-weight of 11.6 million pounds. However, it is unlikely that the Soviets will reach this maximum, as they are currently deploying some SS-17s, which will have a throw-weight of about 5,000 pounds, and they may choose not to MIRV all of their SS-18s. A more likely figure is less than ten million pounds of MIRVed throw-weight.

A reliable megaton-range RV with a CEP (circular error probable, a measure of accuracy) of 0.125 nautical miles has a probability of damage of 85 percent against a silo of 1,500 psi (pounds per square inch) hardness. The targeting of two such RVs on the silo would give a probability of damage of about 92 percent taking into account both reliability and accuracy. An SS-18 missile may have up to eight megaton-range RVs (International Institute for Strategic Studies, *The Military Balance, 1974-75*); thus a megaton-range RV may require around 2,000 pounds of throw-weight. The net throw-weight required, then, to threaten 92 percent destruction of 1,000 hard silos would be approximately 4 million pounds, assuming the Soviets achieve CEPs averaging an eighth of a mile.

A multiple launch-point ICBM system with 600-psi hard shelters or encapsulated missiles in soft shelters would require considerable more throw-weight for its destruction. To barrage attack such a mobile system deployed on 6,000 square nautical miles of land as an area target would require about 19,000 megaton-range RVs to achieve a 92 percent damage level. The throw-weight required for this force would be considered above the Soviet available force. Even as low a damage level as 20 percent would require almost 4,000 megaton-range RVs, a throw-weight of at least 8 million pounds.

Assuming the same factors for accuracy and reliability as used above in calculating the potential results of an attack on silo-based ICBMs, an equal probability of damage (85 percent for a single reliable RV) can be achieved against a 600-psi shelter with a 290-kiloton weapon. Since a Minuteman III, with a total of three RVs of less than 200-kt yield, has a throw-weight of about 2,000 pounds, an RV of 290-kt yield might require about 800 pounds of throw-

Undoubtedly, there are other programs which would also be necessary. In particular, it would seem to be essential, if the Soviet Union is to be permitted an unlimited number of Backfires, that we not grant them a free ride for their bomber forces. This would require a reversal of congressional action limiting support for the AWACS program. But taking everything into consideration, the magnitude of the U.S. effort required would be far less than that which we undertook in the 1957–62 period in response to Sputnik and the then-threatened vulnerability of our bomber force.

VIII

Some of my friends argue that those knowledgeable about such matters should bear in mind the horrors of a nuclear war, and should call for U.S. restraint in the hope the U.S.S.R. will follow our lead. Having been in charge of the U.S. Strategic Bombing Survey team of five hundred physicists and engineers who measured the detailed effects of the two nuclear weapons used at Nagasaki and Hiroshima, the only two such weapons ever used in anger, and having been associated with many of the subsequent studies of the probable effects of the more modern weapons, I am fully sensitive to the first point. But to minimize the risks of nuclear war, it would seem to me wise to assure that no enemy could believe he could profit from such a war.

As to the second point, Helmut Sonnenfeldt, counselor for the State Department, recently described the preconditions for the U.S. détente policy in the following terms:

> The course on which we embarked requires toughness of mind and steadfastness of purpose. It demands a sober view not only of Soviet strengths but of our own. It is an attempt to evolve a balance of incentives for positive behavior and penalties for belligerence; the objective being to instill in the minds of our potential adversaries an appreciation of the benefits of cooperation rather than conflict and thus lessen the threat of war. . . . Interests will be respected only if it is clear that they can be defended. Restraint will prevail only if its absence is known to carry heavy risks.[18]

---

weight. Thus a U.S. deployment of some 10,000 shelters would require 8 million pounds of Soviet MIRVed throw-weight to threaten destruction of 72 percent of the multiple launch-point system. The entire 10-million-pound force would raise the level of destruction to only 77 percent. The cost of adding RVs to the Soviet attack force should be substantially greater than the cost to the United States of adding shelters. In any case, it would appear technologically infeasible to reduce the throw-weight required per RV to less than 300 pounds, even if accuracies were eventually to approach zero CEP.

[18] Helmut Sonnenfeldt, "The Meaning of Détente," *Naval War College Review* (July-August 1975), pp. 3-8.

Unfortunately, I believe the record shows that neither negotiations nor unilateral restraint have operated to dissuade Soviet leaders from seeking a nuclear-war-winning capability—or from the view that with such a capability they could effectively use pressure tactics to get their way in crisis situations.

Hence it is urgent that the United States take positive steps to maintain strategic stability and high-quality deterrence. If the trends in Soviet thinking continue to evolve in the manner indicated by the internal statements of Soviet leaders, and if the trends in relative military capability continue to evolve in the fashion suggested by the prior analysis, the foundations for hope in the evolution of a true relaxation of tensions between the U.S.S.R. and much of the rest of the world will be seriously in doubt.

ASSURING STRATEGIC STABILITY: AN ALTERNATIVE VIEW *

Jan M. Lodal

Appraising many of the ideas advanced by Paul H. Nitze in the previous article, Jan M. Lodal sees little evidence that the Soviet Union is approaching strategic superiority: missile throw-weight can be a misleading indicator of aggregate capability, and the Soviet build-up can be attributed to goals other than strategic superiority. Lodal views the SALT process as useful. Although the agreements reached so far have probably imposed only minor restrictions on deployments by the Soviet Union and none on those by the United States, they are important in preventing an excessive and destabilizing expansion by the U.S.S.R. Additional measures should be undertaken to strengthen the American strategic arsenal, but the United States would be better off if land-based mobile ICBMs were bound by SALT II.

In the coming months, the Ford Administration must decide either to offer the Soviet Union compromises on the Vladivostok SALT Accord, permitting completion of the agreement as a permanent treaty, or to face the prospect of a prolonged period of strategic competition with the U.S.S.R., unconstrained by formal limits on strategic offensive forces. If the agreement is completed, the Congress must then decide on ratification or rejection. While this issue will occupy center stage

---

* Source: *Foreign Affairs* (April 1976), pp. 462-481.

in the strategic debate until it is resolved, the United States also faces a second major decision regarding its strategic program: whether to respond to the ongoing Soviet deployment of new, large, land-based missiles equipped with multiple independently targetable reentry vehicles (MIRVs). This Soviet deployment is not affected by the Vladivostok Accord. Thus, if it is important to respond by adjusting our strategic program, we will have to do so whether the agreement is completed or not.

[In the preceding article], Paul H. Nitze recommends that, in addition to ongoing programs to improve accuracy, two specific major actions be taken by the United States to ensure strategic stability in the next decade: the deployment of a "multiple launch-point" land-based intercontinental ballistic missile system (more frequently called a mobile ICBM), and a greatly expanded civil defense program.[1] He bases these recommendations on a series of considerations, including the nature of recent Soviet strategic force deployments, his view of Soviet motives concerning détente, and his view of the overriding importance of missile throw-weight in determining overall strategic force capability.

With regard to the Vladivostok Accord, Mr. Nitze points out that the agreement will not change the basic nature of the current Soviet force build-up. While apparently resigned to its completion, he nevertheless implies that the accord is probably worse than no SALT agreement at all; he clearly believes it to be worse than the type of agreement he would have preferred—primarily because it fails to limit Soviet missile throw-weight—and finds "without adequate foundation . . . the general belief that while strategic stability may not be assured by the SALT agreements, it is not and will not be substantially endangered." "In sum, the trends in relative military strength are such that, unless we move promptly to reverse them, the United States is moving toward a posture of minimum deterrence in which we would be conceding to the Soviet Union the potential for a military and political victory if deterrence failed."[2]

Clearly, the rate and scale of the present Soviet deployment of MIRVed land-based missiles are disappointing, if not outright suspicious. Furthermore, Soviet behavior in the Middle East, Africa, Southeast Asia, and Southern Europe seems to most Americans far from

---

[1] . . . While advocating expanded civil defense, Mr. Nitze notes that "such a program does not appear to be politically possible at this time.". . .

[2] . . . Mr. Nitze now advises me that he did not intend to state a final conclusion, and that only when all the terms of an agreement based on the Vladivostok Accord have been worked out and published will he judge whether such an agreement is preferable to none at all.

consistent with a genuine relaxation of tensions. For their part, the Soviets argue that certain U.S. actions, such as interference in "internal" Soviet affairs, denial of normal trade relations, and continued heavy overseas U.S. force deployments are also inconsistent with such a relationship.

While this situation makes it clear that the process of establishing a better Soviet-American relationship is not an easy one, I believe that Mr. Nitze's concern that the Soviet Union might be close to obtaining strategic superiority is not justified. In my view, he has considerably overemphasized missile "throw-weight"[3] as an indicator of aggregate strategic capability. Furthermore, Mr. Nitze's recommendations for deployment of land-based mobile ICBMs and large civil defense programs are, in my opinion, both ill-advised; neither should be pursued, either on its merits or in the light of other more modest measures that are available to meet the situation.

Finally, with regard to the Vladivostok Accord, while the agreement contains provisions which are clearly less constraining to the arms build-up of the two sides than many persons had hoped for, its terms are relatively favorable to the United States. If it is completed, it should provide a reasonably good basis for controlling the strategic arms competition between the two sides in the longer term.

II

Let us first review carefully the significance of missile throw-weight, both in general and in the specific terms stressed by Mr. Nitze, that is, a comparison of the throw-weight on both sides that would survive after an assumed Soviet first strike against U.S. strategic forces. Since the early 1960s, when the United States abandoned the Titan ICBM program in favor of the Minuteman ICBM, the Soviets have, by and large, deployed considerably larger missiles than the United States. In the mid-to-late 1960s, the size of these missiles, particularly the SS-7, SS-8, and SS-9, permitted the Soviets to surpass the United States in the aggregate megatonnage carried by the strategic missile forces of each side. This situation generated charges that the United States was slipping into strategic inferiority. How-

---

[3] Throw-weight is, roughly, a measure of the total weight of missile warheads which one side could deliver against the other side. Throw-weight also includes the weight of missile guidance systems, MIRV-dispensing systems, and certain other equipment which is carried out of the atmosphere by a strategic missile. For strategic bombers, the term "throw-weight" is technically inappropriate; the correct analogous term is "payload," and when "throw-weight" is used in reference to bombers, it is usually taken to mean payload. See footnote 8 for comment on Mr. Nitze's slightly different formula for bombers.

ever, reasoned response to these charges eventually led to a widespread understanding that total megatonnage is simply not a very accurate measure, or even a meaningful measure, of strategic force capability. Throw-weight, while a considerably more meaningful measure of capability than megatonnage, can nonetheless be similarly misleading as an indicator of the overall U.S.–U.S.S.R. strategic balance.

In evaluating the importance of a Soviet advantage in throw-weight, one must first ask: What, in a military sense, can the Soviets do with their potential throw-weight advantage? The bulk represented by more throw-weight does permit the deployment of more deliverable weapons, and, up to a point, having more weapons can complicate any effort the other side might make to deploy an antiballistic missile system (ABM). More weapons can also increase the flexibility and target coverage capability of one's force. However, both sides now have adequate throw-weight to deploy essentially all the weapons they could conceivably need—up to at least ten thousand for each side. Thus, the main concern over the large Soviet throw-weight is not that it will permit more weapons, but rather that it permits the deployment of larger-yield warheads on Soviet missiles. Having higher yields, it is argued, will give Soviet missiles the capability to attack U.S. missile silos effectively. Furthermore, additional throw-weight, when used to deploy larger-yield warheads, provides a hedge against uncertainties in achieving, in actual operation, high missile accuracies, the only other way in which one could develop a capability to attack missile silos—that is, a hard-target counterforce capability.[4]

To refute this view, let us examine some specific combinations of size and accuracy. The present Minuteman-III missile has three warheads of a yield of 170 kilotons each. If we assume its accuracy is approximately 0.15 nautical miles,[5] it would have about a 40 percent chance of destroying a missile silo, assuming two warheads were

---

[4] Some also argue that a throw-weight advantage could be militarily significant for attacks against large area targets, such as bomber escape areas and submarine patrol areas. However, "barrage" attacks against bombers and submarines are probably not feasible, even with very large-yield weapons. The Soviets would have to locate our submarines, and there is no indication that they will have such an ability by 1985. Our bombers could probably survive barrage attacks, even today. In any event, attacks against our bomber bases would cause such widespread civilian fatalities that the Soviets would have to assume an all-out U.S. response.

[5] This customary measure of accuracy is called the CEP, or circular error probable. In lay language, a warhead is estimated to have a 50 percent chance of landing within this distance from the designated target.

targeted against each silo.[6] If the new generation of Soviet MIRVs are assumed to have a yield of about six times this amount, or 1 megaton each, yet if their accuracy is only 0.25 nautical miles rather than 0.15, their ability to destroy silos would still be no greater than that of the present Minuteman-III. If by 1985 the Soviets were able to increase this yield to 1.5 megatons and improve accuracy to 0.15 nautical miles, they could increase the probability of destroying a silo with two warheads to about 85 percent. But this is no better than the effectiveness expected from the Minuteman-III once the improved Mark 12A warhead is deployed and certain low-cost accuracy improvements are made. Yet it would take at least three times as much throw-weight per warhead for the Soviets to deploy these 1.5-megaton warheads as it would for the United States to deploy the Mark 12A.

Moreover, when accuracies get better than 0.1 nautical miles, as essentially all experts predict they will by the late 1980s, throw-weight becomes almost completely irrelevant. A 500-kiloton weapon with a 0.06 nautical mile CEP has a 95 percent probability of destroying a missile silo, targeting only two weapons per silo—essentially as high a probability as one could ever obtain. Thus, in this situation additional throw-weight, even enough to permit the deployment of one- or two-megaton MIRVs, is of no advantage whatsoever. Even relatively small weapons, such as the 100-kiloton warhead projected for the new Trident-1 submarine-launched missile, can have quite good antisilo counterforce capabilities at these accuracies.

In sum, there is only a very narrow range of accuracies in which throw-weight is important to a hard-target counterforce capability. Unless accuracies are better than about 0.2 nautical miles, *no* reasonable MIRV system can have much of a counterforce capability; once accuracies are better than 0.1 nautical miles, essentially *any* size missile, even those of relatively low throw-weight, can destroy silos. Since the technology is clearly in hand to permit both sides to obtain accuracies better than 0.1 nautical miles in the late 1980s, limiting throw-weight would at best put off the theoretical vulnerability of land-based missile silos for a few years.[7]

---

[6] For complicated technical reasons related to a phenomenon referred to as "fratricide," force planners usually assume that no more than two warheads can be targeted effectively against any one silo.

[7] Personally, I do not believe that accuracies better than 0.1 nautical miles are likely to be obtained by the purely inertial guidance systems now used by both sides. However, using satellite navigational systems, or perhaps terminal homing systems, it seems quite feasible to develop these accuracies over the next ten years, or perhaps even sooner.

There are other technical problems associated with using throw-weight as the primary measure of strategic force capability. First, throw-weight is difficult to define, especially if one includes an allowance for bombers.[8] Second, one must deal with "range-payload" trade-offs. For example, our new Trident-I missile, which will replace the present Poseidon missiles, will be considerably more powerful in terms of its total lifting capacity than the Poseidon missile. However, all of this additional capability will be used to extend the range of the missile, not to increase its throw-weight. The United States could have just as well increased the throw-weight, had it been thought important to do so. Nonetheless, our military planners—correctly in my opinion—chose to emphasize the survivability of our submarines, and thus to use the additional capability of the missile to extend its range; this extra range gives our submarines a much greater operating area and reduces dramatically any possibility that the Soviets could determine their location and attack them.

Even if one accepts Mr. Nitze's specific criteria for measuring the relative surviving capacity of the two sides—that is, the throw-weight ratio of the two forces on the one hand, and the net throw-weight differential on the other—his figures would be open to challenge because they do not presume that the two sides will act in a manner which will maximize their relative situation according to the very criteria being considered.[9] And in any event, by using the criteria

---

[8] For example, Paul Nitze's calculations assigned our B-52 bombers an equivalent throw-weight of 10,000 pounds and our B-1 bombers 19,000 pounds, although these bombers actually carry significantly more payload than this. Furthermore, he degraded the payload of the U.S. bomber force both for its "alert rate" and for "penetration factors."

While I would agree that some adjustment of gross bomber payload might be appropriate, Mr. Nitze's assumptions go too far in favoring the Soviets. If one were to use gross U.S. bomber payload, the Soviet projected throw-weight advantage in 1984 would disappear. While this is going to the other extreme, it illustrates that by picking a different yet still not absurd definition of aggregate throw-weight, one can obtain radically different views of the relative balance.

[9] The figures assume "an exchange in which the Soviet Union has attacked U.S. forces, and the United States has retaliated by trying to reduce Soviet strategic throw-weight to the greatest extent possible." But if what matters is *net* residual throw-weight, the United States should not try "to reduce Soviet strategic throw-weight to the greatest extent possible," but only to the extent that a pound of U.S. throw-weight knocks out more than a pound of Soviet throw-weight. A similar situation is true with regard to the throw-weight ratio criterion. For example, while it is not possible to tell exactly how Mr. Nitze's calculations were done since the assumptions are not presented, it appears that most U.S. SLBMs were assumed to be used to attack Soviet silos in a retaliatory attack. If the United States simply held in reserve most of these weapons, as well as alert bombers, the "after-attack" residual throw-weight advantage of the Soviets might be considerably less.

and scenarios he has chosen, he obscures the fact that the United States retains a very large force even after any conceivable full-scale Soviet attack.[10] In particular, even if the Soviets destroyed all our land-based ICBMs, nonalert bombers and nonalert submarine-launched ballistic missiles (SLBMs), we would still retain our alert bomber force and our alert SLBM force. These forces alone would be capable of delivering something like 4–5,000 nuclear weapons against Soviet targets. I find it difficult to conceive of a military need for more than 4–5,000 nuclear weapons, albeit weapons much smaller than the relatively large Soviet weapons.

III

Apart from the potential military importance of a Soviet throw-weight advantage, there is the question of Soviet motives behind their throw-weight build-up. While it is possible that, as Mr. Nitze implies, the Soviets have emphasized large land-based missiles in their strategic force deployments in order to gain a measure of strategic superiority over the United States, one need not hypothesize such Soviet motives in order to explain their weapon systems choices. For the last ten years, the Soviets have clearly felt a great need to deploy a new generation of missiles equipped with MIRVs. Yet they lacked the technology to deploy MIRVs efficiently on relatively small land-based missiles or on submarine-launched ballistic missiles. Furthermore, the Soviets have always had great operational difficulties with their SLBM force. This has led them to put much heavier emphasis on land-based missiles relative to sea-based missiles, while the United States has done just the opposite.

The Soviets needed MIRVs for two reasons: first, to increase the target coverage and flexibility of their force; and second, to ensure that they could penetrate potential U.S. antiballistic missile systems. Since the 1972 signing of the SALT I treaty effectively prohibiting ABMs, we have tended to lose sight of the environment in which the generation of Soviet missiles now being deployed was designed. At that time, in the mid-1960s, not too long after the Cuban missile crisis, the United States was very far ahead in ABM technology, and appeared to be moving toward a large ABM deployment. The Soviets were probably aware of MIRVs at the time they first designed these missiles, and recognized that the most effective way to overcome an ABM defense is to launch a greater number of weapons against the

---

[10] The potential importance of residual force levels is mentioned in general terms by Mr. Nitze [at the end of section VI], but without spelling out their significance.

defense than there are interceptors available to the defense, simply exhausting the defense. However, such a tactic is economically feasible only if one can use MIRVs. Thus, this alone would have been good reason for the Soviets to make a major effort to deploy MIRVs on their new missiles.[11]

The Soviets also needed MIRVs to increase the flexibility and target coverage of their force. With only about 2,000 total missiles in their force, considering reliability and the number of missiles that might be destroyed in a strategic exchange, the Soviets could probably count on no more than about 1,000 nuclear warheads available to deliver against U.S. targets. While 1,000 weapons are certainly more than adequate to destroy virtually all the cities of the United States, in more complicated scenarios it might be possible for the United States to use some of its MIRVs to attack Soviet military targets, keeping population damage relatively low, while retaining a clear capability to destroy all the Soviet cities. Without MIRVs, the Soviets would not be in a similar position. Thus, this need for more weapons undoubtedly added to the attraction of MIRVs.

Once the Soviets decided to deploy MIRVs, it is not surprising that they chose to emphasize size and develop the relatively large missiles we now see. Whereas the United States made great use in its MIRV programs of its already-existing capability to develop small on-board computers and small, but relatively high-yield, nuclear warheads, in the mid-1960s the Soviets simply did not have such technologies. Of course, these technologies are now becoming available to them, but they were not when the systems now being deployed were designed.

Additionally, the Soviets' decision to emphasize land-based missiles undoubtedly led them to conclude that they should increase the hardness (that is, the resistance to nuclear attack of their land-based missile silos. In order to do this, they had to make major structural changes in these silos. Relatively small increases in the depth or diameter of the silos could be easily accomplished in conjunction with a silo-hardening program they probably planned to undertake in any event. Since the new Soviet missiles are not much larger in volume

---

[11] Indeed, there is an additional difficulty here with Mr. Nitze's argument about the objectives and strategy behind U.S. nuclear programs in the 1960s. While our actual deployments were indeed wholly consistent with the stated aim of a situation of assured second-strike capabilities on both sides, our research programs, notably on ABM and MIRV, were almost bound to convey a different future signal to Soviet planners, that is, that we might be seriously comtemplating a return to counterforce strategies and our own version of strategic superiority.

than the ones they replaced, these small increases in silo dimensions were adequate to permit deployment of the new missiles.[12]

In conclusion—given the Soviets' difficulty with SLBM technology, their lack of sophisticated miniaturization technology, and their strong military need for MIRVs, both in order to penetrate ABMs and to increase the target coverage flexibility of their force—it is not at all surprising that the current generation of Soviet land-based missiles have large throw-weight and MIRVs. Had the roles of the two countries been switched, with the United States in the position in which the Soviets found themselves, we probably would have made similar decisions, with no necessary intention of acquiring a position of strategic superiority.

This point, of course, applies principally to the Soviet choice of technologies. Similar considerations relate to the rate and scale of the Soviet deployment of big missiles. If one puts oneself in Soviet shoes, one can see that the Russians have faced, and still face, such factors as a major inferiority in the number of deployed warheads (roughly 3,500 versus 9,000 at present), an inability to keep their SLBM force at sea for long periods, and what may be significant problems of reliability. The point, in both areas, is not to argue for complacency about the Soviet build-up; it is simply to note that the technological and numerical factors are not so one-sided as to indicate —to anything like the degree Mr. Nitze contends—an underlying motive of seeking strategic superiority. In my judgment it is simply impossible to tell from Soviet actions alone whether their "true" motives have been other than technological.

IV

Turning now to the Vladivostok Accord, I believe it is first important to review precisely what was settled there and the negotiating history that led up to the agreement reached in November 1974.

The accord calls for an equal numerical limit on two important quantities: the number of strategic delivery vehicles (missiles and strategic bombers), which are limited to 2,400, and the number of missiles equipped with MIRVs, limited to 1,320, with both numbers effective through 1985. As has been pointed out, 2,400 is only slightly below the Soviets' present force levels (about 2,500), and is above what the United States plans to deploy anyway (unless "mothballed"

---

[12] This additional volume of the missiles accounts for some of the large increase in throw-weight we see with the new missiles; however, most of the throw-weight increase is a result of significant improvements made in Soviet missile propellants and other missile technology.

strategic bombers are counted in the total). Furthermore, 1,320 is dramatically above the present Soviet MIRV force level (zero at the time the accord was reached and only 50–100 today), and also above the number of missiles with MIRVs the United States plans to deploy, even assuming all existing Poseidon submarines are retained in the force as the new Trident submarines come on line. Thus, it is clear that neither side gave up much, if any, of its present strategic programs.

We can only speculate about what future Soviet force levels would be without the agreement. But there is some indication that they had planned to expand further with new submarines, bombers, and mobile missiles. Whether or not they would have gone above 1,320 in the number of missiles with MIRVs is also speculative, but the best guess is that they intended to deploy MIRVs on almost all their missiles—a total closer to 2,400 than to 1,320. Thus, the agreement probably would have a restraining effect on Soviet strategic planning.

More importantly, over and above the limited effect on the programs of the two sides, the accord settled a number of issues of basic principle. Perhaps foremost was the issue of equal numerical limits. The Interim Agreement on strategic offensive arms now in force froze the missile levels deployed and under construction by both sides at the time the agreement went into force (3 October 1972). Since the Soviets had more missiles at that time than did the United States, this left them with a numerical advantage in missiles (about 2,350 to our 1,710). In support of the agreement, the Nixon Administration argued that this numerical advantage was offset by several U.S. advantages: our large bomber force (500 B-52s and 72 FB-111s versus about 150 older Soviet bombers); our tremendous advantage in MIRV technology; and other qualitative advantages in our forces. Nevertheless, many in the Congress insisted that in all future agreements there should be numerical equality. As a result, this principle was somewhat ambiguously embodied in the Jackson Amendment (to the joint resolution approving the Interim Agreement), which provided that "the President seek a future treaty that, *inter alia*, would not limit the United States to levels of intercontinental strategic forces inferior to the limits provided for the Soviet Union."

As SALT negotiations resumed after the Interim Agreement went into effect, within the U.S. government both the Joint Chiefs of Staff and the Office of the Secretary of Defense argued strongly that any follow-on SALT agreement should provide for so-called equal aggregates—a term referring to the aggregate sum of strategic land-based missiles (ICBMs), submarine-launched ballistic missiles (SLBMs), and strategic bombers such as our B-52s. The Pentagon's argument was based not so much on the military importance of this measure, which was acknowledged to be minimal, as on its political significance. It was argued that to accept anything less than numerical equality would lead to "political perceptions" of U.S. strategic inferiority.

The Soviets, on the other hand, continued to argue that "equal aggregates" were not reasonable so long as the U.S. maintained large "forward-based systems" (FBS), that is, nuclear-armed aircraft on carriers and at foreign bases capable of striking the U.S.S.R. They also insisted that our British and French allies' nuclear forces be taken into account. This argument was particularly telling with respect to the sixty-four British SLBMs, since these were of American manufacture, carried on submarines built with American assistance, and essentially indistinguishable from the 160 U.S. Polaris missiles which we had already agreed to count. The argument concerning French forces and our own FBS had less intellectual validity, but nonetheless was not completely without merit.

During the period leading up to Vladivostok, the United States strongly pushed one other point—the throw-weight of Soviet missiles —stressing above all the combined effect of throw-weight and MIRVs. The principal argument was the one spelled out above, that the combination of a larger number of weapons and the relatively high yields possible with large missiles (up to two megatons for each warhead) would pose a threat to the survival of our land-based missile silos more quickly than had been anticipated. Thus, the United States insisted that if the Soviets put MIRVs on their large missiles, they agree to deploy a relatively smaller number of these missiles to compensate for their large size. If the number were low enough, the Soviets would simply not have enough weapons to attack Minuteman effectively, regardless of the accuracy of the weapons, and still retain an adequate "assured destruction" reserve. Only then, it was argued, could we avoid the instabilities inherent in retaining a significant component of our force potentially vulnerable to a surprise attack, possibly tempting such an attack in a crisis.

In reaching agreement at Vladivostok, the Soviets yielded on "compensation" for forward-based systems and allied forces, and the United States yielded on controlling the size of Soviet missiles. Many on the U.S. side had argued that both objectives—equal numbers and limits on missile size—were of key importance. Nevertheless, between the two, there was tremendous pressure to make equal numerical limits the *sine qua non*. This position was somewhat ironic, since within the U.S. government almost everyone acknowledged that equal numbers had little military or strategic effect, while controls on the size of Soviet missiles (especially those equipped with MIRVs) could have some potential military and strategic effect—although even this effect was acknowledged to be limited since, as already noted, improved technology would eventually permit higher accuracies, which would eliminate the benefit of big missiles and their large-yield warheads.

One can raise a legitimate question whether the United States should have agreed to this compromise arrangement. Clearly, had the Soviets been willing to agree to very low limits on the number of land-based missiles they would deploy with MIRVs (for example, 400–500 such missiles), or to cut back the size of their MIRVed missiles, we could have put off the day when we have to be seriously concerned about the survivability of our Minuteman ICBMs. Nevertheless, it is difficult to see how any other compromise could have been made. As discussed in detail above, given their present technology the Soviets could not quickly deploy MIRVed missiles with the type of small warheads we have on our missiles. Thus, were they to accept significant constraints on the size of their missiles, they would remain dramatically behind the United States in the more important strategic measure of numbers of available warheads. It seems unlikely that they would have accepted this *de facto* superiority unless the United States made major concessions on FBS and allied nuclear forces— something we were simply not prepared to do.

It is worth reemphasizing that on its face the Vladivostok agreement is relatively favorable to the United States. It does not place great constraints on either side; however, it does require the Soviets to reduce their force levels in terms of aggregate strategic delivery vehicles somewhat, even with the present 2,400 limit. Based on what is known of the results of Secretary Kissinger's January 1976 trip to Moscow, it appears that it might even be possible to obtain a somewhat lower limit—perhaps as low as 2,200. As for the United States, the agreement would not prohibit any program which we now have under way, nor any program we are likely to undertake by 1985. We could increase the throw-weight of our missiles to a level essentially equal to that of the Soviet Union, should we decide it to be important to do so, and, as the agreement's terms now stand, we could deploy mobile ICBMs if we wished. (I shall return later to this point.) We can certainly continue with all our qualitative improvements, including improvements to our bomber force and SLBM force. While the final agreement on cruise missiles may impose some limits on our longer-range sea-based cruise missile force, we have limited strategic need for sea-based cruise missiles (although short-range cruise missiles, which would not be limited, are an important component of our conventional naval forces). What we do have a strong need for are medium-range air-launched cruise missiles to ensure the penetrability of our bomber force, and it seems unlikely that the final Vladivostok limit will compromise our ability to deploy a force of the required size. Thus, as was the case with SALT I, the agreement probably imposes some real, although modest, limits on the Soviet strategic program, but imposes no operational limits on the U.S. program when compared with what we would have done without the agreement.

The agreement also has the major advantage of eliminating "worst case" scenarios from the force planning of both sides. Before the Vladivostok Accord was reached, the intelligence community had projected a possible maximum Soviet deployment of 3,300 strategic delivery vehicles, of which 3,000 would be MIRVed missiles, by 1985. If the agreement is turned into a treaty, there will be no need to plan our actual deployment programs against the possibility of such large Soviet deployments, although we should continue to hedge against Soviet treaty abrogation by maintaining an active research and development program.

Some will argue that the Vladivostok Accord should not be completed because it will permit the Soviets to deploy their Backfire aircraft outside the limits of the agreement. I find this argument somewhat incredible. On the one hand, the same critics frequently argue that our massive strategic bomber force, which costs almost half of our total strategic budget, is not worth much compared to Soviet missiles. On the other hand, the Soviets' Backfire, an aircraft vastly less capable than our B-52s and even more dramatically less capable than our B-1, is alleged to represent a major threat, despite its short range, low payload, low alert rate, and second-strike character.

The Soviets appear willing to make on-the-record assurances that the Backfire is not capable of being used against the United States, will not be used against the United States, and will not be deployed with a companion tanker force which would permit midair refueling. Without such refueling, the aircraft would be limited to one-way, high-altitude, subsonic missions against the United States. Such assurances are consistent with a reasonable interpretation of the aircraft's mission. If the Soviets had intended to develop a new strategic aircraft for use against the United States, they certainly wasted a lot of money building the Backfire. They undoubtedly had the technology to develop at little additional cost an aircraft which would be

412

vastly more capable against the United States. Furthermore, they clearly had a need for an aircraft like the Backfire to replace their aging Badger and Blinder medium-bomber force deployed for use against targets in Europe and China.

Thus, it makes little sense to attribute to the Soviets the sinister motive of attempting to use the Backfire to get around the Vladivostok limits. Arguments over the Backfire should not hold up a new SALT agreement.

V

Based on the analysis presented earlier, I am considerably less concerned with the Soviet throw-weight advantage than is Paul Nitze. Nevertheless, no one can deny that Soviet capabilities are increasing and that Minuteman is becoming vulnerable, albeit more because of improvements in accuracy than because of increases in throw-weight. Thus, the United States must decide whether to react to the Soviet build-up by adjusting its own strategic program; and Mr. Nitze's suggestions for how we should respond deserve consideration even if one disagrees with his reasons for recommending a response.

Mr. Nitze's primary recommendation is that the United States employ a shelter-based land-mobile ICBM system to offset the Soviet throw-weight advantage. He argues that such a system would "absorb" the Soviet throw-weight advantage; if the Soviets were to attempt a first strike against our strategic forces, they would be required to devote a large proportion of their own force to attacking the mobile missiles, reducing their surviving throw-weight.

Again, this argument is open to question on Mr. Nitze's own assumptions concerning Soviet attack strategy. He apparently does not assume that the Soviets would carry out futile attacks against U.S. submarines at sea; why, then, should one assume that they would "waste" their throw-weight in an equally futile attempt to destroy dispersed land-mobile missiles? Yet, if they should not do so, the net Soviet advantage after the assumed attack—Mr. Nitze's main criterion—would not be greatly affected.

On the other hand, the deployment of land-mobile missiles would substantially increase the *absolute* amount of surviving U.S. retaliatory capability. Thus, for reasons somewhat different from Mr. Nitze's, I agree that a mobile land-based system, by reducing the vulnerability of U.S. strategic forces to a counterforce attack, could help to prevent the Soviets from ever attaining strategic superiority.

But even on this basis Mr. Nitze's proposed program would be extravagant and untested, going beyond the degree of threat that now appears likely, and far more costly than other measures, at least as feasible, to improve survivability. Furthermore, it might well set off a new competition in which the Soviets would have all the advantages. Let me address these points in order.

First, there remain serious cost and technical problems associated with such systems. They require either very hard movable capsules to protect the missiles, or very cheap hard shelters, neither of which has yet been proved technically feasible. With regard to cost, it is very unlikely that any feasible technical concept could cost as little as Mr. Nitze's prediction of $12–15 billion over a ten-year period. A much more reasonable estimate, when all costs are considered, would be about $30 billion. Since initial cost estimates of new weapons systems inevitably turn out to be somewhat lower than final costs, this final ten-year cost could easily run as high as $50 billion.

Second, we should not forget that potential Minuteman vulnerabilities are strictly theoretical; these projected vulnerabilities are based on force exchange calculations which are probably extremely conservative. Mounting an operational attack against Minuteman would not be a simple task. No one has ever tested weapons against land-based ICBM silos in an operational environment, so the Soviets would face considerable uncertainties in mounting such an attack. Furthermore, there are many technical problems associated with attacking silos: two examples are the problem of "fratricide" mentioned earlier, which necessitates very precise attack timing, and the possibility that the side being attacked will launch its missiles as soon as it sees the incoming attack.

Third, the United States can make potential force improvements which might significantly reduce Minuteman vulnerability, especially through the use of defense concepts oriented exclusively toward defending silos. While most of these concepts are far from proven technically, the Soviets cannot presume we will be unable to protect the Minuteman force if they are seriously considering striving for a capability to destroy it.[13] While I share some of the concerns raised in the

---

[13] For an example of two of the most intriguing possibilities for reducing Minuteman's vulnerability, see Richard L. Garwin, "How Real Is the Soviet Threat to Minuteman," presented to the Senate Committee on Foreign Relations in answer to staff questions addressed to Mr. Garwin's testimony of 18 September 1975. Mr. Garwin suggests two possibilities: a "bed of nails" defense in which vertical steel rods and radar fuse jamming would disable, respectively, both the ground burst and radar fusing on incoming warheads, and a "pellet" defense in which incoming reentry vehicles would be destroyed while passing through a curtain of steel pellets thrown up by simple explosives and set off upon detection of the reentry vehicle by simple radars.

Congress about the present direction of our missile defense research and development programs, clearly we should not short-change this crucial area.[14]

But in any event the issue is not confined to land-based missiles. The United States has other ways of conserving or increasing its survivable second-strike capability. We maintain large and effective submarine-launched ballistic missile and bomber forces, the alert portions of which are essentially invulnerable to potential Soviet attack. We have active programs to modernize and improve both our SLBM and strategic bomber forces. Perhaps the most important of these programs is the new Trident-I missile. This missile is designed for deployment on both our new Trident submarine and our older Poseidon submarines. It will carry up to eight MIRVs and, with over twice the range of the present Poseidon MIRVed missile, will increase the operating area of our SLBM force by a factor of ten, tremendously reducing its vulnerability.

We also have an active program to ensure the effectiveness of our strategic bomber force. This includes the planned deployment of the B-1 bomber, which I believe should go forward in small numbers, although I see little reason to deploy all 240 B-1s now planned. A better use of our funds would be to cut back the B-1 program somewhat and use the funds freed to modernize our older B-52s, equipping them with a moderate number of medium-range strategic cruise missiles to increase their capability of penetrating advanced Soviet air defenses.[15]

---

[14] One counterargument often made is that the Anti-Ballistic Missile Treaty prohibits deployment of such local defense systems, so why should we waste our money on research and development? But, if an effective technology emerges for a defense exclusively devoted to ICBMs, and if arms control measures cannot be found which will improve the stability of the strategic balance in the longer run, we should seriously consider insisting upon modifications to the ABM treaty which would permit deployment of ICBM defenses which would be capable of defending only hardened military sites, and not capable of defending soft area targets such as cities. In pursuing ICBM defense technology, we should actively investigate new concepts, such as the inexpensive but promising technologies mentioned above. One of the major difficulties with our ABM research and development has been that it remains closely tied to the essentially abandoned Safeguard program, although our ABM objectives have changed completely from those which motivated the design of Safeguard.

[15] Some critics charge that for the United States to develop strategic cruise missiles will simply fuel the arms race and further destabilize the balance between the United States and the U.S.S.R. In my view, this criticism is completely unfounded. These weapons will reduce the total destructive capability of our bombers, since the bomber must carry the weight of the missile in addition to the weight of the bomb carried on the missile. With free-fall gravity bombs, the bomber need not carry the weight of the missile, and can therefore carry a more destructive payload to any given range. Furthermore, cruise missiles should

JAN M. LODAL

Indeed, given these alternatives to the deployment of mobile missiles, and the small chance that a feasible U.S. program can be developed from a technical and financial standpoint, serious consideration should be given to banning such systems in a SALT II treaty. It seems clear from the negotiating record to date that the Soviets would accept an outright ban on all mobile ICBMs as part of a final SALT II agreement. The United States apparently has yet to accept such an approach, primarily because of Pentagon pressure to keep the option for a land-based mobile missile open. While the United States has not yet come up with a feasible land-mobile ICBM program, it is a serious technical option for the Soviets. The Soviets have large uninhabited land areas and no political constraints that would confine the deployment of nuclear weapons to military reservations, as is the case in the United States. In fact, they have already deployed significant numbers of intermediate-range mobile missiles for use against China and Europe, and their newest solid-propellant ICBM, the SS-16, could probably be deployed in a mobile mode almost immediately.

Banning land-based mobiles would close off one additional area for potential arms competition between the two countries, as well as eliminating the potential SALT verification uncertainties presented by mobile missiles. While (like Mr. Nitze) I believe these verification uncertainties are not as crucial as some have made them out to be, they could be serious in some circumstances. In particular, if the Soviet Union chose to deploy a large shelter-based land-mobile system similar to the system Mr. Nitze proposes for the United States, our planners would have to assume that each shelter contains a missile. Since there could be thousands of shelters, such a situation could easily force a complete breakdown in the SALT process and lead to a new level of arms competition.

But a shelter-based mobile ICBM deployment is not one which the Soviets are likely to undertake in the near future, so I see no reason why the Vladivostok agreement should be abandoned if land-mobile ICBMs are permitted within its ceilings. Nevertheless the United States should actively seek to obtain mutual agreement that they be banned.

Mr. Nitze's second major program suggestion is that the United States undertake a large civil defense program. He bases this primarily on his belief that the Soviets have a large and active civil de-

represent a stabilizing influence, since they increase our second-strike retaliatory capability, but add essentially nothing to our first-strike counterforce capability. See Alton H. Quanbeck and Archie L. Wood, *Modernizing the Strategic Bomber Force—Why and How* (Washington, D.C.: The Brookings Institution, 1976).

fense program, designed to give them the possibility of absorbing an American retaliatory attack with an acceptable degree of Soviet fatalities. Mr. Nitze believes we should develop the same capabilities.

There is some question about the actual size and extent of the present Soviet program. However, their present program is not likely to be able to significantly reduce overall fatalities in a U.S. retaliatory attack. Only a small percentage of the Soviet population has been adequately trained in evacuation procedures; fallout shelters are in many cases inadequately stocked and of inadequate size; and many would die from secondary nuclear effects even if they reached the shelters before the attack. Thus, while the U.S.S.R. spends more on civil defense than does the United States, it is not clear that the Soviet Union is anywhere near being able to eliminate our deterrent capabilities through such a program.

An American program would face similar technical difficulties. It would be almost impossible to disperse most of the American population now residing in large metropolitan areas to shelters which could not be attacked, given the very large number of Soviet weapons which will be available by the mid-1980s. Furthermore, protecting these shelters against radiation from fallout, adequately stocking them, and adequately training the population, even if all these were politically possible, represent an almost impossible task from a practical standpoint.

If we continue with the strategic programs I have discussed above, it seems highly unlikely that the Soviets could mount an effective threat to our deterrent force. The Soviets can build larger missiles, deploy more throw-weight, increase their megatonnage, and perhaps even come close to deploying as many weapons as the United States has deployed. However, our submarines and alert bombers should remain invulnerable to Soviet counterforce attacks, and we can seriously complicate any potential Soviet effort to develop a counterforce capability against our land-based missiles. Thus, any advantage they might have in throw-weight or other static capability measures will have essentially no military benefits; its only possible benefit might be to create adverse political perceptions in the rest of the world concerning the relative strengths of the United States and the Soviet Union.

But we must not forget that our own rhetoric largely determines these political perceptions. To the extent that we emphasize measures in which the Soviets have an advantage, such as missile throw-weight, we ensure that others will perceive us to be at a disadvantage. On the other hand, if we pursue sensible programs, designed to protect our deterrent capability, and explain carefully why we have decided to forgo a "throw-weight race" or a "megatonnage race," I see no reason why we should be the subject of adverse political perceptions.

*   *   *

VII

To conclude, the United States has reasonable strategic force alternatives which can ensure our retaliatory capability, deny the Soviets any potential military advantage, and yet which do not require a return to a massive civil defense program or deployment of a costly and perhaps technically infeasible land-based mobile ICBM system. We need not match the Soviets in missile throw-weight, nor, within quite broad limits, need we even worry about their advantage. At the same time, our government must adopt complementary rhetoric, making it clear why we have chosen not to place great emphasis on throw-weight, lest the growing Soviet advantage in this one respect create an adverse perception of the strategic balance throughout the world.

With respect to the Vladivostok SALT Accord, I believe that it should be completed, even if this means compromising our positions somewhat on the Backfire and cruise missile issues. The Vladivostok Accord may well have been disappointing relative to what many of us had expected as a follow-on SALT agreement: it does not limit the threat to the survivability of the land-based missile forces of either side, nor does it provide for significant reductions in the size of existing strategic forces. Rather, it will undoubtedly permit a significant increase in the overall destructive capability of the forces of the two sides. These facts make it easy to criticize the Vladivostok Accord, since one can always compare it to the kind of agreement most of us would have preferred. Furthermore, it is easy to place the blame on the Soviets, ascribing to them a strong effort to obtain strategic superiority.

What is much more difficult is to work out a viable alternative to the Vladivostok Accord. Most of the specific suggestions critics have made for alternative agreements were tried vigorously in one form or another during the three-year period leading up to the accord. Low limits on Soviet MIRVs were unacceptable to the Soviet Union for the obvious reason that this would have left the United States with a militarily significant superiority in this area. Limits on throw-weight were unacceptable because such limits would have effectively prohibited significant MIRV deployments, given existing Soviet technology. Significant reductions were not of interest to either side, perhaps more than any other reason because neither the Soviet leadership nor the U.S. Administration was willing to undertake the internal bureaucratic struggles necessary to decide which component would have to reduce. Finally, the Soviets even today remain quite concerned about U.S. forward-based systems, as we remain concerned about the size of their missiles. Thus, the Vladivostok Accord itself represented a fairly major breakthrough from what appeared to be a completely deadlocked situation.

Given this background, I believe the only serious alternative to completing the Vladivostok Accord is to abandon the SALT process for the time being, at least with respect to offensive forces, hoping that the two sides will trust each other enough to keep their force deployments under control by mutual example, without the benefit of formal agreements.

Such a hope is likely to be disappointed. With no agreements, the probability is that the Soviets will continue to increase their strategic spending, leading to ever-widening disparities in force size. While the thrust of this article has been that many of these disparities are much less meaningful than they are made out to be, at some point the disparities could become large enough to have political, and perhaps even military, consequences. We would then have to increase our force size to keep up, probably beyond the ceilings contemplated at Vladivostok, certainly beyond our present programs.

Some might argue that we need not match the Soviet build-up even roughly. But unless we did so we could hardly expect the Soviets, in renewed negotiations, to accept even Vladivostok-level limits, since they would then be at a far higher level and probably at a comparative advantage at least in numbers.

In short, abandonment of the SALT process, even for a time, would mean unnecessary extension of an arms competition that has gone on too long. Such an extension could only increase Soviet-American tensions and, in my judgment, decrease rather than improve our security.

STRATEGIC STABILITY *

Paul H. Nitze

This letter by Paul H. Nitze addresses issues raised by Jan M. Lodal in the preceding article. Lodal rejected the contention that the Soviet Union is approaching the strategic superiority postulated in Nitze's article "Assuring Strategic Stability." There, Nitze argued that a key determinant of strategic stability is the relationship between U.S. and Soviet nuclear forces after an exchange in which each side reduces its opponent's force to the greatest useful extent. Here, Nitze maintains that his initial analysis of such an exchange accurately represented its outcome: throw-weight was a pertinent measure, and the U.S. forces were deployed in ways that maximized their usefulness.

The article, "Assuring Strategic Stability: An Alternative View" by Jan Lodal, which appeared in the April issue of *Foreign Affairs*, is principally a rebuttal of my article which appeared in the January 1976 issue. I have carefully studied Mr. Lodal's remarks and believe that a rejoinder is necessary.

There are three distinctly different ways, each representing an increasing order of depth and sophistication, in which throw-weight, or any other parameter, can be used as an index of relative capability or of crisis stability:

1. That which each side has *before* a strike;
2. That *surviving* to the United States after an initial counter-force strike by the Soviet side;
3. That remaining to each side *after an exchange* in which the Soviet side attacks U.S. forces and the United States responds by reducing the Soviet side's reserved forces to the greatest useful extent.

The analysis in my January article was specifically based on the third of these methods. It is this method which most clearly brings out the stability, or potential instability, of the relationship. It is the indicated method if one judges that we would not have high-quality deterrence if our only recourse, after a purely counterforce attack by the Soviet Union, were immediately to attack Soviet population and industry. Such a response would concede military victory to the Soviet Union and lead to immeasurable destruction in the United

---

* Source: *Foreign Affairs* (July 1976), pp. 820-823.

States and other parts of the world. In my opinion, a U.S. posture requiring such an immediate response would not provide the high-quality deterrence we need.

Mr. Lodal, on the other hand, emphasizes the adequacy of our deterrent forces, after a Soviet counterforce attack on U.S. forces. Much of his criticism of my article is based either on a confusion of the first or second methods of analysis with the third, or on a misunderstanding of my analysis, using the third method.

Mr. Lodal presents arithmetic showing that hard-target counterforce capability is influenced more by accuracy than by throw-weight. This point would be pertinent if I had used throw-weight as an index in the first method of analysis. The effect of accuracy is fully taken into account in the third method of analysis and should not be a subject of contention between us. The after-exchange balance necessarily takes into account not only the accuracy, but also the yield, number, and reliability of each side's offensive weapons as well as the survivability of the forces being attacked. *After the exchange,* the counterforce hard targets that can be usefully addressed would have been addressed. Hence, *after the exchange* most remaining targets would be relatively soft and many of the originally important parameters, such as accuracy, would become of significantly reduced importance, and throw-weight a much more relevant index.[1]

Mr. Lodal also argues that throw-weight is not a good index because, particularly when bombers are included, it is difficult to define. He asserts that my assumptions regarding this definition "go too far in favoring the Soviets. If one were to use gross U.S. bomber payload, the Soviet projected throw-weight advantage in 1984 would disappear entirely" [footnote 8]. Gross bomber payload, since it bears scant relationship to the weapons which can actually be carried and delivered to target, is clearly not comparable to missile throw-weight. Missile throw-weight, by contrast, is by its definition limited to the useful weight which can be propelled to the assigned target including, in the case of MIRVs, that weight used to distribute RVs among the several assigned targets.

---

[1] I have examined indices, other than throw-weight, including equivalent megatons, countermilitary potential, warheads, single nuclear delivery vehicles, and a more sophisticated index called "Equivalent Weapons" which sums the capability of weapons against the targets they may be called upon to attack, including those that are relatively hard as well as those that are relatively soft; the last is designed to take into account all the relevant characteristics of both the weapons and the targets. Each of these indices produces roughly similar after-exchange results; what is important is not which index is used but whether the third method of analysis, rather than the first or second, is used.

Concluding on this point, Mr. Lodal also contends that it is "difficult" to use throw-weight as an index because of the possibility of "range-payload" trade-offs in, for example, the Trident missile. My analysis is based on U.S. plans as they exist. Mr. Lodal notes that these plans sacrifice throw-weight to get survivability. To give these plans the maximum possible credit, my analysis actually assumes that the at-sea SLBMs are *100-percent survivable* in the after-exchange situation. The alternative, to increase U.S. SLBM throw-weight, would (as Mr. Lodal points out) reduce survivability and hence would improve only the before-strike and not the after-exchange balance.

Next, Mr. Lodal infers [footnote 9] that in my postulated exchange "most U.S. SLBMs were assumed to be used to attack Soviet silos" and argues that if the SLBMs and alert bombers were "simply held in reserve," the " 'after-attack' residual throw-weight advantage of the Soviets might be considerably less." These contentions are based on a misunderstanding of my analysis. Contrary to his suggestion, no SLBMs were used to attack silos on either side. In my analysis, the Soviets were assumed to attack U.S. forces in a manner which would give them the greatest net advantage at the end of an exchange, including U.S. retaliation against the Soviet reserve forces. U.S. retaliation was in the analysis limited so that a pound of U.S. missile throw-weight knocks out more than a pound of Soviet reserve force throw-weight. Where appropriate, SLBMs were used against bomber bases; those SLBMs not used were *retained as reserve and assumed to survive for an unlimited period.*

In my analysis U.S. alert bombers were, however, used in striking Soviet counterforce targets and constituted a significant component of the effectiveness of that attack. They were not assumed to be held in reserve since most of them would then have been subject to destruction similar to that assumed for nonalert bombers. The number of available long runways is not large. The Soviets could deny us these runways at the cost of a very modest amount of their throw-weight. The Soviet side would, therefore, gain in net residual advantage if we attempted to hold our bombers in reserve.

This point bears directly on a key argument made by Mr. Lodal [in the concluding paragraph of section II]: "In particular, even if the Soviets destroyed all our land-based ICBMs, nonalert bombers and nonalert submarine-launched ballistic missiles (SLBMs), we would still retain our alert bomber force and our alert SLBM force. These forces alone would be capable of delivering something like 4–5,000 nuclear weapons against Soviet targets. I find it difficult to conceive of a military need for more than 4–5,000 nuclear weapons, albeit weapons much smaller than the relatively large Soviet weapons." This statement reflects the second method of analysis, not the third method used in my article. Following the initial Soviet attack, approximately half the surviving U.S. weapons and a very large percentage of their aggregate damage potential would be in the surviving bomber force. A prompt decision would then have to be made as to whether to direct these bomber weapons at Soviet urban-industrial targets or at counterforce targets. My method of analysis assumed the latter. The Soviet side, however, would never be certain that we would not exercise the first alternative, immediately to strike their cities and industry, despite the desperate consequences to us and the world of doing so. It is upon this uncertainty that Mr. Lodal's alternative view appears to be based.

In the November 1975 issue of *Communist of the Armed Forces*, the leading Soviet military journal, the following statement appears:

> The premise of Marxism-Leninism on war as a continuation of policy by military means remains true in an atmosphere of fundamental changes in military matters. The attempt of certain bourgeois ideologists to prove that nuclear missile weapons leave war outside the framework of policy, and that nuclear war moves beyond the control of policy, ceases to be an instrument of policy and does not constitute its continuation is theoretically incorrect and politically reactionary.

I find it hard to accept the viewpoint that the United States should be less interested than the Soviet Union in the continuing control of policy over military strategy. To permit one's country to arrive at a position where it could have little choice but immediately to escalate a war to the ultimate violence which modern technology makes possible, does not seem to me to be wise policy, or to be necessary.

In order to assure such crisis stability, rough parity and high-quality deterrence, as measured by the third method of analysis, it is a prerequisite that U.S. deterrent forces be reasonably survivable against a Soviet initial attack. This part of the analysis is covered by the second method emphasized by Mr. Lodal. As a result there is a degree of overlap and correspondence between his judgments and mine. He also would take steps to improve the survivability of our Minuteman forces. But the methods he suggests have been given far less scientific and technical study than the methods I have recommended, namely a so-called multiple launch-point system for our land-based ICBMs. (Incidentally, in a recent discussion, Mr. Lodal agreed that if it were decided to pursue a new basing mode for Minuteman, he would also favor pursuing the approach on which my $15 billion cost estimate was based rather than the one on which his $30 billion cost estimate was based.)

He also would advocate an improvement in U.S. missile accuracy, and suggests that accuracies of 0.06 NM are wholly possible for both sides by the late 1980s. My analysis was based on the less radical estimates for the accuracy of deployed systems given by most responsible authorities for the period up to 1985, that covered by my analysis.

I did not recommend against a SALT agreement based on the Vladivostok Accord. Indeed, my analysis was based on the assumption that such an agreement would be entered into. Mr. Lodal also hopes that such an agreement would not inhibit us from mitigating the effects of permitted Soviet deployments by developing and deploying medium-range air-launched cruise missiles—a point I believe critically important.

As a final point, if one assumes that the immediate response of the United States to a Soviet counterforce attack should be an attack on Soviet population and industry, and that the Soviet Union will have no appreciable ABM defenses, little of our presumed technological advantage would be of much significance. A reasonable number of very large single-warhead weapons, not necessarily of high accuracy, which could be launched on assured warning of attack, to ground-burst in the Soviet Union with maximum fallout effect, would be much more devastating against population and industry and much more difficult for civil defense measures to protect against than the larger number of smaller but more accurate weapons our advanced technology makes possible. For years we have been using our technology to get away from such a high-risk doomsday strategy—I believe correctly.

CAN NUCLEAR DETERRENCE LAST OUT THE CENTURY? *

Fred Charles Iklé

Mutual deterrence, the keystone of America's approach for preventing nuclear war, affects only a fraction of the possible causes of a nuclear war, according to Fred Charles Iklé, though the continual readiness it requires increases the potential for accidents. In addition,

* Source: *Foreign Affairs* (January 1973), pp. 267-285.

this strategy contains two dangerous, archaic dogmas: an emphasis upon swift launch and massive population destruction. Iklé contends that undertaking steps to reduce missile vulnerability, to slow the speed of response, and to end the targeting of civilians would decrease the chance of war.

The autumn of last year [1972] marked half the road from the beginning of the nuclear era to the year 2000. Mankind has been spared nuclear devastation since the annihilation of two Japanese cities by the only two nuclear weapons then existing. But the destructiveness of nuclear arsenals, now increased many thousandfold, has sunk into human consciousness like man's knowledge of his mortality.

We all turn away, however, from the thought that nuclear war may be as inescapable as death, and may end our lives and our society within this generation or the next. We plan and work every day for the twenty-first century—as parents educating our children, as young workers saving for retirement, as a nation that seeks to preserve its physical environment, its political traditions, its cultural heritage. For this larger horizon—encompassing for the younger generation simply the common expectation of a healthy life—we do in fact assume "nuclear immortality." We believe, or we act as if we believe, that thanks to a certain international order, the existing arsenals of nuclear weapons with their almost incomprehensible destructiveness will never be used.

Yet, this order is so constructed that it cannot move toward abolition of nuclear weapons. It demands, as the necessary condition for avoiding nuclear war, the very preservation of these arms, always ready to destroy entire nations.

This ever-present danger once caused great anguish among the informed public in Western countries and evoked a diffused anxiety everywhere. Since the mid-1960s, the concern of both the public and the specialists has become far less acute, even though Soviet strategic forces have grown dramatically. Since 1968, confidence has been encouraged by the prospect of agreement in the Strategic Arms Limitation Talks (SALT) and, in May 1972, by the Moscow accords.

These initial agreements are designed, at least from the American perspective, first to preserve mutual deterrence as the strategic relationship between the United States and the Soviet Union, and second, to stabilize it by curbing the build-up of nuclear forces. As seen by a majority of American government officials, congressional leaders and civilian experts, these two objectives should govern our strategic arms-control policy as well as our own force planning for the foreseeable future. Other objectives (such as protecting cities) are held to jeopardize deterrence, and massive arms reductions or general and complete disarmament are considered utopian as well as dangerous.

According to this view, there are no alternatives to our current approach to mutual deterrence that deserve serious consideration. Even though the military services, government agencies and experts may differ on particular points of doctrine and choices of weapons, the dominant view of the workings of mutual deterrence has come to uphold three far-reaching dogmas:

One: our nuclear forces must be designed almost exclusively for "retaliation" in response to a Soviet nuclear attack—particularly an attempt to disarm us through a sudden strike.

Two: our forces must be designed and operated in such a way that this "retaliation" can be swift, inflicted through a single, massive and—above all—prompt strike. What would happen after this strike is of little concern for strategic planning.

Three: the threatened "retaliation" must be the killing of a major fraction of the Soviet population; moreover, the same ability to kill our population must be guaranteed the Soviet government in order to eliminate its main incentive for increasing Soviet forces. Thus, deterrence is "stabilized" by keeping it mutual.

This third dogma dictates not only our desire that Russian cities should remain essentially undefended, but also our willingness to abstain from defending our cities and even to hobble our capability to destroy Soviet nuclear arms. Proponents of this arrangement argue that it will lead to "arms race stability"; critics maintain that guaranteeing capabilities for Mutual Assured Destruction is indeed a "MAD" strategy.

Soviet military writers, by and large, express other views. Above all, they reject the idea that their forces should be designed for retaliation only, stressing instead the need to be prepared for fighting a nuclear war. Among Americans interested in nuclear strategy, however, only a minority now oppose any of these dogmas, and fewer still would reject them all. Absence of any one of these three elements—it is widely believed—would undermine deterrence, stimulate an arms race, or both.

Yet, these assumed requirements of stable deterrence are to a large extent the heritage of strategic policies from prior decades, now obsolete. They are a perilous way to protect ourselves from nuclear catastrophe and harmful to the prospects of strategic disarmament. Happily, they are dispensable for deterrence. Over the decades to come, we can develop and put into effect a safer and more humane strategy to prevent nuclear war.

II

It was Winston Churchill who in 1955 first expounded the essential ideas of mutual deterrence to the world at large. In that celebrated "balance of terror" speech, he made a "formidable admission," as he himself called it: "The deterrent does not cover the case of lunatics or dictators in the mood of Hitler when he found himself in his final dugout. This is a blank." The most disturbing defect, today, in the prevalent thinking on nuclear strategy is the cavalier disregard for this blank.

An almost exclusive emphasis on deterrence could be defended as a satisfactory long-term policy if it could be convincingly argued that successful deterrence was tantamount to prevention of nuclear war. There exists no rational basis for such an argument. No matter how cataclysmic the threatened "assured destruction," those calculated decisions which our deterrent seeks to prevent are not the sole processes that could lead to nuclear war. We simply cannot know which of the various potential causes is most probable—whether it be a coherently calculated decision to attack, or an "irrational" decision or technical accident. Yet the approach now prevailing puts almost all effort into preventing the "rational" decision.

Moreover, our current strategy explicitly selects for nearly exclusive emphasis a very special type of intended attack. It has thus become the overriding concern of American strategic analysts and force planners to ensure that our intercontinental arms would be capable of "retaliating" after a Soviet attack sought to destroy them. It so happens that the problem of deterring such an attack lends itself to rigorous analysis, *provided* one postulates that a particular type of rationality governs a Soviet decision whether or not to launch it. The fascinating opportunity for such intellectual rigor—so exceptional in military and political affairs—may partly explain why this problem has commanded so dominant a place in American strategic thinking.

This analysis has now become the canonical way of determining the adequacy of our strategic forces. It uses *our* ideas about how surprise attacks could be designed, our estimates of what weapons the Soviets have and how they would perform, our latest findings about the performance of our own weapons, and, as soon as we discover a mistake in these calculations, our corrections. That is to say, we impute to the Soviet military leadership our imaginativeness (or lack of it) in inventing "successful" attacks, our state of knowledge

427

(or ignorance) of how the weapons on both sides would perform in the vortex of a thermonuclear war and our diligence (or carelessness) in calculations.

The results of such calculations are taken most seriously by American defense planners. Should they suggest a way in which our "retaliatory" capability might be jeopardized, we institute remedies: we harden, disperse, or add penetration aids. Should they show that we could still inflict massive destruction, we conclude that all is well. To be sure, we must consider surprise strikes against us based on our understanding of how the relationship between the two strategic forces might be exploited. But we should not disregard all other risks.

Yet this is what the canonical analysis does. It makes a peculiar assumption about the "rationality" of the Soviet decision we need to deter. On the long slope descending from rationality to irrationality, it postulates that only a short stretch needs to be considered. We must prepare—it is argued—for the possibility that Soviet leaders might move so far down this slope as to be tempted to decide on a surprise attack, provided the calculations that we impute to their military staff indicate the attack would "succeed." That is, we prepare for the event that Soviet leaders might judge how a global nuclear war would turn out by relying on such largely untested calculations, trusting their military advisers to have used unbiased estimates and avoided gross mistakes. But we need not prepare for the possibility that Soviet leaders might be somewhat less "rational" and let a cabal of officers mislead them by twisting the enormously complicated data to show that a surprise attack could "succeed" even where our own analysis clearly indicates it would fail.

Or, to put it differently, our analysis implicitly argues that we have to prepare for a certain type of Soviet leader: a man who could be tempted to launch a surprise attack if the calculations we impute to them promise "success"; who would ignore the dangers of long-term radioactive fallout (which our analysis omits) and expect they could stay on top of the postwar chaos (about which our analysis says next to nothing). But we need not prepare—it is argued—for Soviet leaders who might be "less rational" in an acute crisis and who might rely on their ability to launch an attack so designed as to deter us from retaliating. Such a stratagem of "counter-deterrence" would seek to cripple our nuclear forces in a surprise attack while sparing our cities, in order to deter the U.S. President from reprisal against Russian cities lest withheld Soviet forces then devastate American cities.

When leaders of a powerful country are credited with a willingness to gamble on some scheme for nuclear surprise attack—a scheme whose calculations they cannot validate, whose assumptions they cannot test and whose failure would mean the end of their regime or even their country—how rational a decision are we assuming in our posture of deterrence? When the prevailing American view of mutual deterrence postulates that both the Russian nuclear posture and our own must be designed to deter an opponent of such degraded rationality, why stop at this particular degradation in judgment?

The narrowness of our canonical analysis of what it takes to keep deterrence stable can perhaps be traced to the traumatic American experience of the Pearl Harbor attack. By a few easy protective measures we could have denied the Japanese militarists their success in 1941. This lesson we have learned well, and with good reason. We should not permit such a surprise attack to become easy, lest we invite it during some crisis when our antagonist sees himself forced to choose among deadly alternatives.

To make a surprise attack unsuccessful, however, is not necessarily to deter it. By 1945, after all, the Japanese surprise attack had turned into a failure. Shortly before the attack was launched, Emperor Hirohito anticipated such an outcome and asked his military leaders how they envisaged defeating the United States, given its superior industrial might. His question never received an answer.[1] Would hardening, dispersal, and a higher alertness of the American forces in 1941 have made the Japanese military abstain, or merely have driven them to redesign their attack?

Pearl Harbor thus provides a lesson beyond that of the danger of forces vulnerable to surprise attack. The Japanese military evidently expected that the United States, if it were disarmed in the Pacific, would not mount the terribly costly effort of striking back. In choosing this gamble, they were even more "irrational" than future Soviet leaders would have to be to gamble on "counter-deterrence," since our striking back after Pearl Harbor did not invite the devastation of American cities. Yet today, our European-based nuclear arms, for instance, are vulnerable to a "counter-deterrence" attack.

Rather recent history reminds us that men can acquire positions of power who are willing to see their nation destroyed in pursuit of causes which only they and their henchmen espouse. In countries

---

[1] Many other examples can be found of aggressive wars that have been planned without at all considering how they were to end. See the author's *Every War Must End* (New York: Columbia University Press, 1971).

429

that tolerate a dictatorship, a leader might always rise to the top who deems it a virtue, perhaps part of his revolutionary creed, to live dangerously—*vivere pericolosamente,* as Benito Mussolini put it. What a sad irony that the nations that had to fight Hitler to his last bunker should now rely on an interlock of their military postures, making survival depend on the rationality of all future leaders in all major nuclear powers.

III

In the 1950s, prior to the missile age and Russia's massive build-up of her nuclear forces, one heard a great deal about the risk of accidental war. Now, when American and Soviet missiles by the thousands are poised in constant readiness, this concern has curiously diminished. To justify this more relaxed attitude, some might point to the fact that no unauthorized detonation has ever occurred, or cite the American-Soviet agreements of 1971 for improving the hotline or recall the elaborate safeguards with which the military seem to protect nuclear weapons.

But nobody can predict that the fatal accident or unauthorized act will never happen. The hazard is too elusive. It is inherent not only in the ineradicable possibility of technical defects, but also in the inevitable vulnerability to human error of all command and operational procedures—during periods of high alert as well as during the many years of quiet waiting. So exceedingly complex are modern weapons systems, both in their internal mechanisms and in their intricate interactions, that it seems doubtful whether any group of experts could ever ferret out every unintended ramification, discover every lurking danger. Indeed, the very word *system* misleads in that it suggests a clearly bounded combination of parts, their interactions all designed to serve the intended purpose.

The deadly danger is deepened by the fact that latent hazards can only be corrected if they are sought out. To look, day in and day out, for some hidden risk of accident is not a task, however, that captures the attention of top decision makers. It is far from unusual in military operations for serious oversights or occasional incompetence to go undetected or uncorrected until after a major disaster. For example, after the North Korean seizure in 1968 of the American reconnaissance ship *Pueblo,* when the crew had been unable to destroy all the cryptographic material before capture, destructive incendiary devices were suddenly permitted aboard ship. Previously, such devices had been prohibited because of the fire hazard, and the development of safer ones had been neglected. Safeguards rarely come without costs, and often appear to pose counteracting hazards.

Drastic shortcomings in the Defense Department's worldwide communications came to the attention of a congressional subcommittee after the Israeli attack in 1967 on the American ship *Liberty*. At the beginning of the Six-Day War, the joint chiefs of staff decided to order the *Liberty* into safer waters. Over a period of thirteen hours prior to the Israeli attack, they sent their order in at least four messages. Two of the messages were misrouted to the Philippines and one of these was thence sent to the National Security Agency in Maryland, there merely to be filed. Another message was routed over two paths to be doubly sure; in the first path it was lost in a relay station, in the second delayed until many hours after the attack. The fourth message also arrived too late. This failure in emergency communications occurred under almost perfect conditions: no facilities had been disabled, there was no enemy jamming, and no restrictions on the use of available communication modes had been imposed.

It can be argued that safeguards for nuclear arms are likely to be more stringent and more carefully designed than arrangements protecting cryptographic equipment or procedures for transmitting top-level emergency commands. But those Russians and Americans who monitor the safety of strategic arms cannot afford to learn from past accidents to probe for and correct critical hazards. When it comes to defects in safeguards that might lead to an accidental nuclear war, our societies cannot survive by learning through trial and error.

Polaris and Poseidon submarines suffer from communication difficulties so serious that "some of the messages never get delivered," as a senior naval officer put it. To permit "retaliation" after a massive surprise attack, officers on American and Russian missile-carrying submarines must be ready, presumably, to launch their enormously destructive loads even after military communications networks have been destroyed. Yet, they must never inadvertently or deliberately misconstrue an order to launch—during all the long years the submarines will cruise the oceans as part of the "stable" deterrent, as well as during the confusion and turmoil of a global crisis. Will this formidable requirement always be met?

The peril may well be greater on the Soviet side. Since the American military establishment is relatively open to outside scrutiny, pressures to ferret out safety hazards or institute perhaps costly remedies can come from civilians in the executive branch, congressional committees and even the public. Under the compartmentalized, pervasive secrecy of the Soviet military, however, past accidents and

431

present hazards can be kept not only from the public but from senior civilian authorities as well.

Given that occasional incompetence or malfeasance is predictable in large institutions—whether military or civilian—the safety of nuclear armaments remains a constantly pressing uncertainty. Given the huge and far-flung missile forces, ready to be launched from land and sea on both sides, the scope for disaster by accident is immense. Given that our strategic dogmas demand the targeting of populations and denial of defensive measures, the carnage would be without restraint. And as if all this were not terrifying enough, some proponents of these dogmas want to push matters to the brink.

Various influential people have urged that the United States adopt procedures to launch its missile force upon receipt of a warning that a Soviet surprise attack is on the way. . . .

But what might appear as a deliberate attack within the few minutes before the expected impact could have been a false warning; even an actual nuclear explosion could have been accidental. The short time available to execute a "retaliatory" launch-on-warning of our missile forces would not be enough to resolve this uncertainty.

Advocacy of a launch-on-warning policy might be viewed as a passing aberration in a fluid debate, if it were not for institutional pressures among the military that will keep driving in the same direction. Those branches of American and Russian military services that believe they must continue to press the case for land-based missile forces will—because of the increasing vulnerability of these forces—be ever more tempted to stress launch-on-warning as an option. To make this option more acceptable, new warning systems would be acquired; these in turn would strengthen vested interests in favor of this policy.

In Russia, such pressures may be even more compelling, because Soviet strategic thinking continues to consider favorably "preemption," that is, striking at the enemy before he can complete—or even start—his attack. For instance, the 1968 edition of Marshal V. D. Sokolovskii's book on Soviet military strategy refers to surveillance systems for detecting "the adversary's immediate preparations for a nuclear attack" as well as his massive missile launch, making it possible "to bar an aggressor's surprise attack and deliver prompt nuclear strikes against him." As recently as 1971, Defense Minister Grechko stressed the importance of speed for "frustrating an aggressor's surprise blows and successfully carrying out those military tasks, especially by the rocket troops . . . which must be fulfilled in a matter of seconds." In a matter of seconds—through technical accident or human failure—mutual deterrence might thus collapse.

[The United States has consistently] rejected a launch-on-warning policy. However, should one side give the appearance of adopting it, the other might feel compelled to institute faster launch procedures, creating an "arms race" in reducing safeguards against accidental war. Under mounting pressures from Soviet "hawks," and from some American "doves" as well as "hawks," in both countries responsible people in the center may not keep enough influence to halt this race. The very fact that well-informed and well-intentioned advisers now recommend, in essence, that the balance of terror should rest on hair-triggered doomsday machines offers a chilling reminder that we cannot rely on unswerving rationality among those who might affect critical strategic decisions.

The launch-on-warning aberration is only the most conspicuous outgrowth of the belief that to prevent nuclear war we have but to deter it. Our present strategic policy aggravates the risk of accidental war through many less visible practices as well as by its grand design.

IV

While the current overemphasis on mutual deterrence against a "rational" surprise attack dates from the mid-1960s, the other two dogmas of our nuclear strategy are largely the legacy of earlier periods. This is particularly true of the dogma that "retaliation" must be swift, inflicted in an all-out strike.

The world's first nuclear force—the U.S. Strategic Air Command (SAC)—was established in a period when we did not have to deter nuclear attack, but seriously feared the Red Army might move into Western Europe with its preponderant conventional strength. SAC became the remedy for the weakness perceived in the United States because of our extensive unilateral disarmament following World War II. One cannot appreciate the thinking of American leaders at that time, unless one makes an effort to recall how imminent they judged the likelihood that the Russians would launch an all-out ground attack in Europe.

Accordingly, to fight a war seemed at least as important a mission for SAC as to deter one. And in planning to fight a war, American strategists took account of what they had learned from the bombing raids in World War II. Whereas they had found that urban societies could continue to support a war effort as long as the damage was partial and gradual, it still seemed possible that sudden and extensive destruction would produce a collapse. Thus, the strategy that had

433

not fully succeeded against Hitler because of technological limitations now seemed feasible thanks to the atomic bomb. Our new weapons could administer the "knock-out blow" against Russia's cities—the industrial and political centers—in order to halt the Red Army's advance against Western Europe. Hence, to be an effective war-fighting strategy, atomic bombing had to be a concentrated, quick blow.

As the Russians also began to acquire a nuclear capability, American strategists came to fear attack on European or even American cities as an act of "retaliation" should SAC carry out the attack that would leave the advancing Red Army without support from the homeland. Thus, the first priority for SAC in the mid-1950s became the destruction of the Soviet nuclear capability before it could be used. This priority provided a second reason for our nuclear strike to be prompt and massive.

Initially, our strategic forces for this disarming strike lacked intercontinental range; they had to be based in North Africa or Europe to reach their targets. Later, we assigned an increasingly large role in this mission to our growing intercontinental arms, which meant they had to be capable of reaching their targets early enough to prevent the launching of most of the Soviet weapons. Thanks to the new solid fuel technology, our U.S.-based missiles could be launched in minutes and Minuteman became our principal land-based missile force. The requirement for speed, stemming from the disarming mission of our forces protecting Western Europe and appropriate perhaps for the 1950s and early 1960s, was thereby transferred to the arms that were to remain a principal element in our intercontinental deterrent for the 1970s and beyond.

After 1963, however, our dominant strategic philosophy shifted from the emphasis on the disarming strike to the principle of "mutual assured destruction." This shift was primarily motivated by our view of the arms race: we feared that our efforts to maintain a capability for a disarming strike would stimulate a continuing build-up of Soviet forces; and conversely, we hoped that our restraint would be reciprocated. Accordingly, we began to deny ourselves the capability to defend against those Soviet forces that could escape our quick, disarming strike in behalf of NATO, and—further undermining this earlier mission of our strategic forces—we began to curtail our capability to hit Soviet forces. In 1971, for example, the Senate referred explicitly to this new arms-control thinking in voting against funds to improve the accuracy of our missiles.

As a result of these developments, our current strategic posture is afflicted by a deep but strangely concealed contradiction. Those of our forces that serve to protect our NATO allies are still largely designed and operated in accordance with the earlier strategy threatening, in response to a major conventional attack, a nuclear first strike that would seek to disarm. But our global deterrence posture now has to meet the opposite requirement: to eschew, and through agreement mutually to preclude, a nuclear disarming capability. Meanwhile, some of our allies have come to regard our nuclear forces based on their soil as the most tangible symbol committing our entire deterrent forces to their defense, so that our former technological reason for overseas basing has been replaced by a political one. In the midst of the incompatibility between our nuclear strategy for NATO and our global deterrence policy, our so-called "tactical" nuclear weapons—also a legacy of a bygone era—introduce yet another anachronism of obsolete posture and technology.

To make the historical evolution still more complex, starting about 1960 the growing Soviet nuclear capability seemed to threaten more than just vengeful destruction of our cities so as to deter NATO's nuclear "knock-out" response to a Red Army advance. Soviet intercontinental missiles began to pose the canonical threat that figures so prominently in our strategic analysis—the massive suprise attack to disarm the United States. Given that the major portion of our strategic forces had been designed primarily for the prompt disarming strike in response to a Soviet invasion of Europe, they had not been primarily designed to survive a Soviet nuclear attack. For this new mission—"retaliation" in response to the Soviet nuclear strike—our bombers and missiles had to be launched promptly, before they were all destroyed on the ground. Here was the third reason conspiring to keep our strategic thinking riveted to the notion that "retaliation" had to be swift.

V

Clearly distinguishable from the notion that "retaliation" must be a swift, massive strike in any strategy of mutual deterrence is the now equally prevalent dogma that this strike must be designed to kill millions of people. This dogma can also be traced to the technical and conceptual limitations of strategic bombing in World War II. One has to recall the emotions and theories behind Hitler's raids on Coventry and London, and the deliberate bombing of residential areas in Hamburg, Tokyo, Dresden, and Hiroshima, to understand how we could have arrived where we are today. After World War II, military experts began to recognize that the immensely greater destructive power of nuclear weapons could compensate for the inaccuracy of aerial bombing, hence permitting destruction of small-sized military targets. But only if these targets were in unpopulated areas could they be destroyed without the killing of civilian populations. A nuclear weapon small enough to avoid vast civilian damage, yet accurate enough to hit most military targets, was not within the technology of the first nuclear decade.

As our strategic planners began to grapple with the role of nuclear weapons, not only was their vision confined by these technological limitations; but their sensitivity to the distinction between combatants and civilians—long cultivated through civilizing centuries—had become dulled by the strategic bombing in World War II. And given that we were then still planning how to fight—not to deter—a nuclear war, the mass killing of noncombatants came to be viewed as a "bonus effect," a useful by-product of the bombing campaign on which we relied to win in the event of World War III. Our "knock-out blow" would paralyze the Red Army not only by demolishing railroad yards, factories and party headquarters, but also by decimating urban populations and thus (perhaps) crushing Russia's "morale."

This history—not reasoned strategic analysis—led us into the habit of thinking that one had to threaten the killing of millions and millions of people in order to deter an "aggressor." None the less, the question of whether or not cities should be the targets of the "retaliatory" strike remained unsettled. In the late 1950s, a few strategists began to make the case that we should avoid hitting Russian cities in our initial strike responding to Soviet aggression. Instead, we should seek to destroy whatever Soviet nuclear weapons had not yet been used as well as other military targets, holding Soviet cities "hostage" to deter attacks on our cities. This strategy, it was then argued, would not only serve us better if nuclear war should break out for whatever reason, but would be just as effective to deter it.

During his first two years in office, Secretary of Defense McNamara came out in support of this new strategy and advocated military efforts consistent with it, such as civil defense and "counterforce" capabilities. Yet, after 1963, he began to promote the concept of "assured destruction." Initially, he perhaps meant to use this concept primarily as a convenient bureaucratic tactic. By pointing out our overwhelming capability for "assured destruction," he had a precise, statistical measurement for arguing against budgetary pressures from the military services, that we had more than enough arms for deterrence.

What began as a budgetary device within the Defense Department, conveniently fitting the need to shift defense dollars from our strategic forces to Vietnam from 1965 on, ended up as one of the dogmas governing our strategic and arms-control policy. We came to view a "retaliatory" threat to kill a major fraction of the Russian population as necessary for deterrence. And we came to believe that forces tailored to this threat were the only alternative to forces that appeared to jeopardize Russia's nuclear deterrent and hence would stimulate an arms race.

As "assured destruction" became the yardstick of nuclear strategy, the underlying calculations adopted a brutally simplifying index of success. It considered only those hostages whose death from the retaliatory strike would be certain and exactly calculable—those killed by the direct blast and heat effects of our weapons. In gauging the excellence of our deterrent—as reflected in statistics presented to Congress—those Russians who would be killed or injured by fires, fallout, and famine were excluded. *Cognoscenti* call this method of calculation the "cookie cutter"—nuclear weapons are assumed to "take out" hostages in a neat circle, like a piece of dough.

Such tasteless jargon helps to conceal the peculiar reasoning that is implicit in the modern approach to deterrence. We impute to the potential aggressor enough rationality or compassion to be reliably deterred by the prospect that calculable millions of his compatriots would meet prompt and certain death from "direct weapons effects"; we somehow do not trust him to be deterred by the prospect of the less easily measured millions who would suffer and die from radiation sickness, untreated injuries, or starvation. And while destruction of industry has been mentioned as being part of our "assured destruction," the question whether one could spare people and target only industry has scarcely been raised. Yet, by permitting evacuation, for instance, separation of urban industries and populations might be accomplished.

The Nixon Administration properly discontinued flaunting of these gruesome satistics to demonstrate the reliability of our deterrent. None the less, most American strategic experts still use the same calculus.

Our arms-control experts and military planners insulate themselves from the potential implications of their labors by layers of dehumanizing abstractions and bland metaphors. Thus, *assured destruction* fails to indicate what is to be destroyed; but then *assured genocide* would reveal the truth too starkly. The common phrase *deterring a potential aggressor* conveys a false simplicity about the

437

processes that might lead to a nuclear attack, as if we had to worry only about some ambitious despot who sits calculating whether or not to start a nuclear war. A moral perversity lies hidden behind the standard formula: in the event this "aggressor" attacks, we must "retaliate by knocking out *his* cities." Tomas de Torquemada, who burned 10,000 heretics at the stake, could claim principles more humane than our nuclear strategy; for his tribunals found all his victims guilty of having knowingly committed mortal sin.

The jargon of American strategic analysis works like a narcotic. It dulls our sense of moral outrage about the tragic confrontation of nuclear arsenals, primed and constantly perfected to unleash widespread genocide. It fosters the current smug complacence regarding the soundness and stability of mutual deterrence. It blinds us to the fact that our method for preventing nuclear war rests on a form of warfare universally condemned since the Dark Ages—the mass killing of hostages.

Indeed, our nuclear strategy is supposed to work the better, the larger the number of hostages that would pay with their lives should the strategy fail. This view has become so ingrained that the number of hostages who could be killed through a "second strike" by either superpower is often used as a measure of the "stability" of deterrence. Our very motive behind the recent treaty curbing the deployment of missile defenses is to keep this number reliably high.

In the long run, preserving a mutual threat of genocide may impede the reduction of tension and distrust between the two nuclear superpowers that we all hope for. It is far better, of course, for major powers to maintain peace between them by planning for deterrence instead of for war. But to stabilize deterrence by keeping ready arsenals for instant and unrestrained slaughter of men, women, and children is likely to impose a wrenching perspective on the officialdom of both nations. Such a "stabilization" perpetuates an arms-control philosophy that, at its core, is incredibly hostile. How would American-British relations have developed in the nineteenth century if, instead of the Rush-Bagot agreement, we had negotiated the establishment of armaments on each side permanently primed to destroy most cities in the United States and England?

Despite the arcane jargon of modern deterrence theory, ordinary Americans and Russians cannot escape the realization that their generation and their children's generation are destined to remain the chosen target of the nuclear forces on the other side. Toward each other as a people, Americans and Russians harbor practically no feelings of hostility, but by our theories they must indefinitely face each other as the most fearful threat to their future existence.

VI

Mercifully, no inhuman power condemns us to live perpetually in the grim jail of our own ideas. Alternatives can be found, although it may take decades to construct a better order for the prevention of nuclear war and the task will require the work of many minds. This is all the more reason for beginning today.

A good place to begin is to cast out the dogma that to deter nuclear attack, the threatened response must be the mass killing of people. By taking advantage of modern technology, we should be able to escape the evil dilemma that the strategic forces on both sides must either be designed to kill people or else jeopardize the opponent's confidence in his deterrent. The potential accuracy of "smart" bombs and missiles and current choices in weapon effects could enable both sides to avoid the killing of vast millions and yet to inflict assured destruction on military, industrial, and transportation assets—the sinews and muscles of the regime initiating war. Combined with this change in concept and techniques of "retaliation," we must design solutions more stable than in the past to the problem of achieving invulnerable deterrent forces. No matter how accurately each side can aim its own weapons, we want to make it physically impossible for most of the strategic arms to be destroyed by sudden attack.

It is premature to judge whether such a change in capabilities and doctrine might eventually make it desirable for us and the Russians to permit active defenses for urban populations while prohibiting them for military assets other than the nuclear deterrent. If such discrimination were to become technically feasible, its desirability would depend not only on American-Soviet relations at that time, but also on the danger of attack, if any, from other nuclear powers.

The second dogma we have to discard is that response to nuclear attack must be the prompt, even instant, launching of nearly the entire nuclear force. By eliminating the need to design our arms for instant launching, we can reduce vulnerability in many new ways. Precisely how to design forces that are far less vulnerable because they are not meant for instant reaction is a task for future research. We may not now see promising approaches; over all these years we have never made the effort. Arms buried thousands of feet underground come to mind, with provision for reaching the surface—and their targets—weeks or months after attack. By insisting that our strategic arms be capable of swift launch, we have restricted our engineers to such vulnerable arrangements as aircraft in delicately ready conditions and missiles exposed on or near the surface.

If we can eliminate the vulnerability of our strategic arms to surprise attack, we will have broken the vicious circle: that they must be ready for prompt launching because they are vulnerable, and that they are vulnerable because they must be ready. Furthermore, should the Russians come to agree with us, we could jointly decide to replace the doomsday catapults invented in the 1950s with arms that are incapable of being launched swiftly. If the strategic order could be transformed in this way, the dominant fear of surprise attack which drives our arms competition would loosen its grip. Weapons incapable of quick launching tend to be less suitable for surprise; and against truly invulnerable nuclear armaments, surprise would have lost its purpose.

Neither we nor the Russians will suddenly scuttle all our hair-triggered engines of destruction. By abandoning the dogma of speed, however, both of us can shift intellectual energies and budgetary resources to develop different nuclear armaments. Strategic weapons have a long lifetime; between the initial concept and the scrap heap, up to twenty-five years may elapse. What we engineer during this decade will have to prevent nuclear war into the next century.

Discarding the dogma of speed would result in another gain, perhaps even more important than reduced vulnerability. It would go a long way to reduce the danger of accidental war. By eliminating the requirement for launching entire missile forces in a matter of minutes, we can get rid of the triggering mechanisms and sensitive command procedures where some obscure malfunction might lead to cataclysm. Time is the best healer of mistakes, whether technical or human. The insistence on speed leaves insufficient time for double-checking; it denies opportunities for correction. If rapidity becomes the overriding concern, independent monitors tend to get pushed aside. Until about 1950, the Atomic Energy Commission shared in the custody of the nuclear weapons deployed by the military. But the notion that these weapons had to be ready for immediate use led President Truman to turn them over to the sole custody of the military.

Although avoiding the killing of hostages, these changes would not make nuclear war less unacceptable as an instrument of policy. Deterrence would remain: the conventional military might of the aggressor nation—its navy, army and air force with their logistics support—would be the first to suffer "assured destruction." Such a prospect would make even less tempting the planning of nuclear war than today's actual or imagined opportunities for a quick strike to deprive the opponent of his nuclear weapons. And the risk of the destruction of cities would still loom in the background.

Could the Soviet leaders be induced to accept such an evolution? We have lately devoted a major effort to teach our dogmas to the Russians—some feel with considerable success. Certain stubborn positions in Soviet strategic thought, however, manifest a less narrow view of deterrence by showing greater concern for dangers of a nuclear war that cannot be deterred, and reflect a longer time-perspective than we have developed. Once freed from our dogmas, we may discover that the distance in strategic views between us and the Russians is less than it appears today.

The greatest obstacles to the necessary reconstruction of our strategic order may well be intellectual and institutional rigidities. We justify our old habits of thinking because we are so competently familiar with the arguments against change. We are disposed to reject suggestions for improvement by demanding a perfect solution at the outset.

Military services cling to the type of weapons to which they have become accustomed, seeking marginal improvements rather than radical innovation. For instance, the United States Navy in the 1950s was at first reluctant to press ahead with the Polaris program, preferring to stress the strategic mission of carrier-based aircraft. Similarly, the Soviet Strategic Rocket Forces and the United States Air Force will probably want to hold on to their land-based missile forces well beyond the 1970s. Much is made about the importance of preserving our "triad" of strategic forces, as if the fact that we happen to acquire bombers, missiles, and submarines created some sacred trinity. Means outlive their ends among military organizations, for it is to the means that institutional loyalties and intellectual craftsmanship are devoted.

The scholasticism justifying our current policy is full of contradictions. On the one hand, we brush aside the immorality of threatening to kill millions of hostages, assuming that the threat will deter and that to deter means to prevent nuclear war. On the other hand, we argue that we must be poised to carry out "retaliation" swiftly and thus convey determination for irrational vengeance, since all rational purpose of retaliation would have disappeared when its time had come. We want to maintain a vague threat of using nuclear weapons first to deter massive conventional attack; yet, to stabilize mutual deterrence we must not threaten Soviet nuclear arms nor defend against them.

441

The result of such contradictions is a cancelling out of good intentions. In some years, our arms policy is dominated by our pre-occupation with the arms race and the view that we should therefore hobble our forces. In other years, we decide to refurbish our so-called options for attacking Russia's nuclear arms. Left to itself, this pulling and hauling between *yin* and *yang* will not lead the world into a safer era. On the contrary, the bureaucratic struggle may result in the worst compromise among the biases of contending factions. While luck has been with us so far, strategic thinking must and can find a new path into the twenty-first century.

CONTRIBUTORS

LES ASPIN is a U.S. representative from Wisconsin (Democrat) and a former economist with the Department of Defense.

ROBERT L. BARTLEY is editor of the editorial page of *The Wall Street Journal*.

LEONID I. BREZHNEV is general secretary of the Communist Party of the Soviet Union.

ZBIGNIEW BRZEZINSKI is professor of public law and government and director of the Research Institute on International Change at Columbia University.

JOHN S. CHWAT is a reference assistant with the Congressional Research Service of the Library of Congress.

JOHN M. COLLINS is a senior specialist in international relations with the Congressional Research Service of the Library of Congress.

ROBERT CONQUEST is a former research fellow in Soviet affairs at the London School of Economics and senior fellow of Columbia University's Russian Institute.

ALAN CRANSTON is a U.S. senator from California (Democrat).

BRIAN CROZIER is director of the Institute for the Study of Conflict, London.

JOHN ERICKSON is a professor of politics at the University of Edinburgh.

J. WILLIAM FULBRIGHT is a former U.S. senator from Arkansas (Democrat) and chairman of the Senate Committee on Foreign Relations, and is now associated with a law firm in Washington, D.C.

Larry Kahn, research assistant at the American Enterprise Institute, deserves special thanks for his help in producing this volume.

JOSEPH GODSON is coordinator of the Europe-American Conference and a former American Foreign Service officer.

GREGORY GROSSMAN is professor of economics at the University of California, Berkeley.

STANLEY HOFFMANN is professor of government at Harvard University.

FRED CHARLES IKLE is director of the U.S. Arms Control and Disarmament Agency.

HENRY M. JACKSON is a U.S. senator from Washington (Democrat).

AMOS A. JORDAN is deputy to the undersecretary for security assistance in the U.S. State Department and former acting assistant secretary of defense for international security affairs.

GEORGE F. KENNAN is a former U.S. ambassador to the Soviet Union and member of the Institute for Advanced Study at Princeton.

HENRY A. KISSINGER is the U.S. secretary of state.

ROBERT W. KOMER is a senior social science researcher with the Rand Corporation and former U.S. ambassador to Turkey.

LEOPOLD LABEDZ is editor of *Survey: A Journal of East and West Studies*.

MELVIN R. LAIRD is senior counsellor for national and international affairs with *Reader's Digest* and former secretary of defense and U.S. representative from Wisconsin (Republican).

BERNARD LEWIS is Cleveland E. Dodge professor of Near Eastern studies at Princeton University.

JAN M. LODAL is executive vice president of American Management Systems, Inc., and former director of program analysis for the National Security Council.

CHARLES BURTON MARSHALL is a former centennial professor at Texas A & M University and professor of international politics at the School of Advanced International Studies, Johns Hopkins University.

PAUL H. NITZE is a corporation executive and former member of the U.S. delegation to SALT and deputy secretary of defense.

RICHARD M. NIXON was thirty-seventh President of the United States.

G. WARREN NUTTER is Paul Goodloe McIntire professor of economics at the University of Virginia, adjunct scholar of the American Enterprise Institute, and former assistant secretary of defense for international security affairs.

RICHARD PIPES is Frank B. Baird, Jr., professor of history and former director of the Russian Research Center at Harvard University.

ROBERT J. PRANGER is director of foreign and defense policy studies at the American Enterprise Institute and adjunct professor of international politics at Georgetown University's School of Foreign Service.

WILLIAM P. ROGERS was U.S. secretary of state from 1969 to 1973 and now practices law in New York City.

RICHARD ROSECRANCE is Walter S. Carpenter, Jr., professor of international and comparative politics at Cornell University.

DONALD H. RUMSFELD is U.S. secretary of defense.

LEONARD SCHAPIRO is professor of political science at the London School of Economics.

EDWARD SHILS is distinguished service professor of sociology at the University of Chicago and a fellow of Peterhouse College, Cambridge.

ALEXANDER SOLZHENITSYN is a Soviet writer and Nobel Prize laureate.

P. J. VATIKIOTIS is professor of politics at the University of London.

Cover and book design: Pat Taylor